PHILOSOPHY, POLITICS, DEMOCRACY

PHILOSOPHY, POLITICS, DEMOCRACY

Selected Essays

JOSHUA COHEN

HARVARD UNIVERSITY PRESS
Cambridge, Massachusetts, and London, England
2009

Library of Congress Cataloging-in-Publication Data

Cohen, Joshua, 1951–
Philosophy, politics, democracy : selected essays / Joshua Cohen.
p.   cm.
Includes bibliographical references and index.
ISBN 978-0-674-03448-8 (alk. paper)
1. Social sciences—Philosophy.   2. Political science—Philosophy.   3. Democracy.   I. Title.

H61.15.C64 2009
321.8—dc22   2008052224

For Ellen

CONTENTS

7

ACKNOWLEDGMENTS

The essays collected here were written over a period of twenty-two years, between 1986 and 2008. Their footnotes underscore the many debts I have accumulated in writing them. I wish here to add a few acknowledgments that apply to the collection itself.

Some of these essays existed in usable electronic form thanks only to optical scanning. I am very grateful to Paul Gowder and Marilie Coetsee (along with Christine Kim) for their generous assistance in getting the papers in shape. Lindsay Waters, my editor at Harvard University Press, urged me to bring this volume together. Lindsay has made a large contribution—as editor and author—to fostering a more democratic society, so I am very pleased that the book appears on his watch. Tim Scanlon's name appears in many footnotes, because of both the influence of his work and his incisive comments on many of the papers. I taught at MIT for twenty-nine years, and all the papers in this collection were written while I was there (even the final paper was first drafted in 2005). At MIT, I was privileged to have a wonderful group of colleagues and to teach a remarkable bunch of undergraduates and graduate students. I single out Archon Fung, whose imprint appears directly on the work, as research assistant on essay 4, and as coauthor on some of the work that shapes essay 10. I am especially grateful to Joel Rogers and Chuck Sabel, each a coauthor, friend, and inspiring example.

John Rawls's influence is evident throughout. The essays often draw directly on his views, and many ideas presented in them struck me first when I was engaging with his work. More than that, Rawls conveyed, in his writing, his teaching, and his bearing, a sense of the importance of philosophical thought. I have tried to do some justice to that importance.

The essays are presented in the order in which they were written, and I have made only very slight editorial changes: there is some overlap, and I have not tried to eliminate it. Nor have I updated the more empirical materials or the discussion of constitutional cases. Although reviewing them has reminded me of their many flaws, I still hope that others will benefit from reading them. The essays originally appeared in the following publications, and I thank the publishers for their permission to reprint:

Essay 1: "Deliberation and Democratic Legitimacy," in Alan Hamlin and Phillip Petit, eds., *The Good Polity* (Oxford: Blackwell, 1989), 17–34.

Essay 2: "Moral Pluralism and Political Consensus," in David Copp, Jean Hampton, and John Roemer, eds., *The Idea of Democracy* (Cambridge: Cambridge University Press, 1993), 270–291. Copyright © 1993 Cambridge University Press. Reprinted with permission.

Essay 3: "Associations and Democracy" (with Joel Rogers), *Social Philosophy and Policy* 10, 2 (Summer 1993): 282–312. Copyright © 1993 Social Philosophy and Policy Foundation. Reprinted with the permission of Cambridge University Press.

Essay 4: "Freedom of Expression," *Philosophy & Public Affairs* 22, 3 (Summer 1993): 207–263, by Blackwell Publishing Ltd.

Essay 5: "Procedure and Substance in Deliberative Democracy," in Seyla Benhabib, ed., *Democracy and Difference: Changing Boundaries of the Political* (Princeton: Princeton University Press, 1996), 95–119.

Essay 6: "Directly Deliberative Polyarchy" (with Charles Sabel), *European Law Journal* 3, 4 (December 1997): 313–342, by Blackwell Publishing Ltd.

Essay 7: "Democracy and Liberty," in Jon Elster, ed., *Deliberative Democracy* (Cambridge: Cambridge University Press, 1998), 185–231. Copyright © 1998 Jon Elster. Reprinted with the permission of Cambridge University Press.

Essay 8: "Money, Politics, Political Equality," in Alex Byrne, Robert Stalnaker, and Ralph Wedgwood, eds., *Fact and Value* (Cambridge, MA: MIT Press, 2001), 47–80.

Essay 9: "Privacy, Pluralism, and Democracy," in Joseph Keim Campbell, Michael O'Rourke, and David Shier, eds., *Law and Social Justice* (Cambridge, MA: MIT Press, 2005), 15–40.

Essay 10: "Reflections on Deliberative Democracy," in Thomas

Christiano and John Christman, eds., *Contemporary Debates in Political Philosophy* (Oxford: Blackwell, 2009), 247–263.
Essay 11: "Truth and Public Reason," *Philosophy & Public Affairs* 37, 1 (Winter 2009): 2–42, by Blackwell Publishing Ltd.

PHILOSOPHY, POLITICS, DEMOCRACY

INTRODUCTION

The essays collected here are about an ideal of democracy. It is the demanding ideal that we, as equals and on a footing of mutual respect, should guide the conduct of our common affairs through the use of our shared reason.

Although focused on democracy, these essays are animated by a more general conception of the relationship between philosophical reflection and social-political life. I begin this Introduction with some comments about that conception. I then make some semi-autobiographical remarks about the intellectual background that led me to the animating conception of democracy. Next, I describe the substance of the essays, how they are connected, and their lines of evolution. I conclude with some brief comments on whether the essays express an objectionably Panglossian outlook.

1

We all have ideas that belong to political morality. We have some mix of thoughts about rights and responsibilities, about the evil of slavery, cruelty, destitution, humiliation, and intolerance, about the fairness of social inequality and the virtues of open discussion, about religious tolerance and personal privacy, about whether the state is like a large family or something fundamentally different, about the importance of a rule of law and democracy, about when it is acceptable to fight a war and what we owe to people in other places, and about whether justice is somehow fixed by the nature of things or is a human construction.

Moreover, those thoughts, both more abstract and more concrete, play a role in political life. That's because politics is not only—though it is assuredly in (perhaps large) part—a struggle for power and a strategic pursuit of personal and group interests. Particularly in a democracy, politics is also a matter of expressing convictions that belong to political morality and of arguing with others about how we should act in ways that keep faith with our separate and shared convictions.

Consider the response of Alberto Mora, the U.S. Navy's general counsel, to his discoveries about the cruel treatment of prisoners sanctioned by the Bush administration in conducting its "war on terror." Mora thought—and acted on the thought—that "cruelty" and torture, though different, are "equally pernicious." "If cruelty is no longer declared unlawful . . . it alters the fundamental relationship of man to government. It destroys the whole notion of individual rights. The Constitution recognizes that man has an inherent right, not bestowed by the state or laws, to personal dignity, including the right to be free of cruelty. It applies to all human beings, not just in America—even those designated as 'unlawful enemy combatants.' If you make this exception, the whole Constitution crumbles."[1] Here we have an argument—concise and clear, whether correct or incorrect—about the equivalence in political morality of cruelty and torture, concluding that torture and cruelty are both to be condemned as violations of a right to personal dignity. Thoughts such as this, which prompted Mora to concerted action, belong as much to our political life as the pressures that led to the abuses he sought to halt (and as the defenses of torture and cruelty as warranted under special circumstances).

Cynics will say that appeals to normative ideas in political argument are a high-minded sham. They say that we should not, for example, take Lincoln seriously when he says that the country was born in an idea and dedicated to a proposition. They say that the Universal Declaration of Human Rights is a strategy of political control by Western powers or by an emerging class of globe-circling lawyers and bureaucrats. The cynics say that normative conviction and argument provide a smokescreen for the interests of those who have power and a distraction for those who don't. Political struggle, they remind us, is not discussion in the seminar room: it is not an argument about who is right, or a proof of a theorem, or an experiment to test a hypothesis, but a conflict about who will win. Cynicism (tendentiously self-styled as *realism*, sometimes more simply as the grown-up view) strikes me as an implausible position, though its tireless reiteration threatens to turn it into a self-fulfilling prophecy. But I am

1. See Jane Mayer, *The Dark Side* (New York: Doubleday, 2008), 219.

not here arguing for a thesis, only expressing an outlook, the outlook expressed in these essays, which all are premised on a rejection of cynicism about normative political discourse.

Normative political discourse is one thing, however; political philosophy is something else. What do these observations about the place of normative thought in politics have to do with philosophy?

In his *Prison Notebooks*, Antonio Gramsci draws attention to the role of normative ideas in our individual and collective conduct.[2] Formulating the point in striking terms, he says, "Everyone is a philosopher." That is because a "specific conception of the world" underlies our intellectual activity. That conception, Gramsci says, is typically implicit, often adapted from the "external environment," passively internalized rather than worked out "consciously and critically." Gramsci probably overstates the extent to which we each embrace a "specific conception of the world," a comprehensive doctrine with a significant degree of coherence and stability, as distinct from a somewhat more inchoate family of convictions. Still, his comment points to the role of a more or less connected set of ideas in our ordinary understanding and conduct, a conception of the world that comprises normative ideas, even if it is not confined to them.

More to the point, Gramsci's invocation of philosophy suggests continuity between endorsing the conception of the world that shapes our conduct—what he calls a spontaneous philosophy—and pursuing the activity that we call political philosophy.[3] Think of political philosophy as a more reflective engagement with the political morality that shapes our conduct and that we offer in argument to others, an engagement that aims to bring greater coherence, comprehensiveness, and—most importantly—reasoned consideration to that morality. We suppose that our convictions withstand scrutiny, and we think they are worthy of our allegiance—and suitable for political argument—because they do. Political philosophy puts this thought to the test, aiming to judge, for example, whether cruelty and torture are indeed morally on a par, each violating a right to dignity; or whether treating people differently because of race or gender is on a par with treating them differently because of differences in

2. Antonio Gramsci, *Prison Notebooks*, ed. and trans. Quintin Hoare and Geoffrey Nowell Smith (New York: International, 1971), 323.

3. Gramsci distinguishes the possession of a conception of the world from a "second level, which is that of awareness and criticism," and he emphasizes the importance—sometimes the necessity—of ordering "in a systematic, coherent and critical fashion one's own intuitions of life and the world." Ibid., 323, 327.

sexual orientation; or whether the rights that many of us suppose people to be entitled to are really anything more than the conditions for a smoothly functioning liberal, market society; or whether our convictions about the moral significance of political boundaries express an insight about justice or an unreflective prejudice; or whether there really is a morally salient distinction between forcing people to work and taxing their income. Political philosophy, thus understood, is animated by concerns about whether the normative views we are drawn to—views we take to be reasonable and correct and offer in argument to others—are as compelling on reflection and worthy of allegiance as we take them to be.

Because normative thought is part of politics, and political philosophy is continuous with normatively inflected public discussion, political philosophy is continuous with politics. And that continuity is particularly clear in pluralistic societies, where political ideals compete and argumentative challenges to those ideas are settled parts of the political culture. Political philosophy does not, then, aim to *substitute* reflective reason for politics, as if political life itself shared nothing with philosophical argument, as if it were all about power and interests. Nor is political philosophy about judging the political world. Instead, the point of political philosophy is to contribute reflectively to the public reasoning about what we ought to do that always already forms one (sometimes strikingly small) part of political life.

The idea that political philosophy is continuous with politics informs the essays collected here in at least two ways. First, many of these essays grew out of and were engaged with a political controversy. The philosophical argument locates the problem in a larger setting, with the hope of getting some practical guidance in how best to address it. "Freedom of Expression" (essay 4), for example, was prompted by debates in the United States in the 1980s and early 1990s about regulations of pornography and hate speech, campus speech codes, and campaign finance. Reflection on these issues and the conflicting pulls of competing ideas about how to address them—that words are not just vehicles for argument but also instruments of human injury, or that silencing speech is insulting to audiences and destructive to social advance—led to larger questions about the rationale for freedom of expression, all inspired by the hope that that rationale might guide judgment on contested questions. Essay 8, on campaign finance and political equality, started as a presentation to a group working on campaign finance reform, in particular on efforts to secure public financing, which led to considerations about the nature of democracy. Essay 9, on privacy, was part of a debate that resulted from the late 1990s public preoccupation with Bill Clinton's sex life. And several of the essays (3, 6, 10) grew out of public political debates of the past three decades about how to achieve constructive regulation for the common good in democratic societies, given concerns about the capacity of the state to achieve such regulation.

Second, if the concerns in the essays have typically grown out of political argument, they also return to it. Political philosophy is philosophy, but it is also political-practical. Accordingly, I have tried to be attentive to concerns about how the norms and ideals explored in reflection on normative political ideas might be realized in the world, and that put these essays in closer touch with theoretical and empirical materials from the social sciences than is common in much political philosophy. Philosophy does not settle the question of how we ought to live together, but sensible normative political ideas should be workable in the political world as it might be, and concerns about such workability are part of a reflective assessment of their reasonableness and correctness. Political philosophy has always been practical and political as well as philosophical, and these essays reflect an effort to be faithful to the inevitable complexities that result from this attention to both principles and practical possibilities, to the circumstances to which normative reflection is addressed, and to the possibility of realizing ideals from where we are, given who we are.

2

I attended graduate school in the mid-1970s, a period of great creativity in political philosophy. John Rawls's *Theory of Justice* had appeared in 1971, followed soon by Robert Nozick's *Anarchy, State, and Utopia* (1974). This was also a period of political rethinking for people who, like me, identified themselves as democrats and socialists and thought of their socialism as principally a matter of political values—egalitarian, participatory, and antiauthoritarian—rather than more specifically institutional convictions about public ownership or a planned economy.

In 1975–76, I tried to write a PhD dissertation on socialism. The guiding idea was that the socialism worth being concerned about—anyway, the socialism that interested me normatively—had something to do with democracy. The point was to create a more democratic society in many senses of that term, including a more democratic economy: to extend democratic ideas outside the state. And here my political concerns came into contact with my philosophical interests. While I found Rawls's views deeply attractive, I also found it striking that Rawls (not to mention Nozick and others) had very little to say about democracy and was focused instead on individual rights and opportunities, and a fair distribution of income and wealth.[4]

I did not make much headway on the dissertation topic, but I returned to the concern about democracy in a paper I wrote in 1980. The paper sketched a "principle of democratic legitimacy" and tried to show how it could serve as a fundamental political idea, a kind of axiom that would organize other political principles, about liberties, economic democracy, and distributive fairness, which all could be understood as features of a democratic political society. I thought of democracy as a compelling normative idea, requiring that people be treated as equals in the processes of collective decision-making. It also struck me as a demanding one: treating people as equals had implications for outcomes as well as processes, so democracy was both a procedural and a substantive ideal, with a "for the people" as well as a "by the people" dimension.

That paper grew (in much improved form) into the last chapter of *On Democracy*, which Joel Rogers and I wrote in the summer of 1982 and published in 1983. Rogers and I had organized a meeting with a group of academics and other intellectuals, all of whom shared our convictions about the misdirection of American politics under Reagan. In the meeting, Rogers and I kept referring to the shared ideas and convictions of the group. Someone suggested that we draft a statement expressing our sense of what was shared. Responding to the challenge, we drafted the book.

Soon after *On Democracy* appeared, I felt dissatisfied with several parts of the view. Three dissatisfactions are germane here. First, the conception of democracy—with its emphasis on treating people as equals—seemed too thin: not wrong, but too limited to serve the central normative role I had been assigning to it. Second, and not unrelated to the first point, I thought the brief remarks about personal liberties and democracy

---

4. I eventually came to see that Rawls's views were far more deeply shaped by a conception of democracy than I then understood. See Joshua Cohen, "For a Democratic Society," in Samuel Freeman, ed., *Cambridge Companion to Rawls* (Cambridge: Cambridge University Press, 2002), 86–138.

were insufficient and perhaps misguided. Third, I was troubled by the "dualism" in our account of the relationship between the book's normative conception of democracy as an ideal and its structural theory of capitalist democracy. In presenting the account of democracy as an ideal, we appealed to what we understood to be a widely shared set of political values. But those values played no role in our account of politics in a capitalist democracy, which emphasized structural constraints.

Over the next few years, I wrote on Locke[5] and Rousseau[6] with these concerns close at hand, and also explored the idea of an "epistemic" conception of democracy. The results of this exploration appeared in a 1986 essay, "An Epistemic Conception of Democracy."[7] The epistemic conception says, in essence, that democracy is about combining judgments about what we ought to do—in particular, opinions about the common good—not aggregating interests or preferences, even the preferences of people under equal conditions. The critical part of the essay—arguing that William Riker's *Liberalism Against Populism* was too quick to draw large conclusions about democracy from social choice theory—seems right, but I was not convinced (even as I was writing the paper) by the idea that democracy is about offering opinions regarding the right answer to a reasonably well-defined question and then pooling those answers. That conception seemed to be missing something about democracy as a fundamental political value.

The angle of approach that I was eventually drawn to centered on the idea of deliberative democracy. The deliberative democrat emphasizes that democracy is not simply about treating people as equals in a process of collective decision-making, or about fair bargaining among groups, but also about reasoning together as equals on matters of common concern (or it could be described as treating people as equals by relying on our common reason as a basis for justification). Here, I was moved in part by Habermas's ideal of decisions arrived at through a process that reflects no force other than the force of the better argument (though Habermas had not presented this ideal in connection with a conception

---

5. "Structure, Choice, and Legitimacy: Locke's Theory of the State," *Philosophy and Public Affairs* 15, 4 (Fall 1986): 301–324.

6. "Reflections on Rousseau: Autonomy and Democracy," *Philosophy and Public Affairs* 15, 3 (Summer 1986): 275–297.

7. "An Epistemic Conception of Democracy," *Ethics* 97, 1 (October 1986): 26–38.

of democracy). And I was working with the intuitive idea that democracy might be thought of not only as a fair process or as an instrument for achieving just ends but as a way to realize in actual political life an ideal of justification through public reason-giving.

"Deliberation and Democratic Legitimacy" (essay 1) was the result. Originally written in 1986, it located deliberation—understood as a kind of mutual reason-giving—as central to the democratic ideal in its most attractive form. By making such reason-giving central, the deliberative conception of democracy also showed how democracy was connected, so I argued, with ideas of autonomy, equality, and the common good: democracy, understood deliberatively, was both a procedural and a substantive ideal. And also, I thought, a specifically political ideal, not tied to an encompassing moral outlook. The idea was not that people ought to reason about everything, or guide their personal choices by reflective, autonomous judgment, or that the unexamined life is not worth living, but that the legitimacy that emerges from democratic collective choice reflects the role of reason-giving—of a kind of mutual justification—in the process.

3

"Deliberation and Democratic Legitimacy" proposed, then, that the deliberative conception, with its idea of reason-giving among equals, provides the most compelling account of settled elements of the democratic ideal. And this suggested two lines of further evolution.

First, I wanted to see whether and how the idea of deliberative democracy could serve as a unifying normative political ideal. Addressing that issue required filling out its normative content, showing how it provided argumentative traction in addressing disputed issues about liberty, equality, and the common good. I wrote several essays along these lines, which aimed to show how deliberation, understood as a kind of reasoning, was different from simply discussing and how the idea of deliberative democracy could be used to organize an account of other political values. An essential part of the argument, which I developed in "Moral Pluralism and Political Consensus" (essay 2, originally written in 1990), was the idea of reasonable pluralism.

Beginning in the mid-1980s, Rawls emphasized that societies that protect liberties are marked by what he called a "fact of pluralism," a pluralism of distinct and incompatible comprehensive doctrines, religious and philosophical.[8] A conception of justice suited to such societies needed, he argued, to be able to win support from those doctrines, "each from its own point of view,"[9] and this would be aided by confining the conception of justice and the case for it to specifically political matters. I thought that the concern about the fact of pluralism was misplaced. Because justice is not fixed by some sort of de facto consensus, it is not a problem for a conception of justice—a problem that might prompt us to reconsider its correctness—that it cannot win support from the doctrines that people happen to be drawn to, whatever the content of those doctrines.[10] The issue about pluralism, I proposed, was really about reasonable disagreement, about the fact that there are many reasonable views with different fundamental elements, say religious and secular, that people are drawn to. Political argument should, then, take place on a terrain that could be endorsed by people with different reasonable views. Though "Moral Pluralism and Political Consensus" is not specifically about democracy, a notion of reasonable pluralism and reasonable disagreement subsequently played an essential role in my account of deliberative democracy, because I thought that the kinds of reasons that could be used to justify collective decisions needed to be attentive to the pluralism that lies at the heart of democratic societies.

In "Procedure and Substance in Deliberative Democracy" (essay 5), I modified the conception of deliberative democracy to take account of the fact of reasonable pluralism. Democratic deliberation is about reason-giving to others as equals. Reasonable disagreement, then, restricted the range of reasons that could be advanced in political justification. It also led to an account of democracy that was not simply procedural, but had substantive elements as well, with protections of liberties and a concern for the common good emerging as elements of democracy. The paper also explored the implications of the conception of deliberative democracy for some contested issues of democratic politics: how associa-

---

8. See the papers on "The Idea of an Overlapping Consensus," "The Priority of Right and Ideas of the Good," and "The Domain of the Political and Overlapping Consensus," all of which emphasized the importance of the "fact of pluralism." See *John Rawls: Collected Papers*, ed. Samuel Freeman (Cambridge, MA: Harvard University Press, 1999), chaps. 20, 21, 22.

9. Ibid., 479.

10. The paper presents a criticism of Rawls, but the point was to make a case about what he really ought to have been saying in his account of political liberalism and overlapping consensus. Rawls did shift focus to the fact of reasonable pluralism, though he also observes that both facts are relevant. See *Political Liberalism* (New York: Columbia University Press, 1996), 36–37, 58–66.

tions could play a larger regulatory role in advancing the common good without ruining deliberative politics, and electoral finance (issues discussed in much greater detail in essays 3 and 8).

Because deliberative democracy has strong roots in a radical democratic tradition, emphasizing ideas of political autonomy, I was especially concerned to show that and how it provided a way to think about the "liberties of the moderns," including religious and moral liberty. This, as I mentioned earlier, was a gap in *On Democracy*. In "Deliberation and Democratic Legitimacy," I had tentatively suggested (in footnote 22) that those liberties provided protections that bolster the confidence required for independent participation. That thesis had the smell of the lamp. Maybe confidence born of those protections emboldens people. Maybe it privatizes. Who knows? And anyway, the argument assigned a kind of unwanted privilege to political engagement. How could it be that protections of liberties of conscience and of the person are simply a shadow cast by the preconditions of participation? But wasn't that conclusion the natural consequence of an unnatural beginning? If you treat democracy—or, more abstractly still, politically autonomous lawgiving—as basic, and are moved by convictions about the liberties of the moderns, how can you avoid the suspicious result?

To address the issue, I focused initially on freedom of expression. Though my concerns about freedom of expression grew partly out of an interest in exploring the implications and plausibility of the conception of deliberative democracy, I was also independently interested, as I mentioned earlier, in addressing a set of public debates about campus speech codes, pornography, hate speech, and campaign finance. I was troubled by the hate speech, could understand the concerns about pornography, and saw that many people who shared an egalitarian sensibility thought that concerns about regulation required a kind of abstract allegiance to rights or liberty and that their egalitarianism put them on the side of a less expression-friendly position.

After reading lots of constitutional cases and thinking about the differences between American and Western European protections of free expression, I was persuaded that no simple theory founded on a single value or interest (autonomy, for example) would suffice to capture the terrain. I proposed a view that had (to my mind) an attractive complexity, founded on three basic interests—expressive, informational, and deliberative—and a range of plausible judgments about the costs of regulation.

In "Freedom of Expression" (essay 4), I did not present the theory as an illustration of my account of deliberative democracy but as an independently plausible view, which needed subsequently to be fit into the account of democracy, if it could be.[11]

"Procedure and Substance" pointed in the right direction, but I drew out the connections most fully in "Democracy and Liberty" (essay 7), which argues that religious, expressive, and moral liberties are essential parts of democracy, not constraints upon it, that a political society is less democratic to the extent that it fails to protect these liberties, and that those liberties are not destructive of community, but integrative. Once more, the argument turns on the reasons that can be used to defend regulations in a society of equals, assuming the fact of reasonable pluralism. Given the kinds of reasons that are expressed in religious conviction, for example, and the need to justify to others on the basis of reasons that they can reasonably accept, it will generally not be possible to justify regulations of religious exercise. An essential part of the argument was to tie the idea of finding such reasons to democracy itself, to the deliberative idea that democracy is an arrangement of collective decision-making that treats people as equals in part by offering reasons of a suitable kind. The reason-giving among equals essential to deliberative democracy, along with reasonable pluralism, brought the liberties inside the conception of democracy. Deliberation and pluralism shape the content of what, in the paper on "Privacy, Pluralism, and Democracy" (essay 9), I call "democracy's public reason."

I also had been thinking for some time about political equality, which I discussed briefly in "Procedure and Substance." As a way to provide focus, I concentrated my attention on the troubled American system of financing elections (essay 8). Once more—in part prompted by practical engagement with the issue—I sketched an account of political equality and campaign finance largely independent of the general conception of deliberative democracy, drawing on arguments in American constitutional law and empirical research on the role of money in elections. The line of thinking adopted by the U.S. Supreme Court in *Buckley v. Valeo*

---

11. I also wrote a companion piece on pornography, "Freedom, Equality, and Pornography," in Austin Sarat and Thomas R. Kearns, eds., *Justice and Injustice in Law and Legal Theory* (Ann Arbor: University of Michigan Press, 1996), 99–137, and in Jessica Spector, ed., *Prostitution and Pornography: Philosophical Debate About the Sex Industry in the U.S.* (Stanford: Stanford University Press, 2006).

(1976), and preserved more or less consistently thereafter, reflected, I argued, an elite conception of democracy in the tradition of democratic theory associated with Joseph Schumpeter's *Capitalism, Socialism, and Democracy*. The elite conception is defined by a focus on electorally organized competition for office, as the distinctively democratic method of deciding which elites would rule. Correspondingly, the conception is marked by an inattention to the value of fair chances for citizens to exercise various forms of political influence, including influence on public argument. The challenge, I observed, is to find a way to accommodate both the fundamental importance of free political speech, unrestricted by content and viewpoint, and fair chances for equal citizens to influence public discussion and collective decision, not simply to subordinate the latter to the former.

The privacy paper (essay 9) aims to clarify further the place of personal liberties in the deliberative conception of democracy, while underscoring the limits of privacy. I argue that an idea of independent judgment has an important role in democracy's public reason, and that this respect for independent judgment has important implications for authoritative regulation in areas of life, death, and sex. This case for "privacy rights," I argue, does not dependent on philosophical liberalism but is a natural consequence of the reason-giving among equals and reasonable pluralism associated with deliberative democracy. But—and here are the limits—the kinds of restrictions on justification that are appropriate to public, political justification are not to be extended to informal public discussion in civil society, which can be much more open-ended, more agonistic, less confined by standards of civility and norms of reticence. The aim here is to free the ideal of deliberative democracy, with its concerns about justification on common ground, from a cultural conventionalism with which it might be associated.

A second line of thought has moved along a less philosophical track. Two of the essays (4, 6) focus on how to achieve a more deliberative democracy rather than on the ideal itself. In 1988 Joel Rogers and I wrote a long article on "associative democracy." The central intuitive idea was that the nature of associative life—the strength and role of associations intermediate between state and market—made a morally consequential difference to the operations of a capitalist democracy. In part we were concerned about the decline of unions and other kinds of secondary associations in the United States and the implications of that decline for representing interests. But we were also concerned, perhaps more fundamentally, with limits on state capacity and thus focused on the potential for community organizations, environmental groups, NGOs, and worker organizations to play a larger and more constructive role in achieving important regulatory aims. The ideas were connected to Western European and Latin American debates about a successor to corporatism as a scheme of macroeconomic management; in the United States, these ideas were part of a discussion about how to do anything constructive given significantly reduced confidence in state capacity. The full version appeared (with crucial encouragement from Erik Olin Wright) as "Associations in Democratic Governance," in *Politics and Society*.[12] I have included a shorter version here.

The general line of thought—about achieving a reasonably decent, effective, and egalitarian democracy without relying so heavily on the state—still seems promising. But the associative view struck me as limited, both because it paid insufficient attention to deliberation and because it focused too much on the role of associations, as a specific category. The essay on directly deliberative polyarchy (essay 6), jointly authored with Chuck Sabel, sought to remedy those deficiencies. The essay describes a very general architecture of deliberatively democratic problem-solving. The architecture has application to a range of conditions, even without the state's shadow looming, and Sabel and I draw in that architecture in subsequent work on the European Union and on global democracy.[13] It describes a scheme for the provision of important public goods that is disciplined by reason-giving and the need for comparisons but that does not impose the kind of uniformity that is conventionally associated with the state, law, and public administration. It shares with the associative democracy view a willingness to rely less on the state (without endorsing any kind of hostility to politics) but does not depend on enlisting associations as the preferred vehicle for constructive public participation.

12. *Politics and Society* 20, 4 (December 1992): 393–472. The essay was accompanied by replies from Ellen Immergut, Andrew Levine, Jane Mansbridge, Philippe Schmitter, Wolfgang Streeck, Andrew Szasz, and Iris Young.

13. "Sovereignty and Solidarity in the EU" (with Charles Sabel), in Jonathan Zeitlin and David Trubek, eds., *Governing Work and Welfare in a New Economy: European and American Experiments* (Oxford: Oxford University Press, 2003), 345–375; "Global Democracy?" (with Charles Sabel), *New York University Journal of International Law and Policy* 37, 4 (2006): 763–797.

The penultimate essay (essay 10) aims at synthesis of some of the more and the less philosophical arguments. I restate the idea of deliberative democracy, emphasizing the central role of reason-giving, explain why that conception is not inattentive to the facts about political power, and discuss a range of considerations that might lead us to endorse the deliberative view. I then explore some potential tensions between the deliberative conception of democracy and the proposals to secure a more participatory democracy. Deliberation and participation are arguably both important elements of the democratic ideal, but it is easy to see how we might be led to sacrifice the one for the other. The essay then concludes with a discussion of some ways to remedy the tensions.

The concluding essay ("Truth and Public Reason") is the most recent and the most philosophical. Normative discourse, I said at the outset, is part of politics. Moreover, it should be taken at face value, as concerned with what we ought to do, not simply as a mask of attitude and interest. In addition, it is continuous with the reflective, critical engagement with political values characteristic of political philosophy. In this essay, I argue that the concept of truth has a role in public political discourse and present a political conception of truth suited to that role. The kind of common ground that we might aim to occupy in political argument—a ground of public reason—cannot make room for the whole truth. But because it is a form of reasoning about what we ought to do, it cannot disavow a concern for truth. Preserving this concern does not turn practice into theory but affirms the place of reflective normative thought in life.

4

I mentioned that essay 10 is concerned with accommodating the importance of deliberation and participation, which stand in uneasy tension. This concern about reconciling tensions underscores a theme that runs throughout the essays and is an especially important presence in the essays on political equality, procedure and substance, and associative democracy. Much work in political theory points in a very different direction: it draws our attention to the need to make hard choices. In the spirit of Max Weber, Isaiah Berlin, and Bernard Williams, it reminds us that all good things in life do not go together, and reminds us, too, that we sometimes, in a cheerfully Panglossian or romantic spirit, gloss over these tensions.

Such reminders are important. But the essays here are animated by a very different idea. My own experience is not that we are constantly yielding to Panglossian temptations. Quite to the contrary, we are often too quick to suppose that important values cannot be jointly realized, that political life is filled with tragic conflicts between and among important values. So we respond to political ideals with a knowing irony of the intellect and a lassitude of the heart.

In his Gettysburg Address, Lincoln drew attention to the idea that the United States was conceived in liberty and dedicated to a kind of equality. The question whether a country "so conceived and so dedicated" could endure was very much open and not to be resolved through philosophical argument. Still, Lincoln urged in effect that we not be too quick to assume an intractable conflict. Perhaps conscientious and sustained effort at improvement is not doomed to fail; perhaps we live in a perfectible union. And here philosophy, too, has a role. It must not, of course, deny the possibility of conflict between important values. But inspired by hope, guided by reason, and focused on the political world as it might be, philosophy can help us to see the possibility of more fully realizing our largest political ideals.

1

DELIBERATION AND DEMOCRATIC LEGITIMACY

In this essay I explore the ideal of a "deliberative democracy."[1] By a deliberative democracy I shall mean, roughly, an association whose affairs are governed by the public deliberation of its members. I propose an account of the value of such an association that treats democracy itself as a fundamental political ideal and not simply as a derivative ideal that can be explained in terms of the values of fairness or equality of respect.

The essay is in three sections. In section 1, I focus on Rawls's discussion of democracy and use that discussion both to introduce certain features of a deliberative democracy, and to raise some doubts about whether their importance is naturally explained in terms of the notion of a fair system of social cooperation. In section 2, I develop an account of deliberative democracy in terms of the notion of an *ideal deliberative procedure*. The characterization of that procedure provides an abstract model of deliberation, which links the intuitive ideal of democratic association to a more substantive view of deliberative democracy. Three features of the ideal deliberative procedure figure prominently in the essay. First, it helps to account for some familiar judgments about collective decision-making, in particular about the ways that collective decision-making ought to be different from bargaining, contracting, and other market-type

I have had countless discussions of the subject matter of this essay with Joel Rogers, and wish to thank him for his unfailingly sound and generous advice. For our joint treatment of the issues that I discuss here, see Joshua Cohen and Joel Rogers, *On Democracy* (Harmondsworth: Penguin, 1983), ch. 6. The main differences between the treatment of issues here and the treatment in the book lie in the explicit account of the ideal deliberative procedure, the fuller treatment of the notions of autonomy and the common good, and the account of the connection of those notions with the ideal procedure. An earlier draft of this essay was presented to the Pacific Division Meetings of the American Philosophical Association. I would like to thank Loren Lomasky, Alan Hamlin, and Philip Pettit for helpful comments on that draft.

1. I originally came across the term "deliberative democracy" in Cass Sunstein, "Interest Groups in American Public Law," *Stanford Law Review* 38 (1985): 29–87. He cites (n. 26) an article by Bessette, which I have not consulted.

interactions, both in its explicit attention to considerations of the common advantage and in the ways that that attention helps to form the aims of the participants. Second, it accounts for the common view that the notion of democratic association is tied to notions of autonomy and the common good. Third, the ideal deliberative procedure provides a distinctive structure for addressing institutional questions. And in section 3 of the essay I rely on that distinctive structure in responding to four objections to the account of deliberative democracy.

1

The idea of deliberative democracy is a familiar ideal. Aspects of it have been highlighted in recent discussion of the role of republican conceptions of self-government in shaping the American constitutional tradition and contemporary public law.[2] It is represented as well in radical democratic and socialist criticisms of the politics of advanced industrial societies.[3] And some of its central features are highlighted in Rawls's account of democratic politics in a just society, particularly in those parts of his account that seek to incorporate the "liberty of the ancients" and to respond to radical democrats and socialists who argue that "the basic liberties may prove to be merely formal." In the discussion that follows I shall first say something about Rawls's remarks on three such features, and then consider his explanation of them.[4]

First, in a well-ordered democracy, political debate is organized around alternative conceptions of the public good. So an ideal pluralist

2. For some representative examples, see Cass Sunstein, "Naked Preferences and the Constitution," *Columbia Law Review* 84 (1984): 1689–1732; idem, "Interest Groups in American Public Law"; idem, "Legal Interference with Private Preferences," *University of Chicago Law Review* 53 (1986): 1129–1184. Frank Michelman, "The Supreme Court, 1985 Term—Foreword: Traces of Self-government," *Harvard Law Review* 100 (1986): 4–77. Bruce Ackerman, "The Storrs Lectures: Discovering the Constitution," *Yale Law Journal* 93 (1984): 1013–1072.

3. I have in mind, in particular, criticisms that focus on the ways in which material inequalities and weak political parties restrict democracy by constraining public political debate or undermining the equality of the participants in that debate. For discussion of these criticisms, and of their connections with the ideal of democratic order, see Cohen and Rogers, *On Democracy*, chs. 3, 6; Roberto Unger, *False Necessity* (Cambridge: Cambridge University Press, 1987), ch. 5.

4. In the discussion that follows, I draw on John Rawls, *A Theory of Justice* (Cambridge, MA: Harvard University Press, 1971), esp. sections 36, 37, 43, 54; John Rawls, "The Basic Liberties and Their Priority," *Tanner Lectures on Human Values* (Salt Lake City: University of Utah Press, 1982). [The Tanner Lectures were reprinted as Lecture 8 in John Rawls, *Political Liberalism* (New York: Columbia University Press, 1996). I have kept the references to the original here.]

scheme, in which democratic politics consists of fair bargaining among groups each of which pursues its particular or sectional interest, is unsuited to a just society.[5] Citizens and parties operating in the political arena ought not to "take a narrow or group-interested standpoint."[6] And parties should only be responsive to demands that are "argued for openly by reference to a conception of the public good."[7] Public explanations and justifications of laws and policies are to be cast in terms of conceptions of the common good (conceptions that, on Rawls's view, must be consistent with the two principles of justice), and public deliberation should aim to work out the details of such conceptions and to apply them to particular issues of public policy.[8]

Second, the ideal of democratic order has egalitarian implications that must be satisfied in ways that are manifest to citizens. The reason is that in a just society political opportunities and powers must be independent of economic or social position—the political liberties must have a fair value[9]—and the fact that they are independent must be more or less evident to citizens. Ensuring this manifestly fair value might, for example, require public funding of political parties and restrictions on private political spending, as well as progressive tax measures that serve to limit inequalities of wealth and to ensure that the political agenda is not controlled by the interests of economically and socially dominant groups.[10] In principle, these distributional requirements might be more stringently egalitarian than those fixed by the difference principle.[11] This is so in part because the main point of these measures is not simply to ensure that democratic politics proceeds under fair conditions, nor only to encourage just legislation, but also to ensure that the equality of citizens

---

5. Rawls, *Theory of Justice*, 360–361. [The page references to A *Theory of Justice* in essays 1–7 are to the 1971 edition. For a conversion table to page numbers in the revised, 1999 edition, see John Rawls, *A Theory of Justice*, rev. ed. (Cambridge, MA: Harvard University Press, 1999), 517–519.] This rejection is not particularly idiosyncratic. Sunstein, for example, argues that ideal pluralism has never been embraced as a political ideal in American public law. See his "Naked Preferences" and "Interest Groups."

6. Rawls, *Theory*, 360.

7. Ibid., 226, 472.

8. Ibid., 362.

9. Officially, the requirement of fair value is that "everyone has a fair opportunity to hold public office and to influence the outcome of political decisions." Rawls, "Basic Liberties," 42.

10. Rawls, *Theory*, 225–226, 277–278; "Basic Liberties," 42–43.

11. "Basic Liberties," 43. Whatever their stringency, these distributional requirements take priority over the difference principle, since the requirement of fair value is part of the principle of liberty; that is, the first principle of justice. See ibid., 41–42.

is manifest and to declare a commitment to that equality "as the public intention."[12]

Third, democratic politics should be ordered in ways that provide a basis for self-respect, that encourage the development of a sense of political competence, and that contribute to the formation of a sense of justice;[13] it should fix "the foundations for civic friendship and [shape] the ethos of political culture."[14] Thus the importance of democratic order is not confined to its role in obstructing the class legislation that can be expected from systems in which groups are effectively excluded from the channels of political representation and bargaining. In addition, democratic politics should also shape the ways in which the members of the society understand themselves and their own legitimate interests.

When properly conducted, then, democratic politics involves *public deliberation focused on the common good*, requires some form of *manifest equality* among citizens, and *shapes the identity and interests* of citizens in ways that contribute to the formation of a public conception of common good. How does the ideal of a fair system of social cooperation provide a way to account for the attractiveness and importance of these three features of the deliberative democratic ideal? Rawls suggests a formal and an informal line of argument. The formal argument is that parties in the original position would choose the principle of participation[15] with the proviso that the political liberties have their fair value. The three conditions are important because they must be satisfied if constitutional arrangements are to ensure participation rights, guarantee a fair value to those rights, and plausibly produce legislation that encourages a fair distribution according to the difference principle.

Rawls also suggests an informal argument for the ordering of political institutions, and I shall focus on this informal argument here: "Justice as fairness begins with the idea that where common principles are necessary and to everyone's advantage, they are to be worked out from the viewpoint of a suitably defined initial situation of equality in which each person is fairly represented. The principle of participation transfers this no-

12. Rawls, *Theory*, 233.
13. The importance of democratic politics in the account of the acquisition of the sense of justice is underscored in ibid., 473–474.
14. Ibid., 234.
15. The principle of participation states that "all citizens are to have an equal right to take part in, and to determine the outcome of, the constitutional process that establishes the laws with which they are to comply." Ibid., 221.

tion from the original position to the constitution . . . [thus] preserv[ing] the equal representation of the original position to the degree that is feasible."[16] Or, as he puts it elsewhere: "The idea [of the fair value of political liberty] is to incorporate into the basic structure of society an effective political procedure which *mirrors* in that structure the fair representation of persons achieved by the original position."[17] The suggestion is that, since we accept the intuitive ideal of a fair system of cooperation, we should want our political institutions themselves to conform, insofar as it is feasible, to the requirement that terms of association be worked out under fair conditions. And so we arrive directly at the requirement of equal liberties with fair value, rather than arriving at it indirectly, through a hypothetical choice of that requirement under fair conditions. In this informal argument, the original position serves as an *abstract model* of what fair conditions are, and of what we should strive to mirror in our political institutions, rather than as an initial-choice situation in which regulative principles for those institutions are selected.

I think that Rawls is right in wanting to accommodate the three conditions. What I find less plausible is that the three conditions are natural consequences of the ideal of fairness. Taking the notion of fairness as fundamental, and aiming (as in the informal argument) to model political arrangements on the original position, it is not clear why, for example, political debate ought to be focused on the common good, or why the manifest equality of citizens is an important feature of a democratic association. The pluralist conception of democratic politics as a system of bargaining with fair representation for all groups seems an equally good mirror of the ideal of fairness.

The response to this objection is clear enough: the connection between the ideal of fairness and the three features of democratic politics depends on psychological and sociological assumptions. Those features do not follow directly from the ideal of a fair system of cooperation, or from that ideal as it is modeled in the original position. Rather, we arrive at them when we consider what is required to preserve fair arrangements and to achieve fair outcomes. For example, public political debate should be conducted in terms of considerations of the common good because we cannot expect outcomes that advance the common good unless

---

16. Ibid., 221–222. I assume that the principle of participation should be understood here to include the requirement of the fair value of political liberty.

17. Rawls, "Basic Liberties," 45; emphasis added.

people are looking for them. Even an ideal pluralist scheme, with equal bargaining power and no barriers to entry, cannot reasonably be expected to advance the common good as defined by the difference principle.[18]

But this is, I think, too indirect and instrumental an argument for the three conditions. Like utilitarian defenses of liberty, it rests on a series of highly speculative sociological and psychological judgments. I want to suggest that the reason why the three are attractive is not that an order with, for example, no explicit deliberation about the common good and no manifest equality would be unfair (though of course it might be). Instead it is that they comprise elements of an independent and expressly political ideal that is focused in the first instance[19] on the appropriate conduct of public affairs—on, that is, the appropriate ways of arriving at collective decisions. And to understand that ideal we ought not to proceed by seeking to "mirror" ideal fairness in the fairness of political arrangements, but instead to proceed by seeking to mirror a system of ideal deliberation in social and political institutions. I want now to turn to this alternative.

2

The notion of a deliberative democracy is rooted in the intuitive ideal of a democratic association in which the justification of the terms and conditions of association proceeds through public argument and reasoning among equal citizens.[20] Citizens in such an order share a commitment to the resolution of problems of collective choice through public reasoning and regard their basic institutions as legitimate insofar as they establish the framework for free public deliberation. To elaborate this ideal, I be-

18. Rawls, *Theory*, 360.

19. The reasons for the phrase "in the first instance" are clarified below at 29.

20. Since writing the first draft of this section of the essay, I have read Jon Elster, "The Market and the Forum: Three Varieties of Political Theory," in Jon Elster and Aanund Hylland, eds., *Foundations of Social Choice Theory* (Cambridge: Cambridge University Press, 1986), 103–132; and Bernard Manin, "On Legitimacy and Political Deliberation," *Political Theory* 15 (1987): 338–368, which both present parallel conceptions. This is especially so with Elster's treatment of the psychology of public deliberation (112–113). I am indebted to Alan Hamlin for bringing the Elster article to my attention. The overlap is explained by the fact that Elster, Manin, and I all draw on Jürgen Habermas. See Jürgen Habermas, *Legitimation Crisis*, trans. Thomas McCarthy (Boston: Beacon Press, 1975); idem, *Communication and the Evolution of Society*, trans. Thomas McCarthy (Boston: Beacon Press, 1979); and idem, *The Theory of Communicative Action*, vol. 1, trans. Thomas McCarthy (Boston: Beacon Press, 1984). I have also found very helpful the discussion of the contractualist account of motivation in T. M. Scanlon, "Contractualism and Utilitarianism," in Amartya Sen and Bernard Williams, eds., *Utilitarianism and Beyond* (Cambridge: Cambridge University Press, 1982), 103–128.

gin with a more explicit account of the ideal itself, presenting what I shall call the "formal conception" of deliberative democracy. Proceeding from this formal conception, I pursue a more substantive account of deliberative democracy by presenting an account of an *ideal deliberative procedure* that captures the notion of justification through public argument and reasoning among equal citizens and serves in turn as a model for deliberative institutions.

The formal conception of a deliberative democracy has five main features:

D1 A deliberative democracy is an ongoing and independent association, whose members expect it to continue into the indefinite future.

D2 The members of the association share (and it is common knowledge that they share) the view that the appropriate terms of association provide a framework for or are the results of their deliberation. They share, that is, a commitment to coordinating their activities within institutions that make deliberation possible and according to norms that they arrive at through their deliberation. For them, free deliberation among equals is the basis of legitimacy.

D3 A deliberative democracy is a pluralistic association. The members have diverse preferences, convictions, and ideals concerning the conduct of their own lives. While sharing a commitment to the deliberative resolution of problems of collective choice (D2), they also have divergent aims, and do not think that some particular set of preferences, convictions, or ideals is mandatory.

D4 Because the members of a democratic association regard deliberative procedures as the source of *legitimacy*, it is important to them that the terms of their association not merely *be* the results of their deliberation but also be *manifest* to them as such.[21] They prefer institutions in which the connections between deliberation and outcomes are evident to ones in which the connections are less clear.

D5 The members recognize one another as having deliberative capac-

21. For philosophical discussions of the importance of manifestness or publicity, see Immanuel Kant, "Toward Perpetual Peace: A Philosophical Essay," in *Perpetual Peace and Other Essays*, trans. Thomas Humphrey (Indianapolis: Hackett, 1983), 135–139; Rawls, *Theory*, 133 and section 29; Bernard Williams, *Ethics and the Limits of Philosophy* (Cambridge, MA: Harvard University Press, 1985), 101–102, 200.

ities, i.e., the capacities required for entering into a public exchange of reasons and for acting on the results of such public reasoning.

A theory of deliberative democracy aims to give substance to this formal ideal by characterizing the conditions that should obtain if the social order is to be manifestly regulated by deliberative forms of collective choice. I propose to sketch a view of this sort by considering an ideal scheme of deliberation, which I shall call the "ideal deliberative procedure." The aim in sketching this procedure is to give an explicit statement of the conditions for deliberative decision-making that are suited to the formal conception, and thereby to highlight the properties that democratic institutions should embody, so far as possible. I should emphasize that the ideal deliberative procedure is meant to provide a model for institutions to mirror—in the first instance for the institutions in which collective choices are made and social outcomes publicly justified—and not to characterize an initial situation in which the terms of association themselves are chosen.[22]

Turning then to the ideal procedure, there are three general aspects of deliberation. There is a need to decide on an agenda, to propose alternative solutions to the problems on the agenda, supporting those solutions with reasons, and to conclude by settling on an alternative. A democratic conception can be represented in terms of the requirements that it sets on such a procedure. In particular, outcomes are democratically legitimate if and only if they could be the object of a free and reasoned agreement among equals. The ideal deliberative procedure is a procedure that captures this principle.[23]

I₁ Ideal deliberation is *free* in that it satisfies two conditions. First, the participants regard themselves as bound only by the results of their deliberation and by the preconditions for that deliberation. Their consideration of proposals is not constrained by the authority of

22. The distinction between the ideal procedure and an initial-choice situation will be important in the later discussion of motivation formation (see 26–27) and institutions (34–36).

23. There are of course norms and requirements on individuals that do not have deliberative justification. The conception of deliberative democracy is, in Rawls's term, a "political conception," and not a comprehensive moral theory. On the distinction between political and comprehensive theories, see John Rawls, "The Idea of an Overlapping Consensus," *Oxford Journal of Legal Studies* 7 (1987): 1–25.

prior norms or requirements. Second, the participants suppose that they can act from the results, taking the fact that a certain decision is arrived at through their deliberation as a sufficient reason for complying with it.

I2 Deliberation is *reasoned* in that the parties of it are required to state their reasons for advancing proposals, supporting them, or criticizing them. They give reasons with the expectation that those reasons (and not, for example, their power) will settle the fate of their proposal. In ideal deliberation, as Habermas puts it, "no force except that of the better argument is exercised."[24] Reasons are offered with the aim of bringing others to accept the proposal, given their disparate ends (D3) and their commitment (D2) to settling the conditions of their association through free deliberation among equals. Proposals may be rejected because they are not defended with acceptable reasons, even if they could be so defended. The deliberative conception emphasizes that collective choices should be *made in a deliberative way,* and not only that those choices should have a desirable fit with the preferences of citizens.

I3 In ideal deliberation parties are both formally and substantively *equal.* They are formally equal in that the rules regulating the procedure do not single out individuals. Everyone with the deliberative capacities has equal standing at each stage of the deliberative process. Each can put issues on the agenda, propose solutions, and offer reasons in support of or in criticism of proposals. And each has an equal voice in the decision. The participants are substantively equal in that the existing distribution of power and resources does not shape their chances to contribute to deliberation, nor does that distribution play an authoritative role in the deliberation. The participants in the deliberative procedure do not regard themselves as bound by the existing system of rights, except insofar as that system establishes the framework of free deliberation among equals. Instead they regard that system as a potential object of their deliberative judgment.

I4 Finally, ideal deliberation aims to arrive at a rationally motivated *consensus*—to find reasons that are persuasive to all who are com-

24. Habermas, *Legitimation Crisis,* 108.

mitted to acting on the results of a free and reasoned assessment of alternatives by equals. Even under ideal conditions there is no promise that consensual reasons will be forthcoming. If they are not, then deliberation concludes with voting, subject to some form of majority rule.[25] The fact that it may so conclude does not, however, eliminate the distinction between deliberative forms of collective choice and forms that aggregate non-deliberative preferences. The institutional consequences are likely to be different in the two cases, and the results of voting among those who are committed to finding reasons that are persuasive to all are likely to differ from the results of an aggregation that proceeds in an absence of this commitment.

Drawing on this characterization of ideal deliberation, can we say anything more substantive about a deliberative democracy? What are the implications of a commitment to deliberative decisions for the terms of social association? In the remarks that follow I shall indicate the ways that this commitment carries with it a commitment to advance the common good and to respect individual autonomy.

COMMON GOOD AND AUTONOMY

Consider first the notion of the common good. Since the aim of ideal deliberation is to secure agreement among all who are committed to free deliberation among equals, and the condition of pluralism obtains (D3), the focus of deliberation is on ways of advancing the aims of each party to it. While no one is indifferent to his/her own good, everyone also seeks to arrive at decisions that are acceptable to all who share the commitment to deliberation (D2). (As we shall see just below, taking that commitment seriously is likely to require a willingness to revise one's own preferences and convictions.) Thus the characterization of an ideal deliberation procedure links the formal notion of deliberative democracy with the more substantive ideal of a democratic association in which public debate is focused on the common good of the members.

Of course, talk about the common good is one thing; sincere efforts to advance it are another. While public deliberation may be organized around appeals to the common good, is there any reason to think that

25. For criticism of the reliance on an assumption of unanimity in deliberative views, see Manin, "On Legitimacy," 359–361.

even ideal deliberation would not consist in efforts to disguise personal or class advantage as the common advantage? There are two responses to this question. The first is that in my account of the formal idea of a deliberative democracy, I stipulated (D2) that the members of the association are committed to resolving their differences through deliberation, and thus to providing reasons that they sincerely expect to be persuasive to others who share that commitment. In short, this stipulation rules out the problem. Presumably, however, the objection is best understood as directed against the plausibility of realizing a deliberative procedure that conforms to the ideal, and thus is not answerable through stipulations.

The second response, then, rests on a claim about the effects of deliberation on the motivations of deliberators.[26] A consequence of the reasonableness of the deliberative procedure (I2) together with the condition of pluralism (D3) is that the mere fact of having a preference, a conviction, or an ideal does not by itself provide a reason in support of a proposal. While I may take my preferences as a sufficient reason for advancing a proposal, deliberation under conditions of pluralism requires that I find reasons that make the proposal acceptable to others who cannot be expected to regard my preferences as sufficient reasons for agreeing. The motivational thesis is that the need to advance reasons that persuade others will help to shape the motivations that people bring to the deliberative procedure in two ways. First, the practice of presenting reasons will contribute to the formation of a commitment to the deliberative resolutions of political questions (D2). Given that commitment, the likelihood of a sincere representation of preferences and convictions should increase, while the likelihood of their strategic misrepresentation declines. Second, it will shape the content of preferences and convictions as well. Assuming a commitment to deliberative justification, the discovery that I can offer no persuasive reasons on behalf of a proposal of mine may transform the preferences that motivate the proposal. Aims that I recognize to be inconsistent with the requirements of deliberative agreement may tend to lose their force, at least when I expect others to be proceeding in reasonable ways and expect the outcome of deliberation to regulate subsequent action.

Consider, for example, the desire to be wealthier come what may. I

26. Note the parallel with Elster, "The Market and the Forum," indicated in note 20. See also the discussion in Habermas, *Legitimation Crisis*, 108, about "needs that can be communicatively shared," and Habermas, *Communication and the Evolution of Society*, ch. 2.

cannot appeal to this desire itself in defending policies. The motivational claim is the need to find an independent justification that does not appeal to this desire and will tend to shape it into, for example, a desire to have a level of wealth that is consistent with a level that others (i.e., equal citizens) find acceptable. I am of course assuming that the deliberation is known to be regulative, and that the wealth cannot be protected through wholly non-deliberative means.

Deliberation, then, focuses debate on the common good. And the relevant conceptions of the common good are not comprised simply of interests and preferences that are antecedent to deliberation. Instead, the interests, aims, and ideals that constitute the common good are those that survive deliberation, interests that, on public reflection, we think it legitimate to appeal to in making claims on social resources. Thus the first and third of the features of deliberative democracy that I mentioned in discussion of Rawls (17–19 above) provide central elements in the deliberative conception.

The ideal deliberation scheme also indicates the importance of autonomy in a deliberative democracy. In particular, it is responsive to two main threats to autonomy. As a general matter, actions fail to be autonomous if the preferences on which an agent acts are, roughly, given by the circumstances, and not determined by the agent. There are two paradigm cases of "external" determination. The first is what Elster has called "adaptive preferences."[27] These are preferences that shift with changes in the circumstances of the agent without any deliberate contribution by the agent to that shift. This is true, for example, of the political preferences of instinctive centrists who move to the median position in the political distribution, wherever it happens to be. The second I shall call "accommodationist preferences." While they are deliberately formed, accommodationist preferences represent psychological adjustments to conditions of subordination in which individuals are not recognized as having the capacity for self-government. Consider Stoic slaves, who deliberately shape their desires to match their powers, with a view of minimizing frustration. Since the existing relations of power make slavery the only possibility, they cultivate desires to be slaves, and then act on those desires. While their motives are deliberately formed, and they act on

27. Jon Elster, "Sour Grapes," in Sen and Williams, eds., *Utilitarianism and Beyond*, 219–238. For an interesting discussion of autonomous preferences and political processes, see Sunstein, "Legal Interference," 1145–1158, and "Naked Preferences," 1699–1700.

their desires, the Stoic slaves do not act autonomously when they seek to be good slaves. The absence of alternatives and consequent denial of scope for deliberative capacities that defines the condition of slaves supports the conclusion that their desires result from their circumstances, even though those circumstances shape the desires of the Stoic slaves through their deliberation.

There are then at least two dimensions of autonomy. The phenomenon of adaptive preferences underlines the importance of conditions that permit and encourage the deliberative formation of preferences; the phenomenon of accommodationist preferences indicates the need for favorable conditions for the exercise of the deliberative capacities. Both concerns are met when institutions for collective decision-making are modeled on the ideal deliberative procedure. Relations of power and subordination are neutralized (I1, I3, I4), and each is recognized as having the deliberative capacities (D5), thus addressing the problem of accommodationist preferences. Further, the requirement of reasonableness discourages adaptive preferences (I2). While preferences are "formed" by the deliberative procedure, this type of preferences formation is consistent with autonomy, since preferences that are shaped by public deliberation are not simply given by external circumstances. Instead, they are the result of "the power of reason as applied through public discussion."[28]

Beginning, then, from the formal ideal of a deliberative democracy, we arrive at the more substantive ideal of an association that is regulated by deliberation aimed at the common good and that respects the autonomy of the members. And so, in seeking to embody the ideal deliberative procedure in institutions, we seek, *inter alia*, to design institutions that focus on political debates on the common good, that shape the identity and interests of citizens in ways that contribute to an attachment to the common good, and that provide the favorable conditions for the exercise of deliberative powers that are required for autonomy.

3

I want now to shift the focus. While I shall continue to pursue the relationship between the ideal procedure and more substantive issues about deliberative democratic association, I want to do so by considering four

---

28. Whitney v. California, 274 U.S. 357 (1927).

natural objections to the conception I have been discussing, objections to that conception for being sectarian, incoherent, unjust, and irrelevant. My aim is not to provide a detailed response to the objections, but to clarify the conception of deliberative democracy by sketching the lines along which a response should proceed. Before turning to the objections, I enter two remarks about what follows.

First, as I indicated earlier, a central aim in the deliberative conception is to specify the institutional preconditions for deliberative decision-making. The role of the ideal deliberative procedure is to provide an abstract characterization of the important properties of deliberative institutions. The role of the ideal deliberative procedure is thus different from the role of an ideal social contract. The ideal deliberative procedure provides a model for institutions, a model that they should mirror, so far as possible. It is not a choice situation in which institutional principles are selected. The key point about the institutional reflection is that it should *make deliberation possible*. Institutions in a deliberative democracy do not serve simply to implement the results of deliberation, as though free deliberation could proceed in the absence of appropriate institutions. Neither the commitment to nor the capacity for arriving at deliberative decisions is something that we can simply assume to obtain independent from the proper ordering of institutions. The institutions themselves must provide the framework for the formation of the will; they determine whether there is equality, whether deliberation is free and reasoned, whether there is autonomy, and so on.

Second, I shall be focusing here on some requirements for "public" institutions that reflect the ideal of deliberative resolution. But there is, of course, no reason to expect as a general matter that the preconditions for deliberation will respect familiar institutional boundaries between "private" and "public" and will all pertain to the public arena. For example, inequalities of wealth, or the absence of institutional measures designed to redress the consequences of those inequalities, can serve to undermine the equality required in deliberative arenas themselves. And so a more complete treatment would need to address a wider range of institutional issues.[29]

---

29. See Cohen and Rogers, *On Democracy*, chs. 3, 6; Joshua Cohen, "The Economic Basis of Deliberative Democracy," *Social Philosophy and Policy* 6, 2 (1988): 25–50.

SECTARIANISM

The first objection is that the ideal of deliberative democracy is objectionably sectarian because it depends on a particular view of the good life—an ideal of active citizenship. What makes it sectarian is not the specific ideal on which it depends but the (alleged) fact that it depends on some specific conception at all. I do not think that the conception of deliberative democracy suffers from the alleged difficulty. In explaining why not, I shall put to the side current controversy about the thesis that sectarianism is avoidable and objectionable and assume that it is both.[30]

Views of the good figure in political conceptions in at least two ways. First, the *justification* of some conceptions appeals to a notion of the human good. Aristotelian views, for example, endorse the claim that the exercise of the deliberative capacities is a fundamental component of a good human life and conclude that a political association ought to be organized to encourage the realization of those capacities by its members. A second way in which conceptions of the good enter is that the *stability* of a society may require widespread allegiance to a specific conception of the good, even though its institutions can be justified without appeal to that conception. For example, a social order that can be justified without reference to ideals of national allegiance may nonetheless require widespread endorsement of the ideal of patriotic devotion for its stability.

A political conception is objectionably sectarian only if its *justification* depends on a particular view of the human good, not if its stability is contingent on widespread agreement on the value of certain activities and aspirations. For this reason the democratic conception is not sectarian. It is organized around a view of political justification—that justification proceeds through free deliberation among equal citizens—and not around a conception of the proper conduct of life. So, while it is plausible that the stability of a deliberative democracy depends on encouraging the ideal of active citizenship, this dependence does not suffice to show that it is objectionably sectarian.

30. For contrasting views on sectarianism, see Rawls, "The Idea of an Overlapping Consensus"; Ronald Dworkin, *A Matter of Principle* (Cambridge, MA: Harvard University Press, 1985), part 3; Alisdair MacIntyre, *After Virtue* (Notre Dame: University of Notre Dame Press, 1981); Michael Sandel, *Liberalism and the Limits of Justice* (Cambridge: Cambridge University Press, 1982).

INCOHERENCE

Consider next the putative incoherence of the ideal. We find this charge in an important tradition of argument, including Schumpeter's *Capitalism, Socialism, and Democracy* and, more recently, William Riker's work on social choice and democracy. I want here to say a word about the latter, focusing on just one reason that Riker gives for thinking that the ideal of popular self-government is incoherent.[31]

Institutionalizing a deliberative procedure requires a decision rule short of consensus—for example, majority rule. But majority rule is globally unstable: as a general matter, there exists a majority-rule path leading from any element in the set of alternatives to any other element in the set. The majority, standing in for the people, wills everything and therefore wills nothing. Of course, while anything can be the result of the majority decision, it is not true that everything will be the result. But, because majority rule is so unstable, the actual decision of the majority will not be determined by preferences themselves, since they do not constrain the outcome. Instead decisions will reflect the particular institutional constraints under which they are made. But these constraints are "exogenous to the world of tastes and values."[32] So the ideal of popular self-government is incoherent because we are, so to speak, government by the institutions, and not by ourselves.

I want to suggest one difficulty with this argument that highlights the structure of the deliberative conception. According to the argument I just sketched, outcomes in majority-rule institutions reflect "exogenous" institutional constraints and not underlying preferences. This suggests that we can identify the preferences and convictions that are relevant to collective choices apart from the institutions through which they are formed and expressed. But that is just what the deliberative conception denies. On this conception, the relevant preferences and convictions are those that could be expressed in free deliberation, and not those that are prior to it. For this reason, popular self-government *premises* the existence of institutions that provide a framework for deliberation; these ar-

31. See William Riker, *Liberalism Against Populism: A Confrontation between the Theory of Democracy and the Theory of Social Choice* (San Francisco: W. H. Freeman, 1982); for discussion of Riker's view see Jules Coleman and John Ferejohn, "Democracy and Social Choice," *Ethics* 97 (1986): 6–25; Joshua Cohen, "An Epistemic Conception of Democracy," *Ethics* 97 (1986): 26–38.

32. Riker, *Liberalism Against Populism*, 190.

rangements are not "exogenous constraints" on the aggregation of preferences but instead help to shape their content and the way that citizens choose to advance them. And, once the deliberative institutions are in place, and preferences, convictions, and political actions are shaped by them, it is not clear that instability problems remain so severe as to support the conclusion that self-government is an empty and incoherent ideal.

INJUSTICE

The third problem concerns injustice. I have been treating the ideal of democracy as the basic ideal for a political conception. But it might be argued that the ideal of democracy is not suited to the role of fundamental political ideal because its treatment of basic liberties is manifestly unacceptable. It makes those liberties dependent on judgments of majorities and thus endorses the democratic legitimacy of decisions that restrict the basic liberties of individuals. In responding to this objection, I shall focus on the liberty of expression[33] and shall begin by filling out a version of the objection, which I put in the words of an imagined critic.[34]

"You embrace the ideal of a democratic order. The aim of a democratic order is to maximize the *power of the people* to secure its wants. To defend the liberty of expression you will argue that that power is diminished if the people lack the information required for exercising their will. Since expression provides information, you will conclude that abridgements of expression ought to be barred. The problem with your argument is that preventing restrictions on expression also restricts the power

33. For discussion of the connection between ideals of democracy and freedom of expression, see Alexander Meiklejohn, *Free Speech and Its Relation of Self-Government* (New York: Harper and Row, 1948), and John Hart Ely, *Democracy and Distrust* (Cambridge, MA: Harvard University Press, 1980), 93–94, 105–116). Freedom of expression is a special case that can perhaps be more straightforwardly accommodated by the democratic conception than liberties of conscience, or the liberties associated with privacy and personhood. I do think, however, that these other liberties can be given satisfactory treatment by the democratic conception, and would reject it if I did not think so. The general idea would be to argue that other fundamental liberties must be protected if citizens are to be able to engage in and have equal standing in political deliberation without fear that such engagement puts them at risk for their convictions or personal choices. Whether this line of argument will work out on the details is a matter for treatment elsewhere.

34. This objection is suggested by Dworkin, "The Forum of Principle," in A *Matter of Principle*, 61–63. He cites the following passage from a letter of Madison's: "And a people who mean to be their own Governors, must arm themselves with *the power which knowledge gives*" (emphasis added).

of the people, since the citizens may collectively prefer such restrictions. And so it is not at all clear as a general matter that the protection of expression will maximize popular power. So while you will, of course, not want to prevent everyone from speaking all the time, you cannot defend the claim that there is even a presumption in favor of the protection of expression. And this disregard for fundamental liberties is unacceptable."

This objection has force against some conceptions in which democracy is a fundamental ideal, particularly those in which the value of expression turns exclusively on its role as a source of information about how best to advance popular ends. But it does not have any force against the deliberative conception, since the latter does not make the case for expression turn on its role in maximizing the power of the people to secure its wants. That case rests instead on a conception of collective choice, in particular on a view about how the "wants" that are relevant to collective choice are formed and defined in the first place. The relevant preferences and convictions are those that arise or are confirmed through deliberation. And a framework of free expression is required for the reasoned consideration of alternatives that comprises deliberation. The deliberative conception holds that free expression is required for *determining* what advances the common good, because what is good is fixed by public determination, and not prior to it. It is fixed by informed and autonomous judgments, involving the exercise of the deliberative capacities. So the ideal of deliberative democracy is not hostile to free expression; rather, it presupposes such freedom.

But what about expression with no direct bearing on issues of public policy? Is the conception of deliberative democracy committed to treating all "non-political expression" as second-class and as meriting lesser protection? I do not think so. The deliberative conception construes politics as aiming in part at the formation of preferences and convictions, not just at their articulation and aggregation. Because of this emphasis on reasoning about preferences and convictions, and the bearing of expression with no political focus on such reasoning, the deliberative view draws no bright line between political speech and other sorts of expression. Forms of expression that do not address issues of policy may well bear on the formation of interests, aims, and ideals that citizens bring to public deliberation. For this reason, the deliberative conception supports protection for the full range of expression, regardless of the content of that expression.[35] It would violate the core of the ideal of free deliberation among equals to fix preferences and convictions in advance by restricting the content of expression, or by barring access to expression, or by preventing the expression that is essential to having convictions at all. Thus the injustice objection fails because the liberties are not simply among the topics for deliberation; they help to provide the framework that makes it possible.[36]

IRRELEVANCE

The irrelevance objection is that the notion of public deliberation is irrelevant to modern political conditions.[37] This is the most important objection and the one about which it is hardest to say anything at the level of generality required by the present context. Here again I shall confine myself to one version of the objection, though one that I take to be representative.

The version that I want to consider starts from the assumption that a direct democracy with citizens gathering in legislative assemblies is the only way to institutionalize a deliberative procedure. Premising that, and recognizing that direct democracy is impossible under modern conditions, the objection concludes that we ought to be led to reject the ideal because it is not relevant to our circumstances.

The claim about the impossibility of direct democracy is plainly correct. But I see no merit in the claim that direct democracy is the uniquely suitable way to institutionalize the ideal procedure.[38] In fact, in the absence of a theory about the operation of democratic assemblies—a theory which cannot simply stipulate that ideal conditions obtain—there is no reason to be confident that a direct democracy would subject political

35. On the distinction between content-based and content-neutral abridgements, the complexities of drawing the distinction in particular cases, and the special reasons for hostility to content-based abridgements, see Laurence Tribe, *American Constitutional Law* (Mineola, NY: Foundation Press, 1978), 584–682; Geoffrey Stone, "Content-neutral Restrictions," *University of Chicago Law Review* 54 (1987): 46–118.

36. I am not suggesting that the deliberative view provides the only sound justification for the liberty of expression. My concern here is rather to show that the deliberative view is capable of accommodating it.

37. For an especially sharp statement of the irrelevance objection, see Carl Schmitt, *The Crisis of Parliamentary Democracy*, trans. Ellen Kennedy (Cambridge, MA: MIT Press, 1985).

38. This view is sometimes associated with Rousseau, who is said to have conflated the notion of democratic legitimacy with the institutional expression of that ideal in a direct democracy. For criticism of this interpretation, see Joshua Cohen, "Autonomy and Democracy: Reflections on Rousseau," *Philosophy and Public Affairs* 15, 3 (Summer 1986): 275–297.

questions to deliberative resolution, even if a direct democracy were a genuine institutional possibility.[39] In the absence of a realistic account of the functioning of citizen assemblies, we cannot simply assume that large gatherings with open-ended agendas will yield any deliberation at all or that they will encourage participants to regard one another as equals in a free deliberative procedure. The appropriate ordering of deliberative institutions depends on issues of political psychology and political behavior; it is not an immediate consequence of the deliberative ideal. So, far from being the only deliberative scheme, direct democracy may not even be a particularly good arrangement for deliberation. But, once we reject the idea that a direct democracy is the natural or necessary form of expression of the deliberative ideal, the straightforward argument for irrelevance no longer works. In saying how the ideal might be relevant, however, we come up against the problem I mentioned earlier. Lacking a good understanding of the workings of institutions, we are inevitably thrown back on more or less speculative judgments. What follows are some sketchy remarks on one issue that should be taken in this spirit.

At the heart of the institutionalization of the deliberative procedure is the existence of arenas in which citizens can propose issues for the political agenda and participate in debate about those issues. The existence of such arenas is a public good and ought to be supported with public money. This is not because public support is the only way, or even the most efficient way, of ensuring the provision of such arenas. Instead, public provision expresses the basic commitment of a democratic order to the resolution of political questions through free deliberation among equals. The problem is to figure out how arenas might be organized to encourage such deliberation.

In considering that organization, there are two key points that I want to underscore. The first is that material inequalities are an important source of political inequalities. The second point—which is more speculative—is that deliberative arenas that are organized exclusively on local, sectional, or issue-specific lines are unlikely to produce the open-ended de-

---

39. Madison urges this point in the *Federalist Papers*. Objecting to a proposal advanced by Jefferson, which would have regularly referred constitutional questions "to the decision of the whole society," Madison argues that this would increase "the danger of disturbing the public tranquility by interesting too strongly the public passions." And "it is the reason, alone, of the public that ought to control and regulate the government . . . [while] the passions ought to be controlled and regulated by the government." I endorse the form of the objection, not its content. *Federalist Papers*, ed. Clinton Rossiter (New York: New American Library, 1961), 315–317.

liberation required to institutionalize a deliberative procedure. Since these arenas bring together only a narrow range of interests, deliberation in them can be expected at best to produce coherent sectional interests, not a more comprehensive conception of the common good.

These two considerations together provide support for the view that political parties supported by public funds play an important role in making a deliberative democracy possible.[40] There are two reasons for this, corresponding to the two considerations I have just mentioned. In the first place, an important feature of organizations generally, and parties in particular, is that they provide a means through which individuals and groups who lack the "natural" advantage of wealth can overcome the political disadvantages that follow on that lack. Thus they can help to overcome the inequalities in deliberative arenas that result from material inequality. Of course, to play this role, political organizations must themselves be freed from the dominance of private resources, and that independence must be manifest. Thus the need for public funding. Here we arrive back at the second point that I mentioned in the discussion of Rawls's view—that measures are needed to ensure manifest equality—though now as a way of displaying a shared commitment to fairness. Second, because parties are required to address a comprehensive range of political issues, they provide arenas in which debate is not restricted in the ways that it is in local, sectional, or issue-specific organizations. They can provide the more open-ended arenas needed to form and articulate the conceptions of the common good that provide the focus of political debate in a deliberative democracy.

There is certainly no guarantee that parties will operate as I have just described. But this is not especially troubling, since there are no guarantees of anything in politics. The question is how we can best approximate the deliberative conception. And it is difficult to see how that is possible in the absence of strong parties supported with public resources (though, of course, a wide range of other conditions is required as well).

---

40. Here I draw on Cohen and Rogers, *On Democracy*, 154–157. The idea that parties are required to organize political choice and to provide a focus for public deliberation is one strand of arguments about "responsible parties" in American political-science literature. My understanding of this view has been greatly aided by Lee Perlman, "Parties, Democracy, and Consent," (unpublished PhD dissertation, MIT, 1987), and, more generally, by the work of Walter Dean Burnham on the implications of party decline for democratic politics. See, for example, Burnham, *The Current Crisis in American Politics* (Oxford: Oxford University Press, 1982).

4

I have suggested that we take the notion of democratic association as a fundamental political ideal and have elaborated that ideal by reference to an ideal deliberative procedure and the requirements for institutionalizing such a procedure. I have sketched a few of those requirements here. To show that the democratic ideal can play the role of fundamental organizing ideal, I should need to pursue the account of fundamental liberties and political organization in much greater detail and to address a wide range of other issues as well. Of course, the richer the requirements are for institutionalizing free public deliberation, the larger the range of issues that may need to be removed from the political agenda; that is, the larger the range of issues that forms the background framework of public deliberation rather than its subject matter. And the larger that range, the less there is to deliberate about. Whether that is good news or bad news, it is, in any case, a suitable place to conclude.

2

MORAL PLURALISM AND
POLITICAL CONSENSUS

The idea of normative consensus plays a central role in John Rawls's theory of justice. In a well-ordered society, he says, "everyone has a similar sense of justice and in this respect a well-ordered society is homogeneous."[1] But is a consensus on fundamental norms of justice a realistic and attractive prospect for a morally pluralistic society?[2]

Rawls says little about this question in A *Theory of Justice*. Although he is closely attentive there to the diversity of interests and of conceptions of good among citizens in a well-ordered society, he is generally inattentive to the pluralism of moral conceptions that can be expected when expressive and associative liberties are protected. As a consequence, he does not consider the possibility that this pluralism might either exclude consensus on justice altogether or throw its value into question by turning it into mere compromise. Moreover, since the argument in A *Theory of Justice* that justice as fairness is a realistic conception—in particular, the case for the stability of a just society—depends on the idea that a just society features a consensus on principles of justice, the inattention to moral pluralism renders the force of that argument uncertain. So justice as fairness may be, after all, unrealistic and utopian.[3]

To address these concerns and show that the case for justice as fairness

This essay began as comments on an unpublished paper by John Rawls entitled "A Reasonably Realistic Idea of a Well-ordered Society." I have rewritten it to address Rawls's "The Domain of the Political and Overlapping Consensus," which was originally published in *New York University Law Review* 64, 2 (May 1989): 233–255, and reprinted in the book in which my paper originally appeared. I thank Michael Hardimon, John Rawls, T. M. Scanlon, and Judith Thomson for very helpful comments on earlier drafts of this essay.

1. John Rawls, A *Theory of Justice* (Cambridge, MA: Harvard University Press, 1971), 263.
2. Rawls is concerned with forms of diversity that extend beyond the domain of morality, for example, to religious and philosophical matters. Nothing turns on the limitation that I adopt here.
3. The ideal of consensus may, of course, be unrealistic in other ways as well.

can be restated under more realistic assumptions, Rawls introduced the idea of an *overlapping consensus* and, corresponding to this idea, a condition on the acceptability of a conception of justice that I refer to as the "pluralistic consensus test." A society features an *overlapping consensus* on norms of justice if and only if it is a morally pluralistic society with a consensus on norms of justice in which each citizen, holding one of the different moralities that win adherents and persist over time in the society, supports the consensual norms as the correct account of justice. Norms of justice satisfy the *pluralistic consensus test* if and only if those norms could provide the focus of an overlapping consensus in a society regulated by those norms and operating under favorable conditions.[4] A conception of justice that would not be so supported by at least some of the moral doctrines that persist within a society regulated by it, and so could not be the focus of an overlapping consensus, fails to meet the pluralistic consensus test and is, to this extent, unreasonable.[5]

Why unreasonable? Why (if at all) should requirements of justice be realistic? "Because ought implies can" will not do as an answer, because the question concerns justice, not what ought to be done, all things considered. Judgments about what ought to be done, all things considered, must, of course, be sensitive to all sorts of practical matters, since issues of practicality plainly are among the things to be considered. The question is what sorts of constraints on realizability are constitutive of ideal justice. And in matters of justice, realism is an uncertain good. By accepting the "demands" of realism, we may be led to build an accommodation to unhappy, grim, and even hideous facts of political life into the foundations of political justification and into the fundamental principles of justice themselves.

Focusing this general concern about the demands of realism on the pluralistic consensus test, one might say that in aiming for a conception of justice that could realistically be supported by a pluralistic consensus, one in fact undercuts the attraction of the conception that results. Consider the following elaboration of this objection:

> The pluralistic consensus test asks us to evaluate a conception
> of justice in part by asking whether we can realistically expect
> the conception to be supported as the correct account of justice

4. I return to the issue of favorable conditions later.
5. I explain the point of the phrase "to this extent" later.

by the diverse moralities in a well-ordered society. But why should we be concerned with such support? In fact, requiring it forces an accommodation to power at the foundations of a theory of justice—to the power of those who believe the false and spurn the good. Accommodation to power is commonly prudent and often recommended by our all-things-considered judgments about the application of moral ideals to the facts of life. We give money to the thief who threatens our life; we let the rich get richer if that is what's needed to get them to invest; we pay the lion's share of the surplus to the greedy if that is necessary to motivate them to use their talents for the common good (at least in the first case we don't call it "justice"). And we often frame our political arguments and proposals to win broad acceptance, if that is what we must do to keep those who don't believe the true and love the good from making life worse for those of us who do. But adjustments designed to build support do not define ideal justice. To suppose otherwise would be to permit the facts of power to fix the content of the fundamental requirements of justice, thus undercutting their attraction as basic requirements. Philosophers, above all, should resist the confusion of justice with accommodation and a moral ideal with a consensus on principles that accommodate the power of thieves, pirates, and benighted souls. Because if philosophers are not good for that, then just what are they good for?[6]

Responding to this objection, Rawls argues that consensus on justice is both a realistic and an attractive prospect for a morally pluralistic society and that subjecting conceptions of justice to the pluralistic consensus test is not tantamount to substituting mere compromise for genuine moral consensus and through that substitution advancing an account of justice that is "political in the wrong way" (234).[7]

I agree with Rawls's main contentions, and my aim here is to explore the problem itself, to discuss some surrounding issues, and to clarify the grounds of agreement. After some initial points of clarification, I offer a

6. The objection extrapolates on some points made by G. A. Cohen, in a conversation about Rawls's difference principle.

7. All references to "The Domain of the Political" are included parenthetically within the text. Page numbers refer to the *New York University Law Review* edition cited in the unnumbered note at the start of this essay.

generic statement of the problem of moral consensus and pluralism. Then, I discuss some historical background, linking the problem of pluralism, realism, and moral consensus to a line of argument extending from Rousseau through Hegel to Marx. Next, I discuss and criticize one source of concern about imposing constraints of realism and, in particular, imposing the pluralistic consensus test on a conception of justice— that the constraint of realism undermines a substantively egalitarian conception of justice. Although this discussion does not address the concern about pluralism and realism in its most generic form, I include it because I suspect that the energy surrounding the debate about pluralism and political consensus derives importantly from alleged implications of the debate for matters of equality. Finally, I argue in more general terms that the pluralistic consensus condition does not fall prey to the objection I have sketched here. The argument turns on taking what Rawls calls "the fact of pluralism" (235) in a certain way. In particular, I distinguish the fact of pluralism from the fact of reasonable pluralism and, drawing on this distinction, I suggest that in aiming to find a conception of justice that meets the pluralistic consensus test, we are not simply adjusting ideals to the facts of life and to moral pluralism as one such fact. Instead, we are acknowledging the scope of practical reason. Put otherwise, in aiming to find a conception of justice that meets the pluralistic consensus test, we are not accommodating justice to an unfavorable condition of human life, since, as the idea of reasonable pluralism shows, we ought not to count moral pluralism itself among the unfavorable conditions.

The Place of Consensus

Before getting to these issues, I need to clarify one remark I made earlier. I said that a conception of justice that fails to meet the pluralistic consensus test is, *to this extent*, unreasonable. The phrase "to this extent" is meant to indicate the place of the pluralistic consensus test in an account of justice and, in particular, its role in the two-stage strategy of argument that Rawls sketches in "The Domain of the Political."

Rawls emphasizes that the idea of an overlapping consensus and the pluralistic consensus test come into play at the second stage of a two-part argument for a conception of justice. The aim of the first stage is, roughly, to show that the content of a conception is attractive—that it organizes a set of fundamental political values in a plausible way. The aim of the second stage is to determine whether a conception of justice that is in other respects attractive is also realistic—in particular, that it is stable. Showing that it is stable consists in part in showing that it satisfies the pluralistic consensus test: that different people, brought up within and attracted to different traditions of moral thought, might each affirm the conception as the correct account of justice.

But how, more precisely, are we to understand the relationship between the results of the first stage and the argument at the second? What would follow if there were problems at the second stage? Three possibilities suggest themselves: (1) it is *necessary* that the correct account of justice satisfies the pluralistic consensus test; (2) satisfying the test is not necessary, though it does provide *some support* for a conception of justice; or (3) satisfying the test is a *desideratum* that has *no bearing* on the correctness of an account of justice. In case (3), the pluralistic consensus test might be interpreted as a condition on the all-things-considered reasonableness of a conception of justice or perhaps as a test of the *legitimacy* of the exercise of state power, not as a condition on the justice of the institutions through which that power is exercised. On this interpretation, if the best understanding of justice failed to satisfy the pluralistic consensus test even under favorable conditions, we ought to conclude that there is an unhappy divergence between justice and legitimacy—that even under the best conditions we can realistically hope for, it will be illegitimate to secure justice—but not that we should revise our conception of justice.

Interpretation (3) may by suggested by Rawls's emphasis (234) on the importance of separating the two stages of argument and, so, distinguishing questions of justice from issues about the course of the world. But it is, in fact, ruled out by the description of the conclusions of the first stage as "provisionally on hand" (246) and the remark that the argument is "not complete" until the case for stability has been presented (245n27). I am not sure which of the other two views Rawls means to endorse. But for the purposes of this essay, I will assume that (2) is right, that satisfying the pluralistic consensus condition does count in favor of the correctness of a conception of justice, and that while failure to meet it is not a sufficient reason for rejecting a conception, it would provide some reason to modify a view to bring it into conformity with that test.

Consensus and Moral Pluralism

Pluralism takes a variety of forms, and so there is, correspondingly, a variety of ways that it might raise troubles for consensus and social unity. To state the specific problem of pluralism and consensus that I will be considering here, I first need to fix some terminology. Following Rawls, then, I will say that a "well-ordered society" is a society in which it is common knowledge that the members share an understanding of justice and a willingness to act on that understanding. A well-ordered society, that is, features a restricted but important moral consensus. The moral consensus is restricted in that it extends only to certain basic constitutional values and principles and norms of distributive justice, and not to all aspects of the conduct of life. Despite this limitation, the consensus that defines a well-ordered society is a genuinely *moral* consensus. For the norms and ideals on which there is consensus play a reason-giving and an authoritative role in the deliberation and choices of individual citizens.[8]

At the same time, a well-ordered society may be morally pluralistic in that members may have conflicting views about the fundamental norms and ideals that ought to guide conduct in life more generally. In a morally pluralistic society, the members hold different theories about what is valuable and worth doing. Thus understood, moral pluralism is to be distinguished both from cultural pluralism—the existence of groups of people within a single society who share distinct histories and ways of life and who share a common identity as members of a group—and from organizational pluralism—the existence of a plurality of organized groups pursuing distinctive interests or ideals. These forms of pluralism are distinct phenomena and less plausibly understood as a matter of people holding different theories. So the discussion here of moral pluralism and consensus is limited and does not naturally translate into an account of consensus and either cultural or organizational pluralism.

Moving now from terminology to substance: a moral consensus on political fundamentals is a fundamental good for at least three reasons. First, for any conception of justice, the likelihood that social order will stably conform to the conception is increased by the existence of a moral consensus on it.[9]

Second, the existence of a moral consensus supports a variety of specific values of considerable importance. It increases social trust and har-

---

8. I identify moral reasons by their functional role in individual deliberation and choice not by their content. There may be content restrictions as well, but I think that the functional role characterization captures a central aspect of ordinary usage and in any case suffices for my purposes here.

9. See Rawls's "third general fact," 235.

mony, supports social peace, reduces the complexity of decision making, encourages a willingness to cooperate and so reduces the costs of monitoring and enforcement, and—assuming the consensus is reflected in public debate and decisions—reduces alienation from public choices, because citizens embrace the norms and ideals that guide those choices.

Third, a consensus on norms of justice provides a way to reconcile the ideal of an association whose members are self-governing with an acknowledgment of the central role of social and political arrangements in shaping the self-conceptions of citizens, constraining their actions, channeling their choices, and determining the outcomes of those choices.[10] For when a consensus on norms and values underlies and explains collective decisions, citizens whose lives are governed by those decisions might nonetheless be said to be self-governing, because each endorses the considerations that produce the decisions as genuinely moral reasons and affirms their implementation.[11]

But not just any consensus is attractive, as is indicated by reflection on these reasons themselves. If, for example, a moral consensus is attractive because it provides a way to make the ideal of free association consistent with the unavoidable chains of political connection, then the consensus must be a free moral consensus and not simply a form of enforced homogeneity. A free consensus is a consensus arrived at under conditions that ensure the possibility of individual reflection and public deliberation— conditions in which, for instance, expressive and associative liberties are protected.

It is at just this point that a minimal condition of realism appears to undermine either the possibility of consensus or, at least, its attractions as an ideal. For the assurance of expressive and associative liberties—an assurance that is necessary if the consensus is to be free and attractive—will also produce moral, religious, and philosophical pluralism.[12] But can a genuine moral consensus survive this "fact of pluralism" (235)? Or does an insistence on consensus under conditions of pluralism in effect turn political philosophy into a search for a political compromise among people who disagree?

---

10. See Jean-Jacques Rousseau, *On the Social Contract*, trans. Judith R. Masters (New York: St. Martin's, 1978), Book 1, chap. 6.

11. We also need to add that everyone believes with good reason that the decisions express the values.

12. This is what Rawls calls the "first general fact." See 234–235.

Historical Excursus

These concerns about the pluralistic consensus condition ought to have a familiar ring. Earlier I mentioned the problem of reconciling self-government with the chains of political connection. Rousseau identified this problem and thought it could be solved if social order were regulated by a consensual understanding of the common good—a "general will." Rousseau's solution is commonly rejected on the ground that it is inattentive to differences among people and to the diversity of human interests and ideals. In the face of that diversity, according to the objection, consensus on the common good can be achieved only through the unattractive combination of a sectarian conception of virtue and, for those who do not share that conception, enforced subordination and homogeneity in the name of freedom.

Hegel's response to Rousseau was more complex. He agreed that freedom could be reconciled with the chains of political connection and applauded the notion of a general will as the way to achieve that reconciliation.[13] But he also appreciated the force of the critique of Rousseau that I just sketched. His conclusion was that it was necessary to reformulate the classical ideal of a political community organized around a moral consensus in light of the modern distinction between the unity of political society and the diversity of civil society. This distinction shapes Hegel's own political conception in three important ways:

1. He endorsed a fundamental distinction between civic diversity and political unity, associating that distinction with the differentiation between two spheres of social life. While the civil sphere would feature a diversity of aims and ideals and a range of individual and group activities organized around those aims and ideals, the political sphere would be organized around a set of values that both claimed authority over individual concerns and were alleged to lie within the diverse aspirations of civil life and to provide their common ground.[14]

2. His distinction between political unity and civic diversity is associ-

13. Hegel's discussion of Rousseau in the *History of Philosophy* is more balanced than his critical remarks in the *Philosophy of Right*. Compare *Lectures on the History of Philosophy*, vol. 3, trans. Elizabeth Haldane (New York: Humanities Press, 1968) with *Philosophy of Right*, trans. T. M. Knox (Oxford: Clarendon Press, 1952), 156–157.

14. See *Philosophy of Right*, paragraph 261, where Hegel says that the state is both an "external necessity," with respect to the family and civil society, and "the end immanent within them."

ated with an acceptance of substantially inegalitarian forms of civic diversity,[15] as though an acceptance of that distinction and of a social sphere in which people pursue diverse aims itself brings inegalitarian implications in its wake.

3. Concerned to affirm the unity of the state in the face of the tendencies to social fragmentation that might follow from civic diversity, he defended a strong, highly centralized, executive-dominated constitutional monarchy, featuring a corporatist form of representation and special political rights for the landed class.

At least since Marx, critics of Hegel have objected that some or all of these gestures at reinterpreting the ideal of political unity in the face of civic diversity represent unwanted accommodations to de facto power in the formulation of basic political ideals. Marx, for example, objected to all three.[16] Putting Hegel's favored form of state to the side, these allegations of "accommodation" raise two questions that are relevant for our purposes here.

First, does the reformulation of the ideal of consensual political unity with an eye to respecting the diversity of civil society itself represent an objectionable accommodation? Do we find unacceptable accommodation in Hegel's reformulation of the ideal of political society to accommodate the diversity of aspirations characteristic of civil society or in Rawls's broadly parallel idea that a reasonable conception of justice should be supportable by an overlapping consensus?

Second, does the affirmation of moral diversity lead to an accommodation of social and economic privilege? A *Theory of Justice* defended an egalitarian liberalism that departed from Hegel's accommodation to inegalitarian forms of civic diversity. Does this egalitarianism survive the gesture at realism reflected in the pluralistic consensus condition? Put otherwise: the pluralistic consensus condition presumably restricts the content of norms of justice in some way. More demanding norms are less plausibly the object of agreement than less demanding norms. So does

---

15. Hegel did acknowledge the need to regulate property in the name of the general welfare and to avoid certain extreme cases of poverty (see *Philosophy of Right*, paragraphs 234–248). But his view does not appear to countenance the regulation of economic activity with an eye to ensuring that the final distribution of resources is not determined by differences of social background and natural ability.

16. See his "On the Jewish Question," in *Marx-Engels Reader*, 2d ed., ed. Robert Tucker (New York: Norton, 1978), 26–46; *Critique of Hegel's Philosophy of Right*, trans. Joseph O'Malley (Cambridge: Cambridge University Press, 1970).

the importance of accommodating moral diversity lead to a thinner conception of justice that lacks the critical egalitarian dimension of Rawls's earlier position?

Because an affirmative answer to the second question would fuel an affirmative answer to the first, I will begin with diversity and equality.

The Case of Equality

A number of commentators on Rawls's post-*Theory of Justice* work have noted that the many reformulations of his views about political justification have not yet been matched by similar revisions in the substance of the theory. My impression[17] is that lots of people now think that Rawls's discussions of political justification—with their emphasis on the importance of realism, on the practical nature of political philosophy, and on the associated idea of an overlapping consensus—do require a shift in the substance of his theory of justice and, in particular, a shift in an inegalitarian direction.[18]

The reasoning goes something like this: "Rawls recognizes the utopianism of his earlier conception of a well-ordered society. So he now recommends that political justification proceed by identifying the common ground among the diverse moralities and conceptions of justice in our own society. But if we follow that recommendation, we will certainly not find support for the specifically egalitarian aspects of *Theory of Justice*, since there is (to put it mildly) considerable contemporary controversy about egalitarian political views."

This account of the idea of an overlapping consensus, with its emphasis on locating common ground among current political views, is mistaken in several ways. Once we see where it goes wrong, we shall see as well that the concern for realism expressed in the pluralistic consensus test has none of the alleged implications. To make this case, I will begin with a sketch of the egalitarian content of the theory and the strategy of argument for it and then proceed to a discussion of the objection.

17. This impression was confirmed by conversations at the conference at which I presented the first draft of these comments. See also the concerns about the "abstractions, vagueness, and conservatism" of Rawls's later work expressed in Thomas Pogge's *Realizing Rawls* (Ithaca, NY: Cornell University Press, 1989), 4.

18. See, for example, John Gray, "Contractarian Method, Private Property, and Market Economy," in John W. Chapman and J. Roland Pennock, eds., *Markets and Justice, Nomos XXIII* (New York: New York University Press, 1989), 13–58; and William Galston, "Pluralism and Social Unity," *Ethics* 99, 4 (July 1989): 711.

The egalitarian content of A *Theory of Justice* is encapsulated in three requirements: the fair value of political liberty, fair equality of opportunity, and the maximin criterion of distributive equity. These three conditions, which are meant to sever the distribution of advantage from social background and natural difference, represent substantively egalitarian interpretations of more formal and less controversial norms of equal liberty, equal opportunity, and the common good.[19] A contention common to egalitarian liberal political conceptions generally, and advanced in A *Theory of Justice* in particular, is that we are led to these substantively egalitarian interpretations by considering the justification of those more formal and political norms.

The basic strategy of argument for this contention is familiar and proceeds by bootstrapping. Thus, associated with the more formal requirements of equal liberties and assurances of opportunity is a conception of the properties of human beings that is important for the purposes of political justification. That conception of persons supposes that the relevant features are not race, color, cultural creed, sex, religion, and the like. The relevant features are certain potentialities (moral powers)—for example, the capacity to govern one's conduct and to revise one's aspirations—rather than the determinate form in which those potentialities are realized. The rationale for the protection of liberties and formal opportunity, for example, lies in part in the importance of assuring favorable conditions for the realization of the basic potentialities. But—and here is where the bootstrapping comes in—once we acknowledge the need for favorable conditions for realizing the basic potentialities, we are naturally led from the more formal to the more substantively egalitarian requirements, since the latter more fully elaborate the range of favorable conditions.

With this quick sketch as background, I can now state more precisely the concern already noted about the idea of an overlapping consensus. The intuitive objection was that the need to confine fundamental political justification to considerations that lie on common ground would undercut the egalitarian components and result in an unacceptable accommodation to power in the formulation of principles. Is this right? Does the requirement of proceeding on common ground deprive us of the ar-

19. See *Theory of Justice*, 65.

gumentative resources necessary for the bootstrapping argument for an egalitarian form of liberalism?

COMMON GROUND

To see why the answer is no, it is important to note first that the bootstrap argument for the egalitarian view is itself meant to proceed on common ground shared by different moral conceptions in a well-ordered society governed by it. That may seem puzzling, since the conception of potentialities as morally fundamental may strike some as peculiarly Kantian. But the contention of the argument (which I am not evaluating here) is that those ideas will seem attractive for the purposes of political argument to anyone who considers how best to defend the liberties, formal norms of equal opportunity, and the requirement that public powers be exercised for the common good.[20]

Noting this draws attention to a first feature of the notion of an overlapping consensus that is important in assessing the objection. What lies in the intersection of different moral conceptions is not simply a set of policies or a system of norms within which political conflict and competition proceed.[21] Nor is it simply a determinate set of moral principles. Instead, the consensus extends to a view of persons, of the importance of fairness and other political values, of what counts as an advantage, and of which practices are paradigmatically evil (e.g., slavery, religious intolerance, and racial discrimination). In short, what lies at the intersection of different views is a (restricted) terrain on which moral and political argument can be conducted, and not simply a fixed and determinate set of substantive points of political agreement.

To show, then, that an egalitarian conception of justice meets the pluralistic consensus test, one needs to show that the bootstrap argument succeeds and that the terrain on which that argument proceeds could itself be the focus of an overlapping consensus in a society governed by it. One need not deny the obvious fact of disagreement on egalitarian politi-

20. The attribution to Kant in particular of the idea that abstract human potentialities are morally fundamental is also off the mark historically. That idea plays a central role in Rousseau's view and is also suggested in Locke's theory of natural law. The variations on this general theme are complex, as is the evolution of the idea; fortunately, these details are not relevant here.

21. Robert Dahl, for example, emphasizes the importance of "underlying consensus on policy" and on the basic rules of political competition in A Preface to Democratic Theory (Chicago: University of Chicago Press, 1956), 75–84, 132.

cal ideals or the only slightly less obvious fact that such disagreement is likely to persist even under favorable conditions.

CONTEMPORARY SUPPORT

When the case for an egalitarian conception of justice is understood as a bootstrap argument and the common ground is understood in the way that I just sketched, it is not so obvious that an appeal to a wide range of *contemporary* political views will fail to support the substantively egalitarian aspects of the conception. For we do not require de facto agreement on substantively egalitarian norms, but only that the reasoning supporting those norms proceed on common ground. That is, we require that the egalitarian features represent a reasonable extension of what people do agree to—that they "extend the range of some existing consensus" by bringing the best justification of certain fundamental points of agreement to bear on unsettled and controversial matters.[22] That contention is not so implausible, because—as I noted earlier—the bootstrap argument for the egalitarian ideals proceeds principally by reference to points of agreement about the value of the liberties and certain formal requirements of equality.

ROLE OF OVERLAPPING CONSENSUS

While the contention that the resources for defending an egalitarian political conception are implicit in current understandings may not, then, be entirely implausible, it should not be identified with the thesis that an egalitarian liberal political conception can meet the pluralistic consensus test. That test does not require that we rummage through the political culture searching for underlying points of agreement among the views featured in it.[23] Rummaging may serve an important function, and I will say a word about it below. But the pluralistic consensus test does not itself command a search for de facto points of agreement at all, and so the failure to find any would not undercut the force of an egalitarian conception of justice.

Instead it formulates a test on the reasonableness of a political conception that is in other respects attractive. The test is this: consider a pro-

22. See *Theory of Justice*, 582. For elaboration of this strategy, see my "Democratic Equality and the Difference Principle," *Ethics* 99, 4 (July 1989): 727–751.

23. See John Rawls, "The Priority of the Right and Ideas of the Good," *Philosophy and Public Affairs* 17, 4 (Fall 1988): 275–276.

posed conception of justice in operation, and then consider whether the principles, ideals, and terms of argument that figure in it provide moral reasons within the views that could be expected to arise among those who live in a society governed by it. Bringing this to bear on the issue of egalitarian liberalism, then, we are to imagine a society regulated by such a conception and existing across several generations. In such a society, we can reasonably expect moral diversity. We also can expect widespread agreement on the fundamental value of the liberties and on at least formal understandings of equality. But then, if there were such agreement, and if the bootstrap argument had any force, the diverse moral understandings would each still have the resources necessary for supporting the substantively egalitarian conception as the correct conception of justice.

I have, of course, not tried to defend the bootstrap argument here. Instead, I have only argued that the pluralistic consensus test does not undercut the force (whatever its magnitude may be) of that argument. *The acknowledgment of diversity* underscored by the notion of an overlapping consensus does not undercut the *critique of privilege* contained in the egalitarian aspects of egalitarian liberalism.

CONTEMPORARY SUPPORT, AGAIN

I have been emphasizing that the pluralistic consensus test does not itself require a search for implicit points of agreement in current moral views. Nonetheless, the existence of such points might have a certain indirect relevance to justification. For, given that the deliberative liberties now receive some protection, it seems implausible to suppose that existing moral views simply represent accommodations to current and historical injustices and would not continue to have some hold under just conditions. So it would be surprising if we could not already find the resources available in current moral understandings for defending a view of justice that we would also be able to defend under more favorable conditions. And if the pluralistic consensus test is acceptable, then there is also some rationale for taking current points of agreement seriously. But it must be emphasized that when we understand the rationale for an examination of current points of agreement this way, we are not letting anything about justification turn on the mere fact of current consensus. In fact, it is never the case—not in the gesture to current understandings of value and not in the requirement of overlapping consensus—that de facto agreement itself plays a role in justification.

With this last point, I have begun to tread on the issues of the next section and so shall move directly to them.

Realism and Reason

Now we come to the first of the issues about accommodation that I noted earlier: Does the pluralistic consensus test represent an unwanted accommodation to power? I begin my discussion of this question with some distinctions that will play an essential role in my (negative) answer.

REASONABLE PLURALISM

Rawls refers to the fact that the deliberative liberties produce diversity as "the fact of pluralism." I think that this terminology may be misleading because "fact" puts the emphasis in the wrong place.[24] To explain why, I need first to introduce the idea of reasonable pluralism.[25]

The idea of reasonable pluralism is that there are distinct understandings of value, each of which is fully reasonable (235–238). An understanding of value is fully reasonable just in case its adherents are stably disposed to affirm it as they acquire new information and subject it to critical reflection.[26] The contention that there is a plurality of such understandings is suggested by the absence of convergence in reflection on issues of value, which leaves disagreements, for example, about the value of choice, welfare, and self-actualization; about the value of contemplative and practical lives; about the value of devotions to friends and lovers as distinct from more diffuse concerns about abstract others; and about the values of poetic expression and political engagement.

What we ought to suppose about the truth of our beliefs about any subject matter, evaluative or otherwise, in the face of such an apparently "irresoluble rivalry" of reasonable alternative views, is an open philosophical question.[27] But among the rationally acceptable answers to that ques-

---

24. One reason for referring to a fact of pluralism is to distinguish the view that we need to accommodate the diversity of values that follows on the protection of the liberties from the view that that diversity should be accommodated because it is a good thing in itself. Nothing that I say is meant to challenge the propriety of this usage.

25. My discussion of reasonable pluralism is in agreement with Rawls's account of the "burdens of reason" (235–238). The point of the discussion is largely to indicate the special importance of those burdens, as distinct from the four other general facts that Rawls discusses (234–235), in explaining the pluralistic consensus test and in responding to objections to it.

26. I take this formulation from conversations with Mark Johnston.

27. See, for example, W. V. O. Quine, *Pursuit of Truth* (Cambridge, MA: Harvard University Press, 1990), 98–101, from whom I take the phrase "irresoluble rivalry" and the term "sectarian" as it is used in the next sentence.

tion is that it is permissible, even with full awareness of the fact of reflective divergence, to take the *sectarian* route of affirming one's own
view; that is, believing it as a matter of faith. And since believing is believing true, a rationally permissible (though not mandatory) response to an
apparently irresoluble rivalry of evaluative conceptions is to affirm that
one's own view contains the whole truth, while the truths in other views
are simply the subsets of those views that intersect with one's own. This
being one of the options, and the option that creates the most trouble for
the pluralistic consensus test, I will frame the rest of my discussion so that
it is consistent with it.

These remarks about reasonable pluralism suggest two different ways
to understand the fact of pluralism:

> *The simple fact of pluralism:* The protection of the deliberative liber-
> ties will result in moral pluralism.
>
> *The fact of reasonable pluralism:* The protection of the deliberative
> liberties will result in moral pluralism, and some of the moral con-
> ceptions will fall within the set of fully reasonable conceptions.

The reasonable pluralism interpretation does make a factual claim. The
asserted fact, however, is not simply that the protection of deliberative
liberties will result in a plurality of conceptions of value but, further, that
a number of those conceptions will be reasonable and permissibly taken
by their adherents to be true.

THE REASONABLE PLURALISM EXPLANATION

Consider now a conception of justice that we wish to subject to the pluralistic consensus test. We imagine a society regulated by that conception
and in which the condition of reasonable pluralism obtains. The pluralistic consensus test requires that the values and principles used to authorize the exercise of power by the state must be restricted to those that are
compelling to the different reasonable moral views adhered to in the society. Consider some people—call them "us" (or "we")—who hold one
such view and think that others believe what is false about the domain of
value. Should we think that the pluralistic consensus test, which prevents
us from relying on the whole truth in authorizing the use of power, is
simply an accommodation to the de facto power of those others? It depends, and what it depends on is clarified by the distinction between simple and reasonable pluralism.

Suppose that we are impressed by the lack of reflective convergence in understandings of value, that we acknowledge the idea of reasonable pluralism, and at the same time that we embrace (not unreasonably) the sectarian view that our moral views are true. Because these are consistent positions, our sectarianism does not require that we condemn as unreasonable everyone who believes what we take to be false. And this provides a rationale for formulating a conception of justice that is confined to considerations that others also take to be moral reasons.

In particular, when we restrict ourselves in political argument to the subset of moral considerations that others who have reasonable views accept as well, we are doing three things. First, we are advancing considerations that we take to be genuine moral reasons; the adherents of each of the views that support the overlapping consensus hold that *nothing but the truth* lies in the overlapping consensus.

Second, in restricting ourselves to a subset of the true moral reasons—appealing to nothing but the truth, though not to the whole truth—we are not simply acknowledging that those who believe the false and spurn the good have the power to make their voices heard or to make our lives miserable if we fail to heed those voices. Instead, we are acknowledging that their views are not unreasonable, even if they do believe what is false. In short, we are moved not by their power but by an acknowledgment that they are reasonable.

Third, we are taking cognizance of a peculiarity in insisting on the whole (sectarian) truth in the face of our acknowledgment of the idea of reasonable pluralism. For suppose we acknowledge it and affirm the divergence of moralities under reflection. Then we must see that if we were to appeal to the whole truth, that appeal would be, from the standpoint of others who we take to be reasonable, indistinguishable from simply appealing to what we believe. But we already acknowledge that the mere appeal to what we believe carries no force in justification.[28]

Suppose, for example, we believe that welfare is the sole ultimate

---

28. For elaboration of this point, see Thomas Nagel, "Moral Conflict and Political Legitimacy," *Philosophy and Public Affairs* 16, 3 (Summer 1987): 215–240. Joseph Raz has criticized Nagel's point, suggesting that it rests on an untenable distinction between the position of the speaker who advances a justification and the listener to whom it is addressed. See his "Facing Diversity: The Case of Epistemic Abstinence," *Philosophy and Public Affairs* 19, 1 (Winter 1990): 37–39. I am not persuaded by Raz's contention. He is right that the positions of speaker and listener are parallel. But taking up the point of view of the person to whom a justification is addressed is simply a heuristic for understanding the limited force of an argument that appeals to the whole truth. So, far from undermining Nagel's point, the parallelism is essential to drawing the right conclusions from the use of the heuristic.

good, and we understand that view to imply that choice is not an independent final value. In the course of political argument, we affirm: "It is true that welfare is the sole ultimate good." Now others ought not to suppose that what we mean is equally well captured by "We believe that welfare is the sole ultimate good." The indistinguishability at issue is not semantical. The point, rather, is that if others accept the idea of reasonable pluralism, then they notice what we also notice, namely, that what lies between our taking our views to be reasonable (about which there may be no disagreement) and our taking them to be true (about which there is disagreement) is not a further reason, but simply our (rationally permissible) belief in those views. Because there is nothing else that lies in between, an appeal to the whole truth will seem indistinguishable from an appeal to what we believe.

THE SIMPLE-FACT EXPLANATION

Following the reasonable pluralism interpretation, then, when we restrict ourselves to common ground in the face of the fact of diversity, we are acknowledging that reason does not mandate a single moral view and then are refraining from imposing ourselves on others who are prepared to be reasonable. This account of whom we need to accommodate turns on our willingness to acknowledge that some people with whom we fundamentally disagree are not unreasonable. That is why we are not simply accommodating principles to power when we are concerned, to ensure that the conception of justice is acceptable to them as well. This explanation of the pluralistic consensus test might be clarified by contrasting it with another explanation, which is suggested by some of Rawls's remarks but which is not persuasive.

As I indicated at the outset, Rawls emphasizes the importance of realism in the formulation of reasonable ideals. And he suggests that when we confine ourselves to considerations that are reasons for others as well, we are simply adjusting to certain general facts about the social world. Here the emphasis is on the need to be realistic, to find common ground because disagreement is a basic fact of life under free conditions.

To see why this explanation of the need to accommodate diversity is not right, notice that it is a plausible general fact that there will always be people with unreasonable views. But the fact that there are some people with unreasonable views does not require that we adjust our conception of justice so that it can be supported by an overlapping consensus that will appeal to them. While we need to take the fact of disagreement into account in some way in deciding what to do, the pluralistic consensus condition is certainly not the only way to do that and is not mandated by the recognition that there are and will always be such people. Furthermore, if we did embrace the requirement that a conception of justice be able to bring everyone on board—that it restrict itself to reasons embraced by all understandings of value—then it is hard to see what the response would be to the objection that the requirement of an overlapping consensus simply forces an accommodation to power.

The problem with this explanation is that it makes too much of the de facto diversity highlighted in the simple-fact interpretation. The first explanation—which draws essentially on the idea of reasonable pluralism—does not deny the relevance of the fact that under conditions of deliberative liberty there will be diversity. But the response to that fact is not undiscriminating and, in particular, is controlled by the distinction between reasonable and unreasonable understandings of value.

Ensuring that a conception of justice fits the fact of diversity under conditions of deliberative liberty is not, then, an unacceptable accommodation to power. But the reason that it is acceptable is not because diversity is a fact of life, as the simple-fact interpretation of pluralism states, and not because adjustment to general and unalterable facts of social life is always to be distinguished from accommodation to power. Instead, that adjustment is reasonable because some forms of diversity are the natural consequence of the free exercise of practical reason. Once we agree that they are, we will not be inclined to count moral diversity among the unfavorable facts of human life nor to confuse a concern to find a conception of justice consistent with it with a willingness to compromise justice in the face of the course of the world.

EXCLUSION

Answering the charge of unwarranted accommodation, then, commits us to the view that we need not accommodate the unreasonable. Indeed, given the explanation for this view, if we did accommodate the unreasonable in the formulation of fundamental principles, then we would be unacceptably adjusting principles to de facto power.

But this brings me to a different concern about power and political consensus: that the promise of consensus is associated with the practice of arbitrary exclusion. In view of the problem of securing general agreement on anything, claims to speak on behalf of all of the reasonable depend, it will be argued, on drawing arbitrary boundaries around the community of the reasonable.[29] So the charge is that any appeal to the ideal of consensus, in fact, rests on the power to exclude, exercised in this case through the pretense of discovering that some people are unreasonable.

In the case at hand, the exclusion is of a special kind. It does not amount to a deprivation of liberties or of what are conventionally understood to be the advantages of social cooperation. Instead, exclusion lies in the fact that the arguments used to justify the exercise of power depend on norms, values, and ideals that are rejected by some people whose views will as a consequence not belong to an overlapping consensus. Although this does not violate the ideal of consensus, which requires that justification proceed by reference to reasons located on the common ground occupied by all who are prepared to listen to reason, it is exclusion all the same. And it is of a troublesome form. Its implication is that some people will reject the values, ideals, principles, and norms that serve, at the most fundamental level, to justify the exercise of power over them.

These are extremely important and complicated matters, not least because the charge of unreasonableness is commonly a ponderous way to express simple disagreement, or, in the distinctively American political idiom, a thinly disguised signal that one's opponents are poor or female or black. But as important as these issues are, I must be very brief here and intend my comments as a way only to mark out certain issues for further examination and to introduce some doubts about the alleged arbitrariness of characterizations of views as unreasonable.

Consider, then, some views that might end up being excluded in this way, in particular those that would deny the protection of liberties on the basis of the doctrine that "outside the church there is no salvation." Rawls discusses this case and states that it is "unreasonable" to use public powers to enforce this doctrine. I agree. But it is important to distinguish two ways that such enforcement might be unreasonable. Distinguishing them will help illustrate what is involved in exclusion on the grounds of unreasonableness.

The first case is presented by a "rationalist fundamentalist." This is the

---

29. I am indebted to Uday Mehta for many discussions of these issues. For discussion of a variety of different strategies of exclusion, see his "Liberal Strategies of Exclusion," *Politics and Society* 18, 4 (December 1990): 427–454.

person who denies the idea of reasonable pluralism, affirming instead that it lies within the competence of reason to know that salvation is the supreme value, that there is a single path to salvation, that there is no salvation among the damned, and, therefore, that liberty of conscience is to be condemned. This is not a common view, if only because it claims for reason, territory usually reserved for faith.[30] But if someone were to advance the view, then one ought to say that she is simply mistaken. Even if the elements of rationalist fundamentalism are all rationally permissible, reason surely does not mandate them, and in insisting that it does, the rationalist fundamentalist is not acknowledging the facts.

This response will not do in the second case. These are the nonrationalist fundamentalists who accept the limited competence of reason but deny that reason is controlling in the authorization to use power. By contrast with the rationalist fundamentalists, they agree that an appreciation of the value of salvation and of the conditions for achieving it fall outside the competence of reason and that grasping the truth about the proper conduct of life depends on faith. But they affirm that truths accessible only through faith are sufficient to authorize the legitimate exercise of power. What is important is that they are *truths,* and not the mode of access to them available for finite human creatures. Faced with nonrationalist fundamentalists, it will not do to state the case for the idea of reasonable pluralism; they know that case, celebrate the limited competence of reason as a guide in human affairs, and lament the self-imposed disabilities of those who insist on proceeding within its narrow compass.

Still, what they are prepared to do is to impose on those who are outside the faith in a way that—so far as those others can tell—is indistinguishable from the concededly irrational practice of imposing in the name of their beliefs. To resist such imposition is not simply to affirm a disagreement with the nonrationalist fundamentalist. Instead, it is to complain about this fundamental form of unreasonableness. And finding them unreasonable in this way, is sufficient to show that the exclusion is not arbitrary.

Conclusions

I noted earlier that Rawls's problems—the reasonableness of the ideal of a consensual order and of the pluralistic consensus condition—echo a set

30. It is an analog to "creation science," operating in the domain of salvation. The proper response is the same in both cases.

of concerns familiar from Hegel's political philosophy and critical discussion of it. Returning now to these concerns, what conclusions about them can we draw from the discussion here?

First, in *A Theory of Justice*, Rawls proposed a formulation of the distinction between political and civil society and a conception of justice that was meant to accommodate that distinction without carrying the inegalitarian implications that some have thought intrinsic to it. Whatever the merits of that earlier defense of egalitarian liberalism, the pluralistic consensus condition does nothing to weaken it.

Second, Hegel thought that an account of the ideal of a consensual polity suited to modern conditions needed to accommodate the diversity of values and attachments characteristic of civil society.[31] While Hegel emphasized that the universal-particular distinction, and its institutionalization in the separation of civil and political spheres, is a distinguishing feature of modern societies, he did not suppose it to be simply a brute fact about post-Reformation Europe. Instead, his rationalism led him to suppose that this peculiarity represented a historically situated discovery about the operation of practical reason. In accommodating the diversity institutionalized in civil society, then, political philosophy was not simply accommodating the bare fact that people differ in aims and aspirations. Instead, it was acknowledging the diverse promptings of practical reason itself, even as it sought to find within that diversity, the seeds of the set of common values underlying political society.[32] In short, some form of civil-political society distinction is an unavoidable aspect of any attractive ideal, once we see the scope and competence of practical reason. In a Hegelian *Doppelsatz*: we need to accommodate the ideal to the real because the real manifests the ideal.

Rawls's talk about the fact of pluralism, the role of the Reformation in prompting acknowledgment of that fact, and the need for an overlapping consensus can be taken in this same spirit. If we accept the idea of reasonable pluralism, then moral diversity is not simply a bare fact, even a bare general fact about human nature, but, rather, indicates something

---

31. I am not confident that Hegel held the view I attribute to him in this paragraph. It does fit with and make sense out of various pieces of his view, including his account of the relationship between civil society and the state, his conception of the role of reason in history, and his views about the rationality of modern social arrangements. But he does not state it anywhere in the way that I put it here. If I am wrong in thinking that he held it, nothing else in the essay would need to change.

32. See *Philosophy of Right*, paragraph 261.

about the operation and powers of practical reason. With this account of diversity, we have a response to the contention that accommodating different understandings of value in the formulation of basic moral principles for the political domain is tantamount to supposing that justice commands that we turn our money over to thieves. The response is that we are accommodating basic principles not to the reality of power but, rather, to the way that social reality reveals the powers of practical reason.

3

ASSOCIATIONS AND DEMOCRACY

with Joel Rogers

Since the publication of John Rawls's A *Theory of Justice*, normative democratic theory has focused principally on three tasks: refining principles of justice, clarifying the nature of political justification, and exploring the public policies required to ensure a just distribution of education, health care, and other basic resources. Much less attention has been devoted to examining the political institutions and social arrangements that might plausibly implement reasonable political principles.[1] Moreover, the amount of attention paid to issues of organizational and institutional implementation has varied sharply across the different species of normative theory. Neoliberal theorists, concerned chiefly with protecting liberty by taming power and essentially hostile to the af-

This essay is an abbreviated version of "Associations in Democratic Governance" (with Joel Rogers), *Politics and Society* 20, 4 (December 1992): 393–472, published with replies by Ellen Immergut, Andrew Levine, Jane Mansbridge, Philippe Schmitter, Wolfgang Streeck, Andrew Szasz, and Iris Young. That essay was published, along with the replies, in *Associations and Democracy* (London: Verso, 1995). Versions of the longer essay were presented at meetings of the American Political Science Association, the Princeton University Political Theory Colloquium, the Social Organization Colloquium at the University of Wisconsin-Madison, the Society for Ethical and Legal Philosophy, the UCLA Center for History and Social Theory, the University of Chicago Colloquium on Constitutionalism, the University of Maryland Seminar on Political Theory, PEGS (Political Economy of the Good Society), and CREA (Ecole Polytechnique); drafts have also been presented at the conference on "Post-Liberal Democratic Theory" held at the University of Texas at Austin and at the "Associations and Democracy" conference held at the University of Wisconsin-Madison. We are grateful to participants in those discussions for many useful comments and suggestions, and especially to Bruce Ackerman, Suzanne Berger, Owen Fiss, Charles Sabel, Wolfgang Streeck, and Erik Olin Wright, for the same. We also thank the editors of *Social Philosophy & Policy* for comments on an earlier draft of this essay.

1. See John Rawls, A *Theory of Justice* (Cambridge, MA: Harvard University Press, 1971), whose own work is an exception to the generalization made in the text. Another prominent exception is Roberto Unger's *False Necessity*, vol. 2 of *Politics* (Cambridge: Cambridge University Press, 1987).

firmative state,[2] have been far more sensitive to such issues than egalitarian-democratic theorists, who simultaneously embrace classically liberal concerns with choice, egalitarian concerns with the distribution of resources, and a republican emphasis on the values of citizen participation and public debate (we sketch such a conception below in Section 1). Neglect of how such values might be implemented has deepened the vulnerability of egalitarian-democratic views to the charge of being unrealistic: "Good in theory but not so good in practice."

In this essay we address this vulnerability by examining the constructive role that "secondary"[3] associations—labor unions, employer associations, citizen lobbies and advocacy groups, private service organizations, other private groups—can play in a democracy. Our central contention is that, as a practical matter, implementing democratic norms requires a high level of secondary group organization of a certain kind. Roughly speaking, the "level" required is one in which all citizens, irrespective of their initial endowment, enjoy the political benefits of organization; the "kind" required is one which delivers those benefits in ways consistent not only with political equality but also with other democratic norms. The problem is that the required level and kind of group activity do not arise naturally, and those groups that do arise often frustrate, rather than advance, democratic aspirations. Our proposed solution to this problem is to supplement nature with artifice: through politics, to alter the environment, incidence, activity, and governing status of associations in ways that strengthen democratic order. We call this deliberate politics of associations "associative democracy."[4]

We would recommend the pursuit of "associative democracy" for a wide range of administrative and property regimes. Here, however, we assume the context of modern capitalism, where markets are the primary mechanism of resource allocation and private, individual decisions are the central determinant of investment. Admitting the limits this context

2. For examples of the institutional program of "neoliberal constitutionalists" hostile to the affirmative state, see Friedrich A. Hayek, *The Constitution of Liberty* (Chicago: University of Chicago Press, 1960); *idem, The Mirage of Social Justice*, vol. 2 of *Law, Legislation, and Liberty* (Chicago: University of Chicago Press, 1976); and James M. Buchanan, *The Limits of Liberty: Between Anarchy and Leviathan* (Chicago: University of Chicago Press, 1975).

3. So called because they are, by convention, the large residual of the "primary" organizations of family, firm, and state.

4. We share the term "associative democracy" with John Mathews, *Age of Democracy: The Political Economy of Post-Fordism* (New York: Oxford University Press, 1989). But we arrived at the term independently.

places on the satisfaction of egalitarian-democratic norms, our argument is that associative democracy can improve the practical approximation to those norms.

Our argument is animated by concerns about the likely future of even such approximation. Due principally to changes in the organization of capitalism, many of the most important institutional sources of egalitarian achievement under modern capitalism—from strong unions and employer organizations to a variety of popular political organizations—have recently fallen into disarray. The egalitarian project is weakened by a widening organizational deficit at its base. Recognizing that most social clocks cannot be turned backward, that new as well as revived institutional structures are needed, we offer associative democracy as a strategy to rebuild that base—to provide egalitarian democracy with necessary associative supports.

We sketch the associative conception in four steps. First, to identify the need for an associative strategy of democratic reform, we note three barriers to egalitarianism and indicate how each implicates questions of associative order. Second, to underscore the potential contribution of groups to democratic governance, we distinguish four general types of contribution and then draw from comparative experience to illustrate how the potential has been realized in different areas of public policy. Third, we defend the associative strategy for netting this contribution against two objections: that it is impossible, because groups are intractable to reform; and that it is undesirable, because the increase in group power needed to secure contributions poses unacceptably high risks of group abuse of power. Fourth and finally, we illustrate the associative strategy by discussing how it might be used to guide reforms of industrial relations and vocational training in the United States.

1. Why Associative Reform?

Associative democracy aims to further an egalitarian-democratic view of politics defined by simultaneous respect for norms of political equality, popular sovereignty, distributive equity, and deliberative politics and the operation of society for the general welfare. We interpret these norms in the following ways. *Political equality* requires a rough equality across citizens in their chances to hold office and to influence political choices. *Popular sovereignty* requires that the authorization of state action be determined (within the limits set by fundamental civil and political liberties) by procedures in which citizens are represented as equals.[5] *Distributive equity* obtains when inequalities of advantage, if they exist, are not determined by differences of inherited resources, natural endowments, or simple good luck. Collective choice is *deliberative* when it is framed by different conceptions of the common good and public initiatives are defended ultimately by reference to a conception of the public interest. Society operates for the *general welfare* when there is both economic and governmental efficiency.

These norms are routinely frustrated in the everyday politics of contemporary mass democracies. While there are many sources of frustration, here we note three that are of special relevance to our discussion of associations.[6]

THREE PROBLEMS OF EGALITARIAN GOVERNANCE

The first problem is that government programs directed to achieving a more equitable distribution of advantage (e.g., welfare services, active labor-market policies, much economic and social regulation) are widely perceived as unacceptably costly and inefficient. Whatever their theoretical attractions, critics assert, in practice such programs generate economic rigidities, and a wasteful expansion of government aims beyond government capacities. During a period of slowed productivity growth and intensified economic competition, this makes egalitarianism at best an unaffordable indulgence, at worst a betrayal of government obligations to "promote the general welfare."

While claims of government inefficiency are often grossly exaggerated, they have sufficient basis in fact to give popular resonance to their constant amplification.[7] And especially in more liberal societies—where choices about social governance are seen largely as choices between

5. This procedural formulation of the idea of popular sovereignty does not assume a people with a single will and thus is immune to the criticisms directed against that assumption by, for example, William Riker, *Liberalism against Populism: A Confrontation Between the Theory of Democracy and the Theory of Social Choice* (San Francisco: W. H. Freeman, 1982).

6. Among the fundamental issues we will put to the side here are intense national and religious divisions and the destructive conflicts associated with them.

7. For discussion of some prominent exaggerations, see George W. Downs and Patrick D. Larkey, *The Search for Government Efficiency: From Hubris to Helplessness* (New York: Random House, 1986). In the United States, increased public doubt about government capacity to achieve egalitarian ends is coincident with increased support for those ends. The "politics of happiness" that some saw in the reformist projects of the 1960s has been succeeded by a "politics of sadness," in which the public knows that it is not getting what it wants but has no confidence that government can provide it.

states and markets, and no associative alternative is perceived—popular acceptance of those claims is devastating to the practical pursuit of egalitarian ends. Most publics are unwilling to forgo economic growth in the interest of equality. None enjoys literally wasting its tax dollars. So if state programs are successfully defined as inimical to growth and wasteful, and if market governance is the only alternative, egalitarianism is politically doomed.

The second problem is that egalitarian efforts are deeply compromised by representational inequalities. Capitalist property relations are, of course, defined by inequalities in economic power, and political power is materially conditioned. So economic inequalities characteristically translate into political inequalities in violation of the norm of political equality. Until recently, however, at least in most rich, Western, liberal societies, it was possible to speak of a relatively steady advance in the social democratization of capitalist societies. Gains in political equality accrued from gains in the political representation of economically disadvantaged interests.[8]

Today, any such optimistic assessment needs to be revised. Unions and virtually all other mass popular organizations representing working people are in palpable decline, while success in the organized representation of the interests reflected in the "new social movements" of feminism, environmentalism, and racial justice is distinctly limited.[9] With a widening range of interests lacking an effective voice, the defining idiom of much politics is not equality but exclusion.

The third problem is that those whose voice is organized often speak with a strident particularism. On both sides of the many lines of privilege, the narrow assertion of group interest is very nearly a norm. Whether motivated by simple selfishness or fear of cooperation that comes from weakness, the result is a politics of group bargaining that, undisciplined by respect for the common good, inevitably conflicts with norms of popular sovereignty and deliberative politics.[10] Group particularism makes demo-

8. Many saw this as irreversible. See, for example, Jürgen Habermas, *The Legitimation Crisis of Late Capitalism* (Boston: Beacon Press, 1973).

9. On unions, see Jelle Visser, "Trends in Trade Union Membership," *OECD Employment Outlook*, July 1991, 97–134.

10. For the American case, see the classic characterization of the resulting "interest group liberalism" offered by Theodore J. Lowi, *The End of Liberalism: The Second Republic of the United States*, 2d ed. (New York: Norton, 1979).

cratic governance more difficult, and it lessens the appeal of inclusive politics by inspiring doubt that inclusion in fact enhances democracy.

The problems of government incompetence, political inequality, and particularism feed one another. Inequalities in representation diminish support for any egalitarian effort. The particularism of existing groups prompts substantial reliance on statist means in those efforts. The adoption of such means, even where ends could in theory be better accomplished by or with the aid of associations, compromises government efficiency. And the fact and the perception of government inefficiency, working directly or through the consequent erosion of political support, weaken those efforts and thus underscore inequality.

AN ASSOCIATIVE STRATEGY OF REFORM

The idea of associative democracy is to break this cycle by curing the associative disorders that help to fuel it. Using conventional tools of public policy (taxes, subsidies, legal sanctions), as applied through the familiar decision-making procedures of formal government (legislatures and administrative bodies, as overseen by the courts), it would promote associative reform in each of the three problem areas.[11] Where manifest inequalities in political representation exist, it recommends promoting the organized representation of presently excluded interests. Where group particularism undermines democratic deliberation or popular sovereignty, it recommends encouraging the organized to be more other-regarding in their actions. And where associations have greater competence than public authorities for achieving democratic ends, or where their participation could improve the effectiveness of government programs, it recommends encouraging a more direct and formal governance role for groups.

This last point may be the most immediate. In many areas of economic and social concern—from the environment and occupational safety and health to vocational training and consumer protection—egalitarian aims are badly served by the state-market dichotomy that still dominates mainstream debate about how those aims should be pursued. Often, the right

---

11. Throughout, respect for the associational liberties of group members, recognition of the resistance of many groups to change, and rejection of concessionist views of associations mean that the strategy stops well short of legislating associative practice or its relation to the state. Associative democracy is not a distinct form of order, but a strategy to reform aspects of current practice.

answer to the question "Should the state take care of the problem, or should it be left to the market?" is a double negative.

This seems to be so in three ideal-typical classes of regulatory problems. In the first, nonmarket public standards on behavior are needed, and government has the competence to set them, but the objects of regulation are so diverse or unstable that it is not possible for the government to specify just how those standards should be met at particular regulated sites. Much environmental regulation presents problems of this sort. In the second, public standard-setting is needed, and government has the competence to do it, but the objects of regulation are sufficiently numerous or dispersed to preclude serious government monitoring of compliance. Consider the problems of occupational safety and health enforcement. In the third, uniform public standards are needed, but it lies beyond the competence of either markets or governments to specify and secure them, as doing either requires the simultaneous coordination of private actors and their enlistment in specifying the behavior sought. Here, consider the difficulties of getting private firms to agree on standards for vocational training and to increase their own training efforts.

Where these sorts of problems are encountered, associative governance can provide a welcome alternative or complement to public regulatory efforts because of the distinctive capacity of associations to gather local information, monitor behavior, and promote cooperation among private actors. In such cases, the associative strategy recommends attending to the possibility of enlisting them explicitly in the performance of public tasks.

In sum, the idea of the associative strategy is to encourage the use of associations to address concerns about unequal representation, particularism, and excessive cost and inefficiency of egalitarian programs and, through that address, to satisfy more fully egalitarian-democratic norms. In the next two sections, we will explore in more detail the features of associations that provide foundations for the strategy and underlie our assessment of its promise.

2. The Potential Contribution of Groups

The cornerstone of the argument for associative democracy is that groups have a significant contribution to make to democratic governance. In the ordinary operation of mass democracies, groups are generally acknowledged to be capable of performing at least four useful, democracy-enhancing functions: providing information, equalizing representation, promoting citizen education, and implementing alternative governance.

Information. Associations can provide information to policy makers on the members' preferences, the impact of proposed legislation, or the implementation of existing law. As the state has become more involved in regulating society and has extended the reach of its regulation to more diverse sites, technically complex areas, and processes subject to rapid change, this information function has arguably become more important. Good information is needed to assess the effectiveness of a myriad of state policies, commonly operating at some distance from the monitoring of state inspectorates, and to adjust policies to changed circumstances or behaviors. This is especially so given social and policy interdependence—the interaction of social welfare policy and economic growth, for example, or environmental regulation and technical change—which underscores the value of accurate, timely intelligence on policy effects. Because of their proximity to those effects, groups are often well positioned to provide such information. When they do, they contribute to satisfying the norm of popular sovereignty, since good information improves citizen deliberation, facilitates the enforcement of decisions, and clarifies the appropriate objects of state policy.

Equalizing representation. Politics is materially conditioned, and inequalities in material advantage, of the sort definitive of capitalism, translate directly to inequalities in political power. Groups can help remedy these inequalities by permitting individuals with low per-capita resources to pool those resources through organization. In making the benefits of organization available to those whose influence on policy is negligible without it, groups help satisfy the norm of political equality. Similarly, groups can promote a more equitable distribution of advantage by correcting for imbalances in bargaining power that follow from the unequal control of wealth. Groups can also represent interests not best organized through territorial politics based on majority rule. These include functional interests, associated with a person's position or activity within a society; "categoric" interests of the sort pursued by the new social movements; interests whose intensity is not registered in voting procedures; and, at least in systems without proportional representation, the interests of political minorities. Here, groups improve an imperfect system of interest representation by making it more fine grained, attentive to preference intensities, and representative of diverse views. This, too, furthers political equality.

Citizen education. Associations can function as "schools of democracy." Participation in them can help citizens to develop competence, self-confidence, and a broader set of interests than they would acquire in a more fragmented political society. Alexis de Tocqueville provides the classic statement of this educative power of associations: "Feelings are recruited, the heart is enlarged, and the human mind is developed only by the reciprocal influence of men on one another," and under democratic conditions, this influence can "only be accomplished by associations."[12] In performing this educative function, associations help foster the "civic consciousness" on which any egalitarian order, and its deliberative politics, depends. That is, they promote a recognition of the norms of democratic process and equity and a willingness to uphold them and to accept them as fixing the basic framework of political argument and social cooperation, at least on condition that others do so as well.

Alternative governance. Associations can provide a distinctive form of social governance, alternative to markets or public hierarchies, that permits society to realize the important benefits of cooperation among member citizens. In providing a form of governance, associations figure more as problem solvers than simply as representatives of their members to authoritative political decision makers, pressuring those decision makers on behalf of member interests. They help to formulate and execute public policies and take on quasi-public functions that supplement or supplant the state's more directly regulatory actions.

Such associations facilitate cooperative dealings in two ways. First, their sheer existence reduces the transaction costs of securing agreement among potentially competing interests. The background of established forms of communication and collaboration they provide enables parties to settle more rapidly and reliably on jointly beneficial actions. Second, groups help to establish the trust that facilitates cooperation. They effec-

12. Alexis de Tocqueville, *Democracy in America* (New York: Vintage, 1945), vol. 2, p. 117.

tively provide assurances to members that their own willingness to cooperate will not be exploited by others. Often directly beneficial to society, associative governance can also support public efforts to achieve egalitarian aims.

Lessons from comparative experience. While examples of all these sorts of group contributions can be found in the United States, in recent years it is students of comparative politics, in particular the politics of Western Europe, who have been especially attentive to these positive features of associations. They have argued more particularly that certain sorts of group organization play a central role in resolving, in egalitarian fashion, problems of successful governance in mass democracies.

The rediscovery in the 1970s of liberal "corporatist" systems of interest representation in Northern European democracies was the key to one such argument.[13] Students of liberal corporatism suggested that the incorporation of organized interests into the formation of economic policy helped produce, simultaneously, better satisfaction of distributive concerns, improved economic performance, and gains in government efficiency. Of particular note was the negotiation and compromise between organized business and organized labor within such systems, which appeared to permit their joint realization of many gains from cooperation.

The Scandinavian social democracies of Norway and Sweden provided a particularly advanced example of such labor-business cooperation. There, encompassing union and employer federations, both speaking for virtually all of their respective populations of interest, would meet regularly to negotiate the terms of their essentially peaceful coexistence, with the state serving to ratify and support those terms. Unions exchanged wage restraint for guarantees of low unemployment and a high social wage. Employers traded employment security and industrial upgrading for union moderation. The state, backed by both "social partners," calibrated fiscal policy to stabilize employment, social policy to provide in-

---

13. See Philippe C. Schmitter, "Still the Century of Corporatism?," *Review of Politics* 36 (1974): 85–131; Suzanne Berger, ed., *Organizing Interests in Western Europe: Pluralism, Corporatism, and the Transformation of Politics* (Cambridge: Cambridge University Press, 1981); and John H. Goldthorpe, ed., *Order and Conflict in Contemporary Capitalism* (Oxford: Clarendon Press, 1984).

surance against market misfortune, and industrial policy to maintain competitiveness in foreign markets.[14]

More recent discussions, even as they have dissented from claims made about corporatism or have paused to note its devolution or collapse, have also stressed the importance of associative activity to economic performance. Students of the successful alternatives to mass production that are marked, simultaneously, by high wages, skills, productivity, and competitiveness have argued that this success requires a dense social infrastructure of secondary association and coordination. This organizational infrastructure provides the basis for cooperation between management and labor, among firms, and between firms and government on issues of work organization, training, technology diffusion, research and development, and new product ventures. And that cooperation, it is argued, is essential to ensuring economic adjustment that is both rapid and fair.[15]

The reemerging (or more newly visible) regional economies of Western Europe—Italy's Emilia-Romagna, Sweden's Småland, Germany's Baden-Württemburg, Denmark's Jutland peninsula—provide particularly striking examples of such associative economic governance. They feature complex public-private partnerships on training and technology diffusion, flexible manufacturing networks that facilitate inter-firm cooperation in performing discrete and varied production tasks, more formalized consortia and industry associations to realize economies of scale in some functions (e.g., marketing or research and development) among otherwise competing firms, joint training activities among firms, occupational credentialing of labor through industry-wide or regional labor and

14. For useful description and analysis of such coordination in Scandinavia, see Walter Korpi, *The Democratic Class Struggle* (London: Routledge and Kegan Paul, 1983); Gøsta Esping-Andersen, *Politics against Markets* (Princeton: Princeton University Press, 1985); for a good comparative treatment of the Swedish and German cases, and the role played by corporatist institutions in facilitating wage stability and industrial upgrading, see Peter Swenson, *Fair Shares: Unions, Pay, and Politics in Sweden and West Germany* (Ithaca: Cornell University Press, 1989); and Lowell Turner, *Democracy at Work: Changing World Markets and the Future of Labor Unions* (Ithaca: Cornell University Press, 1991). For a general review of problems that have beset social democracies since the mid-1970s, see Fritz W. Scharpf, *Crisis and Choice in European Social Democracy* (Ithaca: Cornell University Press, 1991).

15. See Charles F. Sabel, "'Flexible Specialization and the Re-emergence of Regional Economies," in Paul Q. Hirst and Jonathan Zeitlin, eds., *Reversing Industrial Decline: Industrial Structure and Policy in Britain and Her Competitors* (Oxford: Berg, 1989), 17–70; and Wolfgang Streeck, "On the Institutional Conditions of Diversified Quality Production," in Egan Matzner and Wolfgang Streeck, eds., *Beyond Keynesianism: The Socio-Economics of Production and Employment* (London: Edward Elgar, 1991), 21–61.

management associations, and close linkages between regional development and welfare policies. Indeed, the object of state economic development policy in most of these regions prominently includes efforts to build the private associative framework upon which such efforts rely.[16]

For an example of the sorts of associations being fostered, consider CITER, an association of small knitwear firms in the town of Carpi, in Emilia-Romagna. Its six hundred dues-paying member firms are generally tiny, averaging fewer than eight workers each. But by pooling resources in the association itself, as well as in countless joint-production schemes facilitated by the association, they are able to flourish in the fiercely competitive and unstable business of international fashion. Through CITER, they share information on trends in technology, production processes, and emerging markets, underwrite a sophisticated forecasting service on fashion trends, gain access to and training in the use of sophisticated business software, and enjoy other services no one firm could afford on its own. CITER is not a cartel. Its member firms still compete with one another. They simply do not forsake the obvious gains to all that can come from associative cooperation.[17]

The virtues of associative forms of governance are, however, not confined to economic cooperation. Associative governance has also been credited with achieving more effective social regulation and welfare delivery. Within the heavily procedural and litigious "command and control" regulation favored in more liberal systems and particularly dominant in the United States, groups commonly appear to frustrate regulatory efficiency. Evidence from systems in which associations are assigned a more central and open governance function, however, suggests that they can powerfully contribute to the success of regulatory programs. Instead of acting only or chiefly as "special interests" intent on either capturing public powers or limiting their efficacy, groups supplement traditional public authority by helping to define policy, to monitor its imple-

---

16. For examples of state policy, see Stuart A. Rosenfeld, *Technology Innovation and Rural Development: Lessons from Italy and Denmark* (Washington: Aspen Institute, 1990). We emphasize that state policy is needed in all these cases. The appropriate infrastructure does not emerge naturally from the interactions of economic actors or from favorable cultural tradition. For further discussion, see Section 3 below.

17. For this and other examples of "flexible manufacturing networks," see C. Richard Hatch, *Flexible Manufacturing Networks: Cooperation for Competitiveness in a Global Economy* (Washington: Corporation for Enterprise Development, 1988).

mentation, and to enforce it. Rather than acting as obstructions, they serve as private multipliers on public capacities.

Associations have been shown to play this role for a wide range of regulatory purposes, extending from the enforcement of occupational safety and health, wage and hour, and environmental regulation to the promotion of curricular reform and better learning opportunities in education and training systems. Admitting variations in national success, the general result appears to be a style of regulation and the affirmative promotion of egalitarian ends, at once more effective, flexible, and efficient than command and control or simple state administration of programs.

Consider occupational safety and health. Instead of relying exclusively on a centralized state inspectorate to enforce occupational safety and health laws, virtually all European systems supplement their inspectorates with mandated workplace health and safety committees. These committees operate with delegated public powers: they monitor, and in some measure are empowered to enforce, compliance with the regulatory regime. While bringing new costs in its train (e.g., the costs of training worker deputies), the general result of this strategy is a health and safety policy more effective and efficient than an inspectorate-alone approach. It is more effective because it supplements public capacities for monitoring compliance with the capacities of workers themselves. It is more efficient because it permits public efforts to be left largely to standard setting and enlists the local knowledge of regulated actors in devising the least costly means, in particular settings, of satisfying such standards.[18]

Or consider the use of associations in education. A striking example is provided by the German system of youth apprenticeship. Employer associations and unions determine training standards and requirements, monitor the provision of training at both school and work, and provide much of the workplace-based instruction. The role of the state is essentially to inform the social partners about emerging labor-market trends, ratify the results of their deliberations, help enforce the occupational

18. For a review of worker participation in safety regulation focusing on Europe, see the contributions to Sebastiano Bagnara, Raffaello Misiti, and Helmut Wintersberger, eds., *Work and Health in the 1980s: Experiences of Direct Workers' Participation in Occupational Health* (Berlin: Edition Sigma, 1985); for a particularly useful country study, see Bjørn Gustavsen and Gerry Hunnius, *New Patterns of Work Reform: The Case of Norway* (Oslo: Universitetsforlaget, 1981); for the contrast with the United States, see Charles Noble, *Liberalism at Work: The Rise and Fall of OSHA* (Philadelphia: Temple University Press, 1986); and Eugene Bardach and Robert Kagan, *Going by the Book* (Philadelphia: Temple University Press, 1982).

standards that result, and encourage widespread participation in the associative effort. From top to bottom, the system is driven by the associations, albeit acting in concert with public authority. The result is generally recognized as the most successful and inclusive vocational training program in the developed Western world.[19]

Taken together, these different investigations and examples underscore the range of important contributions associations can make to a functioning democratic order. What assures that contribution, moreover, is not the sheer "quantity of associability" found in such systems but the care of public authorities within them in matching the qualitative characteristics of different groups to public functions and in working with groups to encourage the appropriate qualitative characteristics.[20] The deliberate conditioning of state fiscal and welfare assistance on the outcomes of wage bargaining under corporatism; the explicit state efforts to build the associative infrastructure of regional economies; the laws mandating the workplace safety committees; the support provided by the German state to the social partners in education: here we have examples of the sort of public encouragement of appropriate group forms recommended by the associative strategy.

3. Impossibility and Undesirability: A Response to Objections

Thus far we have discussed problems of government incompetence, political inequality, and particularism that now thwart egalitarian-democratic politics; we have proposed that a partial remedy for those problems lies in an improved organization of secondary associations pursued through a politics of associations; and we have presented some analytical considerations and comparative experience to support and illustrate our proposal. We want now to consider a pair of related objections to it. Both objections accept (at least for the sake of argument) the attractiveness of egalitarian-democratic norms and both agree that associations can contribute to the satisfaction of those norms. But they reject the use

19. For a close examination of the different public powers enjoyed by the "social partners" in the German case, see Wolfgang Streeck, Joseph Hilbert, Karl-Heinz van Kevelaer, Frederike Maier, and Hajo Weber, *The Role of the Social Partners in Vocational Training and Further Training in the Federal Republic of Germany* (Berlin: European Center for the Development of Vocational Training, 1987).

20. The phrase and the point come from Philippe C. Schmitter, "Interest Intermediation and Regime Governability in Contemporary Western Europe and North America," in Berger, ed., *Organizing Interests*, 285–327.

of an associative strategy to engender the "right" sort of associative environment. According to the first objection, it is not possible to create a favorable associative environment through politics; according to the second, efforts to create such an environment are more dangerous than the disease they aim to cure.

IMPOSSIBILITY

The argument for impossibility begins with the assumption that groups are a product of nature or culture or some other unalterable substrate of a country's political life. Just as some countries are blessed with good topsoil or a temperate climate, others are blessed with the "right" kinds of groups, at the right level of organization. In countries that are so blessed, group contributions of the sort we note are observed. But since patterns of group organization and behavior lie beyond politics, the observation provides no support at all for an associative strategy for addressing the problems of egalitarianism. Indeed, precisely by highlighting the importance of a favorable social basis for egalitarian democracy, they explain why equality does not travel well.

We think that this objection exaggerates the fixity of the associative environment. Groups are, after all, in important ways political artifacts. Their incidence, character, and patterns of interaction are not merely the result of natural tendencies to association among citizens with like preferences. They reflect structural features of the political economy in which they form—from the distribution of wealth and income to the locus of policy making in different areas. And they reflect variations across the members of that society, along such dimensions as income, information, and density of interaction. Existing political institutions and "culture" may crystallize around certain structural features and patterns of variation along these dimensions. But those features and variations are in no sense natural. They can be changed through public policy.

Public policy can, for example, make the background distribution of wealth and income more or less uneven. It can shift the locus of public decision making from regional to national levels or concentrate it in a single department, in ways that encourage different sorts of group formation and discourage others. The availability of information can be widened or constricted. The density of interaction among similarly situated citizens can be increased or decreased. The cost of administering joint efforts, or navigating the negotiation antecedent to them, can be subsidized or not. Those subsidies can simply be provided to the most powerful or tied to antecedent satisfaction of certain requirements of behavior. Consistent with the continued supremacy of formal political institutions, groups can also be assigned public functions, including the power to issue complaints for violations of administrative regulation, to take emergency action in correcting violations, to establish standards for licensing and training in different occupations and industry standards on production, to establish eligibility criteria for receipt of other sorts of benefits (including welfare benefits), and to apply such licensing procedures, standards, and eligibility criteria as part of a general regulatory regime.

All such changes in the environment of group formation, the incentives available to individual groups, and the governing status of groups can manifestly change the group system.

The experience of countries that are now recognized as having the "right" kinds of groups, moreover, bears out the importance of such deliberate efforts to shape the group environment. While corporatist systems of wage bargaining and peak negotiation may have benefited from preexisting religious solidarities, they were commonly built, deliberately, on the wreckage of much more contentious industrial relations. While regional economies may be furthered by the social linkages of independent agrarian communities, today those linkages are fabricated by efforts to seed joint projects and lower information costs. While apprenticeship vocational training may draw on longstanding traditions of craft production and employer obligation, the organizational base of such training, and the base of craft production itself, is secured through legally required memberships in organizations and protection of small producers. There is nothing "natural" about such efforts to secure appropriate associative ends and nothing in "nature" that has precluded their success.

UNDESIRABILITY

Still, efforts to enlist associations in democratic governance may be undesirable. While groups can contribute to democratic order, and while their contribution can be secured through public policy, they can also work to undermine democratic order. This threat of "faction" was evident in our own inventory, offered earlier, of the practical problems now faced by democratic egalitarianism. Each problem suggested an impairment of democracy produced by the existing system of secondary association. If our associative strategy entails the further cultivation of groups, and the ceding to them of further public powers, does it not risk making faction truly ruinous?

Before addressing this question, we need to enter some background remarks aimed at clarifying the issues it raises.

The problem of faction has been a particular preoccupation of American politics and democratic theory ever since James Madison announced it as the key issue of American constitutional design.[21] But it must be faced by any liberal order, by reason of one of the defining features of such order: the protection of associative liberties. Once associative liberties are protected, associations inevitably follow. And, inevitably, legitimately, and without malfeasance, some of those associations will use their powers in pursuit of their aims in ways that frustrate the satisfaction of basic democratic norms. They will represent members in ways that undermine political equality; they will capture areas of policy in ways that undermine popular sovereignty and promotion of the general welfare; in "doing their job" of advancing member interests, they will inevitably promote particularism in place of deliberative politics. The threat of faction is, then, inescapable in any regime with associative liberties. Moreover, since those liberties are fundamental, the issue is how to mitigate that threat, not how to remove it.

The characteristic forms of faction were suggested earlier. There is, first, a pathology of inequality. Given inequalities in organization arising naturally from the background of market capitalism, group efforts to represent the interests of members may simply compound political inequality rather than relieve it. Political inequality may then compound material inequality, as groups use their political powers to improve their material position, in a vicious cycle of privilege. Second, there is a pathology of particularism. Groups are, by their very nature, to some degree particularistic. Only some citizens are represented in them, group leaders are (at best) accountable to their members and not others, and the interests and ideals of groups are not shared by all citizens. Representing their members faithfully, particular groups thus often seek policies that impose costs to the society at large, even as they provide gains for their own members, and promote a politics of narrow advantage and bargaining that corrupts the ideal of public deliberation about the common good. Commonly, inequality and particularism both thrive, as over-

21. See James Madison, Federalist 10, in *The Federalist* (New York: G. P. Putnam's Sons, 1907), 51–60. We are concerned here only with what Madison called "minority" faction.

represented interests bargain with one another, divide the political spoils, and so preserve their privileges until the next round of bargaining begins.

The problem of faction is serious, then; it is also inevitable so long as associative liberties are preserved. Since threats of faction are inevitable, it would be a mistake to attribute them to the associative strategy or to expect that strategy to eliminate faction. But since those problems are serious, it would be objectionable if the associative strategy increased the threat of faction. The question raised by the second objection, then, is whether pursuit of associative strategy would make the problem of faction worse.

To address this question fully, we would need to consider the likely effects of the associative strategy on each of the defining norms of egalitarian democracy: popular sovereignty, political equality, distributive equity, deliberative politics, and the operation of society for the general welfare. In the interests of space, we propose to focus here solely on the norm of popular sovereignty, though our treatment of it will suggest the shape of our more general response. Recall that that norm requires that the authorization of state action be determined (within the limits set by fundamental civil and political liberties) by procedures in which citizens are represented as equals. Our question then becomes: Would the pursuit of our associative strategy undermine the ultimate authority of the people in the formation of policy?

In answering this question, we assume that all associations, including those vested with quasi-public powers, will operate within a political system with encompassing formal institutions organizing representation along traditional territorial lines. We assume, then, a possibility of "exit" from the group-based system of interest representation to the more traditionally organized system. Moreover, we assume that the group system is itself regulated by the traditional system. Final formal authority resides with traditional institutions. Associations will depend on them for authorizations of certain of their powers and for material support in carrying such authorizations out.

With these background assumptions in mind, we want first to indicate four sorts of positive-sum relationships between associations and the democratic state—four ways, that is, that the fuller and more explicit incorporation of groups into governance roles might actually enhance the exercise of popular sovereignty through the traditional institutions and practices of territorial representation.

First, groups provide the state with information, thus permitting better definition of problems and greater precision in the selection of means for addressing them. By thus sharpening policy instruments and enabling them to be applied with greater precision, groups promote the capacity of the people to achieve their aims. Second, groups provide additional enforcement power, thus increasing the likelihood that decisions made by the people will be implemented.[22] Third, in mitigating enforcement problems, groups remove one important constraint on political debate. Instead of proposals being short-circuited with the claim that they are unenforceable, a wider range of proposals can be seriously discussed. Fourth, a more open politics of associations makes explicit a condition, which is already a standing feature of even the most liberal of societies, namely, that secondary associations do in fact perform a variety of functions that affect the conditions of political order. The associative strategy "exposes and brings out into the open, it institutionalizes a factor in law-making that we have, eagerly in fact, attempted to obscure."[23] By bringing the role of associations "into the open," it would make the exercise of power by associations more accountable. In combination, better and more flexible means, better enforcement, less constrained debate about ends and their achievement, and more openness and accountability in the exercise of power all count as important gains for popular sovereignty.

These four contributions are, however, accompanied by three sources of serious concern—of negative-sum relations between the powers of associations and the egalitarian-democratic order.

First, there are problems of disjunction of interest between the leaderships of groups and their members—the problem of the "iron law of oligarchy." A dense world of association may make the government more informed about, and more responsive to, the interests of group "oligarchs" but not those of its members. Second, there is the problem of independent powers—what might be called the "Frankenstein" issue. Endowed with quasi-public status, and commonly subsidized by the state, groups that at one point in time contribute to decent policy may continue to exercise power after outgrowing their usefulness, use that power to freeze their position, and so work to distort future debate and choice. Third, in-

22. See, for example, the discussion of "fire alarm" enforcement in Mathew D. McCubbins and Thomas Schwartz, "Congressional Oversight Overlooked: Police Patrols vs. Fire Alarms," *American Journal of Political Science* 28 (1984): 165–179.

23. Louis Jaffe, "Law-Making by Private Groups," *Harvard Law Review* 51 (1937): 220–221.

creasing the extent of policy making outside of formal legislative arenas increases threats of improper delegation. In particular, powers delegated to associations are bound to be vague. As in the context of legislative delegations to administrative agencies, then, there are problems about the abuse of the discretion permitted by such vagueness.

What are we to make of these problems? To make the case for associative democracy, it should be clear, we do not need to show that the strategy will solve these problems. They already exist and will remain in place so long as freedom of association is guaranteed. It is enough to show that associative democracy will not plausibly make the problems worse. Moreover, if the same deliberate politics of association that harnesses group contributions can mitigate the threat of faction, that should count as an added support for the argument. In considering the three problems just noted, it appears to us that this burden can be carried and that the promise of actual advance on curbing faction can be redeemed.

Beginning with internal democracy, the chief threat of the associative strategy appears to be its potential encouragement of large, encompassing, bureaucratic associations of the sort capable of taking broad responsibility for the coordination of social interests. These, it might be thought, are likely to suffer from even greater problems of internal responsiveness than the existing population of organizations. A recurrent example used in critical discussions is the distant, professionalized leadership of centralized trade union federations, whose "social responsibility" in dealings with employers and the state is seen to come at the expense of the concerns of actual members.

Given the decline of centralized union bargaining, the example may be of diminished empirical relevance. But it suffices to carry the concern. And it remains an instructive test of the intuitive assumption that responsiveness of leadership to group membership must decline as group encompassingness, size, and social responsibility increase. For, in fact, it suggests that the intuitive assumption is without foundations. There is no correlation between the opportunities for voice and exit that encourage responsiveness and the conditions necessary for peak bargaining. On a variety of measures of internal union democracy, for example, the Norwegian union movement, among the most centralized and encompassing in the world, is more internally democratic than unions in the United Kingdom, comprising one of the least centralized union movements, which are in turn more democratic than the unions of West Germany, which are intermediate in their level of centralization.[24]

If the union case is credited, internal responsiveness need not come at the expense of external capacity. Moreover, internal responsiveness can be designed into large organizations through their internal procedures. In combination, these points suggest that oligarchy is more plastic than the "iron law" suggests. More immediately, they suggest a natural response to the problem of disjunction: require greater use of internal democratic procedures among groups that are granted quasi-public status. Operationally, the requirement should be that groups accorded this status provide evidence that they in fact represent their members by showing that they actually use some mechanism of responsiveness. Infinite gradations in degree and differences in judgment are certainly imaginable here, just as they are in ongoing disputes over the representativeness of electoral systems. But as the case of electoral systems also suggests, it is possible to articulate a general principle of legitimacy, in this case internal responsiveness, and to use that general principle to guide debate about specific proposals.

Our second problem, the "Frankenstein" problem of independent powers, also carries a natural response, namely some variant of "sunset legislation." The quasi-public status of groups (and subsidies to them) should be reviewed on a regular basis, with a rebuttable presumption that the status (or subsidies) will be withdrawn or amended as group behavior, or perceived social needs, warrants. The general requirements are reasonably clear, though their precise elaboration is not. On the one hand, the threat of withdrawal must be sufficiently credible, and the gains associated with public status sufficiently great, to induce groups to meet accountability requirements and other conditions on their conduct. On the other hand, since continuity in bargaining relations is an important prerequisite of gains, the requirements must not be so exacting as to make them impossible to satisfy.

Of course, the ultimate guard against independent powers is the vital-

24. See Peter Lange, *Union Democracy and Liberal Corporatism: Exit, Voice, and Wage Regulation in Postwar Europe*, Cornell Studies in International Affairs, Occasional Paper No. 16. The measures include rules governing election to union councils, intermediate organizations, and national office; incidences and support of informal caucuses; and procedures for debate and vote on strikes, contracts, and other sorts of concerted action.

ity of the system dispensing the powers in the first place. This fact is precisely what gives normative force to our assumption, above, that systems relying heavily on group-based representation still rest final authority in encompassing territorial organizations. For evaluating associative democracy, the narrow issue here is whether, *ceteris paribus*, that system is made more or less vital by the increase in its democratic capacity that would follow on its enlistment of the energies of representative groups. And to ask that question is to answer it.

Finally, we offer two thoughts on the third problem noted above: the problem of vague delegations of power and the attendant risks of abused discretion. The first of these is simply a plea for realism and fairness in evaluation. The threat of vague delegations of powers in our associative scheme should be contrasted not with some ideal world but with the one that exists and the alternative reform proposals for that world. When it is, the contrast does not seem particularly damning. In the existing world, there is already much vague delegation to and exercise of discretion by administrative agencies. If we consider a scheme of more limited government as a means to cabin discretion, then we need to keep in mind that such a scheme is unlikely to serve the egalitarian democratic aims at issue here. If we consider a scheme with stronger legislative controls—less vagueness in delegating and more sharpness in formulating legislative standards—then we should consider familiar cautions that it may lead to an unwelcome politicization of legislative instruction, reflected in unreasonable goals, improbable deadlines on their achievement, or simple legislative deadlock.[25] Nor is there any reason to think that such reasonable requirements as clarity in the statement of statutory goals will be inconsistent with the associative scheme.

Moving now to a more positive engagement with the issue, we propose to address the problem of delegation through performance criteria. Where associations are involved in the enforcement and administration of policy, public institutions should formulate clear performance standards for groups to enforce and administer, while avoiding detailed specification of the means to be used in meeting those standards. For example, in the area of workplace health, there might be performance stan-

---

25. These effects are noted in Cass Sunstein, "Constitutionalism after the New Deal," *Harvard Law Review* 101 (1987): 480–481: "The movement toward increased congressional control is not without risks of its own [since] . . . undue specificity may produce regulation riddled by factional tradeoffs."

dards in the form of permissible exposure limits for hazardous chemicals, while decisions about the means for implementing those limits would fall to health and safety committees. When associations are involved in the formation of policy, the discretion ingredient in grants of quasi-public status can again be addressed by setting performance criteria—for example, minimum standards for skills, knowledge, courses, and examinations in vocational training programs whose operation is coordinated by labor and business in particular sectors. Even where groups do not enjoy subsidies for their performance of quasi-public duties, they should be regulated in the conduct of those duties. Where they are officially granted quasi-public status, or material state assistance, performance criteria can be more exacting.

In sum, then, our response to the undesirability objection is that dangers of faction in the area of popular sovereignty could be mitigated by requirements on internal democracy, legislative and judicial oversight, sunset laws that threaten a group with competition for its position, and performance standards. Moreover, we think that similar measures of internal accountability, external oversight, and competition could be deployed to mitigate problems of faction that arise on the other dimensions of democracy (political equality, for example). But we have not, of course, argued this here, and to that extent the discussion of faction is importantly incomplete. It might, for example, be argued that an associative strategy for equalizing political representation would generate cartels or other concentrations of economic power that would, in turn, present intolerable threats to economic efficiency. We disagree with this objection and think that some of the comparative evidence discussed in Section 2 speaks against it. Nevertheless, we think it raises a serious problem and that a fuller discussion of the associative idea would need to show in detail how it could be met.

4. The American Case

Thus far we have argued that associative solutions are, in the abstract, attractive ways of advancing democratic ideals and that the factional potential of such solutions can be tamed by the same strategy of constructive artifice that enlists group contributions. Still, the idea of associative democracy may seem of little relevance to the United States. More than any other economically advanced mass democracy, the United States has a strongly anti-collectivist political culture, a weak state, and a civil society dominated by (relatively disorganized) business interests. The potential for artifice granted, this context poses obvious problems for the associative strategy. At best, it might be thought, the absence of any initial favoring conditions makes the strategy irrelevant. There is simply not enough to get started down the path of democratic associative reform. At worst, it might be feared, pursuit of the strategy under these conditions would be a political nightmare. Giving new license to a congeries of group privilege and particularism, it would exacerbate inequalities and further corrupt and enfeeble the state.

Such concerns have considerable force and deserve a fuller answer than we can provide here. Briefly, however, while we acknowledge the anti-collectivism of much American political culture, we also see considerable experimentation now going on with associative solutions to policy problems in such areas as regional health and welfare service delivery, local economic development, education and training, and environmental regulation, among many others.

There is, for example, a tradition of delivering many welfare and social services through secondary associations—community organizations, churches, volunteer agencies, and the like. While such organizations often have substantial autonomy in designing the appropriate service mix for the communities they are asked to serve, they are also increasingly inextricably dependent on government fees for such services for their own survival.[26] Much "public" input in local economic development is decided, for good or ill, in "community development corporations," heavily subsidized by government grants, representing different admixtures of independent neighborhood associations and business firms.[27] In education, parent-teacher associations are commonly vested with substantial powers in determining the budget and curriculum of elementary and secondary public schools, and those schools increasingly look to local business interests for support in setting standards on student performance.[28] In train-

26. For an instructive discussion of the role of nonprofit organizations in welfare-state service delivery, emphasizing the increased dependence of many of these agencies on their ties to government, see Steven Rathgeb Smith and Michael Lipsky, *Nonprofits for Hire: The Welfare State in the Age of Contracting* (Cambridge, MA: Harvard University Press, 1995).

27. A useful (though not impartial) survey of local economic development strategies is provided in R. Scott Fosler, *Local Economic Development* (Washington: International City Management Association, 1991).

28. For an enthusiastic review of some of the emerging linkages between schools and private business associations, see Anthony Carnevale, Leila Gainer, Janice Villet, and Shari Holland, *Training Partnerships: Linking Employers and Providers* (Alexandria: American Society for Training and Development, 1990).

ing, the largest single training program in the United States, the Job Training Partnership Act (JTPA), is almost wholly administered through "private industry councils" dominated, by statute, by local business interests.[29] In environmental regulation, from the deliberate promotion of bargaining among industry and environmental groups as a prelude to standard setting at the federal level, to the promotion of bargaining between business and community organizations over the appropriate implementation of environmental standards in local neighborhoods and regions, policy is rife with secondary associations exercising de facto public powers.[30]

Some of these efforts display the great strengths of associative governance; others display its many dangers. Our point here is simply that such governance in fact goes on, widely, even in this liberal culture. And its incidence provides a natural basis for more deliberate, and democratic, associative strategies.

Moreover, while we acknowledge the weakness of the American state, we think that at least some sorts of associative reforms can make it stronger. Particularly given a weak state, it is important that group empowerment proceed in a way that is reliably positive-sum with state power. But this merely requires judgment in the choice of associative strategies. It does not generally bar pursuit of them. And while we acknowledge, finally, the overwhelming business dominance of the American polity, we think this again simply constrains choice in the groups that are advantaged through the associative strategy. If business is too powerful, then associative resources should be provided to labor or other nonbusiness-dominated groups; the current imbalance is not an argument for abandoning the general idea.

Most generally, we agree that the United States has high levels of inequality, a less-than-competent government, and weak cooperative institutions—that, in brief, it does not work well as a democracy. This, in fact,

29. JTPA has been widely criticized as insufficiently accountable to public needs. Among others, see John D. Donahue, *Shortchanging the Workforce: The Job Training Partnership Act and the Overselling of Privatized Training* (Washington: Economic Policy Institute, 1989); United States General Accounting Office (GAO), *Job Training Partnership Act: Inadequate Oversight Leaves Program Vulnerable to Waste, Abuse, and Mismanagement*, GAO/HRD-91–97 (Washington: General Accounting Office, 1991).

30. Some of the federal experience is reviewed in Charles W. Powers, *The Role of NGOs in Improving the Employment of Science and Technology in Environmental Management* (New York: Carnegie Commission on Science, Technology, and Government, May 1991); the experience of local communities in fostering such environmental bargaining among organized groups is reviewed in Valjean McLenighan, *Sustainable Manufacturing: Saving Jobs, Saving the Environment* (Chicago: Center for Neighborhood Technology, 1990).

is the very problem that provides our point of departure. We move, then, to some examples of how an associative strategy might proceed from this point of departure in this distinctive polity. We offer two illustrations of the general look and feel of the associative project: the reform of worker representation and industrial relations in the United States, and the reform of vocational training. In each case we sketch some problems that need to be addressed, indicate the ways that a richer associational setting might help in addressing them, and discuss some measures that might now be taken to promote that setting.

WORKER REPRESENTATION

Our goal here—controversial and surely bitterly contested—would be to improve the organization of American workers. Such improvement would plausibly contribute to the satisfaction of democratic norms in a variety of ways. By extending and deepening the benefits of organized representation to those who are now unorganized or under-organized, it would advance the goal of political equality. It would also have a fair chance of improving distributive equity and economic performance in the United States. At the same time, properly structured worker organization is of particular importance, because work is important. The associative framework that determines how it is organized, distributed, and rewarded sets the background and tone for associative action throughout much of the society. So other reforms are more likely to succeed if reforms here succeed.[31]

The system of worker organization in the United States currently suffers from two related problems. First, very few substantive benefits are provided to workers in their role as citizens. We have a low "social" wage. Most benefits are instead provided through individual firms. But benefits are costly and firms compete. So there are obvious incentives to skimp on the provision of benefits. The result is comparatively low and uneven substantive protection for workers.

Second, the system discourages cooperation between employers and employees. Part of the reason for this is the generally low level of worker organization. Genuine cooperation is based on mutual respect, which typically depends on recognition of mutual power. With the disorganization of workers limiting their power, however, employees are commonly

31. The force of this claim will emerge in our discussion of the role of associations in vocational training.

incapable of extracting from employers the sorts of institutionalized respect for their interests (e.g., a serious commitment to job security or consultation in advance of work reorganization) needed to elicit genuine cooperation. The other part of the reason has to do with the structure of union organization. In general, mimicking the decentralized benefit system, unions themselves are highly decentralized. Where they have power, then, they have incentives to free-ride on the interests of others and to seek maximum reward for their particular labor. Decentralization does permit wildcat cooperation. More commonly, however, it—in conjunction with the low social wage—promotes an economistic job-control unionism unfavorable to cooperation. Altogether, then, an environment featuring low social wage, low union density, and highly decentralized union organization is dense with incentives for collectively irrational conflict.[32]

This diagnosis suggests four related steps of associative reform of this system: (1) lower the barriers to unionization, (2) encourage alternative forms of self-directed worker organization, (3) raise the social wage, and (4) promote more centralization in wage bargaining, while permitting high levels of decentralization in bargaining over specific work conditions. We consider these in turn.

Even within the current framework of U.S. labor law—which centers on collective bargaining between elected and exclusive worker representatives (unions) and employers—strategies for reducing barriers to worker representation are clear enough. Elections of representatives could be simplified and expedited, bargaining obligations could attach early and survive the arrival of successor employers, the right to use economic force could be enhanced, and, throughout, violations of labor regulation could be remedied with compensatory damages rather than with toothless "make whole" remedies. In a more ambitious scheme of reforms, representation might be awarded upon a simple demonstration of support from a majority of affected workers rather than upon the elaborate demonstration now required; individual rights of workplace members of unions without majority status might be enhanced; restraints on the coor-

32. For a general review of the U.S. industrial relations system emphasizing these interactions, see Joel Rogers, "Divide and Conquer: 'Further Reflections on the Distinctive Character of American Labor Law,'" *Wisconsin Law Review* (1990): 1–147. For a review of the state of the American labor movement, see the contributions to George Strauss, Daniel G. Gallagher, and Jack Fiorito, eds., *The State of the Unions* (Madison: Industrial Relations Research Association, 1991).

dination of unions in using economic force could be relaxed; greater attention to the practical requirements of union "security" in maintaining a workplace presence could be given; current restraints on the use of member dues for organizing the unorganized, and for political action, could be relaxed.[33]

Even with such reforms in place, however, most of the economy would remain nonunion, leaving most workers without representation. We would suggest, then, that forms of workplace representation alternative to, though not in direct competition with, unions also be encouraged. This could be achieved directly through a mandate of workplace committees with responsibilities in, for example, occupational health and safety, training, or areas of concern apart from wages. Alternatively, or as a supplement, government purchasing contracts might be used to enhance worker voice. Eligibility for such contracts could be conditioned on successful employer demonstration of the existence of a works council or some other acceptable form of autonomous employee representation with real powers in the administration of the internal labor market.

The increased levels of worker organization that could be expected to follow on these two changes would mitigate one of the barriers to cooperation noted earlier, namely the weakness of labor organization. With labor stronger, it is possible to imagine a new social contract in the internal labor market, one that will promote cooperation. The terms of the contract are simple enough: labor offers flexibility on internal labor-market work rules and greater job commitment in exchange for management's commitment to consultation and heightened job security.

To ensure fairness, however, and to promote the stability of associations that contributes to their beneficial effects, a system of multiple worker organizational forms would require an increase in the social wage—our third initiative. For workers, an increased social wage would provide some assurances of fair treatment and security external to the firm. Aside from its direct distributional benefits, this increase would relieve pressures for the internal rigidity and the defensiveness associated with job-control unionism. It would make more flexible, productivity-enhancing strategies of work organization more appealing. For employ-

---

33. There are many such statements of possible labor-law reform. A good guide to the issues involved, containing both more and less ambitious recommendations for reform, is provided by Paul Weiler, *Governing the Workplace: The Future of Labor and Employment Law* (Cambridge, MA: Harvard University Press, 1990).

ers, the mitigation of job-control consciousness (and the likely reduction of labor costs) among organized workers would remove one powerful incentive to resist worker association in their firms.

Finally, greater coordination of wage contracts would be needed to overcome a second barrier to cooperation and to reap the full benefits for economic performance. As noted earlier, the American system of contract negotiation is highly decentralized. It is unreasonable to expect the United States to approximate the corporatist peak bargaining of the late 1970s (especially since corporatist systems themselves no longer approximate that). Still, some measures could be undertaken to encourage more encompassing associations than now exist, thus generating an environment better suited to some greater centralization and coordination of wage negotiations (at least on a regional basis).

One step would be to amend the law governing multi-employer bargaining, shifting the presumption away from the voluntariness and instability of such arrangements toward their requirement. In addition, pressures within the union movement for consolidation could be strengthened by selective incentives, for example, in the form of funds for (re)training, conditioned on inter-union cooperation. Government support for business cooperation—for example, consortia pursuing joint research and development strategies—could be conditioned on efforts to consolidate wage policies. Or, following common practice in most systems, "extension laws" on bargaining contracts could be enacted, generalizing their results to nonunion settings.

The effect of this combination of increasing the social wage and promoting more generalization of wage patterns across firms would be to discriminate more sharply between the focus of bargaining within the firm and the focus of bargaining outside it. Within the firm, unions would come to look more like employee-participation schemes, and employee-participation schemes would look more like unions. Worker representation would be secured, but with a particular focus on regulating the internal labor market and increasing productivity within it, through innovation on issues of job design, work organization, access to training on new firm technology, and the like. Outside the firm, more encompassing organizations suited to handling matters affecting workers in general rather than workers in a particular firm—would be more empowered to pursue that object. They would focus more on securing generalizable wage agreements and the content of the social wage.

Such a system, which relies on associative empowerment and artifice throughout, would likely be a vast improvement on current American industrial relations. It would improve representation, increase productivity, generalize the benefits of cooperation, and better integrate the industrial relations system with state economic and welfare policies.

VOCATIONAL TRAINING

Our second example of constructive group artifice comes from the area of vocational training. In the United States, as in most other rich countries, intensified international competition and rapid technological change have underscored the need for improvements in workforce skills. To preserve living standards in the face of low-wage competition from abroad, labor must be made substantially more productive, and firms must become increasingly adept at such "nonprice" aspects of product competition as quality, variety, customization, and service. Success here will require, *inter alia*, that "frontline" production and nonsupervisory workers be equipped with substantially higher and broader skills than they presently possess.

The vocational training problem in the United States consists in the fact that such skills are being provided in insufficient quality and quantity by schools and firms, and insofar as they are provided, they are directed to college-bound youths and managers. In the public school system, very little occupational training is provided for the "forgotten half" of each high school cohort that does not go on to college or the "forgotten three-quarters" of each cohort that does not complete it. And U.S. employers provide their frontline workforce with far less training than do leading foreign competitors. Moreover, the training they do provide is generally narrower than is desirable—for the economy as a whole, for innovative firms drawing from the external labor market, and for individual workers, who typically change employers several times in their working lifetimes.[34] With skills more essential than ever to compensation, the failures of U.S. training have powerfully contributed to the decline in production and

---

34. For general reviews of U.S. training problems, making all these points, see U.S. Congress, Office of Technology Assessment, *Worker Training: Competing in the International Economy*, OTA ITE-457 (Washington: Government Printing Office, 1990); and *Commission on the Skills of the American Workforce, America's Choice: High Skills or Low Wages!* (Rochester: National Center on Education and the Economy, 1990).

nonsupervisory worker wages experienced over the last generation and to rising inequality in U.S. market incomes.[35]

The problems in the American training system lie on both the "demand" and "supply" sides. We will concentrate here on the supply side, focusing in particular on two central issues.[36]

First, the quality of public school vocational training is limited by the absence of effective linkages with the economy itself. Most public vocational training in the United States is essentially "stand alone" classroom-based instruction, and while such instruction is certainly important for any training system, it has intrinsic limits.[37] As a general matter, the system will lag behind industry practice in its provision of skills. It will be baffled by the need to make large expenditures on capital equipment, of the sort needed to replicate factories inside schools. And it will have difficulty conveying to students the active knowledge they need to flourish in, and can only acquire from, real-world production situations.

35. For a good review of wage trends in the United States and the more general decline in living standards among nonsupervisory workers, see Lawrence Mishel and David M. Frankel, *The State of Working America*, 1990–91 edition (Armonk: M. E. Sharpe, 1990).

36. A word of explanation on the focus. Demand by American employers for high and broad frontline workforce skills is extremely weak and uneven. Unless this changes, supply-side innovations geared to improving skill delivery to frontline workers will risk having all the effect of "pushing on a string." Moreover, competitive pressures acting alone cannot be counted on to change the structure of employer demand in the desired way, since employers can choose to respond to those pressures by reducing wages, increasing firm productivity through changes in work organization that "'dumb down" most jobs while increasing the human-capital component of a well paid few, or simply moving away from high-end markets. Most U.S. firms, in fact, have chosen some combination of these "low wage, low skill" competitive strategies. To remedy the demand-side problem, it is essential to foreclose this option. The most obvious way to do this is to build stable floors under wages and effective linkage between productivity improvements and wage compensation, thus forcing employers to be more attentive to strategies for increasing the productivity of their labor (e.g., skill upgrading). Direct state action can help here, by increasing minimum-wage floors. As regards more specifically associative reform, however—and this is why we do not linger on the demand side—we believe the most important actions are those already outlined in the recommendations just made on improving industrial relations. Deeper and more encompassing worker organizations, especially ones shaped by social interests in improved cooperation, would help create the needed wage floors, wage-productivity linkages, and pressures within firms to upgrade. Moreover, they could be expected to do so in a way that not only raises the aggregate demand for skills and their compensation but also improves the distribution of both. The basic problem on the demand side is that the interests of the bulk of the population, workers, are simply not now centrally in the picture. They are barely represented in the economy and only very imperfectly represented in the state. The basic solution to under-representation is to improve the conditions of their organization in ways consistent with other democratic norms.

37. The importance of these limits rises where, as in the United States, the public training system lacks any effective industry-based-training complement.

To remedy these problems, denser linkages must be forged between schools and students, on the one side, and between employers and their workers, on the other. Through such linkages can flow that which the classroom system now lacks: up-to-date knowledge on industry trends, loans and grants of current equipment on which to train, and, all important, access to actual workplaces, and their principals, for work-based instruction complementary to what goes on in the classroom.

Second, while the quantity of training supplied by government could be expected to increase as a result of the reform of worker representation discussed earlier, the effort by employers must also be substantially increased and improved. Here, the problem is in part that employers are uncertain about the sorts of broad-banded skills that would be appropriate to provide and in part that they have no confidence that they would capture the returns to providing training in such skills. Employer training suffers, that is, both from a lack of agreed-upon standards for coordinated training and from the positive externalities that accompany an open external labor market, in which workers are able to move freely among firms, so that one firm's trainee can become another firm's asset. The externalities problem is particularly acute for high and broad skills. Since such skills are, by definition, of use in a wide variety of work settings, their possession increases the potential mobility of workers, enabling one firm to appropriate the benefits of another firm's training efforts. This is part of the reason that when firms do train, they train narrowly, in job-specific or firm-specific skills.

To remedy the problem of coordination, a mechanism for setting common standards and expectations is necessary. To remedy the externality problem, there are two basic solutions. One is to reduce worker mobility across firms. This permits firms to train workers with the confidence that they will recoup any investments made. In effect, this is what is done in Japan. The other solution is to socialize the costs of private-firm training, so that individual employers will not care about worker mobility. This can be done with the assistance of the tax system—for example, in the form of "train or tax" rules, requiring firms either to train or to pay into some general fund. Or it can be done through the private collective organization of employers to a point that they can discipline free riders or, at high levels of joint participation (where close to all relevant competitors or poachers train), become indifferent to them. In effect, this is what is done in successful European training systems, which, like those in the

United States, operate with relatively open external labor markets and high rates of inter-firm worker mobility.

As the second European strategy makes clear, the presence of competent, encompassing employer and labor associations immensely aids both in addressing the problem of linkage between the worlds of school and work and in increasing the level and quality of employer-sponsored training.

Facilitating linkage, associations provide the state with timely information on emerging industry trends and practices, new technologies, skill needs, and access to the insides of firms. They permit industries to speak with a unified voice to public training providers, to negotiate authoritatively with the state over training curricula, access to firms, requirements on skills certification, rules on the use of equipment, and the like. They permit the state to get closure and enforcement on decisions once made—"If you don't like it, talk to your association" being a far more effective retort to second-guessing firms than, "Well, that's just what we decided to do"—while providing monitoring and enforcement capacities to supplement any public training effort. And being broad in their representation, and accountable to members, associations are natural vehicles for developing general standards, of wide applicability, of the sort that protect the training investment made by employees themselves.

Facilitating employer training efforts, industry associations help in part by setting general standards on skills—something no single firm can do. The identification of commonly desired competencies assures workers that acquiring those competencies will improve their position on the external labor market. This leads to increased take-up rates on training, assuring employers of a large pool of workers with high and common skills. And this assurance encourages more proactive industry strategies of upgrading and inter-firm cooperation in implementing those strategies.

But associations also act to facilitate employer training efforts by mitigating the externality problem that discourages those efforts. They require training as a condition of membership, or of receipt of its benefits. They monitor the training that goes on, relieving fears of "suckering." They ease the flow of information about new technology and work practices among members, providing a natural vehicle for voluntary industry benchmarking that creates upward pressures on existing standards. They share training facilities and curricula among themselves, reducing per capita training costs. More elusive, but not less important, they help define and sustain—through means ranging from social gatherings and award dinners to insider gossip and plum subcontracting deals—common norms of "accepted practice." As such norms congeal into obligatory industrial cultures, those who undersupply training come to be seen less as clever businessmen than as social pariahs, to be punished with loss of status and business. This can powerfully discourage even temptations to defect, making the consideration of cooperation more familiar, extending and securing its reach, and lowering monitoring costs. In all these ways, a strong employer association, especially one "kept honest" by a strong union, can provide a powerful boost to the quality and the extent of firm training efforts.

How might associative supports be enlisted for a revamped vocational training system in the United States? In general terms, the problems and the instruments at hand to solve them are clear enough. Both labor and employer associations are relatively weak in the United States. Both need to be strengthened, at least in their capacity to discipline their own members and to deal with one another and with the state effectively, on training matters. Very little public money now goes directly to these purposes, even though the lessons of comparative experience clearly indicate their virtues. Public supports—in the form of direct cash assistance, technical assistance, greater participation in curriculum development, increased legal powers to enforce obligations against their own members—can be provided in exchange for help in carrying out the important public task of training the workforce.

For example, significant improvement in the quality of vocational training will require some recognized occupational standards. But outside a few specialized trades, these do not exist. Joining with public training providers, existing unions and employer associations could be invited, on an industry-by-industry basis, to develop such standards. Their work could be facilitated by the state, in the form of modest financial supports and technical assistance. And it should not be accepted by the state without independent evaluation. But some product should finally be accepted and enforced as a standard. Such enforcement will naturally be advanced by the primary authors themselves. Employers would look to demonstrated competence, according to these standards, when awarding jobs in internal labor markets. Unions would center on them in wage negotiations or in rules governing job assignments in those markets. But such private actions could also be supplemented through public means.

The standard could be made applicable to all federally funded vocational training programs, for example, and adopted as a standard in arbitration and judicial decisions in labor and employment law.[38]

The competency of labor and trade associations to provide training services to members may be explicitly promoted by public policy as well. Public subsidies and technical assistance to such organizations for this purpose, utterly routine in other countries and already tried with some success with a handful of trade and labor organizations in the United States, would be a natural supportive policy. Antitrust law could be relaxed for joint training activities of member firms;[39] additional amendments might be needed in labor law, to permit union-management cooperation in training activities involving nonunion firms.[40]

Both of the examples just presented involve efforts to improve training by strengthening existing associations. But the formation of new associations around training might be encouraged as well. Industry or regional training consortia composed of firms and unions, for example, could be encouraged through demonstration grant assistance, technical aid, and discounts on public training services provided to their members.[41] These supports would properly be conditioned on those associations providing training services, participating in setting standards, mounting outreach programs to public schools, providing such schools with technical assistance, expanding existing apprenticeship programs (the best, albeit much neglected, example of vocational training in the United States), and otherwise cooperating with public providers, and each other, to move to more aggressive and inclusive training agenda. The goal again would be to bring more order, and a critical mass, to private training efforts and to improve effective linkages to schools.

Given the present weakness of associations in the United States, addressing the externality problem probably requires direct government ef-

38. The Department of Labor's Office of Work-Based Learning is already making qualified moves in this direction—"qualified" in that outside more heavily unionized industries, it remains unclear what, if any, organized voice workers in the industry will have.

39. Following current practice for joint research and development activities.

40. Recommendations on how to do this are made in Margaret Hilton, "Shared Training: Learning from Germany," *Monthly Labor Review* 114, 3 (March 1991): 33–37.

41. An experiment along these lines is under way in Milwaukee, where several firms (nonunion and unionized), unions, and public training providers have come together around a Wisconsin Manufacturing Training Consortium designed to do just these things. See Joel Rogers and Wolfgang Streeck, *Recommendations for Action* (Madison: Center on Wisconsin Strategy, 1991).

forts at socializing costs—through unqualified payroll levies or "play or pay" levy structures. The revenues, however, could be used in ways that strengthen future private capacities for self-governance. Funds might, for example, be given to associations for redistribution. The effect would be to create enormous temptations to associations to organize themselves to take a more active role in training and for firms and unions to join associations—in effect, an inducement to encompassingness of the sort desired. Or, in a "play or pay" scheme, tax relief could be granted to firms that demonstrate that the training they provide conforms to the standards set by industry associations. This would have the same effect of strengthening a collective associative hand in setting standards and strengthening the associations themselves.

There are many paths to virtue, but this should be enough to make the point. In principle, at least, the associative supports for a more successful vocational training system could be achieved in the United States with fairly standard policy instruments. Those supports would benefit both workers and "better" firms (i.e., those firms interested in upgrading). And, far from engendering further corruption of the state, they would strengthen public capacities to address problems of manifest public concern.

Conclusion

The examples just given provide no more than a couple of illustrations of the directions an associative democratic strategy might take in the United States. But they suffice to underscore the sorts of concerns that define that strategy and the considerations relevant to its execution. What we have argued in this essay, and what is displayed in the examples just given, is straightforward enough. To proceed, egalitarian politics must once again be shown to work. To work, it requires associative supports. Those supports can be developed. And developing them, and realizing their contribution to democratic governance, requires neither a naive view of associations as free from the threat of faction nor a dangerous view on the surrender of encompassing public authority. Faction can be mitigated through the same artifice that enlists associative contributions, and the strength and the competence of public authorities can be enhanced by this enlistment.

More broadly, by assuring greater equality in organized representation among private citizens, and by more effectively recruiting the energies of their organizations into public governance, the aim of the associative strategy is to forge an egalitarian-democratic order without an oppressive state. That is nice work if you can get it—and we have suggested that you can.

4

FREEDOM OF EXPRESSION

Introduction

In April 1989, students at the University of Michigan walked into a class and were faced with a blackboard that read: "A mind is a terrible thing to waste—especially on a nigger." This message followed closely on the appearance of a flier at the University declaring "open season on Blacks." A month later, an African student at Smith College found a message slipped under her door, which read: "African nigger do you want some bananas? Go back to the jungle."[1]

Responding to a pattern of such incidents and the longstanding American traditions of racial hatred and violence reflected in them, a substantial number of colleges and universities have adopted codes regulating racist and other forms of hate speech. These regulations have been the object of intense controversy. Denounced by some as the work of "tenured radicals,"[2] they have also been the target of more serious criticism.

I have presented talks based on earlier drafts of this essay at Haverford College, the University of California (Davis), the John F. Kennedy School of Government, Wellesley College, the University of Illinois (Chicago), Northwestern University, the Jerusalem Philosophical Encounter, Amherst College, New York University, the Inter-Africa Group Symposium "On the Making of the New Ethiopian Constitution," and the Society for Ethical and Legal Philosophy. I am grateful to audiences at these talks for their criticisms and suggestions. I would also like to thank C. Edwin Baker, Randall Forsberg, John Rawls, John Simmons, and Cass Sunstein for comments on previous versions, Sunstein for making available successive drafts of his *Democracy and the Problem of Free Speech* (New York: Free Press, 1994), and Archon Fung for his research assistance. More generally, I am very much indebted to Tim Scanlon's papers on freedom of expression, in particular his "Freedom of Expression and Categories of Expression," *University of Pittsburgh Law Review* 40 (1979): 519–550.

1. See Charles Lawrence, "If He Hollers Let Him Go: Regulating Racist Speech on Campus," *Duke Law Journal* (1990): 431–483; Mari Matsuda, "Public Response to Racist Speech: Considering the Victim's Story," *Michigan Law Review* 87 (1989): 2320–2381; Richard Delgado, "Campus Antiracism Rules: Constitutional Narratives in Collision," *Northwestern University Law Review* 85 (1991): 343–387.

2. See for example George Will, "Curdled Politics on Campus," *Newsweek*, 6 May 1991, 72; Chester E. Finn, "The Campus: 'An Island of Repression in a Sea of Freedom,'" *Commentary*, September 1989, 17–23.

The University of Michigan's own speech code was found constitutionally infirm by Judge Avern Cohn.[3] Considering the University's record in implementing that code, Cohn's objections were well-taken.[4]

Still, critics commonly sweep too widely. The United States is, after all, unique internationally in its legal toleration of hate speech.[5] And the Michigan rule is not the only model. Consider, for example, Stanford's regulation on discriminatory harassment. The Stanford behavior code regulates "speech or other expression" that:

(1) is *intended* to insult or stigmatize individuals on the basis of their sex, race, color, handicap, religion, sexual orientation, or national and ethnic origin.

(2) is addressed *directly* to the individual or individuals whom it insults or stigmatizes.

(3) makes use of insulting or *"fighting words"* or non-verbal symbols that are "commonly understood to convey direct and visceral hatred or contempt for human beings on the basis of their sex, race, etc."

Expression is only regulable if it meets all three conditions. So here we have a not very restrictive regulation that can be endorsed consistent with a strong commitment to freedom of expression and to the toleration associated with that commitment.[6] It does restrict some expression, but it is not very restrictive.[7] There is no violation if a student in a course or at a political rally says, "The Holocaust is a Zionist fraud," or "Slavery was a great civilizing influence." Indeed, the regulation does not prohibit very

3. Doe v. University of Michigan, 721 F. Supp., 852 (E.D. Michigan, 1989).

4. See ibid. for discussion of cases of enforcement against comments made in the course of classroom discussion.

5. See David Kretzmer, "Freedom of Speech and Racism," *Cardozo Law Review* 8 (1987): 445–513; Eric Stein, "History Against Free Speech: The New German Law Against the 'Auschwitz'—and Other 'Lies,'" *Michigan Law Review* 85 (1986): 275–324; Kenneth Lasson, "Racism in Great Britain: Drawing the Line of Free Speech," *Boston College Third World Law Journal* 6 (1987): 161–181; Robert Sedler, "The Constitutional Protection of Religion, Expression, and Association in Canada and the United States: A Comparative Analysis," *Case Western Reserve Journal of International Law* 20 (1988): 577–621; Matsuda, "Public Response to Racist Speech"; Delgado, "Campus Antiracism Rules."

6. But it does appear to be inconsistent with the current view of the Supreme Court on permissible forms of state regulation of speech. See R. A. V. v. St. Paul, 122 S. Ct. 2538 (1992). I will discuss this view in Section 5.

7. In saying that it is not very restrictive, I do not mean to say that it is, therefore, an acceptable restriction. "No one whose first name includes the letters 'z' and 'y' may criticize Impressionist painting" is not very restrictive, but it is also not acceptable.

much at all—for example, probably not the Michigan or Smith cases I mentioned at the outset.

Putting the extent of prohibition to the side, what is the rationale for it and similar regulations? The aim is not to encourage civility, to shelter people from offensive comments, or to punish malign ignorance. The regulations are motivated instead by various costs associated with discriminatory harassment: direct psychological injury, indirect injury from encouragement to assaults on targeted groups, and, in particular, damage to prospects of equality that comes from undermining equality of educational opportunity within the university and from contributing to an environment in which unacceptable forms of discrimination seem reasonable. Judge Cohn's opinion in *Doe v. Michigan* gives special notice to concerns about equality. He begins by noting that it is an "unfortunate fact of our constitutional system that the ideals of freedom and equality are often in conflict." Responding to this unfortunate fact, he indicates in the concluding section of his opinion that the Court is "*sympathetic* to the University's obligation to ensure equal educational opportunities for all of its students" but emphasizes that "such efforts must not be at the *expense* of free speech."[8]

Why not? What is this "expense" of regulating free speech? Why is the expense of such magnitude that, in the face of it, concerns about such substantial values as equality rise only to the level of "sympathetic" concern?

My aim here is to address these and related questions. To that end, I leave aside for now the immediate controversies about speech codes, though I will return to the Stanford code at the end, indicating why a pallid endorsement of it is consistent with an affirmation of stringent protections of expressive liberties. Principally, however, I will be arguing for the pallor of the endorsement by discussing some reasons for the protections. The discussion will show that support for such regulations need not reveal a disdain for the values of freedom of expression and that a lack of enthusiasm for them need not reveal indifference to the destructive potential of hate speech. To claim otherwise—to draw a line of principle around regulations of this kind—is to provoke a divisive and unnecessary division between liberal and egalitarian commitment.

I start (Section 1) by describing what I mean by "stringent protections of expressive liberties." Then (in Section 2) I sketch and criticize two

---

8. Doe v. Michigan, 721 F. Supp., 853, 868, emphases added. Cohn did not indicate the sorts of measures that might be consistent with the First Amendment.

strategies for defending such stringency. The first, which I will call "minimalist," holds that expression deserves stringent protection, not because it is so valuable but because it is costless ("just speech"), or because the costs it imposes cannot permissibly be taken into consideration by the state, or because government is especially untrustworthy when it comes to regulating expression: the common thread running through the several variants of minimalism is that the defense is to proceed without recourse to the thesis that expression has substantial value. "Maximalist" views, by contrast, concede the costs of stringent protections but argue that the transcendent value of expression guarantees that it trumps the costs (except when they are of equally transcendent value).

Minimalism and maximalism are not formal theories about freedom of expression. Still, each represents an important tendency of thought in this area.[9] Moreover, their attractive simplicity encourages the assumption that they exhaust the field of justifications. Because neither is compelling, nihilism about freedom of expression lives parasitically off their defects—the nihilism urged, for example, in Stanley Fish's claim that "there's no such thing as free speech and it's a good thing, too."[10] Put less colorfully, the nihilist claims that all there really is—all there could be—when it comes to decisions about restricting or permitting speech is an *ad hoc* weighing of costs and benefits in particular cases using the scales provided by "some particular partisan vision."[11] No general presumption in favor of protection can withstand inspection.

But minimalism and maximalism do not exhaust the strategies of argument for stringent protections.[12] The central burden of my argument (in Sections 3 and 4) is to present an alternative to maximalist and minimalist outlooks and, thereby, to defuse some of the temptations to nihilism. Less simple than the alternatives, this view proposes that stringent protections emerge as the product of three distinct considerations:

(1) That certain fundamental interests—expressive, deliberative, and informational—are secured by stringent protections of expressive liberty.

9. As much in informal conversations about these issues as in the legal and philosophical literature.

10. See *Boston Review* 17 (January-February 1992): 3–4, 23–26. I mean "nihilistic" not as a tendentious label or a term of criticism, but rather as a term that captures the "there is no such thing" point in the quotation in the text. The view could be called "pragmatism" about expression, but this misses its critical edge.

11. Ibid., 26.

12. For a response to nihilism, see below, 128–131.

(2) That the costs of expression can, in an important range of cases, be addressed through—as Justice Brandeis put it—"more speech."

(3) That certain features of human motivation render expression vulnerable to underprotection, and so rigid protections are recommended for it.[13]

Stringent protections, then, help to advance a set of fundamental interests and are recommended principally by the importance of those interests, by the prospects of using expression as a preferred strategy for combating the costs of expression, and secondarily—but only secondarily—by concerns about our tendency to underprotect expression or mistrust government regulations of it.[14] I see no rationale that is at once simpler and as compelling. To be sure, the complexity opens the view to the charge of manipulability—of providing a set of relatively unstructured elements that, with suitable adjustments, can be made to deliver any result. I do not think the view has quite that defect. In any case, I think things are just this complex and see no gain in substituting an arbitrary truncation of relevant considerations for a complex but hard-to-manage structure.[15]

One feature of the account that I want especially to emphasize is that the defense of stringent protections of expression does not depend on a free-standing preference for liberty over all competing values—not, in particular, on a free-standing preference for liberty over equality and an associated condemnation of any restrictions of expression that (like hate-speech regulations) are undertaken in the name of the value of equality.[16] The idea that a commitment to freedom of expression depends on a free-standing preference for liberty over equality is, I believe, a serious mistake, because it fosters an unnecessary and destructive hostility to freedom of expression among friends of equality and an unnecessary and

---

13. See, for example, Vincent Blasi, "The Pathological Perspective and the First Amendment," *Columbia Law Review* 85 (1985): 449–514.

14. For an argument based more fundamentally on mistrust, see Richard Epstein, "Property, Speech, and the Politics of Distrust," *University of Chicago Law Review* 59 (1992): 41–90. For criticisms, see Frank Michelman, "Liberties, Fair Values, and Constitutional Method," *University of Chicago Law Review* 59 (1992): 91–114.

15. Cass Sunstein criticizes my view along these lines. He suggests that the legal principles that emerge from it might be "simply too complex, ad hoc, and unruly." See *Democracy and the Problem of Free Speech*, 146. I try to address this concern in my discussion of specific issues in Sections 4 and 5.

16. For the suggestion that it does so depend, see Ronald Dworkin, "Two Concepts of Liberty," in Edna Ullman-Margalit and Avishai Margalit, eds., *Isaiah Berlin: A Celebration* (London: Hogarth Press, 1991), 100–109.

destructive hostility to equality among friends of expressive liberty. Where reconciliation is possible, it promotes division; where disagreement is possible on common ground, it insists on drawing false lines of principle.

This point bears special notice because of the state of debate about freedom of expression. For much of the past century, egalitarians of the political left have been among the most insistent defenders of stringent protections of expressive liberty, arguing that freedom of expression is both an intrinsic aspect of human liberation and a precondition of popular democratic politics. Over the past three decades, this conjunction of egalitarian and libertarian commitment has been subjected to increasingly severe strain. Regulations of political spending aimed at enhancing the voice of less wealthy citizens have been condemned as unacceptable abridgements of expressive liberty. And free-speech values have been advanced as obstacles to regulating pornography and hate speech. Because these regulations, too, are in part about promoting equality, the suggestion has emerged that egalitarian and libertarian commitment have come to a parting of the ways. I disagree, and aim to state a case for stringent protections of expressive liberty in the tradition of free-speech egalitarianism.

Finally, I explore some of the implications of the view. In particular, the basic framework of argument for stringent protections suggests a different treatment of hate-speech regulations than that advanced in Justice Scalia's opinion in the 1992 case of *R. A. V. v. St. Paul*. So in Section 5, I discuss some reasons for rejecting Scalia's reasoning and explore as well the consistency of a certain style of pornography regulation with the view advanced here. Finally, I return to the Stanford regulation (Section 6), indicating how an endorsement of it is consistent with the bases for stringent protections of freedom of expression advanced here.

One last introductory point: throughout, I help myself freely to examples, terms, and ideas drawn from First Amendment law.[17] My aim, however, is not to present an interpretation of the Constitution but to present a rationale for stringent protections.

1. Stringent Protections

I will begin by explaining what I mean by "stringent protections of expressive liberties." My explanation proceeds by setting out four familiar themes suggested by the free-speech tradition. Nothing I say about these

17. In this connection I wish to thank C. Edwin Baker for pointing out a number of blunders that marred the penultimate draft of the paper.

themes will be original or even unfamiliar; each could be expressed in different ways; and not much will turn on the particular formulations. But I do need some statement of themes at hand to fix the idea of stringent protections sufficiently to be able to consider the bases for it.

PRESUMPTION AGAINST CONTENT REGULATION

It is common to distinguish regulations of expression that focus on content—including viewpoint and subject matter—from those that are content-neutral. A prohibition on advocating adultery restricts viewpoint; a prohibition on discussing adultery restricts subject matter; a prohibition on debating the merits of adultery (or anything else) on my street at 3:00 a.m. is content-neutral. The first theme, then, is that there is an especially strong (if rebuttable) presumption against regulating expression in virtue of subject matter and, still more particularly, viewpoint: a presumption against regulations animated by a concern for what a person says or otherwise communicates, or consequences that flow from what he or she says.[18]

CATEGORIZATION

Despite this general presumption, some kinds of content regulation seem intuitively less troubling—as with regulations of express, direct incitement, truth in advertising, private libel, fighting words, bribery, espionage, and nonobscene child pornography.[19] Because content regulation is in general objectionable, it is important to confine these exceptions. So a second main theme recommends a special approach to handling

18. The classic statement of the general concern is Justice Marshall's in Police Department of Chicago v. Mosley, 408 U.S. 92, 95–96 (1972): "Above all else, the First Amendment means that government has no power to restrict expression because of its message, its ideas, its subject matter, or its content." On viewpoint discrimination, see Texas v. Johnson, 491 U.S. 397, 414 (1989). For discussion, see John Hart Ely, "Flag Desecration: A Case Study in the Roles of Categorization and Balancing in First Amendment Decisions," *Harvard Law Review* (1975): 1482–1508; Geoffrey Stone, "Restrictions of Speech Because of its Content: The Peculiar Case of Subject-Matter Restrictions," *University of Chicago Law Review* 46 (1978): 81–115, and "Content-Neutral Restrictions," *University of Chicago Law Review* 54 (1987): 46–120; and T. M. Scanlon, Jr., "Content-Regulation Reconsidered," in Judith Lichtenberg, ed., *Democracy and the Mass Media* (Cambridge: Cambridge University Press, 1990), 331–354.

19. For example, on incitement, see Brandenburg v. Ohio, 395 U.S. 444 (1968); on commercial speech, Virginia State Board of Pharmacy v. Virginia Citizens Consumer Council, 425 U.S. 748 (1976); Central Hudson Gas and Electric v. Public Service Commission of New York, 447 U.S. 557 (1980); Posadas de Puerto Rico Associates v. Tourism Company of Puerto Rico, 106 S. Ct. 2968 (1986); on fighting words, Chaplinsky v. New Hampshire, 315 U.S. 568 (1942); on child pornography, Ferber v. New York, 458 U.S. 747 (1982).

content regulations. Sometimes called "categorization,"[20] the approach singles out a small set of categories of expression—in First Amendment law, for example, child pornography, commercial speech, obscenity, fighting words, and express incitement—for lesser protection, specifying conditions for permissible regulation of expression in each category.[21] For content-neutral regulations, by contrast, the second theme asserts that there ought to be a more or less explicit balancing, with a thumb in the scale for speech, and an especially heavy thumb when the burden of a content-neutral regulation is especially great for groups with restricted means to convey their views.[22] (I will revisit this last point about "weighted balancing" below, in discussing fair access.)

COSTLY PROTECTIONS

Expression sometimes has unambiguous costs.[23] It is sometimes offensive, disgusting, or outrageous; it produces reputational injury and emotional distress; it requires protection from hecklers; when it is delivered through leaflets, someone has to clean up the mess; and, concentrated in sufficient numbers on billboards, telephone poles, and buses, it can add to the general ugliness of an urban environment. But—here is the third theme—the presence of such costs does not as a general matter suffice to remove protection from expression. Neither offense, nor cleanup costs for taxpayers, nor reputational injury, nor emotional distress, for example, suffice by themselves to deprive expression of protection.[24]

I am not suggesting that all libel law is inconsistent with stringent protections of expression, or that the intentional infliction of emotional distress always deserves protection, or that fines for littering always offend the ideal of freedom of expression.[25] I mean only that even uncontested

20. I emphasize that I am using this protean term exclusively as a label for the approach to content regulation described here.

21. For doubts about the virtues of categorization, and corresponding skepticism about categorically formulated prohibitions on content regulation, see John Paul Stevens, "The Freedom of Speech," *Yale Law Journal* 102 (1993): 1293–1313.

22. For a subtle discussion of the structure of argument about content-neutral regulations, and of the extent to which the thumb gets put in the balance for different sorts of regulations, see Stone, "Content-Neutral Restrictions."

23. By "costs," I mean, quite generically, conditions that it is reasonable to want to avoid.

24. See Schneider v. State, 308 U.S. 147 (1939) (on cleanup costs); New York Times v. Sullivan, 376 U.S. 254 (1964) (on reputational injury); Cohen v. California, 403 U.S. 15 (1971) (on offense); Hustler v. Falwell, 485 U.S. 46 (1988) (on intentional infliction of emotional distress).

25. Say, a fine for leaving a pile of leaflets sitting on a bench for people to pick up.

facts of reputational injury or emotional distress or mess are not always sufficient to deprive expression of protection—as when the target of expression is a public figure, or when the expression focuses on a subject of general interest. When, for example, *New York Times v. Sullivan* required a showing of "actual malice" in order for a public figure to win a libel judgment,[26] or when *Hustler v. Falwell* required actual malice in cases of the intentional infliction of emotional distress,[27] there was no suggestion that actual malice is necessary for reputational injury or emotional distress. Instead it was held, in effect, that the values associated with a system of free expression outweighed those injuries.

FAIR ACCESS

A system of stringent protections of expressive liberties must assure fair opportunities for expression: that is, that the value of expressive liberties must not be determined by a citizen's economic or social position.[28] Taking the unequal command of resources as a fact, a system of stringent protections must include measures aimed expressly at ensuring fair access to expressive opportunities. Such measures might include keeping traditional public forums (parks and streets) open and easily accessible; expanding the conception of a public forum to include airports, train stations, privately owned shopping centers, and other places of dense public interaction; affirming the importance of diverse broadcast messages and the role of fair access in contributing to such diversity; financing political campaigns through public resources; and regulating private political contributions and expenditures. The requirement of fair access supports a strong, general presumption against content-neutral regulations that have substantially disparate distributive implications—when, as with regulations on the distribution of handbills, or on the use of parks and sidewalks, they work to disproportionately burden those who otherwise lack the resources to get their messages out.

Several preliminary comments on this inclusion of fair access in the account of stringent protections are in order.

---

26. 376 U.S. 254, 279–280 (1964).

27. 485 U.S. 46, 50 (1988).

28. On the idea of the value of liberty, see John Rawls, *A Theory of Justice* (Cambridge, MA: Harvard University Press, 1971), 204–205. On the rationale for requiring a fair value for political liberty in particular, and the permissibility of (content-neutral) regulations of political speech in order to ensure that fair value, see John Rawls, "The Basic Liberties and Their Priority," *Political Liberalism* (New York: Columbia University Press, 1993), lecture 8, secs. 7, 12.

First, the measures I listed for ensuring fair access are all content-neutral, and all are addressed to remedying problems of unfair access that reflect inequalities of material resources. But it is a serious and open question whether, and to what extent, fair access can be assured through content-neutral remedies. For a lack of fair access—social and political exclusion—is sometimes said to result precisely from what others say and not from the distribution of resources.[29] This tension between demands of content-neutrality and fair access lies at the heart of Catharine MacKinnon's argument for the regulation of pornography on grounds that its content silences women and so prevents fair access.[30] Here I want simply to call attention to this concern. Later, I will suggest some ways to address it and so broaden the range of cases in which values of fair access and content-neutrality can be reconciled (135–140).

Second, it might be objected that the inclusion of requirements of fair access abuses the phrase "stringent protection"—that ensuring fair access is really a matter of "positively" expanding expressive opportunities rather than "negatively" protecting expressive liberties. I have a more formal and a more substantive response to this objection.

The formal response is that my four points define "stringent protection" for the purposes of this essay. So the terminological issue does not interest me very much. More substantively, I disagree that this represents an abuse or stretching of the term "protection." When owners of shopping malls wish to prevent people from leafleting on the premises, and the state bars them from doing so, the state *is* protecting at least some expression from efforts (by the owners) to silence it. It is tendentious to describe this as an effort by the state to expand opportunities for the leafleteers (rather than as an effort to protect their liberty from intrusion), because that description imports a presumptive right of owners to exclude into the distinction between protection and expansion.[31] The real

29. See Frank Michelman, "Universities, Racist Speech, and Democracy in America," *Harvard Civil Rights-Civil Liberties Law Review* 27 (1992): 352.

30. See, for example, Catharine MacKinnon, "Francis Biddle's Sister," in her *Feminism Unmodified* (Cambridge, MA: Harvard University Press, 1987), 163–197; for discussion of the silencing argument, see Frank Michelman, "Conceptions of Democracy in American Constitutional Argument: The Case of Pornography," *Tennessee Law Review* 56 (1989): 291–319; and the critical appraisal in Ronald Dworkin, "Liberty and Pornography," *New York Review of Books* 38, 14 (1991): 12–15.

31. For an extended elaboration of the importance of this point for free-speech doctrine, see Cass Sunstein's discussion of a New Deal for speech in "Free Speech Now," *The University of Chicago Law Review* 59 (1992): 255–316, esp. 263–277, 316.

issue—about which I do not claim to have said anything thus far—is whether fair access to expressive arenas ought to be ensured as a matter of right to citizens, including those who otherwise lack the resources for participating in such arenas. In grouping these four themes together as "protections," I do not mean to have answered or even to have addressed that question.

So here we have four components of a system of stringent protections of expressive liberty: strong presumption against content regulation; categorization as a method for handling such regulation; rejection of the view that a showing of costs suffices to remove protection from expression; and assurances of a fair distribution of expressive opportunities. Let's now consider some reasons for endorsing a scheme of stringent protections, thus understood.

2. Two False Starts

Earlier I briefly sketched minimalist and maximalist styles of argument for stringent protections. Taking "stringent protections" now to be defined by the four features I presented in the last section, I want to discuss these strategies in more detail.

MINIMALISM

Generically described, minimalism aims to defend stringent protections without attaching any elevated importance to expression, instead concentrating, so to speak, on the magnitude of the evil those protections prevent rather than on the magnitude of the good they protect. One familiar minimalist strategy—I will call it "no-cost minimalism"—rests on a distinction between expression and action. Relying on that distinction, the minimalist argues that expression—as distinct from action—is not *in itself* costly or harmful and that the harms that may flow from it *in conjunction with* its surrounding conditions can always be addressed without abridging expression. The no-cost case does not rest on attaching an especially significant value to expression itself: the harm principle suffices to generate the protections.

Other minimalists emphasize as well the remedial side of stringent protections, arguing that they are required by the pervasive tendency of people generally (or, in some versions, of political officials) to silence expression for insubstantial or impermissible reasons: for example, to protect officials from criticism or for reasons that are moralistic or in other ways demeaning to the targets of regulation. Ronald Dworkin, for example, has argued that a right to consume pornography is one implication of a general ban on the enforcement of preferences about the proper way for other people to conduct their lives; the right serves as a protective device against the legal imposition of moralistic preferences, such imposition constituting a demeaning denial of the abstract right of citizens to be treated as equals.[32] This defense of the right to consume pornography is minimalist because it turns not on any special value of expression generally, or of sexual expression in particular, nor on the claim that restrictions of expression are exceptionally burdensome, but on only the abstract right to be treated as an equal, the claim that that right is violated by the legislative imposition of external preferences, and the factual assumption that regulations of expression that emerge from the democratic process commonly are rooted in such preferences.

Minimalism makes two important points: it registers a concern about tendencies to excessive abridgement; and it emphasizes the importance of avoiding the injuries of expression by means other than the restriction of expression, where that is possible. Both points will figure in my own account. But minimalism generally, and "no-cost" minimalism in particular, is pretty much hopeless as a foundation for stringent protections.

Consider for example the third element in the scheme of stringent protection: using "expression" in its ordinary English sense, expression is sometimes harmful, and so protecting it has a price.[33] Denying the cost is simply insulting to those who pay it. Moreover, protecting people with unpopular messages and assuring outlets for expression is costly: sometimes you have to pay for police protection or to sweep the streets to clean up leaflets. It is not clear how no-cost minimalism proposes to capture these components of the idea of a scheme of stringent protections. The minimalist might, of course, be understood as introducing a new

32. "Do We Have A Right to Pornography?" in *A Matter of Principle* (Cambridge, MA: Harvard University Press, 1985): 335–372. For an excellent discussion of the limits of this argument, see Rae Langton, "Whose Right? Ronald Dworkin, Women, and Pornographers," *Philosophy and Public Affairs* 19 (1990): 311–359. Dworkin's recent discussions of expressive liberty seem less minimalist. In "What is Equality? Part 3: The Place of Liberty," he ties the value of expressive liberties to the formation of "authentic preferences." See *Iowa Law Review* 72 (1987): 34–36. And in "The Coming Battles over Free Speech," he notes the importance of an active side to personal responsibility. See *New York Review of Books*, 11 June 1992, 57.

33. For criticism of the project of founding an account of freedom of expression on a prior expression-action distinction, see Scanlon, "A Theory of Freedom of Expression," *Philosophy and Public Affairs* 1 (1972): 205–208.

technical sense of expression—call something "expression" only if it carries no costs. But then minimalism will offer no help in understanding the rationale for stringent protections of expression as characterized here, since they protect expressive liberty in a much wider sense than the technical one just noted—that is, even when expression has costs.[34]

Or consider the style of minimalism that supplements the case for stringent protections by emphasizing a concern for tendencies to restrict expression for demeaning reasons. This still seems insufficient as a rationale for a system of free expression. It is difficult, for example, to see the rationale for a "thumb-in-the-scale" for expression in the case of content-neutral regulations or in the face of a wide range of costs of expression, unless we premise an *affirmative value* for expression and not simply a requirement to abjure demeaning justifications for restrictions of liberty. Consider some content-neutral reasons for restricting expression: to keep the streets clean, the clutter under control, the noise level down, and traffic flowing smoothly. Nothing here seems to involve a troubling, demeaning failure to treat people as moral equals. The problem with, for example, sharp restrictions on political demonstrations enacted for these reasons is that they give insufficient weight to the value of expressive liberty.[35] It is true, as I indicated earlier, that content-neutral regulations are sometimes troubling because of their disparate impact, as they are especially burdensome on citizens who lack the means to get their message out. And it might be thought such unequal burdensomeness signals the presence of a demeaning rationale for the regulations. But in the absence of an antecedent reason for treating expressive liberties as fundamental, I doubt that the conclusion can be supported, unless all forms of disparate impact are demeaning.[36]

Finally, none of the forms of minimalism seems to provide a good rationale for the fourth feature of stringent protections: assurances of fair access to expressive opportunity.

MAXIMALISM

Maximalism inverts the minimalist strategy. Generically described, the maximalist proposes that expression merits stringent protection because

---

34. Indeed, as Scanlon emphasizes, the central task for a theory of freedom of expression is to explain why this should be so. See ibid., 204.

35. See Schneider v. State, 308 U.S. 147, 161 (1939).

36. To put the point in a constitutional slogan: you cannot derive the First Amendment from the equal protection clause of the Fourteenth Amendment.

its great value guarantees that the benefits of protection trump the costs.[37] The maximalist might, for example, argue that the dignity of human beings as autonomous and responsible agents is so immediately at stake in any act of expression and/or so immediately threatened by any regulation of expression—or at least any regulation of expression on grounds of its communicative impact—that abridgements of it represent intolerable violations of human dignity.[38]

The maximalist view has something right, and I will say what it is when (in Section 3) I discuss fundamental expressive and deliberative interests. Still, maximalism is too simple to capture the contours of freedom of expression. In its simplicity, it either exaggerates the stakes in particular cases of the regulation of expression or else manipulates the notion of autonomy to make it fit the complexity of the terrain.[39]

For example, maximalism does not help us to understand why there are cases in which considerations of costs do seem relevant to the justification of regulations: why regulations of group libel might be more problematic than restrictions on individual libel, why it might make sense to distinguish the treatment of reputational injury to public and nonpublic figures, or why autonomy does not simply trump reputational injury altogether. Similarly, maximalism does not seem to be a promising route to understanding why false or misleading advertising seems less worthy of protection than false or misleading claims offered in the course of political or religious argument.[40] In each of these cases, maximalism

37. The maximalist need not hold that the value is intrinsic, nor that there is just a single value associated with expression. I am indebted to Connie Rosati for urging this clarification.

38. See, for example, Scanlon's listener-autonomy theory in "A Theory of Freedom of Expression," 204–226; and his criticisms of that theory in "Freedom of Expression and Categories of Expression," 534–35. In "Persuasion, Autonomy, and Expression," *Columbia Law Review* 91 (1991): 334–371, David Strauss aims to rescue a version of Scanlon's theory from these criticisms. Strauss condemns restrictions of speech justified by reference to the harmful results of the speech's persuasive power as inconsistent with listener autonomy.

39. This complaint is registered in Scanlon, "Freedom of Expression and Categories of Expression"; Steven H. Shiffrin, *The First Amendment, Democracy, and Romance* (Cambridge, MA: Harvard University Press, 1990), chap. 4. On the contrast between the complexity of the terrain and the simplicity of familiar theories, see Harry Kalven, *A Worthy Tradition: Freedom of Speech in America*, ed. Jamie Kalven (New York: Harper and Row, 1988), 23.

40. In "Persuasion, Autonomy, and Expression," Strauss argues that persuasion is "a process of appealing, in some sense, to reason" (335), and that we ought not to regulate expression when its harmful effects come from its power to persuade. Thus false advertising gets reduced protection because it does not work by persuasion (as though we were in no danger of being persuaded by liars); nonobscene pornography is protected because it does work by persuasion (as though the scenes of the Washington Monument and the American flag featured at the start of some triple-X movies were representative). Here I lose hold of his conception of persuasion and so of the argument about commercial speech.

has troubles with an intuitive idea, or distinction. Perhaps there is, in the end, nothing more to these "intuitions" than second nature masquerading as first. But they do have some presumptive weight and so raise troubles for maximalism.

Furthermore, if considerations about the transcendent value of expression are understood to provide only reasons for rejecting regulations on grounds of communicative impact, then they will provide no limit at all on content-neutral regulations—no weighted balancing—and no basis for a concern with fair access. On the other hand, if considerations of autonomy are understood to ground a uniform presumption against all regulation of expression because of the uniform connection of expression with the value of autonomy, then either the uniform presumption will be very low and the protections will be weak, or the uniform presumption will be very high, and we will all have lots of listening to do.

More fundamentally, the main idea behind the variant of maximalism I have focused on here is that expression always trumps other values because of its connection with autonomy. And this suggests that a commitment to freedom of expression turns on embracing the supreme value of autonomy. But this threatens to turn freedom of expression into a sectarian political position. Is a strong commitment to expressive liberties really available only to those who endorse the idea that autonomy is the fundamental human good—an idea about which there is much reasonable controversy? I am not doubting that such a strong commitment *is* available to those whose ethical views are of this kind, but I reject the claim that such views are really necessary. The force of this concern about sectarianism will become clearer as I describe an alternative to minimalism and maximalism. Suffice it to say for now that it would be desirable to frame an account of the values at stake that is capable of receiving wider support, an account that would free the doctrine both from the insulting idea that expression is costless and from the sectarian idea that it is priceless.

3. An Alternative Strategy: Foundations

The difficulties with maximalist and minimalist strategies recommend a different angle of approach: one which gives stringent protections as a conclusion but does not assume that expression is costless or priceless. More precisely, I will present a view that not only gives more weight to the value of expression than minimalism, while retaining its emphasis on the desirability of nonrestrictive remedies for harms and its concern with tendencies to overregulate, but also discriminates more finely than maximalism, while preserving its emphasis on the importance of expression. I propose that three kinds of consideration work together to generate upward pressures for protection and so to provide the basis for the scheme of stringent protections.

(1) An idea of the fundamental *interests* that are protected by a system of freedom of expression.

(2) An account of the structure of the *costs* of these protections.

(3) A set of more or less commonsense factual claims that I will refer to as *fundamental background facts*.

I will consider each of these in turn, beginning with the fundamental interests, and then in the next section discuss the case for protection produced by their joint operation.

INTERESTS

Freedom of expression is commonly associated with such values as the discovery of the truth, the self-expression of individuals, a well-functioning democracy, and a balance of social stability and social change.[41] I do not wish to dispute these associations but rather to connect more transparently the importance of expression with certain fundamental interests.

In particular, I distinguish three interests that are protected by stringent assurances of expressive liberty and whose importance makes the demand for substantial protection reasonable. I will call them the *expressive, the deliberative,* and *the informational* interests. Before describing those interests, however, I want to highlight the background of my account of them.

Earlier I accused maximalism of sectarianism. Because I want to steer clear of that sectarianism, my presentation of these interests, and of their importance, is framed to accommodate what I will call "the idea of reasonable pluralism."[42] In brief, the idea of reasonable pluralism is that

41. See, in general, Thomas Emerson, *The System of Freedom of Expression* (New York: Vintage, 1971). Lee C. Bollinger emphasizes as well the importance of encouraging tolerance in *The Tolerant Society* (Oxford: Oxford University Press, 1986); and Vincent Blasi examines the role of freedom of expression as a check on official misconduct in "The Checking Value in First Amendment Theory," *American Bar Foundation Research Journal* 3 (1977): 521–649.

42. For fuller discussion, see my "Moral Pluralism and Political Consensus," in *The Idea of Democracy,* ed. David Copp, Jean Hampton, and John Roemer (Cambridge: Cambridge University Press, 1993), 281–287 [essay 2 in this volume]; also see John Rawls, *Political Liberalism,* 35–38.

there is a plurality of distinct, conflicting, fully reasonable understandings of value. An understanding of value is fully reasonable—which is not the same as true[43]—just in case its adherents are stably disposed to affirm it as they acquire new information and test it through critical reasoning and reflection.[44] I emphasize that "test through critical reasoning and reflection" is itself a normative notion: so a view is not reasonable simply because of the dogged persistence of its adherents, who preserve their disposition to affirm it after hearing (though not listening to) all the arguments. The contention that there is a plurality of such understandings is suggested by the absence of convergence in reflection on issues of value—the persistence of disagreements, for example, about the values of autonomy, welfare, and self-actualization; about the value of devotions to friends and lovers, as distinct from more diffuse concerns about abstract others; and about the values of poetic expression and political engagement.

Acknowledging the pluralism of reasonable evaluative conceptions has important implications for political justification. It suggests in particular that we ought to conduct such justification in terms of considerations that provide compelling reasons within other views as well. For when we restrict ourselves in political argument to the subset of moral considerations that others who have reasonable views also accept, we are acknowledging that their views are not unreasonable, even if they do believe what we take to be false.

Premising reasonable pluralism, then, I look to characterize interests whose importance provides a basis for stringent protections and that are located on common ground shared by different reasonable conceptions. Because different views disagree in their substantive characterization of what is valuable, the basic interests will inevitably be presented in abstract terms. But this abstractness is no metaphysical or philosophical predilection; instead, it is the natural consequence of taking seriously the diversity that issues from the free exercise of practical reason.

First, then, there is the *expressive* interest: a direct interest in articulating thoughts, attitudes, and feelings on matters of personal or broader human concern and perhaps through that articulation, influencing the

43. There is, for example, this logical distinction: two inconsistent views may both be fully reasonable, though they cannot both be true.
44. I take this formulation from Mark Johnston.

thought and conduct of others.[45] When we think of expression quite generally as a matter of outwardly indicating one's thoughts, attitudes, feelings (or at least what one wants others to believe those inner states are), then the importance of the expressive interest may seem elusive. Drawing some distinctions within the general category of expression, however, will clarify the asserted importance of the interest and one source of the burdensome quality of regulations of expression.

A feature shared by different evaluative conceptions is that the conceptions themselves single out certain forms of expression as especially important or urgent; the conception itself implies that the agent has weighty reasons for expression in certain cases or about certain issues.[46] The failure to acknowledge the weight of those reasons for the agent—even if one does not accept them—reflects a failure to appreciate the fact of reasonable pluralism. Consider in particular three central cases in which agents hold views that state or imply that they have very strong, perhaps compelling, reasons for expression, and so three central cases illustrating the importance of the expressive interest.

(1) In a range of cases, the limiting instance of which is a concern to "bear witness," the agent endorses a view that places her under an *obligation* to speak out, to articulate that view—and perhaps to urge on others a different course of thought, feeling, or conduct. Restricting expression in such cases would prevent the agent from fulfilling what she takes to be an obligation; it would impose conditions that the agent reasonably takes to be unacceptable. Here, expressive liberty is on a footing with liberty of conscience, and regulations are similarly burdensome.[47]

(2) In a second class of cases, expression addresses a matter of political justice. Here the importance of the issue—indicated by its being a matter of justice—provides a substantial reason for addressing it. The

45. I say "perhaps" because expression often has nothing to do with communication. See C. Edwin Baker, *Human Liberty and Freedom of Speech* (Oxford: Oxford University Press, 1989), 51–54. I am grateful to Randall Forsberg for her helpful comments on an earlier draft in which I characterized the expressive interest much too narrowly.

46. My emphasis on reasons in the description of the expressive interest distinguishes my treatment from conventional discussion of the value of self-expression and self-fulfillment. When someone fulfils what they take to be an obligation (as specified by their moral views, for example), it is wrong to treat this as a matter of self-expression or self-fulfillment.

47. Here I follow a suggestion advanced in Rawls's discussion of liberty of conscience: that the rationale for liberty of conscience lies in obligations that religious and moral views assign to those who hold them, and that this rationale can, in some measure, be extended to other liberties. See Rawls, *Theory of Justice*, 206.

precise content and weight of the reason is a matter of controversy. Brandeis, for example, urged that "public discussion is a political duty."[48] Perhaps so, but even if expression on such issues is not a matter of duty, still, it is a requisite for being a good citizen—in some cases, for sheer decency—and as such, is characteristically supported by substantial reasons within different moral-political conceptions, even though those conceptions may disagree about the precise importance of civic engagement and about the occasions that require it.

(3) In a third class of cases, expression is not a matter of personal obligation, nor does it address issues of justice; rather, it is moved by concerns about human welfare and the quality of human life. The evident importance of those concerns provides substantial reasons for the expression. A paradigm here is expression about sexuality—say, artistic expression (whether with propositional content or not)[49] that displays an antipathy to existing sexual conventions, the limited sensibilities revealed in those conventions, and the harms they are perceived as imposing. In a culture that is, as novelist Kathy Acker says, "horrendously moralistic," it is understandable that such writers as Acker challenge understandings of sexuality "under the aegis of art, [where] you're allowed to actually deal with matters of sexuality."[50]

Another paradigm is social satire (or analogously, caricature). Lenny Bruce's biographer described him as a "man with an almost infantile attachment to everything that was sacred to the lower-middle class. He believed in romantic love and marriage and fidelity and absolute honesty and incorruptibility—all the preposterous absolutes of the unqualified conscience . . . Lenny doted on human imperfection: sought it out, gloated over it—but only so he could use it as a *memento mori* for his ruthless moral conscience . . . The attempt to make . . . him a hippie saint or a morally transcendent *artiste*, was tantamount to missing the whole point of his sermons, which were ferociously ethical in their thrust."[51]

There are further important cases here—including an interest in creat-

---

48. Whitney v. California, 274 U.S. 357, 375 (1927) (Brandeis concurring).

49. See, for example, Barnes v. Glen Theatre, Inc., 111 S. Ct. 2456 (1991) (White dissenting).

50. See Kathy Acker, "Devoured by Myths: An Interview with Sylvère Lotringer," in *Hannibal Lecter, My Father* (New York: Semiotext(e), 1991); and the interview of Acker in *Angry Women*, ed. Andrea Juno and V. Vale (San Francisco: Re/Search, 1991), 184–185.

51. Cited in Edward de Grazia, *Girls Lean Back Everywhere: The Law of Obscenity and the Assault on Genius* (New York: Random House, 1992), 459–460.

ing things of beauty. But the three I have mentioned are central cases of the expressive interest and suffice to underscore the basis of its importance. They work outward from the case of fully conscientious expression, the paradigm of expression supported by substantial reasons from the agent's point of view. To be sure, diverse evaluative conceptions carry different implications about what is reasonable to say and do. But common ground is that they assign to those who hold them substantial reasons for expression, quite apart from the value of the expression to the audience, even if there is no audience at all.

One alternative line of argument about freedom of expression focuses entirely on public discussion and locates the contribution of expression to public debate at the core of the ideal of freedom of expression. Such views miss the parallels between expressive liberty and liberty of conscience. As a result, they are insufficiently attentive to the weight of the expressive interest and are likely to be too narrow in the scope of their protections.

Cass Sunstein, for example, has recently restated the case for a two-tier conception of freedom of expression, in which political speech occupies the upper, stringently protected tier.[52] Although Sunstein's immediate focus is the proper interpretation of the First Amendment, his case rests in part on general political values and so intersects with my concerns here.[53] Sunstein defines speech as political when "it is both intended and received as a contribution to public deliberation about some issue."[54] This conception of political speech is very broad and is understood to encompass "much art and literature," because much "has the characteristics of social commentary."[55] It is not boundless, however, in that it excludes from highest level protection commercial speech, bribery, private libel, and obscenity.

Because of the breadth of this conception of political speech, the practical differences between Sunstein's approach and mine may, in the end, turn out to be rather subtle. Still, it strikes me as a mistake to make core protection contingent on the role of expression in contributing to public

52. See his "Free Speech Now" and his *Democracy and the Problem of Free Speech*.

53. See in particular his four reasons for special protection for political speech, only the first of which is concerned specifically with constitutional interpretation, *Democracy and the Problem of Free Speech*, 132–137. Of course, his view is also controversial as constitutional interpretation.

54. Ibid., 130.

55. Sunstein, "Free Speech Now," 308.

discussion, in particular on how it is received. Should the level of protection of, for example, Kathy Acker's literary exploration of sexuality be made to depend on whether people find her *Hannibal Lecter, My Father* or *Blood and Guts in High School* challenging or instructive rather than offensive, disgusting, or, simply, out-of-control, post-modernist, identity-deconstructive raving?[56] Should the level of protection of a doctor's conscientious efforts to advise a pregnant patient on the alternatives available to her depend on that advice being intended or received "as a contribution to public deliberation" about reproductive choice?[57] Expression of these kinds is often supported by very substantial reasons, quite apart from how it is *received*. As my discussion of the expressive interest indicates, an account of freedom of expression ought not to disparage those reasons.

In response it might be urged that the justification for establishing an upper tier occupied by political speech does not depend on an assessment of the relative *value* of different sorts of speech but rather on an assessment of their relative *vulnerabilities*: because the government has such strong incentives to regulate political speech, it is especially vulnerable; because it is so vulnerable, it requires especially strong protections.[58]

This response is not convincing. The evidence of special vulnerability is at best uncertain.[59] And in any case, it is a mistake to reduce the special protection for expression to a matter of vulnerability. As I have indicated in my discussion of the expressive interest, there *are* very substantial interests at stake. I see no compelling reasons—of political theory, general constitutional theory, or American constitutional tradition—to de-emphasize the weight of those interests and shift focus to assessments of vulnerability.[60]

---

56. Just for the record, I think it is neither instructive nor raving.

57. Expression that falls outside the upper tier is not for that reason without protection. Thus the formulation in terms of "level of protection."

58. See Sunstein, *Democracy and the Problem of Free Speech*, 136.

59. Absent a precise delineation of the category of political speech, the empirical issue is hard to adjudicate. But some reasons for doubting the case for special vulnerability are suggested in de Grazia, *Girls Lean Back Everywhere*; and in William Noble, *Bookbanning in America* (Middlebury: Erikson, 1990).

60. On the issue of American constitutional tradition: Sunstein associates his own conception of freedom of expression with Brandeis's focus on deliberation rather than Holmes's marketplace of ideas. See *Democracy and the Problem of Free Speech*, 23–28. But Brandeis's concurrence in Whitney v. California, 274 U.S. 357, 373–378 (1927), is perhaps the classic statement of the very great constitutional weight of the interests protected by the right to freedom of expression; it is not about the special vulnerability of political speech to government restriction.

Let us proceed, then, to the second basic interest: the deliberative interest. This interest has two principal aspects. The first is rooted in the abstract idea—shared by different evaluative conceptions—that it is important to do what is best (or at least what is genuinely worthwhile) not simply what one now believes best (or what one now believes to be worthwhile). For this reason, we have an interest in circumstances favorable to finding what is best, or at least what is worthwhile: that is, to finding out which ways of life are supported by the strongest reasons.

The second aspect of the deliberative interest is rooted in the idea that it is important that one's evaluative views not be affirmed out of ignorance or out of a lack of awareness of alternatives. So alongside the interest in doing what is in fact supported by the strongest reasons, there is also an interest in understanding what those reasons are and the nature of the support they give. This, too, leads to an interest in circumstances favorable to such understanding.

The connection between these two aspects of the deliberative interest and expression lies in the familiar fact that reflection on matters of human concern typically cannot be pursued in isolation. As Mill emphasized, it characteristically proceeds against the background of an articulation of alternative views by other people.[61] So here, again, there is an interest in circumstances suited to understanding what is worth doing and what the reasons are that support it—e.g., circumstances featuring a diversity of messages, forcefully articulated.[62]

Finally, and most straightforwardly, I assume a fundamental informational interest in securing reliable information about the conditions required for pursuing one's aims and aspirations.

Having described these three interests, I want to return to the com-

---

61. This is the force of Mill's contention that censorship robs the human race, and that for this reason, it does not matter whether all censor one or one censors all. Mill does not focus on the harm or robbery to the person who is censored. See *On Liberty* (Indianapolis: Hackett, 1978), 16 (chap. 2, par. 1).

62. Robert Post has suggested a tension among various conditions required for satisfying the deliberative interest in a diverse community. In particular, deliberation depends on civility, but requiring civility puts the community in danger of making one particular understanding of civility authoritative for the community. I am not sure how deep this tension goes. To be sure, civility has its place in public deliberation. But so do anger, disgust, bitter criticism, and open expressions of hostility. Post's immediate concern is with a parody of Reverend Jerry Falwell in Larry Flynt's *Hustler* magazine. Suffice it to say here that the parody of Falwell was, in my view, a contribution to public debate, even if it was not civil and was not an invitation to Falwell to have a conversation with Larry Flynt. See Robert Post, "The Constitutional Concept of Public Discourse: Outrageous Opinion, Democratic Deliberation, and *Hustler Magazine v. Falwell*," *Harvard Law Review* 103 (1990): 601–686.

plaint I registered earlier about the sectarianism of autonomy-based, maximalist views of freedom of expression. For it may now seem that my own view is not, after all, so sharply distinct from them. I will respond briefly by noting three sorts of difference.

First, autonomy has a capaciousness that strikes me as a vice in an account of expressive liberty. Each of the basic interests that I have mentioned is sometimes included within the value of autonomy, but each is importantly different. Bringing out these differences helps both to clarify the ways that those interests can be seen to be important within different evaluative conceptions and to provide the basis for a theory of expressive liberty that is able to capture intuitive distinctions among different sorts of expression. Second, I am not supposing—with the maximalist—that the three interests always trump other values. Nor, third, do I assume that the interests are uniformly implicated in different sorts of expression. For example, I do not think that they are equally at stake in commercial, political, and artistic expression. (I will return to this point in my discussion of categorization in Section 4.)

There are, then, at least these three basic interests rooted in diverse, determinate evaluative conceptions and in the second-order concerns collected under the deliberative rubric.[63] A first component of the case for stringent protection, then, lies in the ways that such protection secures favorable conditions for advancing these fundamental interests. In the case of the expressive interest, the grounds for protecting expression lie in the importance of the expressive activity itself, as specified by the agent's reasons; in the case of the deliberative and informational interests, the grounds for protecting expression lie in the importance of the interests to which expression contributes. In short: the reasons for protection are partly intrinsic, partly instrumental. I see no basis for deciding (nor any reason to decide) which is more fundamental.

I will return later to a more detailed discussion of connections. But, first, the costs and background facts.

63. Joseph Raz proposes that part of the case for a right to freedom of expression turns on the "fundamental need for public validation of one's way of life" together with the fact that acts of expression serve the purpose of "validation" in three ways: (1) they inform the public about "ways of life common in certain segments of the public," (2) they reassure "those whose ways of life are being portrayed that they are not alone," and (3) they provide a "stamp of public acceptability" for those ways of life. See "Free Expression and Personal Identification," *Oxford Journal of Legal Studies* 11 (1991): 311, 324. I agree with Raz about the importance of the interest in validation, but I believe that it can be accounted for in terms of expressive, deliberative, and informational interests.

COSTS

What then of the costs of expression? Commentators since Justice Holmes have noted that protection for expression cannot be premised on faith in its impotence.[64] As Harry Kalven put it, "Speech has *a price*. It is a liberal weakness to discount so heavily the price. [It] is not always correct to win [the protection of speech] by showing danger [it threatens] has been exaggerated."[65] Underscoring Kalven's point about the price of speech and the weakness of characteristic arguments for protection, recent "outsider" jurisprudence has portrayed the injuries that hate speech imposes on its targets by narratively recounting those injuries.[66] If we abjure both the minimalist denial of the price and the sectarian route of maximalism, then the idea of stringent protections may seem just indefensible, and the skeptical response—"there's no such thing"—may seem a natural alternative.

What then are some of the kinds of costs that expression imposes? In answering this question, I want to organize costs along just one axis, distinguishing three types by the pattern of their etiology.

First, there are direct costs. Here I have in mind cases in which, intuitively, nothing intervenes in between the expression and its price, where "the very utterance inflicts injury":[67] I shriek at a neurasthenic with a weak heart; disrupt the peace and quiet with loud shouting; falsely tell an elderly parent that her child has just died; spread defamatory falsehoods about a colleague; use offensive language in a public setting; offer a raise or a higher grade in return for sex. When I have said my piece, the damage is done, and it is done by what I said—and in the latter four cases, by its content.

A second category of costs are "environmental." Thus expression may help to constitute a degraded, sickening, embarrassing, humiliating, obtrusively moralistic, hypercommercialized, hostile, or demeaning environment. It might, for example, combine with other expressive actions to

64. Abrams v. U.S., 250 U.S. 616, 629 (1918) (Holmes dissenting).

65. Cited from Kalven's notes in the "Editor's Introduction" to *A Worthy Tradition*, xxii.

66. See in particular Matsuda, "Public Response to Racist Speech"; Charles Lawrence, "If He Hollers Let Him Go"; Delgado, "Campus Antiracism Rules."

67. Chaplinsky v. New Hampshire, 315 U.S. 568, 571–572 (1942). Or, where the "evil" is "created by the medium of expression itself," as in the case of signs posted on utility poles, as distinct from leaflets handed to individuals. See City Council v. Taxpayers for Vincent, 466 U.S. 789, 810 (1984).

contribute to an environment of racial or national antagonism or to one in which dominance and submission are erotized. Here the harm is not the expression by itself, since in the absence of other similar sayings, the environment would not be degraded, hypercommercialized, or hostile; nor can we trace particular harmful or injurious consequences to particular acts of expression that help to constitute the unfavorable environment.[68] Instead, the price of the expression lies in its contribution to making an environment hostile to, for example, achieving such fundamental values as racial or sexual equality.

Finally there are straightforwardly indirect costs. Here the injury results from the expression causing (by persuading, suggesting, or providing information) someone to do something harmful, as when someone persuades others to purchase too much of a scarce resource or to join the Ku Klux Klan or to support a war that results in massive death and destruction.

BACKGROUND FACTS

To complete the picture of the bases of stringent protections, I now come to the background facts.[69] These facts are the set of sociological and anthropological claims that plays a central role in arguments about freedom of expression, though often only as an implicit, half-articulated, and so easily manipulable background.[70] Whatever their common treatment, their importance will eventually become clear. My aim here is simply to make them explicit.

I will group the facts into three broad categories, which I label the Facts of Reasonableness, the Bare Facts of Life, and the Unhappy Facts of

68. A work environment, for example, may be actionably hostile under Title VII of the Civil Rights Act because of either the severity or the pervasiveness of conduct. See Meritor Savings Bank v. Vinson, 477 U.S. 57, 67 (1986). For discussion of severity and pervasiveness, see Ellison v. Brady, 924 F.2d 872 (9th Circuit, 1991).

69. Scanlon discusses the importance of "linking empirical beliefs" in arguments about right to expressive liberty. His discussion overstates, I believe, the importance of beliefs specifically about the role of government in suppressing expression. See "Freedom of Expression and Categories of Expression," 534.

70. For a general discussion of the tendency of legal-doctrinal argument to suppress reference to background factual assumptions, see Roberto Unger, *The Critical Legal Studies Movement* (Cambridge, MA: Harvard University Press, 1982). In the case of freedom of expression, Bollinger claims that the "fortress model" of speech protection presumes a set of irrational tendencies to suppress speech that conflicts with the assumption of rational competence that drives the ideal of an open market of ideas. So the conjunction of these two doctrines in a justification of free expression is untenable because it requires inconsistent background beliefs. See *The Tolerant Society*, 92–93.

Life. Intuitively, the difference among the three categories is that the facts of reasonableness are considerations that would favor the protection of speech even under fully ideal conditions; the bare facts favor protection and are unalterable; the unhappy facts of life are considerations that now favor protection but that we might hope are alterable features of our circumstances.

Among the Facts of Reasonableness are:

(1) The Fact of Reasonable Pluralism: Under conditions of expressive liberty, people will arrive at conflicting, reasonable evaluative convictions.

(2) The Fact of Reasonable Persuasion: People have the capacity to change their minds when they hear reasons presented, and sometimes they exercise that capacity. This is the assumption of Brandeis's remark that "if there be time to expose through discussion the falsehood and fallacies, to avert the evil by the process of education, *the remedy to be applied is more speech*, not enforced silence."[71] But for the Fact of Reasonable Persuasion, more speech would be a diversion rather than a remedy.

As Bare Facts of Life, we have:

(1) The Fact of Resource Dependence: Expression depends on resources, and the access to those resources is commonly unequally distributed.

(2) The Fact of Innocent Abuse: If expression is relatively uninhibited, people will sometimes—even without malign intent—say things that are false, offensive, insulting, psychically injurious, emotionally distressing, and reputationally damaging. As James Madison put it, "Some degree of abuse is inseparable from the proper use of everything."[72]

(3) The Cold (Chilling) Facts: If sanctions are attached to expression for being false, offensive, insulting, psychically injurious, for example, then people will be reticent to express themselves (chilled), even if they think their expression is true, inoffensive, not insulting, or the like. Moreover, if the regulation of expression proceeds in ways that are highly uncertain—because standards are vague

71. Whitney v. California, 274 U.S. 357, 375–376, 377 (1927) (concurring).
72. Cited in New York Times v. Sullivan, 376 U.S. 254, 271 (1964).

(e.g., if sanctions attach to remarks that are offensive, deeply disturbing, "outrageously" insulting)[73] or their application depends on a weighing of competing considerations in each case—then many people will be reticent to express themselves, even if their views deserve protection.

Finally, I count among the Unhappy Facts of Life:

(1) The Fact of Power: Most people—and those with power in particular—do not like to be criticized or disagreed with, and are tempted to use the means at their disposal to avoid criticism or disagreement.[74]

(2) The Fact of Bias: We tend, as a general matter, to confuse what we would prefer other people to do with what would be best for them to do or with what they must do on pain of immorality.[75]

(3) The Fact of Disadvantage: In a society with relatively poor and powerless groups, members of those groups are especially likely to do badly when the regulation of expression proceeds on the basis of vague standards whose implementation depends on the discretion of powerful actors.

(4) The Fact of Easy Offense: Putting sociopaths to the side, everyone is offended by something.[76]

(5) The Fact of Abuse: Against a background of sharp disagreement, efforts at persuasion sometimes proceed through exaggeration, vilification, and distortion.[77]

4. An Alternative Strategy: Implications

I want now to bring the different pieces together into a case for a scheme of stringent protections. I will proceed through the four themes discussed

73. On the problems of regulating outrageous insults, see Hustler v. Falwell, 485 U.S. 46 (1988).

74. This is, of course, true of public officials but hardly unique to them. It is commonly said that they are especially untrustworthy, but I know of no evidence for the claim that political power breeds arrogance more surely than economic power.

75. As Mill put it: "No one acknowledges to himself that his standard of judgment is his own liking." See On Liberty, chap. 1, par. 6. The point is not that standards of judgment are, in general, simply matters of liking and disliking, but rather that even when they are, we do not see them that way.

76. Bollinger in effect argues that there is a fundamental conflict between appealing to the Facts of Reasonableness and to the Unhappy Facts of Life. See The Tolerant Society, 92–93. I do not see the conflict.

77. Paraphrasing Justice Roberts in Cantwell v. Connecticut, 310 U.S. 296, 310 (1940).

in Section 1, showing how each can be explained by reference to the elements I have just sketched. In my explanation I place principal emphasis on the expressive and the deliberative interests and on the Facts of Reasonableness. The aim is to show that stringent protections are driven principally by the substantive value of expression and the possibilities of using speech to combat the harms of speech; such protections are only secondarily remedial, only secondarily driven by fear and mistrust underwritten by our tendency—or the tendency of government—to undervalue or suppress expression.

CONTENT REGULATION

Take first the presumption against content regulation. This presumption is driven in part by the fundamental expressive and deliberative interests. Content regulation presents the possibility that regulation may effectively exclude certain views from the marketplace, not only driving them into another market niche but also driving them out altogether. Content-neutral regulation may present that possibility as well, but the threat from content-discriminatory regulations is greater because the targeting is more precise. Because of this threat, content regulations pose a more substantial danger that people will be prevented from expressing views despite, as they see it, the existence of substantial reasons for such expression. In short, they represent a direct threat to the expressive interest.

Moreover, the limits imposed by content regulations on the range of messages threaten the deliberative interest. By directly reducing the diversity of expression, they distort, as Meiklejohn said, the "thinking process of the community."[78] More immediately, by restricting the range of views and establishing official dogma, they limit reflection on alternative views and so on the reasons for holding one's own views. The problem is *not* that content regulation keeps people from being persuaded to change their minds; rather, it prevents us from figuring out just what our minds are on some subject and what the reasons are for not changing them.

The Fact of Power points in the same direction. Those with power often wish to insulate themselves from criticism, and the power to regulate content is an especially refined instrument of such insulation. This is particularly true of viewpoint regulation. By contrast, content-neutral regulations are more blunt and so less desirable instruments of insulation. To

---

78. Alexander Meiklejohn, *Political Freedom* (New York: Harper & Brothers, 1960), 27.

be sure, blunt instruments are still instruments. And if someone expects the distribution of messages to be unfavorable, that someone will want to reduce the level of expression. Moreover, content-neutral regulations can have more or less transparently discriminating effects as to classes of speaker. So content-neutral regulations, too, raise serious concerns. But the point suggested by the Fact of Power remains: there is typically no motivation to reduce the quantity of expression of the same kind and intensity as the motivation to target certain topics, or more particularly, certain messages. So content-neutral regulations are often less troublesome.

These considerations about the interests and the Fact of Power indicate why content regulation is especially troubling. Given those troubles, the Fact of Reasonable Persuasion helps to secure the case for a presumption against such regulations. It suggests that the damaging consequences of expression with objectionable content can—apart from the case of direct costs—be addressed with more expression. Because such address is preferable to imposing sanctions, we ought to establish a general presumption in favor of relying on it.

In the case of political speech, for example, these pressures for protection exercised by the basic interests, and the Facts of Power and Reasonable Persuasion are very strong. So some rule of the sort advanced in *Brandenburg v. Ohio* is naturally suggested: that advocacy of violent political change can legitimately be restricted only when "such advocacy is directed to inciting or producing imminent lawless action and is likely to incite or produce such action."[79] Advocacy of the kind recorded in this rule is not the only kind that threatens harm, nor is the expected value of the harm necessarily the greatest. But it is the only case in which circumstances prevent the pursuit of the preferred remedy.

CATEGORIZATION

We come next to categorization as an approach to handling content regulations. Recall that the idea of categorization is to confine exceptions to a general presumption against content regulation by singling out a small set of categories of expression—for example, child pornography, commercial speech, obscenity, fighting words, and express incitement—for lesser protection, specifying conditions for permissible regulation of expression in each category. The rationale for this strategy divides naturally into two parts.

79. Brandenburg v. Ohio, 395 U.S. 444, 447 (1968).

We need first to account for the distinctions between more and less important kinds of expression. Judgments of importance proceed principally by considering the connection of the expression to the fundamental interests and secondarily by considering the prospects of addressing the harms through more expression and the fragility of expression given the Bare and the Unhappy Facts of Life.

Political expression, for example, is especially important because it is so closely connected to each of the basic interests and because of its fragility in light of the Fact of Power. Because it is commonly a form of political speech, expression that libels a group is more strongly connected to expressive and deliberative interests than expression that threatens individual libel is; the injuries are also more easily remedied with group libel than with individual libel. For these reasons it is important to confine reduced protection to a category of individual libel, even though people may be harmed by libeling groups to which they belong or with which they identify. The idea that group libel ought to be more strongly protected than individual libel is not contingent on a liberal individualist failure to acknowledge the possibility of harm through group libel, any more than the protection of the libel of public figures requires a denial of its harm.[80]

Commercial speech can be a source of information. But it is less important than political expression, because it is not so closely connected to the expressive or the deliberative interests.[81] Moreover, the Cold Facts and the Fact of Limited Understanding have much less force in the case of commercial speech.[82] The economic interests that fuel commercial speech ensure that it is less susceptible to a regulatory chill, while the fact that commercial advertisers are best situated to know the accuracy of

80. Here I disagree with the defense of group libel laws in Note, "A Communitarian Defense of Group Libel Laws," *Harvard Law Review* 101 (1988): 682–701. The main reason for rejecting regulations of group libel is not that such libel is harmless. See, for example, Justice Black's dissent in Beauharnais v. Illinois, 343 U.S. 250 (1952). Black does not deny the costs but emphasizes the extensive "inroads" on expression that would result from accepting regulations of group libel.

81. C. Edwin Baker proposes that commercial speech ought to have no First Amendment protection, in part because such speech reflects the coercive logic of profit-maximization rather than the choice of the speaker. This explanation strikes me as a strained defense of the idea that regulations of commercial speech are less burdensome, not least because it suggests that advertising by price-setting monopolists, which is less subject to the coercive demands of profit-maximization, ought to be more protected. See Baker, *Human Liberty and Freedom of Speech*, chap. 9.

82. See Virginia State Board of Pharmacy v. Virginia Citizens Consumer Council, 425 U.S. 748, 771 (n. 24) (1976), and 777–781 (Stewart concurring).

their claims reduces concern about the chilling effects of requiring accuracy in commercial speech.

But—and here we come to the second part of the case—even if we can provide an account of relative importance, why filter judgments of relative importance by categorization rather than proceed case by case?[83] Here the main burden is carried by the Chilling Facts and the Unhappy Facts of Power, Bias, and Disadvantage. Together they induce an expectation that ad hoc regulation will err on the side of excessive interference, on the side of underprotection of what should be protected. Moreover, ad hoc judgments are likely to raise greater concerns about chilling expression. Categories, then, serve as a protective device—a device of self-binding—against excessive interference in a context in which a very substantial value is at stake.

To elaborate: unless expression falls into a less protected category, we impose very high barriers to regulating it. And before we can consider more substantial regulation of some act of expression, we need to find a general category into which it falls such that we are prepared to reduce the protection for all expression in that general category. The result may be greater protection for some expression than we are inclined to think suitable.[84] But—if the facts are right—then the alternative would be insufficient protection to some expression. Of course, the claim that categorization plays this role premises that the categories are—whether for semantical or psychological reasons—not so utterly manipulable and indeterminate that they serve no channeling function at all. If they are not, if the facts are as stipulated, and if the choice of regulatory form does have the proposed consequences, then it is reasonable to pursue the strategy of protection through categorization.

DIGRESSION: NIHILISM REDUX

Earlier I mentioned free-speech nihilism: the idea that "there is no such thing as free speech." The pieces are now in place for a response to it. So I will digress here to provide a reply.

What does the nihilist denial of free speech come to? Echoing Holmes's remark that "every idea is an incitement" and Kalven's "speech has a price," Fish explains it this way: "There is no such thing as 'speech alone' or speech separable from harmful conduct, no such thing as 'mere

---

83. My discussion here is influenced by Ely, "Flag Desecration," 1496–1502.
84. This concern is expressed in Hustler v. Falwell, 485 U.S. 46 (1988).

speech' or the simple nonconsequential expression of ideas."[85] Beginning from these familiar observations, Fish arrives at the conclusion that decisions about the permissibility of speech always require a balancing of benefits and costs in particular cases by reference to "some particular partisan vision."

I have two disagreements with this conclusion: first, with the idea that decisions about cases are always a matter of ad hoc balancing, and second, with the idea that such balancing must proceed by reference to a particular partisan vision.

As to the first: Fish in fact acknowledges the importance of general categories and principles in deciding how to handle particular cases, and for roughly the reasons I just sketched in my remarks on categorization. He says that "free speech principles function to protect society against over-hasty outcomes; they serve as channels through which an argument must pass on its way to ratification."[86] This acknowledgement of the role of "free speech principles" in protecting against "over-hasty outcomes" shows that Fish is not really—as it might have seemed—offering balancing as the mandatory way to resolve particular cases. Neither metaphysics nor politics condemns the resolution of cases by reference to general, "free speech principles" that serve (as we see it) to tie our hands against "over-hasty outcomes." So the mere fact that speech is consequential carries no implications at all about the proper—much less the necessary—forms for the regulation of expression.

If free-speech nihilism is not nihilism about principles and a corresponding embrace of ad hoc balancing as the proper form of regulation, then perhaps it registers a point about the justification of the principles used to decide cases: that because speech is "never free of consequences,"[87] any justification of principles for resolving cases must take into account the values that a scheme of restrictions and permissions promotes and the costs it imposes.

This thesis is indisputable, but it is also uncontested. Justice Black, for example, urged free-speech absolutism as a doctrine about *decision-making under* the First Amendment—"no law" means "no law"—not as a theory about the *justification of* that amendment. He did not deny the

---

85. Stanley Fish, "There's No Such Thing as Free Speech and It's a Good Thing Too," *Boston Review* 17, 1 (1992): 3–4, 23–26.
86. See ibid., 26. I am indebted to Duncan Kennedy for discussion of this point.
87. Ibid.

importance of a "balancing of conflicting interests" at the level of the justification of the First Amendment prohibition on laws restricting freedom of speech; he just thought that the authors of the First Amendment did all the balancing necessary when they settled on the phrase "shall make no law."[88]

Perhaps, then, free-speech nihilism consists neither in the rejection of principles as guides to decision-making, nor simply in the claim that a justification of such principles must take the consequences of speech into account. Perhaps it is the claim that justification must always proceed in terms of the aims, interests, and aspirations of particular groups, in terms of "some particular partisan vision":[89] i.e., there are no common or shared interests that can serve as a basis for justification. Thus understood, nihilism suggests a pair of practical precepts: If you are weak, argue as forcefully as you can for an encompassing protection of speech in the hope of gaining some political space for your vision; if you are strong, "refashion" principles "in line with your purposes," and then "urge them with a vengeance."[90]

But—here I come to my second disagreement—expressive, deliberative, and informational interests do, I claim, provide common ground among a range of genuinely different views and "particular partisan vision[s]." Of course neither those interests nor any other general scheme of values resolves all controversy about specific cases. But if nihilism amounts only to the thesis that judgments in this area are controversial and contestable, then it wins a quick and uninteresting victory.

Some views, to be sure, do deny the importance of expressive and deliberative interests, so it might be said that the endorsement of those interests is itself partisan. But partisanship in this sense—not being accepted by all—is consistent with holding that these interests provide common ground for a wide range of *distinct* moral-political views; they are not the exclusive possession of one particular partisan vision. As to the views that deny these interests, we need to consider actual cases in order to see whether the positions have any serious claim to be reasonable, and whether the partisanship they embrace is not still more narrow and particular. In short, we need to consider cases to decide whether the partisanship is really troubling.

88. Black, "The Bill of Rights," *New York University Law Review* 35 (1960): 879.
89. Fish, "There's No Such Thing," 26.
90. Ibid.

Take, for example, the case of the "rationalist fundamentalist."[91] This is the person who denies the idea of reasonable pluralism, affirming instead that it lies within the competence of reason to know that salvation is the supreme value, that there is a single path to salvation, that there is no salvation among the damned, that there are no expressive and deliberative interests, and that free expression is to be condemned along with liberty of conscience. This is not a common view, if only because it claims for reason territory more commonly reserved for faith.[92] But if someone advances it, then one ought to say that she is simply mistaken about the powers of reason.[93] Even if the views of the rationalist fundamentalist are all rationally permissible, reason surely does not mandate them, and in insisting that it does, the fundamentalist is not acknowledging the facts. So the fact that expressive and deliberative interests are not recognized by the rationalist fundamentalist does not seem very troubling.[94] To be sure, other cases may present greater difficulties. But that needs to be shown. It is not enough simply to point to the fact of disagreement and conclude that there are only particular partisan visions.

Let us now return to the case for stringent protections.

COSTLY PROTECTIONS

What, then, about protecting expression despite its costs? Why is the fact that expression imposes conditions that are reasonable to want to avoid not sufficient to remove the presumption of protection from it?

To address this question, let us start with the special case of offensive expression—in particular, expression that shocks the sensibilities. There is no way to ensure fair opportunities for expression while at the same time protecting people generally from offensive expression. Given the Fact of Easy Offense and the associated ubiquity of offense, such protection would have to take the form of substantially restricting expression. But the weight of the interests that underlie expression—the expressive

91. I take this example from "Moral Pluralism and Political Consensus," 286.

92. It is an analog to "creation science," operating in the domain of salvation. The proper response is the same in both cases.

93. Most fundamentalists are not rationalist fundamentalists, and would I think agree with this response.

94. I offer the rationalist fundamentalist simply as one illustration. The case of the nonrationalist fundamentalist—who affirms that the basis of religious conviction lies in faith—is more complicated. The latter may wish to distinguish truths delivered by faith from the bases of political justification, and so may be prepared to acknowledge expressive and deliberative interests, at least in the context of political argument.

and deliberative interests—is much greater than the weight of the interest in not being offended, so those restrictions would be intolerable. Moreover, it will not help to confine efforts to regulate to the "grossly offensive"—then we will run into troubles because of the chilling effects of vagueness. The likely vagueness in regulations of the "grossly offensive," that is, threatens to chill acceptable expression.[95]

I do not deny that there is a cost or "price" to offensive expression; indeed the cost is direct. Instead, I claim that the costs of avoiding offense are to be borne by those subject to it—they must, for example, "avert their eyes."[96]

Offensive expression is, as I said, a special case. Moving beyond it, then, the general strategy in deciding whether to protect expression despite its price is to consider the importance of the expression (with attention to the role of categories), the directness and seriousness of the harm, and the vulnerability of the expression to underprotection, given the background facts. Let me illustrate with three kinds of case.

In cases of the first type, expression belongs to an important category, it is vulnerable, and the costs are either environmental or indirect. Then the reasons against restriction are especially strong, even if the cost is substantial.

Consider, for example, the pornography ordinances adopted in Minneapolis and Indianapolis in the 1980s. According to the Indianapolis ordinance, pornography is the "graphic, sexually explicit subordination of women, whether in pictures or in words," which also meets one of the following conditions:

> (i) women are presented as sexual objects who enjoy pain or humiliation; or (ii) women are presented as sexual objects who experience sexual pleasure in being raped; or (iii) women are presented as sexual objects tied up or cut up or mutilated or bruised or physically hurt; or (iv) women are presented being penetrated by objects or animals; or (v) women are presented in scenarios of degradation, injury, torture, shown as filthy or inferior, bleeding, bruised, or hurt in a context that makes these conditions sexual; or (vi) women are presented as sexual objects for domination, conquest, violation, exploitation, possession, or

95. See Hustler v. Falwell, 485 U.S. 46 (1988).
96. See Cohen v. California, 403 U.S. 15 (1971).

use, or through postures or positions of servility or submission or display.[97]

As this language indicates, those ordinances—by contrast with obscenity regulations—included no provision for the artistic, literary, scientific, or political value of the expression they sought to regulate. So they were inattentive to the importance to the expressive, deliberative, and informational interests associated with expression on issues of sexuality. But expressive interests are important in this area because advancing views about human sexuality is supported by substantial reasons from the point of view of the expresser. I noted this in my earlier discussion of expressive interests. Moreover, deliberative and informational interests are at stake as well:

> [The existence of pornography] serves some social functions which benefit women. Pornographic speech has many, often anomalous, characteristics. One is certainly that it magnifies the misogyny present in the culture and exaggerates the fantasy of male power. Another, however, is that the existence of pornography has served to flout conventional sexual mores, to ridicule sexual hypocrisy and to underscore the importance of sexual needs. Pornography carries many messages other than woman-hating: it advocates sexual adventure, sex outside of marriage, sex for no other reason than pleasure, casual sex, anonymous sex, group sex, voyeuristic sex, illegal sex, public sex.[98]

Apart from their inattention to basic interests, the ordinances were vaguely drawn, suggesting inattention to the historical vulnerability of sexual expression to overregulation for moralistic reasons.[99] And they did not consider alternative ways to address the injuries that they associated with pornography. For example, if the problem with pornography is that it sexualizes and thereby legitimates abuse, then one natural step would

97. Indianapolis, Ind., City-Council General Ordinance No. 35 (June 11, 1984), cited in MacKinnon, *Feminism Unmodified*, 274, n. 1.

98. Lisa Duggan, Nan Hunter, and Carole Vance, "False Promises: Feminist Antipornography Legislation," in *Caught Looking: Feminism, Pornography, and Censorship* (East Haven, CT: Long Rivers Books, 1992), 82. The authors were members of the Feminist Anti-Pornography Task Force.

99. Though the rationale for the regulations was emphatically not moral. See Catharine MacKinnon, "Not a Moral Issue," in *Feminism Unmodified*.

be to target sexual abuse—the abuse of women as women—directly and seriously. Such targeting might, for example, include a tort of domestic sexual harassment modeled on workplace sexual harassment—including elements of quid pro quo and hostile environment harassment.[100] If the injury of pornography is that it silences women, then—taking seriously Brandeis's idea of combating the harms of speech with more speech— there could be regular public hearings on sexual abuse, perhaps subsidies for women's organizations to hold such hearings,[101] or easier access of women to broadcast licenses.

To be sure, the regulations of pornography did claim to be addressed to the harms of pornography. But in the face of the breadth of coverage of the regulations, and given the importance of what they were targeting, the claims about costs seem too speculative to sustain the case for regulation.

But these criticisms of the speculative character of the connections between the widespread consumption of pornography and its alleged costs derive their force in part from the broad sweep of the regulations and so from the importance of the expression they sought to regulate. The case does not rest entirely on freestanding doubts about the speculative quality of the connections between the expression and the costs. Less sweeping regulations, drafted with more attention to the value of sexual expression, ought to trigger correspondingly less concern about the need for a conclusive showing of injury and so demand less exacting scrutiny.

Consider, for example, a regulation targeted on the "pornographically obscene": the subset of the constitutionally obscene (prurient, offensive, and minimally valuable expression) that erotizes violence. The case against this regulation would be weaker, because of the weak relation of obscenity to the fundamental interests. Given that weak relation, it is less important that the costs are not direct and the arguments in support of the costs are speculative.[102] (I will provide a more detailed case for this conclusion later on.)

100. I take the proposal from Duncan Kennedy, "Sexual Abuse, Sexy Dressing and the Eroticization of Domination," *New England Law Review* 26 (1992), 1318.

101. For a more general discussion of associative approaches to reconciling egalitarian and liberal commitment, see Joshua Cohen and Joel Rogers, "Secondary Associations and Democratic Governance," *Politics and Society* 20 (1992): 393–472.

102. See, for example, Cass Sunstein's proposal in "Pornography and the First Amendment," *Duke Law Journal* 4 (1986): 589–627. He sharply narrows the class of pornographic expression, defining the class in a way that aims to make it low value. It amounts, more or less (and implicitly), to substituting "erotizes violence and subordination" for "offensive" in the definition of obscenity.

I come now to a second type of case: here, expression belongs to an important category and is vulnerable, but the costs are direct and unavoidable. It is still to be protected. Paradigms here are expressions that cause emotional distress or reputational injury to public figures.

Consider, for example, the case of *Hustler v. Falwell.* In a *Hustler* parody of a Campari ad, Reverend Jerry Falwell was represented as having had his first sexual encounter while drunk in an outhouse with his mother. Falwell won a substantial settlement for the intentional infliction of emotional distress. The Supreme Court overturned the settlement, rejecting the idea that tort law protections should define the scope of expressive liberty. Without denying the reality of Falwell's distress, or dismissing it as merely "mental" or emotional, or disputing *Hustler's* responsibility for it,[103] the Court nevertheless argued that the parody was protected, absent a showing of actual malice. The decision did not simply protect offensive expression; emotional distress is not a matter of being offended. Nor did it reflect the view that the liberty to inflict emotional distress is *in general* of greater weight than the injury of such distress. The decision turned instead on Falwell's standing as a public figure and the importance of freewheeling, sharp criticism of public figures. In a world in which carefully crafted personal images play a central role in politics, and in which fundamental interests are dependent on the operation of the political arena, equally well-targeted efforts at deflation deserve strong protection. By requiring actual malice, the Court in effect licensed increased emotional distress in order to protect the values associated with expressive liberty.

In a third type of case, importance and vulnerability diminish, and there are direct costs. Here, restriction is permitted. Take, for example, the case of libel of private figures. The vulnerability of reputations, the difficulty of repairing them through more speech, and the fact that such libel is typically not supported by weighty expressive or deliberative interests combine to reduce the appropriate level of protection.

FAIR ACCESS

Finally, we come to the requirement of ensuring fair access to expressive opportunities. Three main lines of argument converge on this conclusion.

The first begins by underscoring the central role played in the ac-

---

103. There was, for example, no suggestion that Falwell was really responsible for the distress because of a hypersensitivity to accusations of sin.

count of stringent protections by the Fact of Reasonable Persuasion and Brandeis's associated counsel that we remedy the harms of speech with more speech. By holding out the hopeful prospect of reconciling stringent protection of expressive liberties with other substantial political values (including the value of equality), Brandeis's point helps to remove the sectarian edge from freedom of expression. Instead of winning arguments by always insisting that the "danger has been exaggerated," we take the costs seriously and embrace expression as the preferred strategy for addressing them.

But if we help ourselves to Brandeis's thesis, then we must also take its implications on board. When Brandeis urged more speech in the case of *Whitney v. California*, the context was subversive advocacy.[104] But his remarks were not addressed to the advocates: Anna Whitney was using speech; the state was shutting her up. Brandeis was reminding political elites of the vast means at their disposal for addressing arguments for revolutionary change: they might, for example, try to cure the social ills that prompt them or to argue the case against a revolutionary solution.

Addressed to less powerful groups, with restricted access to means of expression, the easy injunction "More speech!" loses its edge. If we insist that "more speech" is the preferred remedy for combating the harms of speech, and appeal to the Brandeisian injunction as part of a case against content regulation, then we also have an obligation to ensure fair access to facilities of expression where the additional speech might plausibly help the "deliberative forces" to "prevail over the arbitrary."[105] Put otherwise, any argument in which Brandeis's thesis figures as a premise must count assurance of fair access among its conclusions. It is simply unacceptable to impose a high burden on justifying restrictions on expression, to justify that burden in part in terms of the possibilities of combating the harms of speech with more speech, and then not to endorse the requirement of ensuring such facilities.

A second line of argument for fair access is rooted in the expressive interest. The argument follows a generic egalitarian strategy of argument for substantively egalitarian norms. Described abstractly, the strategy begins with a more formal and less controversial political norm—for example, the norm of formal equality of opportunity—and then argues that the best justification for that norm actually provides a rationale for

104. Whitney v. California, 274 U.S. 357 (1927) (Brandeis concurring).
105. Ibid., 375.

a more egalitarian norm—for example, substantive equality of opportunity.[106]

To put the point less abstractly and apply it to the issue at hand: the rationale for the more formal requirement of an equal right to expressive liberties rests centrally on a conception of the human interests served by that guarantee. More specifically, the reason for protecting expressive liberties against content regulation or other forms of undue restriction lies in part in the importance of assuring favorable conditions for the pursuit of the expressive interest. But once we acknowledge the need for favorable conditions for realizing this basic interest, we are naturally led from a more formal to a more substantively egalitarian requirement, since the latter more fully elaborates the range of favorable conditions. In particular, given the Fact of Resource Dependence, favorable conditions for realizing the expressive interest will include some assurance of the resources required for expression and some guarantee that efforts to express views on matters of common concern will not be drowned out by messages of better endowed citizens.

The deliberative interest provides the foundation for a third, and more instrumental, rationale for fair access. The cornerstone of this deliberative case is provided by the Millian thesis that favorable deliberative conditions require a diversity of messages. Such diversity might be encouraged in a variety of ways, but one natural means to diversity is to ensure that all citizens have fair opportunities for expression, with the expectation that the breadth of messages will increase if the extent of expressive opportunity is not determined by economic or social position.[107]

I have already indicated some ways to achieve fair access in a world of unequal resources (supra, 106–108). One requirement is to endorse a more "functional" conception of a public forum,[108] rejecting the conception of such forums as places that are by tradition or explicit designation open to communicative activity, and instead accepting a presumption

106. As, for example, in Rawls's argument that reflection on the ideal of natural liberty leads to the ideal of democratic equality. See *Theory of Justice*, 65–74; and my discussion of the bootstrapping strategy in "Moral Pluralism and Political Consensus," 278–279.

107. Reasoning of broadly this kind can be found in Metro Broadcasting, Inc. v. FCC, 100 S. Ct. 2997 (1990), where the Court upholds an FCC program aimed at increasing broadcast diversity, by increasing the number of minorities with broadcast licenses. For criticisms, see Charles Fried, "*Metro Broadcasting, Inc. v. FCC*: Two Concepts of Equality," *Harvard Law Review* 104 (1990): 107–127.

108. See Owen Fiss, "Silence on the Street Corner," *Suffolk University Law Review* 26 1 (1992): 13–14.

that any location with dense public interaction ought to be treated as a public forum that must be kept open to the public.[109] Another condition of fair access is a heightened presumption against content-neutral regulations that have substantially disparate distributive implications—when, as with regulations on the distribution of handbills, or on the use of parks and sidewalks, they work to impose disproportionate burdens on those who otherwise lack the resources to get their message out.

Furthermore, fair access recommends financing political campaigns through public resources—at least to ensure reasonable floors—and regulating private political contributions and expenditures.[110] In *Buckley v. Valeo*, the Supreme Court drew a sharp distinction between regulations of contributions—which are acceptable because they help to prevent the appearance and reality of corruption—and regulations of expenditures, which are an unacceptable burden of expressive liberty.[111] In arguing against expenditure limits, the Court appealed in part to the greater burdensomeness of such regulations. More fundamentally, however, the majority condemned restrictions (even if content-neutral) on expressive liberty imposed in the name of "enhanc[ing] the relative voice of others" and thereby "equaliz[ing] access to the political arena."[112] The Court did not deny that expenditure limits would work to "equalize access," but instead held that regulations of expression aimed at such equalization were "wholly foreign to the First Amendment."[113]

Whatever their connection to the First Amendment, it is difficult to understand how any plausible account of expressive liberty would regard content-neutral regulations enacted in the name of fair access as foreign to its concerns. In any case, I have suggested that requirements of fair ac-

---

109. Current tendencies in doctrine are, more or less, opposite to the suggestion here. See U.S. v. Kokinda, 110 S. Ct. 3115 (1990); and the discussion in Fiss, "Silence on the Street Corner."

110. For an argument—close to the perspective in this essay—that the current private scheme of campaign financing violates requirements of equal protection, and a sketch of alternative directions of reform, see Jamin Raskin and John Bonifaz, "Equal Protection and the Wealth Primary," *Yale Law and Policy Review* 11 (Winter 1993): 273–332. For an instructive discussion of campaign finance that focuses more or less exclusively on the deliberative interest, see Charles Beitz, *Political Equality* (Princeton: Princeton University Press, 1989), chap. 9.

111. 424 U.S. 1 (1976). It is consistent with *Buckley* to move to a system of voluntary public financing, with matching funds for candidates whose opponents opt to spend private contributions, or to spend their own money. For a sketch of such a system, see Ellen S. Miller, "Money, Politics, and Democracy," *Boston Review* 18 (March/April 1993): 5–8.

112. 424 U.S. 1, 48–49 (1976).

113. Ibid.

cess share a common justification with other stringent protections of expressive liberty; rather than being "wholly foreign," they are on a par.

Thus far I have focused on measures for ensuring fair access that are content-neutral and concerned to remedy the effects of inequalities of material resources on access to expressive opportunities. But as I indicated in the discussion of fair access in Section 1, it is not clear that content-neutral regulations suffice when it comes to addressing problems of fair access that do not reflect the distribution of material resources. In the case of pornography, for example, the mechanisms of exclusion have been tied directly to what is said. Consider the argument that pornography works by silencing women. Responding to the Brandeisian "more speech" argument, MacKinnon explains the problem of silencing and the consequent tension between content-neutrality and fair access this way:

> The situation in which women presently find ourselves with respect to the pornography is one in which more *pornography* is inconsistent with rectifying or even counterbalancing its damage through speech, because so long as the pornography exists in the way it does there *will not be more speech by women*. Pornography strips and devastates women of credibility, from our accounts of sexual assault to our everyday reality of sexual subordination. We are stripped of authority and devalidated and silenced. Silenced here means that the purposes of the First Amendment, premised upon conditions presumed and promoted by protecting free speech, do not pertain to women because they are not our conditions. . . . Any system of freedom of expression that does not address a problem where the free speech of men silences the free speech of women, a real conflict between speech interests as well as between people, is not serious about securing freedom of expression in this country.[114]

I agree with the last claim about the implications of a serious commitment to freedom of expression, and later I will present a style of pornography regulation that is less encompassing than MacKinnon's proposals but consistent with the perspective I have advanced in this essay. I do wish, however, to resist jumping too quickly to the conclusion that con-

114. MacKinnon, "Francis Biddle's Sister," 193.

tent regulation is the only way to ensure fair access. Other measures of empowerment that are more affirmative than regulations of expression may show real promise in addressing silencing and exclusion—at least as much promise as restricting pornography. In particular, alongside efforts to address the general unjust inequalities of men and women—to overcome the division of household labor and the labor-market segregation of women[115]—alternative ways to meet the problems of silencing directly should be explored. Earlier, for example, I mentioned a tort of domestic sexual harassment, regular public hearings on sexual abuse, perhaps subsidies for women's organizations to hold such hearings, or easier access of women to broadcast licenses.

Indeed, it is not clear that MacKinnon would disagree with the plausibility of these remedies. Responding to the Brandeisian idea of addressing the harms of speech with more speech, she asks: "Would more speech remedy the harm [of pornography]?" Her response is instructive: "In the end, the answer may be yes, but not under the *abstract system* [my emphasis] of free speech, which only enhances the power of pornographers while doing nothing to guarantee the free speech of women, for which we need civil equality."[116] MacKinnon is right in saying that a serious commitment to freedom of expression cannot be sharply distinguished from a program of civil equality. For that reason, the proposals I have mentioned are not exclusively about "the abstract system of free speech"; they aim directly to enhance the speech of women and are part of a program of "civil equality." So it is unclear why they should not be expected to do as well as a more restrictive strategy for addressing the harms at issue.

5. Hate Speech, Pornography, and Subcategorization

At several points in the discussion—for example, in my remarks on regulating the pornographically obscene—I have suggested that a commitment to stringent protections of expressive liberty is consistent with a certain style of restriction on expression. Other examples of the style—apart from regulations of pornographic obscenity—are regulations of racist fighting words or "sexually derogatory fighting words."[117] The idea of

115. For discussion, see Susan Moller Okin, *Justice, Gender, and the Family* (New York: Basic Books, 1989).

116. "Francis Biddle's Sister," 193.

117. I take the term from R. A. V. v. St. Paul, 112 S. Ct. 2538, 2546 (1992).

such regulations is to restrict expression within a less important class (obscenity, fighting words) by targeting a particular subcategory (pornographic, racist, sexually derogatory) of the broader class on grounds of the special harmfulness of that subclass. For example, rather than targeting fighting words generally, regulations focus on racially insulting fighting words; rather than targeting obscenity generally, they focus on obscenity that erotizes violence. Subcategorization is a distinctive and controversial style of regulation because—to put the point abstractly—the defining features of the subcategory would not provide a permissible basis for regulation outside the less protected category. To be a little less abstract, the strategy raises the following question: Why is it permissible to regulate hateful fighting words or pornographic obscenity, while acknowledging that a general regulation of hate speech or pornography would not be acceptable?

The acceptability of subcategorization will be important to my concluding comments on the Stanford regulation. But it has recently been the target of sharp criticism by Justice Scalia, writing for the Court in *R. A. V. v. St. Paul*. While I am not concerned here with the constitutional issue as such, Scalia's objection raises important issues about regulating expression that are not narrowly constitutional. I propose here to address those issues.

BACKGROUND

The facts in *R. A. V. v. St. Paul* are straightforward and uncontested. R. A. V. (Robert A. Viktora, a juvenile at the time of prosecution) and his friends burned a cross in the yard of a black family; he was arrested, and charged under a St. Paul Bias-Motivated Crime Ordinance. The ordinance provides that:

> Whoever places on public or private property a symbol, object, appellation, characterization or graffiti, including, but not limited to, a burning cross or Nazi swastika, which one knows or has reasonable grounds to know arouses anger, alarm or resentment in others on the basis of race, color, creed, religion or gender commits disorderly conduct and shall be guilty of a misdemeanor.[118]

118. Minnesota Legislative Code §292.02 (1990), cited in ibid., 2541.

R. A. V. challenged the ordinance, arguing that it was overbroad and impermissibly content-based. The Minnesota Supreme Court rejected the challenge. Central to the Court's holding was its construction of the phrase "arouses anger, alarm or resentment in others" as restricted to "fighting words." As defined in *Chaplinksy v. New Hampshire*, such words are directed to individuals, form "no essential part of any exposition of ideas," and their "very utterance inflicts injury" or "tends to incite an immediate breach of the peace."[119] Premising that First Amendment protection does not extend to fighting words,[120] the Minnesota Court held that the ordinance was neither overbroad nor an impermissible form of content regulation.

The Supreme Court rejected the conclusions of the Minnesota Court and agreed unanimously on the infirmity of the St. Paul ordinance. This consensus, however, emerged from a convergence of two distinct lines of argument about the sources of that infirmity. Writing for the Court, Justice Scalia maintained that the regulation, understood to be restricted to fighting words, was an impermissible form of content discrimination; rejecting this contention, the separate concurrences by Justices White and Stevens held that it was not really restricted to fighting words and so was objectionable because overbroad.[121] I am concerned here with the majority's claim: that, *even as restricted to fighting words*, the regulation is impermissibly content-discriminatory. To state the problem more exactly: assuming, as the majority does, that fighting words are a proscribable category of expression, is it permissible to focus a regulation on the particular subcategory of fighting words mentioned in the ordinance? Let us call the subcategory "hateful fighting words." We have two competing proposals: (1) a regulation of hateful fighting words represents an impermissible regulation of subject matter (and perhaps viewpoint), and (2) a regulation of hateful fighting words represents a permissible targeting of a subcategory of concededly low value and regulable expression on grounds of the special injuriousness of that subcategory.

---

119. 315 U.S. 568, 571–572 (1942). For doubts about the fighting words doctrine, see Note, "The Demise of the *Chaplinsky* Fighting Words Doctrine: An Argument for its Interment," *Harvard Law Review* 106 (1993): 1129–1146.

120. This is the basis of the reasoning by the Minnesota Court. Scalia's opinion emphatically rejects this claim. See R. A. V., 112 S. Ct. 2543.

121. The Minnesota Court said it was restricted to fighting words. But the concurrences rejected that Court's construal of the fighting words test. Ibid., 2558–2560.

THREE POINTS OF AGREEMENT

To locate the disagreement between these two proposals more precisely, we need first to clarify three points of common ground:

Proscribable Expression Is Not without Protection. From the fact that the government could proscribe a whole category of expression—say, child pornography—it does not follow that every less inclusive regulation proscribing a subclass and permitting the rest is also acceptable: think of a child pornography statute restricted to kiddie porn in which at least one actor wears an "I like Dan Quayle" button, or a regulation of obscenity produced after supper. Regulations targeted on those subcategories are unacceptable. So the argument for restricting hateful fighting words cannot count among its premises the claim that every subcategory of a proscribable category can be targeted permissibly.

Subcategories Can Sometimes Be Restricted on the Basis of Their Content. Agreeing that fighting words (along with obscenity and defamation) are proscribable because of their content, the majority accepts further that regulations can target certain subcategories of proscribable expression in virtue of the distinctive content of those subcategories. The federal government, for example, can "criminalize only those threats of violence that are directed against the President."[122] So the argument against regulating hateful fighting words cannot count among its premises the claim that *all* content-based regulations of subcategories of fighting words are impermissible.

Taking these first two points together: the disagreement is about the specific subcategory singled out by the St. Paul ordinance. That disagreement, in turn, is sharpened by a third point of agreement between the two positions:

It Is Impermissible to Proscribe All Speech That Arouses Anger, Alarm, or Resentment on the Basis of Race, Color, Creed, Religion, or Gender.[123] Such a regulation would aim at and almost certainly produce an unac-

122. Ibid., 2546.
123. See ibid., 2558–2560 (White dissenting). This point is not very controversial, even among defenders of hate-speech regulations. See, for example, Charles Lawrence, "If He Hollers Let Him Go."

ceptable "suppression of ideas." The issue, then, is whether a regulation targeted specifically at fighting words that "arouse anger, alarm. . . ." is acceptable.

REGULATING HATEFUL FIGHTING WORDS

With these three points in place, we can fix the precise disagreement and assess the alternative positions.

The first view is that a regulation of hateful fighting words will trigger exactly the same suspicion about the suppression of ideas as a *general* hate-speech regulation will, directed to all speech that arouses anger, alarm, or resentment in others on the basis of race, color, creed, religion, or gender. The underlying principle that bars a general regulation of hate speech (the third point of agreement) is that hateful messages are not proscribable because of their content. They do not forfeit that immunity because they travel in a vehicle that is, for reasons other than the hate message, dangerous. Thus, immediate provocative speech can be regulated. But the fact that a hateful message is conveyed, for example, in an immediately provocative way does not make it permissible to target it as distinct from other messages conveyed in an equally (or more) provocative way.

Content regulation threatens the official suppression of ideas; so the question is always whether the "official suppression of ideas is afoot."[124] And that question—according to the first view—loses none of its force when a regulation is targeted on a proscribable category of speech; the fact that expression falls into a less-protected category does not make it permissible to use a regulation of such expression as a device to restrict concededly protected messages.[125]

The alternative view is that there is indeed less concern about content discrimination—less concern about the suppression of ideas—when regulated speech falls into a proscribable category. Why? The neatest answer would be this: "How could there be any concern about the suppression

---

124. R. A. V., 112 S. Ct. 2547.

125. Even this misses the full subtlety of the majority view. They suggest that the Title VII ban on hostile work environment sex discrimination "may" permissibly regulate "sexually derogatory 'fighting words,' among other words" (ibid., 2546). But, it is permissible to regulate sexually derogatory fighting words in the workplace only as an "incidental" effect of a general protection against hostile work environments. The fact that the regulation of speech was an incidental part of a general code of conduct would immediately answer the concern that the speech itself was being regulated because of its message rather than because of its harmful effects.

of ideas? Expression in proscribable categories conveys no ideas." But that will not do; different obscene movies, for example, can convey competing ideas about the pleasures of different sorts of sex.[126] More to the point, if hateful fighting words did not communicate anything, there would be no point targeting them. Nor would it be right simply to insist that if a category is proscribable, then we should be less concerned about protecting it. That is, of course, true in some way. But it does not indicate any reason for reduced concern about content discrimination, and it threatens to fly in the face of the first point of agreement noted earlier: that proscribable expression has some protection. The explanation for the reduced concern about content regulation cannot lie in the bare fact that expression belongs to a proscribable category but must, instead, be provided by the reason for treating it as proscribable in the first place.

Consider, then, the category of fighting words. Provocations directed to individuals, such words comprise "no essential part of the exposition of ideas." For that reason, concerns about the official suppression of ideas are naturally reduced when regulations are targeted on them; it is, intuitively, difficult to see how a regulation targeted on expression that is not an essential part of the exposition of ideas could seriously threaten to drive certain ideas, topics, or viewpoints from the marketplace of ideas or the forum of political debate.[127]

More specifically, recall the reasons for being especially troubled about regulations targeted on content (125–126 above): They represent especially serious threats to the deliberative and expressive interests; the relative precision of their targeting raises the specter of the abuse of power in an especially acute way; and, even if such regulations are targeted on real evils, the Fact of Reasonable Persuasion should lead us to trust more speech to address those evils.

Because fighting words are insults or provocations directed to individuals, they do not make a significant contribution to discussion. The threat to deliberative interests seems, then, relatively small. Moreover, insofar as they serve as vehicles for expression—for advancing the expressive interest—proscribing them leaves a wide range of alternative vehicles. And

126. Thus Scalia's firm distinction between "no part" of the exposition of ideas and "no essential part" of that exposition, ibid., 2544. Implicit in these remarks is the suggestion that the concurrences endorse the tempting but implausible view that I note in the text.

127. There is certainly no "prohibition of public discussion of an entire topic." Boos v. Barry, 485 U.S. 312, 319 (1988).

the reasons for expression in the form of fighting words do not seem especially substantial. Taking these points together, it seems much less plausible that a regulation targeted on hateful fighting words would severely suppress ideas or would be motivated by a desire to suppress them than that a regulation targeted on hate speech generally would have that unacceptable effect or illegitimate motivation. So there does appear to be a substantial difference in the fears about suppression that would reasonably be triggered by a general regulation of hate speech and a regulation targeted specifically on the hateful subset of fighting words.

Of course, given the Facts of Power, Easy Offense, and Abuse, concerns about suppression could be revived if a regulation were focused on a relatively insignificant harm. But racial subordination, for example,[128] is a serious evil; and it is at least plausible that racist fighting words play some role—plausibly a significant role—in maintaining racial inequality. They contribute to an environment of fear, suspicion, hostility, and mistrust that makes racial division so resistant to remedy. So the regulation picks out not an arbitrary class of fighting words but a class that is especially damaging to fundamental political values, for example the value of racial equality. Finally, it seems especially implausible that the injuries produced by hateful fighting words can be remedied with more speech. The anger, the fear, and the suspicion that they produce are not kinds that can be easily addressed by verbal reassurances.

The regulation, then, is targeted on a category with only a minimal connection with the fundamental deliberative and expressive interests; and within that category it focuses on a subcategory that is plausibly more injurious than other elements of the category and whose effects are plausibly more recalcitrant to expressive cure.

There are three responses to this argument, each of which aims to reinstate suspicions about the suppression of ideas in a hateful fighting words regulation.

The first is that there is a straightforward basis for the suspicion: it is agreed, as I indicated earlier, that a *general* hate-speech regulation would

---

128. I say "for example" because the St. Paul ordinance was not simply addressed to racial hate speech nor, more particularly, to racial hate speech targeted on African Americans or other groups subordinated on the basis of race. For the suggestion that such a narrow and "openly asymmetric regulation" might have been less constitutionally suspect—in light of the Thirteenth Amendment ban on badges of servitude—see Akhil Reed Amar, "Comment: The Case of the Missing Amendments: R. A. V. v. City of St. Paul," *Harvard Law Review* 106 (1992): 155–161. See also my discussion of the asymmetry in the Stanford regulation, 152–153 below.

threaten the suppression of ideas. But if it is unacceptable to single out hateful words for special regulation, why isn't it also unacceptable to restrict the hateful subset of fighting words? Contrast that restriction with one that singles out the fighting words that are especially likely to incite breach of the peace. Fighting words are low value in part because they tend to incite breach, so there could be no objection to singling out those fighting words that threaten, in more extreme form, the very evil that prompts the reduced protection in the first place.[129] But a regulation of hateful fighting words (arguably) does not pick out the especially provocative, so it is objectionable.

The problem with this objection is that it fails to take into consideration the bases for reduced protection for fighting words and the reasons for special concerns about content regulation. The category of fighting words is such that the restriction of expression within the category does not present a substantial threat of the suppression of ideas. But the suppression of ideas is the main threat posed by content regulation. So the explanation of the reduced protection for fighting words also explains why a regulation of hateful fighting words does not threaten the suppression of ideas and so accounts for the legitimacy of a form of content discrimination that would be unacceptable outside the limited context of fighting words.

A second reason for the concern might be a familiar "camel's nose" concern: that once we allow the suppression of some subcategory of hate speech, we will then be tempted to regulate hate speech generally. But that regulation is not legitimate.

The problem here is that the argument proves too much: it provides a case for an absolute ban on content regulation, a position that no one in the debate occupies (see the second of the three points of agreement noted above). Moreover, while the concern about excessive regulation is real, the point of carving out such less protected categories as fighting words, obscenity, and commercial speech is precisely to address that concern. To endorse the strategy of categorization as a device against temptations to overregulate and then to revisit concerns about those temptations in the context of regulating subcategories, strikes me as an exaggerated

---

129. See R. A. V., 112 S. Ct. 2545: "When the basis for the content discrimination consists entirely of the very reason the entire class of speech is proscribable, no significant danger of idea or viewpoint discrimination exists."

form of distrust, and one that runs up against the premise—accepted by the Court majority—that fighting words themselves are low value.

The third reason is that, while hateful fighting words are certainly offensive and insulting, even gross offensiveness and insult cannot provide a basis for regulation.[130] But to say that the "price" is offensiveness, represents a tendentious misstatement of the harms. The harms of hateful fighting words are several and include the role of such words in sustaining racial division and preserving racial inequality.[131] This is a very great harm. Of course, not every restriction of expression that contributes to avoiding it is, for that reason, acceptable. But a regulation that may contribute, and do so without threatening the suppression of ideas (for example, a regulation of hateful fighting words), is acceptable.

PORNOGRAPHIC OBSCENITY

In introducing this discussion of regulations of hateful fighting words, I presented such regulations as one example of the more general strategy of regulation by subcategorization. I have now indicated why the strategy is, as a general matter, unobjectionable. To clarify the basis of this view, I want now to say more about an example I discussed earlier—the case of pornographic obscenity.

I will assume the *Miller* test for obscenity.[132] According to that test, a work is obscene just in case the average person, applying community standards, finds that the work, taken as a whole, appeals to the prurient interest; moreover, the work must present an offensive depiction of sexual conduct; and, finally, it must lack serious literary, artistic, political, or scientific value. The intuition is that sexually preoccupied, offensive junk does not merit stringent constitutional protection. It is an interesting question, which I will not pursue here, why the sexual preoccupation makes a difference.[133] It does not appear to diminish the value of the ex-

---

130. This appears to be the force of Scalia's remark that "what makes the anger, fear, sense of dishonor, etc. produced by violation of this ordinance distinct from the honor fear, sense of dishonor, etc. produced by other fighting words is nothing other than the fact that it is conveyed by a distinctive idea, conveyed by a distinctive message." Ibid., 2548.

131. Here I agree with Amar that a cleaner focus on the nature of the harms and a more discriminating discussion of the differences among the categories mentioned in the ordinance— "race, color, creed, religion, or gender"—would have sharpened both the regulation and the Court's assessment of it. See Amar, "The Case of the Missing Amendments," 155–160.

132. Miller v. California, 413 U.S. 15 (1973).

133. See Roth v. United States, 354 U.S. 476, 512 (Douglas dissenting), and Harry Kalven, "The Metaphysics of the Law of Obscenity," *The Supreme Court Review: 1960*, ed. Philip B. Kurland (Chicago: University of Chicago Press, 1960), 18–19.

pression, which by stipulation is not very great; furthermore, since the costs lie in offensiveness, and expression can be offensive without being sexually preoccupied, the sexual content is not required for the costs. So why is it not permissible to regulate violence-preoccupied, offensive junk? Or offensive junk preoccupied with frightening people? Or preoccupied with money making? Or cruelty? Leaving these questions for another occasion, I will assume for the sake of argument that obscenity merits reduced protection. I want to ask about the implications of that assumption for the regulation of subcategories of the obscene.

Consider, then, three obscenity regulations. The first targets all obscene forms of expression. The second targets obscene expression in which women are subjected to violence—what I referred to earlier as the "pornographically obscene." I stipulate a regulation covering all obscenity in which women are subjected to violence, rather than obscenity in which that violence is applauded, because I want the regulation to be content-based but viewpoint neutral.[134] The third regulation targets "grossly" obscene expression, by which I mean expression that is obscene and *grossly* offensive by the lights of the community—perhaps golden-shower movies and movies featuring oral sex with animals fall into this class.

Paralleling the earlier discussion of hateful fighting words, let us distinguish two natural responses to these regulations. The first is constructed on analogy with a view that accepts a regulation targeted on extremely provocative fighting words but not one targeted on hateful fighting words. So it would accept regulations of all the obscene or of only the grossly obscene, but not of only the pornographically obscene.

Why would a regulation focused on the grossly offensive subcategory be acceptable? Although the determination of gross offensiveness is a matter of content (prohibitions on golden-shower movies and movies displaying oral sex with animals are subject-matter restrictions), and content regulations are generally objectionable, offensiveness is precisely the reason for reducing the protection of the obscene in the first place. So if it is permissible to target all offensive, prurient junk without engendering concern about the suppression of ideas, then surely it is permissible to target the *grossly* offensive, prurient junk without engendering such suspicion.

134. I am not sure that an obscene movie could present violence against or humiliation of women in an unfavorable light, because by so doing, it would plausibly have serious political value, thus defeating the categorization as obscene.

A regulation of the pornographically obscene is, like a regulation of the grossly obscene, not subject matter neutral. But, this first line of response emphasizes, it singles out for regulation, a subcategory of the obscene on the basis of considerations other than those that render it obscene in the first place; the subclass of the violent may not correspond to the subcategory that is either *especially* prurient or *grossly* offensive in its prurience. Moreover, a general regulation of pornography seems unacceptable, for the reasons I indicated earlier. Because the feature that defines the subcategory is unrelated to obscenity, and because that feature *would* trigger concern about the suppression of ideas if applied outside the context of obscenity, it might be thought to trigger that concern here. Defenders of the regulation will, to be sure, argue that the regulation is justified by reference to the distinctive harms of the pornographically obscene. But if those alleged harms cannot provide the rationale for a general regulation of pornography, then why should they provide an acceptable rationale for a regulation of the pornographically obscene?

Here again we meet the central concern: the fact that a whole category of expression is proscribable does not imply a reduced concern about the evil of a kind of content discrimination that would be unacceptable if applied to a wider category of expression.

Once more, however, an alternative view—constructed on analogy with the position that approves a regulation of hateful fighting words—seems more plausible. This alternative would accept the regulation of the pornographically obscene.[135] The contention fueling this second line of argument is that *if* obscenity is low value in the first place, then it is permissible to restrict pornographically obscene representations on grounds that such representations are injurious (though not on grounds of viewpoint), *even though* the alleged injuries would be insufficient to sustain the regulation of pornography generally. The reason is this: a regulation of pornography generally does, for reasons I discussed earlier, present a substantial threat to fundamental expressive and deliberative interests. (This might be conceded even by those who argue that the threat is overpowered by injuries reasonably attributed to pornography.) But the basis for treating obscenity as low value is that it contributes little to the fundamental interests. Because it does, a regulation of it would not

135. Indeed, I suspect that many who hold this second view would be more inclined to regulate the pornographically obscene than the grossly obscene. But I will put this matter to the side.

present a substantial threat to those interests. Because it would not, the concerns that provide the basis for opposing content discrimination are diminished. Because they are diminished, the injuries associated with the fusing of sex and violence by the pornographically obscene provide sufficient basis for regulation. Indeed there is a better case for this regulation—which is focused on genuine harms—than either for the regulation of obscenity generally or for the regulation of grossly offensive obscenity. For those regulations aim to prevent the uncertain evil of offensiveness rather than the genuine evil of injuries to women.

6. *Reflections on the Stanford Case*

Finally, I come back to the Stanford regulation. At the beginning of this essay, I promised to fit a pallid endorsement of it into the conception of freedom of expression I have outlined here. Everything I have said thus far should suffice to explain the lack of enthusiasm (though I will add a few more considerations). What are the bases for the endorsement?

Recall that the regulation restricts "speech or other expression" that: (1) is *intended* to insult or stigmatize individuals on the basis of their sex, race, color, handicap, religion, sexual orientation, or national and ethnic origin; and (2) is addressed *directly* to the individual or individuals whom it insults or stigmatizes; and (3) makes use of insulting or *"fighting words"* or nonverbal symbols that are "commonly understood to convey direct and visceral hatred or contempt for human beings on the basis of their sex, race, etc."

My endorsement reflects three features of the regulation, each of which indicates sensitivity to the case for stringent protection that I have presented here.

(1) The regulation is directed to remarks that are *intended* to insult, and the insult must be directed to an individual or small group. So the regulated expression bears at most a loose connection to the fundamental expressive and deliberative interests.

(2) The insult must be conveyed through fighting words and in particular, words that insult or stigmatize on the basis of sex, race, color, and the like. Because of the requirement of immediate provocation and injury associated with fighting words, some of the costs are direct, and there is no deflecting them with "more speech."

(3) The rule singles out an exceptional category and does not repre-

sent an open-ended invitation to balancing the benefits and costs of expression. So it is attentive to concerns about vulnerability.

Given the minimal interests, direct costs, and attention to potential abuse, the supports for protection are substantially reduced, and it seems appropriate (or at least permissible) to shift the burden of restraint to the speaker.

To be sure, the regulation is not without its troubles, principally because (as interpreted) it would be viewpoint-discriminatory; for example, racist remarks addressed to black students may (depending on conditions) count as a form of discriminatory harassment; racist remarks to white students do not.[136] Is the general presumption against such discrimination rebuttable in this case?

In assessing the troublesomeness of the viewpoint discrimination, we need to keep in focus the requirements of intent and fighting words, and the stipulation that the words be directed to an individual or group with the intent to insult or stigmatize. Expression meeting these conditions has only a marginal claim to protection in the first place. So—as I indicated in the discussion of hateful fighting words—it seems *permissible* to deny protection to a subcategory of it in order to promote the substantial value of ensuring equality of educational opportunity for the groups singled out in the regulation.

Of course "permissible" does not imply "recommended." Other considerations are relevant to deciding that issue. How much injurious expression would actually be avoided? Would the regulation be at all effective in combating the underlying problems reflected in hate speech? Furthermore, apart from addressing these questions about the regulation itself, we need to consider the wisdom of focusing energy and attention on regulating hate speech (or pornography) rather than on taking more affirmative measures to combat the harms that the regulation aims to avoid. The focus of regulating expression has at least three defects: it can serve as a distraction of energy from other measures; it divides people who are allied in their commitment to equality; and it suggests a depressingly profound loss of constructive, egalitarian, political, and social imagination.

136. According to a clarification offered in a debate in the Stanford faculty senate. See the discussion in Nadine Strossen, "Regulating Racist Speech," *Duke Law Journal* (1990): 494 n. 110; and the less measured discussion in Charles Fried, "The New First Amendment Jurisprudence: A Threat to Liberty," *University of Chicago Law Review* 59 (1992): 22ff.

Together these considerations strike me as good grounds for skepticism. To be sure, such skepticism is not costly for those of us who are not now targets of hate speech.[137] This point has some force, and so I do not treat my skepticism about effectiveness as a basis for rejecting the regulations as inconsistent with a commitment to stringent protections of expressive liberty.

But ineffectiveness may in turn lead to pressure for more stringent regulations in the name of equality. And this could represent a serious challenge to the conception of freedom of expression I have sketched here. For if the harms of subordination cannot be fought with more speech and other nonrestrictive remedies, then—the world being as it is—a commitment to substantive equality simply cannot be reconciled with a strong affirmation of expressive liberties. If my account of the basis of freedom of expression is correct, then that conclusion will not show that we ought to give up on the value of equality; for as I indicated early on, nothing in the defense turns on a freestanding preference for liberty over all competing values, and in particular a freestanding preference for liberty over equality. Nor would it show that we ought to give up on the value of liberty. Instead, we would face a grim standoff between concerns about expressive liberty and concerns about equality.

So those of us who celebrate the values of equality, toleration, and expressive liberty—and the remedial powers of speech in reconciling these values—ought to conduct our celebration by getting to work.

---

137. I say "not now" because I was frequently called "kike," "bagel-bender," and the like when I was growing up.

5

PROCEDURE AND SUBSTANCE
IN DELIBERATIVE DEMOCRACY

The fundamental idea of democratic legitimacy is that the authorization to exercise state power must arise from the collective decisions of the members of a society who are governed by that power.[1] More precisely—and stated with attention to democracy's institutional character—it arises from the discussions and decisions of members, as made within and expressed through social and political institutions designed to acknowledge their collective authority. That is an abstract statement of the concept of democracy, and deliberately so. Democracy comes in many forms, and more determinate conceptions of it depend on an account of membership in the people and, correspondingly, what it takes for a decision to be collective, to be made by citizens "as a body."

Take a political community in which adherence to a comprehensive moral or religious doctrine,[2] perhaps rooted in national tradition, is a

I would like to thank John Rawls, Charles Sabel, T. M. Scanlon, Cass Sunstein, and Iris Marion Young for illuminating comments on earlier drafts of this essay. The "Deliberative Democracy" section draws on my "Deliberation and Democratic Legitimacy," in Alan Hamlin and Phillip Petit, eds. *The Good Polity* (Oxford Blackwell, 1989), 17–34 [reprinted as essay 1 in this volume]. The "Three Principles" section draws on my review of Robert Dahl's *Democracy and Its Critics* (New Haven: Yale University Press, 1989) in *Journal of Politics* 53, 1 (1991): 221–225; and on my "Pluralism and Proceduralism," *Chicago-Kent Law Review* 69, 3 (1994): 589–618. The "Realizing Democracy" section draws on Joshua Cohen and Joel Rogers, *Democracy and Association* (London: Verso, 1995).

1. "Governed by" rather than "affected by." Democracy is about justifying authority not about justifying influence. See Michael Walzer, *Spheres of Justice* (New York: Basic Books, 1983); and Christopher McMahon, *Authority and Democracy* (Princeton: Princeton University Press, 1994). Alternatively stated, authorization must come from the popular will, where "popular will" is understood as indicating the ultimate authority and responsibility of citizens as a body not as implying a collective ranking of alternatives that preexists institutions and seeks authentic expressions through them. See William Riker, *Liberalism Against Populism* (San Francisco: W. H. Freeman, 1992).

2. On the notion of a comprehensive doctrine, see John Rawls, *Political Liberalism* (New York: Columbia University Press, 1996 [1993]), 13.

condition of full membership. Authorization, then, will require congruence with that view, and only decisions exhibiting such congruence can properly be deemed "collective." For that reason, the test for democratic legitimacy will be, in part, substantive—dependent on the content of outcomes, not simply on the processes through which they are reached.

What happens, though, when the idea of collective authorization is set against a different background: where there is no shared comprehensive moral or religious view, members are understood as free and equal, and the national project, such as it is, embraces a commitment to expressing that freedom and equality in the design of institutions and collective choices?[3] Does this shift in background drive us to an entirely procedural view of democracy and collective decision? I think not. But before explaining why, I want to say something about the interest of the question and the terms in which it is stated.

My question about the effects of a shift in background is prompted by the aim of formulating a conception of democracy suited to the kind of human difference captured in the "fact of reasonable pluralism"[4]—the fact that there are distinct, incompatible understandings of value, each one reasonable, to which people are drawn under favorable conditions for the exercise of their practical reason. The good-faith exercise of practical reason, by people who are reasonable in being concerned to live with others on terms that those others can accept, does not lead to convergence on one particular philosophy of life.

The claim about reasonable pluralism is suggested by persistent disagreements about, for example, the values of choice and self-determination, happiness and welfare, and self-actualization; disputes

3. American national identity is commonly tied to such a conception, as in Lincoln's claim that the nation was conceived in liberty and dedicated to the proposition that all men are created equal. Some regard this abstract national self-definition as exceptionally American. Considering the conflictual conditions under which modern nationalism evolved, I doubt that this claim can be sustained without substantial qualification. Claims about the content of national identity—like all claims about identity—are endlessly contested: they are as much moves in social and political conflicts aimed at establishing the authority of a particular nationalist understanding as they are intellectual discoveries. For every person who will claim that the conception of people as free and equal is foreign to their particular national identity, we can always find someone who shares the national self-definition and will deny that foreignness.

4. For discussion of this fact, see my "Moral Pluralism and Political Consensus," in *The Idea of Democracy*, ed. David Copp, Jean Hampton, and John Roemer (Cambridge: Cambridge University Press, 1993), 270–291 [reprinted as essay 2 in this volume]; John Rawls, *Political Liberalism*; and my "A More Democratic Liberalism," *Michigan Law Review* 92, 6 (May 1994): 1502–1546.

about the relative merits of contemplative and practical lives and the importance of personal and political engagement; and disagreements about the religious and philosophical backgrounds of these evaluative views. Apart from the sheer fact of disagreement, there is, moreover, no apparent tendency to convergence generated by the exercise of practical reason; furthermore, we have no theory of the operations of practical reason that would lead us to predict convergence on comprehensive moralities, nor can I think of any marginally attractive social or political mechanisms that might generate such agreement.

This fact of reasonable pluralism gives shape to the conception of citizens as free and equal that constitutes part of the conception of democracy I want to explore here. To say that citizens are free is to say, inter alia, that no comprehensive moral or religious view provides a defining condition of membership or the foundation of the authorization to exercise political power. To say that they are equal is to say that each is recognized as having the capacities required for participating in discussion aimed at authorizing the exercise of power.

What, then, are the implications of reasonable pluralism for a conception of democracy? It is natural to suppose that by excluding a comprehensive consensus on values, the fact of reasonable pluralism leads to a procedural conception of democracy. According to such a conception, the democratic pedigree that lies at the source of legitimacy can be settled by looking exclusively to the processes through which collective decisions are made and to the values associated with fair processes: for example, values of openness, equal chances to present alternatives, and full and impartial consideration of those alternatives. The fact of reasonable pluralism appears to require a procedural conception because it deprives us of a background of shared moral or religious premises that could give determinate content to the idea of popular authorization or constrain the substance of genuinely collective choices. Without that background, we are left, it may seem, with no basis for agreement on anything more than fair procedures—and perhaps not even that.

I think this conclusion is not right and will sketch a view that combines an assumption of reasonable pluralism with a more substantive conception of democracy. Moreover, I will argue that this combination is a natural result of a particular way of thinking about democracy—a "deliberative" understanding of the collective decisions that constitute democratic governance. Before discussing the deliberative conception, though, I need first to fix the concerns about procedure and substance more precisely, distinguish a deliberative from an aggregative conception of democracy, and show how aggregative conceptions lead to proceduralism.

Liberties, Ancient and Modern

Consider a familiar dilemma associated with the idea of tracing legitimacy to popular authorization.[5] On the one hand, democracy may seem too much a matter of procedure to provide a basis for an account of legitimacy; some democratic collective choices are too execrable to be legitimate, however attractive the procedures that generate them. On the other hand, the idea of democracy appears to exclude any competing basis of legitimacy. Democracy appears to be the form of collective choice mandated by the fundamental idea that citizens are to be treated as equals. So democracy is commonly thought to be the way we must decide how other political values are to be ordered; it is not simply one political value that is to be combined with others.

This dilemma is familiar from discussions of democracy and the "liberties of the moderns"—religious liberty, liberty of conscience more generally, liberty of thought and expression, rights of person and personal property. Lacking any evident connection to conditions of democratic procedure, such liberties are commonly understood as constraints on democratic process. Not so with political liberties. A constitution disabling government from restricting political participation or regulating the content of political speech can be interpreted as safeguarding, rather than constraining, democratic process. Assurances of such political liberties help to preserve the connection between popular authorization and political outcome—to preserve the continuing authority of the people, and not simply the majority of them.[6] These liberties—the liberties of the ancients—are constitutive elements of democratic process.

Things are different when it comes to abridgments of religious liberty or restrictions on expression whose content can be construed as political only on a uselessly capacious construal of "political." In these cases, disabling provisions in a constitution appear simply to limit democracy, not to be among its preconditions, either implicit or explicit.

5. By "tracing legitimacy to popular authorization," I mean treating such authorization as a sufficient condition for the exercise of political power.

6. See John Hart Ely, *Democracy and Distrust* (Cambridge, MA: Harvard University Press, 1980); and Robert Dahl, *Democracy and Its Critics*.

The liberties of the moderns appear, then, to be founded on values entirely independent from the values of democracy. And that appearance may prompt one of two undesirable conclusions. The first is that the political liberties are merely instrumental, of value just insofar as they protect the liberties of the moderns; when they fail to ensure such protection, an authority external to the people ought to do so. Here, a conflict between democracy and other political values is easily translated into a conflict between democratic and nondemocratic procedures of political decision making.[7]

A second view holds that the liberties of the moderns have no standing deeper than contingent popular consensus. Although abridgments of nonpolitical liberties that emerge from a fair democratic process may be unjust, then, they face no problems of democratic legitimacy.[8]

We are pushed into this dilemma by a particular understanding of democracy, which I will call "aggregative"—as distinct from deliberative.[9] According to an aggregative conception, democracy institutionalizes a principle requiring equal consideration for the interests of each member; or, more precisely, equal consideration along with a "presumption of personal autonomy"—the understanding that adult members are the best judges and most vigilant defenders of their own interests.[10] To criticize processes as undemocratic, then, is to claim that those processes failed to give equal consideration to the interests of each member. The natural method for giving such consideration is to establish a scheme of collective choice—majority or plurality rule, or group bargaining—that gives equal weight to the interests of citizens, in part by enabling them to present and advance their interests. And that requires a framework of rights of participation, association, and expression.

7. See Dahl's concerns about judicial review in *Democracy and Its Critics*, 183.

8. It is, of course, open to a democratic pluralist to hold that such infringements are unjust and that the people ought to reject them.

9. On the distinction between aggregative and deliberative views, and its bearing on the possibility of reconciling commitments to values of liberty and equality within a conception of democracy, see my review of Dahl's *Democracy and Its Critics*. For discussion of the related distinction between strategic and deliberative conceptions, see David Estlund, "Who's Afraid of Deliberative Democracy? On the Strategic/Deliberative Dichotomy in Recent Constitutional Jurisprudence," *Texas Law Review* 7, 7 (June 1993): 1437–1477. Estlund identifies strategic theories with views that make use of the idea of utility-maximization. I think that the crucial issue is whether a conception of democracy emphasizes the idea of providing reasons acceptable to others.

10. In *Democracy and Its Critics*, chaps. 6–8, Dahl derives conditions on democratic procedure from a principle of equal consideration and a presumption of personal autonomy.

Arguably, the aggregative view can be extended beyond such straight-forwardly procedural rights to some concerns about outcomes. For it might be said that collective choices that depend on discriminatory views—on hostility or stereotyping—do not give equal weight to the interests of each who is governed by them. And when we face outcomes that disadvantage people who are the likely targets of such views, we have strong evidence of a failure of the process to give equal consideration to the interests of each.[11]

This procedural reinterpretation of important political values can, however, go only so far. Religious liberty, for example, has no apparent procedural basis. To be sure, abridgments of freedom of worship are sometimes troubling because they result from discriminatory (anti-Catholic, anti-Semitic) attitudes. When they do, protections of religious liberties will emerge from the requirement of equal consideration. But the failure to give appropriate weight to religious convictions need not reflect hatred, discrimination, or stereotyping—nor must it depend on any other of the conventional ways of demeaning a person or failing to treat her as an equal. The problem may have a different source: it may trace to a failure to take seriously the stringency or the weight of the demands placed on the person by her reasonable moral or religious convictions—not the intensity with which she holds those convictions, which does figure in aggregative views, but the stringency or the weight of the demands imposed by the convictions, given their content.[12] It is precisely this stringency that compels reasons of especially great magnitude for overriding those demands. But such considerations about the relative stringency of demands are absent from the aggregative conception; so, therefore, is the

11. When, for example, legislation relies on racial classifications—or at least on malign racial classification—we have reason to suspect that discriminatory preferences prompted the legislation. And if they did, then the procedural-democratic pedigree of the regulation is arguably corrupt. See Ely, *Democracy and Distrust*, chap. 6; and Ronald Dworkin, *Law's Empire* (Cambridge, MA: Harvard University Press, 1986), chap. 10. For a less social-psychological view of unacceptable procedural pedigree, see Bruce Ackerman, "Beyond Carolene Products," *Harvard Law Review* 98 (1985): 713–746. Unfortunately, the Supreme Court has endorsed the view that "malign racial classification" is a pleonasm, and "benign racial classification" a contradiction in terms. See Richmond v. Croson, 488 U.S. 469 (1989); Shaw v. Reno, 113 S. Ct. 2816 (1993); and Miller v. Johnson, slip op. (1995). For an alternative view, see Metro Broadcasting v. FCC, 497 U.S. 547 (1990).

12. The distinction between rights required to prevent discrimination and rights required to protect fundamental interests plays a central role in equal protection doctrine. See Laurence Tribe, *American Constitutional Law* (Mineola, NY: Foundation Press, 1988), chap. 16. On the importance of paying attention to the content of views in an account of free exercise, see Ronald Dworkin, *Life's Dominion* (New York: Knopf, 1993), 162–166.

need to find reasons of great weight before overriding those demands. That is a fundamental deficiency, and it lies at the source of the dilemma I sketched earlier.

A deliberative conception of democracy does not face the same troubles about reconciling democracy with nonpolitical liberties and other substantive, nonprocedural requirements. While accepting the fact of reasonable pluralism, it is attentive to the stringency of demands to which agents are subject, and therefore does not present its conception of democracy or collective decision in an exclusively procedural way. To make this case, I will first sketch the main ideas of a deliberative view; then I will show how, on the deliberative conception, we can accommodate the fact of reasonable pluralism without endorsing a wholly procedural conception of democracy. In particular, I will show how the liberties of the moderns and other substantive conditions are themselves elements in an institutional ideal of deliberative democracy.

Deliberative Democracy

The deliberative conception of democracy is organized around an ideal of political justification. According to this ideal, justification of the exercise of collective political power is to proceed on the basis of a free public reasoning among equals. A deliberative democracy institutionalizes this ideal. Not simply a form of politics, democracy, on the deliberative view, is a framework of social and institutional conditions that facilitates free discussion among equal citizens—by providing favorable conditions for participation, association, and expression—and ties the authorization to exercise public power (and the exercise itself) to such discussion—by establishing a framework ensuring the responsiveness and accountability of political power to it through regular competitive elections, conditions of publicity, legislative oversight, and so on.[13]

I will come back later to the conditions for institutionalizing deliberation in greater detail. First, though, I want to say more about the idea of deliberative justification itself.

A deliberative conception puts public reasoning at the center of political justification. I say "public reasoning" rather than "public discussion" because a deliberative view cannot be distinguished simply by its emphasis on discussion rather than on bargaining or voting. Any view of democ-

13. On the role of the idea of democracy as more than a political idea, see Gordon Wood, *The Radicalism of the American Revolution* (New York: Knopf, 1992), esp. 232.

racy—indeed any view of intelligent political decision making—will see discussion as important, if only because of its essential role in pooling information against a background of asymmetries in its distribution. Nor is it marked by the assumption that political discussion aims to change the preferences of other citizens. Though a deliberative view must assume that citizens are prepared to be moved by reasons that may conflict with their antecedent preferences and interests, and that being so moved may change those antecedent preferences and interests,[14] it does not suppose that political deliberation takes as its goal the alteration of preferences. Nor is it distinguished by its endorsement of an epistemic conception of voting, according to which votes are interpreted as expressions of beliefs about the correct answer to a political question, rather than as preferences about what policy is to be implemented.[15]

The conception of justification that provides the core of the ideal of deliberative democracy can be captured in an ideal procedure of political deliberation. In such a procedure participants regard one another as equals; they aim to defend and criticize institutions and programs in terms of considerations that others have reason to accept, given the fact of reasonable pluralism and the assumption that those others are reasonable; and they are prepared to cooperate in accordance with the results of such discussion, treating those results as authoritative.

Which considerations count as reasons? A suitable answer will take the form not of a generic account of reasons but of a statement of which considerations count in favor of proposals in a deliberative setting suited to free association among equals, where that setting is assumed to include an acknowledgment of reasonable pluralism. This background is reflected in the kinds of reasons that will be acceptable. In an idealized deliberative setting, it will not do simply to advance reasons that one takes to be true or compelling: such considerations may be rejected by others who are themselves reasonable. One must instead find reasons that are compelling to others, acknowledging those others as equals, aware that they have alternative reasonable commitments and knowing something about the kinds of commitments that they are likely to have— for example, that they may have moral or religious commitments that im-

---

14. See Cohen, "Deliberation and Democratic Legitimacy," 24.

15. On the idea of an epistemic conception, see Jules Coleman and John Ferejohn, "Democracy and Social Choice," *Ethics* 97, 1 (October 1986): 6–25; and Joshua Cohen, "An Epistemic Conception of Democracy," *Ethics* 97, 1 (October 1986): 26–38.

pose what they take to be overriding obligations. If a consideration does not meet these tests, that will suffice for rejecting it as a reason. If it does, then it counts as an acceptable political reason.

To be sure, the precise characterization of the acceptable reasons, and of their appropriate weight, will vary across views. For that reason, even an ideal deliberative procedure will not, in general, produce consensus. But even if there is disagreement, and the decision is made by majority rule, participants may appeal to considerations that are quite generally recognized as having considerable weight, and as a suitable basis for collective choice, even among people who disagree about the right result: when participants confine their argument to such reasons, majority support itself will commonly count as reason for accepting the decision as legitimate.

To underscore this point about the importance of background context in the account of acceptable political reasons, I want to highlight a difference between the idea of reasonable acceptance at work here and the idea of reasonable rejection in Scanlon's contractualism.[16] Scanlon characterizes the wrongness of conduct in terms of the idea of a rule that "no one could reasonably reject," and he advances this characterization as part of a general account of the subject matter of morality and the nature of moral motivation. So his account of reasonableness—of reasonable grounds for rejecting principles—is required to work quite generally, even in settings with no ongoing cooperation, institutional ties, or background of equal standing as citizens.

My concern is not with reasons generally, or morality generally, or with political deliberation generally, or with the reasons that are suited to democratic discussion quite generally, but with a view about the implications of democracy given a specific background. And that background constrains what can count as an acceptable reason within a process of deliberation. For if one accepts the democratic process, agreeing that adults are, more or less without exception, to have access to it, then one cannot accept as a reason within that process that some are worth less than others or that the interests of one group are to count for less than those of

16. T. M. Scanlon, "Contractualism and Utilitarianism," in Amartya Sen and Bernard Williams, eds., *Utilitarianism and Beyond* (Cambridge: Cambridge University Press, 1982). The point of contrast in the text is prompted by Scanlon's discussion of the role of maximin reasoning in moral contractualism in *What We Owe to Each Other* (Cambridge, MA: Harvard University Press, 1997), 223–229.

others. And these constraints on reasons will limit the substantive outcomes of the process; they supplement the limits set by the generic idea of a fair procedure of reason giving.

I am not here raising an objection to Scanlon's view. He has a different topic—morality generally, as distinct from democratic legitimacy. Instead, I am urging that this difference in background makes a difference to the kinds of reasons that are suited to the two cases.

To conclude these general remarks about the deliberative view, I want to emphasize that its virtues are allied closely with its conception of binding collective choice, in particular with the role in that conception of the idea of reasons acceptable to others who are governed by those choices and who, themselves, have reasonable views. By requiring reasons acceptable to others, the deliberative view suggests an especially compelling picture of the possible relations among people within a democratic order.

To see the character of those relations, notice first that the deliberative conception offers a more forceful rendering than the aggregative view of the fundamental democratic idea—the idea that decisions about the exercise of state power are collective. It requires that we offer considerations that others (whose conduct will be governed by the decisions) can accept, not simply that we count their interests in deciding what to do, while keeping our fingers crossed that those interests are outweighed. Thus the idea of popular authorization is reflected not only in the processes of decision making but also in the form—and, we will see later, the content—of political reason itself.

This point about the force of the deliberative view and its conception of collective decisions can be stated in terms of the idea of political community. If political community depends on sharing a comprehensive moral or religious view, or a substantive national identity defined in terms of such a view, then reasonable pluralism ruins the possibility of political community. But an alternative conception of political community connects the deliberative view to the value of community. In particular, by requiring justification on terms acceptable to others, deliberative democracy provides for a form of political autonomy: that all who are governed by collective decisions—who are expected to govern their own conduct by those decisions—must find the bases of those decisions acceptable. And in this assurance of political autonomy, deliberative democracy achieves one important element of the ideal of community.

Not because collective decisions crystallize a shared ethical outlook that informs all social life, nor because the collective good takes precedence over the liberties of members, but because the requirement of providing acceptable reasons for the exercise of political power to those who are governed by it—a requirement absent from the aggregative view—expresses the equal membership of all in the sovereign body responsible for authorizing the exercise of that power.

To explain the deliberative ideal more fully, I want now to explore some of its implications: the conditions that need to be met by social and political arrangements that, within the setting of a modern state, institutionalize deliberative justification. What conditions will such arrangements need to satisfy, if they are to sustain the claim that they establish the conditions for free reasoning among equals, and they root the authorization to exercise state power in those conditions?

As a partial answer, I will indicate why deliberative democracy needs to ensure the liberties of the moderns. Then I will connect the deliberative view to conceptions of the common good and political equality.

Three Principles

The aggregative conception of democracy promises the protections required for a fair process of binding collective choice, including protections against discrimination that would undermine the claim of the process to ensure equal consideration. I said earlier that the deliberative view will provide a basis for wider guarantees of basic liberties. It is time to make good on that claim. The main idea is that the deliberative conception requires more than that the interests of others be given equal consideration; it demands, too, that we find politically acceptable reasons—reasons that are acceptable to others, given a background of differences of conscientious conviction. I will call this requirement the "principle of deliberative inclusion."

Consider, for example, the case of religious liberty. Religious views set demands of an especially high order—perhaps transcendent obligations—on their adherents; moreover, if we see these requirements from the believer's point of view, then we cannot think of them as self-imposed. Instead, the requirements are fixed by the content of the convictions, which the agent takes to be true. Reasonable adherents, then, cannot accept as sufficient, reasons in support of a law or a system of policy, considerations that would preclude their compliance with those demands. What, then, about people who do not share those views? (I will describe the issue from the point of view of citizens who have fundamental moral convictions but no religious convictions. Broadly parallel remarks could be made from the standpoint of citizens with different religious convictions.) They might regard all religious views that impose such stringent demands, whatever their content and foundation, as unreasonable. I see no rationale for this view. Or they might treat the religious demands as intense preferences, to be given equal consideration along with other preferences of equal intensity. This reductive response indicates an unwillingness to see the special role of religious convictions from the point of view of the person who has them, an unwillingness to see how the religious view, in virtue of its content, states or implies that the requirements provide especially compelling reasons.

Alternatively, they might take seriously that the demands impose what the adherent reasonably regards as fundamental obligations, accept the requirement of finding reasons that might override these obligations, and acknowledge that such reasons cannot normally be found. The result is religious liberty, understood to include freedom of conscience and worship. It emerges as the product of the demanding character of religious requirements—which are seen, from the point of view of those who are subject to them, as matters of fundamental obligation—together with the requirement of finding reasons that those who are subject to those requirements can reasonably be expected to acknowledge, and the fact that citizens who are not religious have fundamental convictions that they take to impose especially compelling obligations.

Suppose, then, that we prevent others from fulfilling such demands for reasons that they are compelled—by the lights of a view that commands their conviction—to regard as insufficient. This is to deny them standing as equal citizens—full membership in the people whose collective actions authorize the exercise of power. And that, according to the deliberative conception, is a failure of democracy. We have failed to provide a justification for the exercise of power by reference to considerations that all who are subject to that power, and prepared to cooperate on reasonable terms, can accept. There are many ways to exclude individuals and groups from the people, and this surely is one.

These points about religious liberty—essentially about its free exercise—do not say anything about how to handle claims for religious exemption from general obligations with a strong secular justification (including obligations to educate children), or about whether special provision is to be made for specifically religious convictions, as distinct from conscientious ethical convictions with no religious roots.[17] My aim here is not to resolve or even address these issues: any view that recognizes rights of free exercise will need to face those hard questions. My aim is to show only that a deliberative conception of democracy is not barred—by its structure—from acknowledging a fundamental role for rights of religious liberty; indeed, it must provide a place for such rights.[18]

Finally, I emphasize that the point of guarantees of religious liberty, which fall under the requirement of deliberative inclusion, is not narrowly political: it is not to enable people to participate in politics—or to participate without fear—nor is the aim to improve public discussion by adding more diverse voices to it.[19] The idea instead is that abridgment of such liberties would constitute denials to citizens of standing as equal members of sovereign people, by imposing in ways that deny the force of reasons that are, by the lights of their own views, compelling. The reasons for abridgment are unacceptably exclusionary because they are unsuited to the ideal of guiding the exercise of power by a process of reason giving suited to a system of free and equal citizens.

The principle of deliberative inclusion extends naturally from religious liberty to a wide guarantee of expressive liberty.[20] In this respect, it con-

17. On this last point: the key to the case for religious liberty is that the content of a view assigns stringent obligations to a person who holds it. But specifically *religious* content is not essential.

18. This account of religious liberty may seem to rest on the idea of a natural right to religious liberty: to say, in effect, that reasons will count as acceptable in a deliberative process only if they accept this right. If the idea of a natural right to religious liberty simply comes to the claim that there is a right that can be abridged only on pain of illegitimacy, then the deliberative view includes natural rights. But natural rights views have claimed more than this: they offer an explanation of the basis of fundamental rights in human nature, in natural law, or in a prepolitical normative order to which political society must conform. The idea of democratic legitimacy does not depend on that explanation, though it asserts nothing inconsistent with it. It suffices that religious liberties have an explanation tied to the idea of democratic legitimacy. For the purpose of political argument, nothing more needs to be said, positively or negatively.

19. Roberto Unger argues that a system of immunity rights is one component of a democratic order, because "freedom as participation presupposes freedom as immunity." Rejecting the view of "critics of traditional democratic theory," who hold that "participatory opportunities [are] a more than satisfactory substitute for immunity guarantees," Unger sees immunity rights as necessary if a citizen is to have the "safety that encourages him to participate actively and independently in collective decision-making." In *False Necessity* (Cambridge: Cambridge University Press, 1987), 525. I agree with Unger's observations, but I think that a conception of democracy can make a less instrumental place for certain liberties, even when those liberties are not procedural.

20. This discussion draws on my "Freedom of Expression," *Philosophy and Public Affairs* 22, 3 (Summer 1993): 207–263 [reprinted as essay 4 in this collection].

trasts with a more familiar strand of free speech theory that traces the foundations of stringent guarantees of expressive liberty to the need to assure a democratic framework of collective choice but guarantees stringent protection only for political speech.[21] This limit is in tension with the requirement of deliberative inclusion.

Confining stringent protection to political speech seems natural, once one has decided to base rights to free expression on the importance of requiring government accountability and responsiveness to citizens as a body. But as my remarks on the religion case suggest, a deliberative conception of democracy cannot accept such a limit. To be sure, the idea of discussion aimed at reaching reasonable agreement is fundamental to the deliberative view. But it does not follow that the protection of expression is to be confined to speech that contributes to such discussion.

Consider expression that is not part of any process of discussion or persuasion—that is not "intended and received as a contribution to public deliberation about some issue"[22]—but that, nevertheless, reflects what a citizen takes, for quite understandable reasons, to be compelling reasons for expression.[23] This might be so in cases of bearing witness, with no expectation or intention of persuading others, or giving professional advice, with no expectation or intention of shaping broader processes of collective decision making. The deliberative view extends stringent protection to such expression, as a way to acknowledge the weight of those reasons. Given the background of reasonable pluralism, the failure to do so—to give due weight to an expressive interest that does not serve as input to political discussion—will constitute a denial of equal standing, and decisions that fail to ensure those stringent protections are not suitably collective.

The tradition that traces protections of expressive liberty to democratic ideals and then restricts stringent protection to contributions to debate in the public forum conflates the general strategy of providing a case for freedom of expression rooted in the idea of democracy with one ele-

21. See Alexander Meiklejohn, *Free Speech and Its Relation to Self-Government* (New York: Harper and Row, 1948); and Cass R. Sunstein, *Democracy and the Problem of Free Speech* (New York: Free Press, 1993). Also, Robert Bork, "Neutral Principles and Some First Amendment Problems," *Indiana Law Journal* 47, 1 (Fall 1971): 1–35; Ely, *Democracy and Distrust*; and Owen Fiss, "Why the State?" *Harvard Law Review* 100 (1987): 781–794.

22. This is Sunstein's account of political speech, in *Democracy and the Problem of Free Speech*, 130.

23. I do not mean to suggest that stringent protection ought to be confined to expression animated by such compelling reasons. The conventional democratic defense of rights of expression also provides a basis for stringent protection. My aim is to supplement that rationale.

ment of that strategy: the need to protect *inputs* to a process of discussion. But as with religious liberty, so, too, with expressive liberty: the deliberative view also ties protections to acceptable *outcomes* of a deliberative process, outcomes, that is, that can be justified given the requirement on finding reasons acceptable to others under conditions of reasonable pluralism.

Earlier I suggested a connection between the deliberative conception and the value of community. That suggestion may now seem strained in light of the connections between the requirement of acceptable reasons and the protection of nonpolitical liberties. For such liberties are commonly represented as—for better or worse—the solvent of community.

But the deliberative view suggests a need for caution about that representation. Given conditions of reasonable pluralism, the protection of the liberties of the moderns is not a solvent of community. Reasonable pluralism itself may be such a solvent: at least if we define community in terms of a shared comprehensive moral or religious view. But once we assume reasonable pluralism, the protection of the liberties of the moderns turns out to be a necessary, though insufficient, condition for the only plausible form of political community. As the phrase "principle of inclusion" indicates, those liberties express the equal standing of citizens as members of the collective body whose authorization is required for the legitimate exercise of public power.

Turning now to the common good: aggregative views of democracy are conventionally skeptical about conceptions of the common good. Robert Dahl, for example, has suggested that in pluralistic societies, conceptions of the common good are too indeterminate to provide guidance, determinate but unacceptable because they lead us to "appalling results" in conditions that "are by no means improbable,"[24] or determinate and acceptable because purely procedural—because they define the common good as a democratic process.[25] On the deliberative conception, this skeptical outlook is unwarranted, yet it is another reflection of the absence of constraints beyond the requirement of fair aggregation.

A deliberative account of the principle of the common good begins by observing that citizens have good reason to reject a system of public policy that fails to advance their interests at all. (I say a "system of policy" because I do not wish to exclude the possibility that particular laws, regu-

24. *Democracy and Its Critics*, 283.
25. Ibid., 306–308.

lations, or policies that are not attentive to the interests of some citizens may be justifiable as part of an overall package of laws and policies that is.)[26] This minimal constraint—of advancing the interests of each—comes out of the generic conception of a deliberative process and suffices to establish a pareto-efficiency requirement, as one element of a conception of democracy.

But as I have emphasized, the deliberation that plays a role in the conception of deliberative democracy is not simply a matter of reason giving, generically understood. The background conception of citizens as equals sets limits on permissible reasons that can figure within the deliberative process. For suppose one accepts the democratic process of binding collective choice, agreeing that adults are, more or less without exception, to have access to it. One can then reject, as a reason within that process, that some are worth less than others or that the interests of one group are to count for less than the interests of other groups. That constraint on reasons will, in turn, limit the outcomes of the process, adding to the conditions set by the generic idea of deliberation. In particular, it provides a case for a public understanding about the distribution of resources that severs the fates of citizens from the differences of social position, natural endowment, and good fortune that distinguish citizens.

John Rawls's difference principle provides one illustration of such an understanding.[27] Treating equality as a baseline, it requires that inequalities established or sanctioned by state action must work to the maximal advantage of the least advantaged. That baseline is a natural expression of the constraints on reasons that emerge from the background equal standing of citizens: it will not count as a reason for a system of policy that that system benefits the members of a particular group singled out by social class or native talent or any other feature that distinguishes among equal citizens. I do not wish to suggest here that Rawls's difference principle is the uniquely acceptable conception of the common good. But there is an especially strong case for it, both because it accepts the pre-

---

26. The vices of a sales tax, for example, depend on the nature and level of exemptions, the presence (or not) of tax credits, and the nature of the policies that the revenue pays for.

27. See John Rawls, A *Theory of Justice* (Cambridge, MA: Harvard University Press, 1971), 513. For discussion of the connections between the difference principle and an ideal of democracy, see my "Democratic Equality," *Ethics* 99, 4 (July 1989): 736–743. Another view that might be used to illustrate the points in the text is Dworkin's equality of resources. See Ronald Dworkin, "What Is Equality? Part 2: Equality of Resources," *Philosophy and Public Affairs* 10, 4 (Autumn 1981): 283–345.

sumption of equality that emerges from the special constraints on reasons within the deliberative democratic view and because it insists, roughly speaking, that no one be left less well off than anyone needs to be—which is itself a natural expression of the deliberative conception.

I want finally to connect the deliberative view with the rights of participation—the liberties of the ancients. More particularly, I want to show how the deliberative view accommodates a "principle of participation."[28] According to that principle, democratic collective choice—institutionalizing the tie between deliberative justification and the exercise of public power—must ensure equal rights of participation, including rights of voting, association, and political expression, with a strong presumption against restrictions on the content or viewpoint of expression; rights to hold office; a strong presumption in favor of equally weighted votes; and a more general requirement of equal opportunities for effective influence.[29] This last requirement condemns inequalities in opportunities for office holding and political influence that result from the design of arrangements of collective decision making.[30]

Notice first that the mere fact that decisions are to be made in a generically deliberative way does not go very far toward establishing a case for the principle of participation.[31] Perhaps an ideal deliberative procedure is best institutionalized by ensuring well-conducted political debate among

28. See Rawls, A Theory of Justice, 36–37.

29. On the requirement of opportunities for effective influence, see Rawls, Political Liberalism, 327–330. For a discussion of the constitutional dimension of the problem, see Davis v. Bandemer, 478 U.S. 109, 132 (1986). The Court here acknowledges equal protection troubles when the "electoral system is arranged in a manner that will consistently degrade a voter's or group of voters' influence on political process as a whole." Low-Beer distinguishes a requirement of equally weighted votes, at stake in apportionment issues, from equally meaningful votes, at stake in gerrymandering cases. The value threatened by gerrymandering is better understood, I believe, as political influence more generally, not simply as voting strength. See John Low-Beer, "The Constitutional Imperative of Proportional Representation," Yale Law Journal 94, 1 (November 1984): 163–188.

30. Among the concerns that fall under this requirement are vote dilution due to racial and political gerrymandering and unequal influence due to campaign finance arrangements, restrictive rules on ballot access, and regulations of political parties.

31. Historically, the deliberative conception of politics was associated with highly exclusivist forms of parliamentarism. Moreover, according to one influential line of thought, mass democracy destroyed the possibility of deliberative political decision-making. According to Carl Schmitt, "The belief in parliamentarism, in government by discussion, belongs to the intellectual world of liberalism. It does not belong to democracy." Moreover, "the development of modern mass democracy has made argumentative public discussion an empty formality." See The Crisis of Parliamentary Democracy, trans. Ellen Kennedy (Cambridge, MA: MIT Press, 1985), 6, 8.

elites, thus enabling people to make informed choices among them and the views they represent, without any special provision for more substantive political equality, understood as requiring equally weighted votes and equal opportunities for effective influence.[32] How, then, does the deliberative view connect to concerns about participation and political equality?

Three considerations are important.

First, given the principles of deliberative inclusion and of the common good, the deliberative view can avail itself of conventional instrumental reasons in support of equal political rights. Such rights provide the means for protecting other basic rights and for advancing interests in ways that might plausibly promote the common good. Moreover, absent assurances of effective influence, such promotion seems an unlikely result. And it would be especially unlikely if inequalities in effectiveness corresponded to underlying social or economic inequalities in the society.[33]

In making this instrumental case, I may appear to be shifting to a bargaining conception of politics, with assurances of equal power working to ensure a political equilibrium with fair outcomes. But that gets the instrumental rationale and the mechanism wrong. The idea instead is that ensuring that all citizens have effective political rights serves as a reminder that citizens are to be treated as equals in political deliberation and, by reducing inequalities of power, reduces the incentives to shift from deliberative politics to a politics of bargaining.

A second consideration is that many of the conventional, historical justifications for exclusions from or inequalities of political rights—justifications based on race and gender, for example—will not provide acceptable reasons in public deliberation. This consideration will not exclude all reasons for inequality—for example, if votes are of unequal weight because the political system relies, as in the case of the U.S. Senate, on a

32. Thus Beitz's account of political equality connects the interests in recognition and equitable treatment with assurances of equally weighted votes and fair access. What he calls the "deliberative interest," by contrast, simply requires well-conducted political debate. See *Political Equality* (Princeton: Princeton University Press, 1989).

33. See the discussion of the interest in equitable treatment in Beitz, *Political Equality*, 110–114. This interest plays an important role in the apportionment cases decided by the Supreme Court in the early 1960s. "No right is more precious in a free country than that of having a voice in the election of those who make the laws under which, as good citizens, we must live. *Other rights, even the most basic, are illusory if the right to vote is undermined.*" Wesberry v. Sanders, 376 U.S. 1 (1964), cited in Reynolds v. Sims, 377 U.S. 533, 558 (1964). Or again: "Especially since the right to exercise the franchise in a free and unimpaired manner is *preservative of other basic civil and political rights*, any alleged infringement of the right of citizens to vote must be carefully and meticulously scrutinized." Reynolds v. Sims, 562.

scheme of territorial representation, in which districts correspond to political subdivisions. But it establishes a further presumption in favor of the principle of participation.

Finally considerations analogous to those we met with in the case of religion and expression strengthen the case for equal political rights, with assurances of equal opportunities for effective influence. A characteristic feature of moral and religious convictions is that they give us strong reasons for seeking to shape our political-social environment. The comprehensive views underlying those reasons range from Aristotelian views about the central role of civic engagement in a good life, to Rousseauean claims about the connection between personal autonomy and participation, to views, founded on religious convictions, about the commanding personal responsibility to ensure social justice and the corresponding personal sin of failing in that responsibility. It is common ground, however, that citizens have substantial, sometimes compelling, reasons for addressing public affairs. Because they do, the failure to acknowledge the weight of those reasons for the agent and to acknowledge the claims to opportunities for effective influence that emerge from them reflects a failure to endorse the background idea of citizens as equals.

Realizing Democracy

The deliberative conception of democracy captures the role of "undemocratic" as a term of criticism applying to results as well as processes: it provides common roots for the "by the people" and "for the people" aspects of the ideal of democracy. But this incorporation of important substantive requirements into the conception of democracy gives rise to a problem of its own. The concern is that if we offer an interpretation of democracy that treats all good things as ingredient in the idea of democracy—requirements of political equality, considerations of common good, and liberties of the moderns—then we may appear to integrate procedural and substantive values at the cost of practical guidance. What are we to do when the many elements of deliberative democracy come into conflict? Common foundations in deliberative democracy do not provide any insurance against conflict in practice. For example, the liberties mandated by the requirement of deliberative inclusion may conflict with the equal political liberties that fall under the requirement of participation. Why does it help to have all these elements ingredient within the ideal of democracy, given conflicts among them?

The answer is that by underscoring common foundations, we highlight the need to find ways to accommodate the different requirements, so far as accommodation is possible. That may be more often than we are inclined to think, though how often is a function of politics. To make this point less telegraphic, I will sketch some examples. I want to focus the discussion on two cases in which the various requirements arguably conflict and see what might be said about their reconciliation in these cases.

My first case is campaign finance. The central problem arises from a familiar dilemma: on the one hand, restrictions on political expenditures by candidates, individual citizens, and organizations appear to burden expressive liberty, particularly given a background expectation that such expenditures are permissible; arguably, burdens also result from very stringent limits on contributions to political campaigns. Moreover, restrictions on candidate and party expenditures, even when they are accepted as a condition for receiving public financing, may reinforce incumbency advantages, resulting in a less competitive electoral system, less capable of holding elected officials accountable and so of ensuring public authorization of the exercise of power.[34] On the other hand, a regime of unrestricted expenditures is a regime in which political influence—chances to hold office and to affect the outcomes of political contests—reflect economic position, and that means inequalities in opportunities for effective influence.[35]

Thus the familiar conflict about restrictions on political spending. Some reject restrictions, even if they are content-neutral and motivated by a sincere desire to ensure greater equality of political influence. In an infamous sentence in the majority opinion in *Buckley v. Valeo*, the Supreme Court said that "the concept that government may restrict the

34. This may seem puzzling. Making the safe assumption that incumbents have advantages in raising funds, it might seem clear that challengers would fare better under a system of spending restrictions. But, according to one influential line of argument, background incumbency advantages make challengers more dependent on money. Thus a challenger is better off running with $300,000 against an incumbent with $500,000 than running with $250,000 against an incumbent with $250,000. See Gary Jacobson, "Enough Is Too Much: Money and Competition in House Elections," in Kay Lehman Schlozman, ed., *Elections in America* (Boston: Allen and Unwin, 1987), 173–195. For criticisms of Jacobson's view, see Donald Philip Green and Jonathan S. Krasno, "Salvation for the Spendthrift Incumbent: Reestimating the Effects of Campaign Spending in House Elections," *American Journal of Political Science* 32, 4 (November 1988): 884–907.

35. I say a "regime" of unrestricted expenditures because the choice among systems of financing is a choice among alternative schemes of permissions and restrictions, not a choice between regulation and nonregulation.

speech of some elements of our society in order to enhance the relative voice of others is wholly foreign to the First Amendment";[36] as a result, they were unwilling to find any basis beyond concerns about quid pro quo corruption for regulating political spending.[37] Others, concerned to insist on the importance of fair political equality, argue that limits are essential.

The first idea—that it is impermissible to restrict the voice of some in order to enhance the relative voice of others—seems bizarre. My earlier account of the bases of rights of expression and political participation suggested a common foundation for both; so there is no basis for the subordinate role of political equality. Moreover, once we have accepted a presumption in favor of equally weighted votes—one person/one vote— we are already committed to precisely such restrictions and enhancements.[38]

Still, focusing on the permissibility of restrictions may be putting the emphasis in the wrong place. Given the bases of rights of expression in the principles of participation and deliberative inclusion, it would be desirable to promote equality of opportunity for effective influence through less restrictive means than expenditure limits, should such means be available.[39] And the natural route to such reconciliation is to establish a scheme of public financing. The idea of such a system is to rely principally on "floors" rather than "ceilings"—subsidies rather than limits— to remedy violations of the principle of participation.[40] By establishing

36. 424 U.S. 1 (1976), 48–49.

37. *Buckley*, 26–27.

38. See Gray v. Sanders, 372 U.S. 368 (1963); *Wesberry v. Sanders*; and *Reynolds v. Sims*. The tension between the apportionment decisions and *Buckley* is noted in Rawls, *Political Liberalism*, 361; and David A. Strauss, "Corruption, Equality, and Campaign Finance Reform," *Columbia Law Review* 94, 4 (May 1994): 1382–1383. The Court itself has retreated from the *Buckley* position, acknowledging possibilities of corruption involving unfair influence without quid pro quo and the permissibility of regulating expenditures—at least in the case of for-profit corporations—in order to avoid such corruption. See Austin v. Michigan Chamber of Commerce, 494 U.S. 652, 660 (1990).

39. A problem with relying principally on spending restrictions is the capacity of contributors and candidates to maneuver around restrictions. See Frank Sorauf, *Inside Campaign Finance: Myths and Realities* (New Haven: Yale University Press, 1992). Increase the level of public subsidy, and you reduce the incentives to such maneuvering.

40. The United States is one of four OECD countries with contributions limits. All the other political systems rely more substantially than the United States does on public financing; the Scandinavian countries have no contribution or expenditure limits and rely entirely on public funding. See Ellen S. Miller and Joel Rogers, *The World of Campaign Finance* (Madison and Washington, D.C.: Center for a New Democracy and Center for Responsive Politics, 1992).

floors, a suitable scheme of public financing helps to make office holding more widely available; by reducing dependence of parties and candidates on private resources, it assures greater equality of opportunity for influence.[41] The effectiveness of floors in providing such assurance may depend on making the availability of support conditional on accepting spending limits. But limits of this kind may be unnecessary, given a regime with substantial public financing.

Of course a wide range of public financing schemes are possible: support can be provided to candidates or to parties[42] or to individual voters (as citizen vouchers)[43] or, in the case of initiatives and referenda, to nonparty organizations; funds can be made available for electoral activity or for more general party support; and support can be provided in the form of free media access. And in deciding among such schemes, it is important to consider their effects on deliberation as well as opportunities for effective influence. Citizen vouchers are especially promising, I think. But I do not propose to go into such details here. The point is to state the main principles, emphasize the importance of finding some accommodation of them in view of their common basis in the value of democracy, and indicate that the strategy of accommodation is, roughly stated, a strategy of empowerment, not of restriction.

My second case concerns possible tensions between a deliberative politics and the principles of participation and the common good—and the role of a strategy of "associative democracy" in blunting those tensions.[44]

41. For a description of a scheme of public financing animated by concerns about equality and deliberation, see Jamin Raskin and John Bonifaz, "The Constitutional Imperative and Practical Superiority of Democratically Financed Elections," *Columbia Law Review* 94, 4 (May 1994): 1160–1203.

42. For an interesting public financing proposal, built around support for parties that would be distributed by congressional leadership, see Daniel Hays Lowenstein, "The Root of Evil Is Deeply Rooted," *Hofstra Law Review* 18, 2 (Fall 1989): 351–355.

43. On voucher systems, see Bruce Ackerman, "Crediting the Voters: A New Beginning for Campaign Finance," *American Prospect* (Spring 1993); and Edward Foley, "Equal Dollars Per Voters: A Constitutional Principle of Campaign Finance," *Columbia Law Review* 94, 4 (May 1994): 1204–1257.

44. A broadly parallel concern arises in connection with the role of race-conscious measures in drawing lines around electoral districts. Given a background of racial bloc voting, the principle of participation may suggest a need for race-conscious districting to ensure opportunities for effective influence. But race-conscious districting arguably works against deliberative politics. According to Lani Guinier, cumulative voting would address this tension. Like other forms of proportional representation, cumulative voting combines increased chances of effective minority influences with voluntary constituencies that may encourage deliberation. See her "Second Proms and Second Primaries: The Limits of Majority Rule," *Boston Review* 17, 5 (September-October 1992): 32–34; and *The Tyranny of the Majority* (New York: Basic Books, 1994).

The problem here is less straightforward, as is the proposed solution. So I first need to set some background.[45]

Begin, then, with two familiar premises. First, any well-functioning democratic order satisfying the principles of participation and the common good requires a social base. Beyond the world of voters and parties, secondary associations—organized groups intermediate between market and state—are needed both to represent otherwise underrepresented interests (as in the case of trade unions or other independent worker organizations) and to add to public competence in advancing the common good (think of the role played by unions and employer associations in establishing standards on worker training in any well-functioning training system). Representing underrepresented interests helps to ensure political equality; adding to public competence helps to promote the common good.

Second, the right kinds of association do not naturally arise, for the purposes of either addressing problems of underrepresentation or performing more functional tasks: there is, for example, no natural tendency for an emergence of secondary associations to correct for inequalities of political opportunity due to underlying economic inequalities or to ensure the regulatory competence needed to advance the common good.

Now put together the need for a favorable associative environment with the fact that such an environment is not naturally provided. This conjunction suggests a strategy for addressing the associative deficit: a strategy of associative democracy that would use public powers to encourage the development of the right kind of secondary association. For example, where manifest inequalities in political representation exist, the associative strategy recommends promoting the organized representation of presently excluded interests. Where associations have greater competence than public authorities have for advancing the common good, it would recommend encouraging a more direct and formal governance role for groups. So trade unions and employer associations that took on responsibility for the joint development of training curricula, for example, might be encouraged by public grants contingent on their assumption of such responsibilities.

But here we arrive at the tension. In seeking to meet the principles of

45. This section of the essay draws on Joshua Cohen and Joel Rogers, "Solidarity, Democracy, Association," in Wolfgang Streeck, ed., *Staat und Verbaende*, special issue of *Politischen Vierteljahresschrift* (Wiesbaden: Westdeutscher Verlag, 1994), 136–159.

participation and the common good by fostering governance roles for groups, we may heighten the role of group affiliation in defining political identity. And that may encourage a factionalized politics of group bargaining—albeit under more fair conditions—rather than a more deliberative politics.[46]

Standard responses to this problem are to encourage greater insulation of the state from groups or to give up on egalitarian political values because no agent has the capacity to advance them. The idea of associative democracy suggests a different line of response. It begins by rejecting the implicit assumption that solidarities formed outside formal political arenas must be narrowly focused on particular groups, and it proposes some institutional invention guided by that rejection. To explain the bases for rejecting that assumption and the relevant kinds of invention, I will make some very sketchy remarks about the idea of a deliberate use of associations in regulation.

Generally speaking, the idea of a regulatory role for associations reflects a sense of the limited capacity of the state to regulate for the common good. Those limits appear in four kinds of cases:

1. Where government has the competence to set specific regulatory terms, but the objects of regulation are sufficiently numerous, dispersed, or diverse to preclude serious government *monitoring* of compliance. Many workplace regulations—on appropriate wages and hours, compensation, and especially the appropriate organization of work, pertaining for example to occupational health and safety—provide instances of this monitoring problem.

2. Where government has the competence to set general standards of performance, but the objects of regulation are sufficiently diverse or unstable to preclude government specification of the most appropriate *means* of achieving them at particular regulated sites. Much environmental regulation is of this kind.

3. Where government may (or may not) be able to enforce standards once set but cannot set appropriate *ends* itself.[47] Often, an appropriate

---

46. This concern emerges naturally from criticisms of modern pluralism. See, for example, Theodore Lowi, *The End of Liberalism: The Second Republic of the United States*, 2d ed. (New York: Norton, 1979). For discussion of associative democracy as a response to the problem of faction, see Joshua Cohen and Joel Rogers, "Secondary Associations in Democratic Governance," *Politics and Society* 20, 4 (December 1992): 393–472.

47. Or it can set them only in very abstract terms, for example, as requirements of "reasonableness" or "due care."

standard can be determined only by those with local knowledge not readily available to government, or it can be specified only as the outcome or in the context of prolonged cooperation among nongovernment actors. Industry standards on product or process uniformity and performance are often of this kind, as are standards on training. The appropriate norm shifts constantly; the content of the norm derives from cooperation in the process of establishing it.[48]

4. Where problems are substantially the product of multiple causes and are connected with other problems, crossing conventional policy domains and processes. In such cases, the appropriate strategy requires *coordination* across those domains as well as cooperation from private actors within them. Urban poverty, local economic development, and effective social service delivery are among the familiar problems in this class. None can be solved without cooperation across quite different institutions and groups—lending institutions, health care providers, technology diffusers, education and training establishments, housing authorities, community development corporations, neighborhood associations—operating wholly or substantially outside the state itself. These and other parties involved in the problem and its proposed solution, however, typically have distinct, if not competing, agendas and different identities and interests.

To address such problems, the associative approach recommends explicitly relying on the distinctive capacity of associations to gather local information, monitor compliance, and promote cooperation among private actors. When problems are more or less *functionally specific*—corresponding roughly to the first three classes of cases described earlier—associative governance is not uncommon. As a general matter, it is best developed in the areas of workplace regulation and training, and it relies on institutions controlled by the traditional "social partners" of labor and capital. The use of plant committees to enforce occupational safety and health regulations, for example, or groupings of trade unions and employers to facilitate technology diffusion, or employer and union associations to set standards on training, is familiar. The lessons of practice in these areas might be more explicitly generalized to include nontraditional parties.

48. For discussion of the problem of shifting standards as it applies to the more general problem of measures of business performance, see Charles Sabel, "A Measure of Federalism: Assessing Manufacturing Technology Centers," in *Research Policy* 25, 2 (March 1996): 281–307.

As the scope of associative efforts moves beyond functionally specific problems to issues that are decidedly more sprawling and open-ended—as in the urban poverty or regional economic development examples—models are less clear. Here the associative strategy recommends the construction of new arenas for public deliberation that lie outside conventional political arenas[49] and that aim to establish the desired coordination.

Notice, however, that both the inclusion of nontraditional stakeholders and the development of deliberative arenas suggest a new possibility: that of constructing new bases of social solidarity through a process of defining and addressing common concerns. It is one thing for a well-funded union to be asked to participate in the design of training standards of obvious concern to it as well as to the rest of society. It is quite another for a nascent or an underfunded community environmental organization to gain significant resources (and thus greater organizational life) if it assists in designing an environmental early warning system that is expected to take notice of emerging environmental problems before they become unmanageable. In this case, support is tied to public service. Or for a neighborhood association and an economic development corporation in a poor community to receive assistance conditional on their jointly organizing a training program for parents and a child care program for trainees as part of a broader job-training effort: once more, participation and support are tied to a project of public advantage.

The solidarities characteristic of such efforts will be the bonds of people with concerns—say, a concern to address persistent urban poverty—who treat one another as equal partners in addressing those shared concerns.[50] In short, these efforts—which could have very wide scope—have the potential to create new "deliberative arenas" outside formal politics that might work as "schools of deliberative democracy" in a special way. Deliberative arenas established for such coordination bring together people with shared concrete concerns, very different identities, and considerable uncertainty about how to address their common aims. Successful cooperation within them, fostered by the antecedent common concerns of participants, should encourage a willingness to treat others with re-

---

49. Though to the extent that they receive public support, they are to be subject to constitutional constraints, in particular to guarantees of equal protection.

50. This claim depends, of course, on the background assumption of a democratic state protecting basic liberties and ensuring equal protection.

spect as equals, precisely because discussion in these arenas requires fashioning arguments acceptable to those others. Assuming fair conditions of discussion and an expectation that the results of deliberation would regulate subsequent action, the participants would tend to be more other-regarding in their outlook. The structure of discussion, aimed at solving problems rather than pressuring the state for solutions, would encourage people to find terms to which others could agree. And that would plausibly drive argument and proposed action in directions that would respect and advance more general interests. Moreover, pursuing discussion in the context of enduring differences among participants would incline parties to be more reflective in their definition of problems and proposed strategies for solution and would tend to free discussion from the preconceptions that commonly limit the consideration of options within more narrowly defined groups.

If this is right, then a social world in which solidarities are formed in part by reference to such arenas is different from a social world whose associational life is narrower and factionalized. And that means that it may be possible to use the associative strategy to advance the principles of participation and the common good without thereby encouraging particularistic group identities that turn politics from deliberation to bargaining.

Conclusion

The fact of reasonable pluralism does not, I have argued, mandate a procedural account of democracy and collective choice. Conjoined with a deliberative conception of justification, it is compatible with a substantive account of democracy whose substance—captured in principles of deliberative inclusion, the common good, and participation—includes values of equality and liberty. Moreover, such a deliberative conception offers an attractive rendering of the idea of collective choice, tying that idea to a view of political community. Finally, we are not without resources for addressing possible tensions between and among the values of liberty, equality, and community built into the deliberative conception. But whether those resources are exploited is, of course, a matter of politics.

6

DIRECTLY DELIBERATIVE POLYARCHY

with Charles Sabel

1. Introduction

In this essay we defend a form of democracy that we will call "directly deliberative polyarchy." We argue that it is an attractive kind of radical, participatory democracy with problem-solving capacities useful under current conditions and unavailable to representative systems. In directly deliberative polyarchy, collective decisions are made through public deliberation in arenas open to citizens who use public services or who are otherwise regulated by public decisions. But in deciding, those citizens must examine their own choices in the light of the relevant deliberations and experiences of others facing similar problems in comparable jurisdictions or subdivisions of government. Ideally, then, directly deliberative polyarchy combines the advantages of local learning and self-government with the advantages (and discipline) of wider social learning and heightened political accountability that result when the outcomes of many concurrent experiments are pooled to permit public scrutiny of the effectiveness of strategies and leaders.

One starting point for our argument is a commonplace of contemporary political debate: that current economic and political institutions are not solving problems they are supposed to solve, in areas of employment, economic growth, income security, education, training, environmental regulation, poverty, housing, social service delivery, or even basic personal safety. A second point of departure is the intrinsic appeal of collec-

We presented earlier versions of this essay at the University of Lausanne, the European University Institute, and the University of Chicago. We thank participants for instructive comments. We also wish to thank Frank Michelman, Norman Daniels, Michael Dorf, Mark Barenberg, and Sam Bowles for helpful criticisms and suggestions.

tive decision-making that proceeds through direct participation by and reason-giving between and among free and equal citizens. Directly deliberative polyarchy is the natural consequence of both beginnings: desirable both in itself and as a problem-solver. That is what we hope to show, or at least make plausible.

But obstacles lie along both paths. However commonplace the recognition of institutional failures in problem-solving, the conventional categories used to explain those failures and defend strategies of repair obscure important developments that suggest the plausibility of a directly deliberative alternative. Moreover, gestures at radical democracy invite skeptical observations about the "dark side" of localism or the scarcity of evenings. And the force of such observations will only be deepened by adding improbable claims about the problem-solving powers of participatory self-government in vast, heterogeneous societies. To take the chill of manifest implausibility from our project, therefore, we start by discussing the limits of current debate as revealed in the promising developments it overlooks (or misrepresents) and by specifying the criticisms of radical democracy to which we must respond if we are to offer more than a consoling prospect for democrats in hard times.[1]

Consider first the conventional interpretations of institutional failure and the projects of reconstruction associated with them. On one interpretation, these failures reveal the limits of state regulation and suggest possibilities for a more comprehensive commodification of social life that will finally lift the political fetters from the free exchange of individuals. To fulfill this promise, we need only remove the detritus of twentieth-century political failure. And that means constraining government from doing anything wrong by constraining it from doing much at all: by fracturing political power both vertically and horizontally, setting stricter

1. For background on diagnosis and remedies, see Joshua Cohen and Joel Rogers, *Associations and Democracy* (London: Verso, 1995), especially the concluding chapter; Joshua Cohen, "Procedure and Substance in Deliberative Democracy," Seyla Benhabib, ed., *Democracy and Difference: Contesting the Boundaries of the Political* (Princeton: Princeton University Press, 1996), 95–119 [reprinted as essay 5 of this volume]; and Charles Sabel, "Learning by Monitoring: The Institutions of Economic Development," in Neil Smelser and Richard Swedberg, eds., *Handbook of Economic Sociology* (New York and Princeton: Russell Sage and Princeton University Press, 1995). For a companion essay on the constitutional and institutional implications of directly deliberative polyarchy, see Michael Dorf and Charles Sabel, "A Constitution of Democratic Experimentalism," *Columbia Law Review* 98, 2 (1998): 267–473.

constitutional limits on government, and interpreting the rule of law as a law of rigid rules.[2]

A counter-interpretation sees comprehensive commodification as a threat to political arrangements carefully crafted earlier in this century to provide goods collectively that will not be provided individually, protect the weak from the strong, and ensure that our destinies in life are not determined by the vicissitudes of market success. The correlative political project is to protect the increasingly fugitive state from attack and hope that a turn in the political cycle will restore public confidence in collective political action.[3]

Yet a third interpretation condemns the false dichotomy of state and market. Well-functioning markets and well-ordered political institutions can, it observes, be mutually reinforcing. Both, however, require prior bonds of trust that can be undermined, but not created or sustained, by self-interested market exchange or selfishly exercised political influence. Those bonds depend, rather, on protecting family, church, and voluntary association—the pre-contractual, pre-political background responsible for accumulating the social capital we need to preserve our economic and political artifice.[4] But because such social solidarities are understood as anterior to both economy and state—preconditions for the proper functioning of both (on any conception of such proper functioning)—the implications of such rebuilding for economic or political institutions are entirely indeterminate.

We are skeptical about these contending diagnoses and remedies. A

2. See Friedrich Hayek, *The Constitution of Liberty* (Chicago: University of Chicago Press, 1960); James Buchanan, *The Limits of Liberty* (Chicago: University of Chicago Press, 1975); Antonin Scalia, "The Rule of Law Is a Law of Rules," *University of Chicago Law Review* 56, 4 (Fall 1989): 1175–1188; William Riker, *Liberalism Against Populism* (San Francisco: Freeman, 1982); William Riker and Barry Weingast, "Constitutional Regulation of Legislative Choice: The Political Consequences of Judicial Deference to Legislatures," *Virginia Law Review* 72, 2 (1988): 373–401.

3. See Robert Kuttner, *Everything for Sale: The Virtues and Limits of Markets* (New York: Knopf, 1997).

4. See Robert Putnam, *Democracy and the Civic Community: Tradition and Change in an Italian Experiment* (Princeton: Princeton University Press, 1992); idem, "Bowling Alone: Democracy in America at the End of the Twentieth Century," *Journal of Democracy* 1 (1995): 35–50. Michael Sandel's remarks on a new public philosophy mix the sociological anxiety characteristic of much communitarianism with the concerns about the political economy of citizenship that are closer to our own focus on new arrangements of democratic governance: see Michael Sandel, *Democracy's Discontent: America in Search of a Public Philosophy* (Cambridge, MA: Harvard University Press, 1995), 324–328.

number of emergent solutions to problems as varied as public safety and public education seem not to result from either a shift in the balance between "state" and "market" forms of coordination or a shift in the balance between these taken together and civil society. Instead of the state's retreat, or the market's resurgence, or even the transfer of functions from government to non-governmental organizations, secondary associations, civil society more broadly, or some other third something alongside state and market, these phenomena suggest a set of changes that disrupts those categories, the social-political boundaries they express, and the associated idea that an effective polity is one that balances responsibilities optimally among the arrangements that fall within those boundaries.

Consider, for example, community policing: a strategy for enhancing public security that features a return of police officers to particular beats, regular discussions between them and organized bodies in the communities they are policing, and regular coordination between those bodies and the agencies providing other services that bear on controlling crime.[5] Or consider forms of school decentralization that—while shrinking school size and permitting parents to choose schools—replace close controls by central bureaucracies with governance mechanisms in which teachers and parents play a central role. Or arrangements for local and regional economic development, which include strong components of training and service provision, and whose governance includes local community interests, service providers, representatives of more encompassing organizations, as well as local representatives of regional or national government. Or, closely related to these arrangements, consider firm-supplier relations that transcend episodic exchange to establish long-term collaboration coordinated through regular discussions, disciplined by reference to officially recognized standards—standards that commonly emerge in regular discussions between and among groups of firms and suppliers

---

5. The Chicago experiment in community policing—the Chicago Alternative Policing Strategy (CAPS)—involves assignments of police officers to single beats (30 square block areas) for an entire year; neighborhood-based organizations called "problem-solving groups" that work in partnership with police in each beat; and open meetings with community and police each month. The emphasis on community participation distinguishes the Chicago scheme from other strategies that share the label "community policing." See Archon Fung, *Empowered Participation* (Princeton: Princeton University Press, 2004).

and that may include public research, technical assistance, or training facilities as well.[6]

These new arrangements suggest troubles for the standard categories of analysis and remedy. The arrangements are not conventionally public because, in solving problems, they operate autonomously from the dictates of legislatures or public agencies; they are not conventionally private in that they do exercise problem-solving powers and their governance works through discussion among citizens rather than assignment of ownership rights. At the same time, they do not presuppose a successful, densely organized, trust-inspiring network of associations. Indeed, they often emerge precisely against a background of associative distress. Nor are these new arrangements mere intellectual curiosities. They are attractive because they appear to foster two fundamental democratic values—deliberation and direct citizen participation—while potentially offering advantages as problem-solvers that programs conceived within the limits of conventional representative democracies do not. Indeed, if the same properties made them both democratically and pragmatically attractive, we would have a compelling case for the novel form of public governance that we call *directly deliberative polyarchy.*

Because these new governance arrangements resonate so strongly with the (often implicit) programmatic suggestions associated with radical democratic criticisms of the modern state, a straightforward and appealing generalization of them seems at hand. Congenitally hostile to the market inequalities and economic subordination, but always suspicious of an overweening state as the best defense against them, radical democracy emphasized the deficiencies of centralized power, the virtues of decentralization, the expressive and instrumental values of participation, and the values of citizen discussion both as an intrinsically attractive form of politics and as a good method of problem-solving.[7]

But evoking the core features of the radical democratic tradition—its emphasis on direct participation and deliberation—immediately suggests three lines of criticism. First, that in a large-scale political system, wide-

6. For discussion, see Charles Sabel, *Local Development in Ireland: Partnership, Innovation, and Social Justice* (OECD, 1996); idem, "Milwaukee Jobs Initiative Consortia Employment Project Description," (unpublished, on file with author, 1996).

7. See, for example, Hannah Arendt, *On Revolution* (New York: Penguin, 1973); Jürgen Habermas, *Between Facts and Norms,* trans. William Rehg (Cambridge, MA: MIT Press, 1996); we discuss our differences with Habermas and Arendt in section 5.

spread participation in decision-making is organizationally or administratively impossible, so the ideal of radical democracy is vacuous. Second, if participation could be ensured, the mutual reason-giving that constitutes deliberation depends on a higher degree of homogeneity among citizens than can reasonably be assumed in a large-scale, pluralistic democracy. And third, direct decision-making requires a localism incompatible with the constitutional safeguards needed to ensure equal treatment for citizens.

Here, the threads of our argument come together: guided by the experience of emerging problem-solving institutions and mindful of the values associated with radical democracy, our aim is to sketch the alternative social-political world of directly deliberative polyarchy in sufficient detail to meet these objections. We start (section 2) by presenting an account of the ideal of democracy and explaining why the properties of directness and deliberativeness make highly participatory forms of direct democracy especially compelling realizations of that ideal. To be sure, the classical institutions of direct, assembly democracy are unavailable as realizations of directness and deliberativeness. But by separating those properties from their familiar institutional expressions, we suggest that they might still guide current institutional reform. In section 3, we describe the current practical impasse in problem-solving and propose that the roots of that impasse lie in part in the mismatch between current arrangements of constitutional democracy and fundamental properties of unsolved problems. In section 4, we describe the new form of state that would result from the generalization of deliberative problem-solving arrangements and foster their successful operation. We conclude with some reflections on the idea of the public, indicating contrasts with the radical-democratic views of Habermas and Arendt.

Our approach is conjectural. We are guided by political values, a view of current failures, and some hunches about promising developments. But our aim is neither to articulate a set of normative principles and deduce institutional conclusions from them nor to predict the course of current institutional evolution. Still less is it to explain fully the causes of the failures of representative democracy or the origins of the new arrangements. Instead, we take the very existence of these arrangements as a sign of the insufficiency of theories that explain what democracy can do and try to imagine what democracy could be from the vantage point of the possibilities suggested by their presence.

2. What's Good about Democracy?

Democracy is a political ideal that applies in the first instance to arrangements for making binding collective decisions.[8] Generally speaking, such arrangements are democratic just in case they ensure that the authorization to exercise public power—and that exercise itself—arises from collective decisions by the citizens over whom that power is exercised.

The ideal of democracy comes in several variants, which are associated with different interpretations of "authorization" and "collective decision." Our principal aim in this section is to sketch and defend a directly deliberative interpretation of the democratic ideal. We begin by exploring the virtues associated with democracy quite generally, and we then consider the special advantages of directly deliberative democracy, as against representative-aggregative democracy. We conclude by returning to the conventional criticisms of directly deliberative democracy, thus setting the stage for our later efforts to describe a form of radical democracy that can answer these criticisms.

Before pursuing these competing interpretations, however, we want to clarify the relationship between those democratic ideals and the conventional institutions of electoral democracy. Following Robert Dahl, we use the term "polyarchy" to cover political systems in which virtually all adults have rights of suffrage, political expression, association, and officeholding, as well as access to diverse sources of information; in which elected officials control public policy, and citizens choose those officials through free and fair elections.[9] Continuing to follow Dahl (and subsequent writers), we note that polyarchy has considerable value, both for its intrinsic fairness and its instrumental success in keeping the peace and protecting certain basic rights. It is not of value simply because it establishes the conditions required for achieving some greater ideal. Furthermore, under the modern circumstances of political scale and social pluralism, polyarchal institutions are necessary for realizing fully an ideal of democracy, however that ideal is specified. Though polyarchies can be more or less democratic, making them more so does not require ne-

---

8. The ideal of democracy also has considerable force for organizations whose collective decisions are not binding. But the rationale for democratic decision-making is most compelling in the case of binding collective choices: that is, when members of the collectivity are expected to regulate their own conduct in accordance with its decisions.

9. Robert Dahl, *Democracy and Its Critics* (New Haven: Yale University Press, 1989), 221–222.

gating, sublating, or otherwise transcending the political institutions definitive of polyarchy. This said, however, polyarchy is insufficient for full democracy—or full political equality—because, for example, it is compatible with inequalities in opportunities for effective political influence that would be condemned by any plausible statement of the ideal.

Building on these three considerations, then, we use the term "directly deliberative polyarchy" for a form of polyarchy distinguished by the presence of a substantial degree of directly deliberative problem-solving. (As we will see later, this presence transforms the role and the function of conventional polyarchal institutions.) And we use the term "directly deliberative democracy" for our account of the democratic ideal: fully democratic arrangements that feature a substantial degree of directly deliberative problem-solving. Directly deliberative polyarchies, then, more closely approximate the ideal of directly deliberative democracy than existing forms of polyarchy do, but—like polyarchies *sans phrase*—need not have the entire range of qualities necessary for full democracy.

THREE VIRTUES

Consider an ideal society whose members are free and equal and treat one another as such. Very roughly, they are equal in that they all have, to a minimally sufficient degree, a set of capacities whose possession makes persons free.[10] These freedom-making capacities include: the capacity to regulate their conduct by reference to a conception of justice and a set of ends with which they identify, to use practical reason to bring both to bear on individual and collective conduct, to reflect on the plausibility of both, and to adjust their aims to the requirements of justice. Though actual societies do not fully achieve this social ideal, modern democracies impute these capacities to their citizens and arguably aspire to the ideal. Assume now that the association needs to make binding collective decisions. Why should a free association of equals make such decisions democratically?[11]

10. Locke says that people are naturally equal in that all have the natural right to freedom. See *Second Treatise* (Cambridge: Cambridge University Press, 1988), §54. For related discussion, see John Rawls, *Political Liberalism* (New York: Columbia University Press, 1993), lectures 1 (sec. 5) and 2; Charles Beitz, *Political Equality* (Princeton: Princeton University Press, 1989), chap. 5.

11. In addressing the question for this case, we do not mean to suggest that democracy is important only when these background assumptions are in place, but that the answer for different cases will vary and that important considerations are likely to get lost if we confine attention to answering the more general question.

Recall that democracies, abstractly conceived, are systems in which decisions to exercise collective power are made in institutions that treat those subject to such power as the ultimate authors. To that end, democracies need at least to satisfy the conditions of polyarchy—to protect constitutive liberties of participation, association, and political expression, establish direct or indirect electoral control of public policy, and ensure adequate information. That said, the reasons for democratic authorization divide naturally into goods intrinsic to the process and goods that arguably result from it.[12]

First, democratic arrangements have the intrinsic virtue of treating those who are subject to binding collective decisions with respect, as free and equal: "The person of the humblest citizen is as sacred and inviolable as that of the first magistrate."[13] Thus, the judgments of citizens, who are expected to govern their conduct in accordance with collective decisions, are treated by the processes of collective decision as equally authoritative. Though decisions will rarely, if ever, be unanimous, no one's judgment of the proper rules of cooperation is treated as having greater weight. Given the background conception of citizens as free and equal, any assignment of differential weights to the views of different citizens is a form of disrespect (unless it can be provided with a suitable justification).[14] Furthermore, the protection of the basic expressive and associative liberties establishes favorable conditions for reflecting on the plausibility of alternative views about justice and on which ends are worth pursuing. And the assurance of adequate and diverse information contributes to the exercise of practical reason, in working out the implications of conceptions of justice and of suitable ends.

Second, democratic arrangements are instrumentally important: they help protect the basic rights of citizens and advance their interests, as de-

---

12. A common rationale for democracy is that it treats people as equals by giving equal consideration to their interests. Dahl, *Democracy and Its Critics*; Thomas Christiano, *The Rule of the Many* (Denver: Westview, 1996). We avoid this rationale because the idea of equal consideration of interests is normatively implausible in as much as it may conflict with the equal consideration owed to persons.

13. Rousseau, *Social Contract*, trans. Victor Gourevitch (Cambridge: Cambridge University Press, 1997), Book 3, chap. 14.

14. In the case of the U.S. Senate, for example, votes are of unequal weight because the political system relies on a scheme of territorial representation in which districts (in this case states) correspond to political subdivisions: in this case, the inequality seems less objectionable because it can be provided with a rationale that does not offend against the requirement of treating members as equals.

fined by the ends and projects with which they identify. Thus, democracies provide mechanisms for regular, popular authorization of exercises of public power: in a representative democracy that means (at a minimum) regular elections of legislators; in a direct democracy it means regular opportunities to review past decisions and evaluate the performance of officials responsible for implementing those decisions. Such regular renewal serves to make the exercise of collective power accountable to the governed in the formal sense that the governed can impose sanctions of removal from office on government. More fundamentally, an accountable system for the exercise of collective power, in which citizens are treated as equals, arguably helps ensure peaceful transitions of power, restrain the exercise of power by protecting majorities from minority rule, avoid at least some egregious violations of minority rights, and foster greater responsiveness of government to the governed.[15]

Both arguments—intrinsic and instrumental—are strengthened when we consider, third, the educative aspects of democracy. Thus, by establishing the position of equal citizen, with associated entitlements to participate in determining the terms of association, democratic arrangements not only respect but also provide instruction in fundamental political values—in particular, the value of equality itself and the conception of citizens as free and equal. By participating, citizens acquire political ideas in the light of which democracy itself is justified. Furthermore, by opening debate to all and addressing problems through public discussion—rather than through market exchange or bureaucratic command—democracy not only assumes adequate information but also helps ensure it. Democracy provides a way to pool dispersed information relevant to problem-solving and to explore the range of possible solutions to practical problems: in short, a framework for collective learning. As Rawls puts it, within a democracy: "Discussion is a way of combining information and enlarging the range of arguments. At least in the

---

15. Such instrumental considerations played an important role in the U.S. Supreme Court's classic apportionment decisions, which urged that the same instrumental reasons that support universal political rights also support equally weighted votes. Thus, in *Wesberry v. Sanders*: "No right is more precious in a free country than that of having a voice in the election of those who make the laws under which, as good citizens, we must live. Other rights, even the most basic, are illusory if the right to vote is undermined." Cited in Reynolds v. Sims, 377 U.S. 533, 558. Or in *Reynolds v. Sims* itself: "Especially since the right to exercise the franchise in a free and unimpaired manner is preservative of other basic civil and political rights, any alleged infringement of the right of citizens to vote must be carefully and meticulously scrutinized." *Reynolds*, 562.

course of time, the effects of common deliberation seem bound to improve matters."[16]

TWO DIMENSIONS OF DEMOCRACY

We said that political institutions are democratic just in case they link the authorization to exercise public power—and that exercise itself—to collective decisions of citizens, understood as free and equal. There are, of course, very different ways to interpret this abstract ideal of democracy, corresponding to different interpretations of the notions of *collective* and *authorization*.

Democratic collective decision-making can be either aggregative or deliberative, depending on how we interpret the requirement that collective decisions treat citizens *as equals*. Understood aggregatively, a democratic decision is collective just in case the procedure gives equal consideration to the interests of each person: it treats people as equals *by* giving their interests equal weight in making a binding decision. Conventional rationales for majority-rule as a method of collective decision rest on the idea that it gives direct expression to this requirement of equal consideration.[17]

Understood deliberatively, democratic decisions are collective just in case they proceed on the basis of free public reasoning among equals: interests unsupported by considerations that convince others carry no weight. Put otherwise, in deliberative decision-making, decisions are to be supported by reasons acceptable to others in the polity of decision-makers; the mere fact that decisions are supported by a majority of citizens, deciding on the basis of their interests, does not suffice to show that the decisions are democratically authorized. On the deliberative interpretation, then, democracy is a framework of social and institutional conditions that both facilitates free discussion among equal citizens by providing favorable conditions for expression, association, and discussion and ties the authorization to exercise public power—and the exercise itself—to such discussion, by establishing a framework ensuring the responsiveness and accountability of political power to it.

To be sure, discussion may not—and often does not—issue in agreement. So even in a deliberative democracy, collective decisions must of-

---

16. John Rawls, A *Theory of Justice* (Cambridge, MA: Harvard University Press, 1971), 359.

17. According to an epistemic conception of majority rule, the rationale is that decisions supported by a majority are more likely to be right, not simply that the process visibly assigns equal weight to the interests of each.

ten be made through voting, under some form of majority rule. But it may be argued that if collective decision-making concludes in a vote, then participants—anticipating that final stage—will not have any incentive to deliberate earlier on and instead will simply seek allies for their position. Though we cannot resolve the issue here, this outcome hardly seems necessary. Even if all parties know that, at the end of the day, heads may be counted, they still may accept the importance of finding considerations that others acknowledge as reasons: they only need accept that something other than a resolution that advances their antecedent interests matters to them. They may, for example, believe that reason-giving is an important expression of respect or that deliberation sometimes yields solutions that could not have been achieved if discussion were purely strategic. If they do, they will be willing to deliberate in the stages leading up to the vote. In short, the objection supposes that, once voting is in prospect, interaction must turn strategic. But this view is no more plausible than the claim that moral advantages and possible mutual gains from deliberation eliminate all strategic maneuvering.

As to authorization to make collective decisions, we have again two distinct understandings: in representative democracy, popular authorization proceeds through a choice by citizens of representatives who decide on content of public decisions. Citizens vote as individuals for persons who will participate in making binding collective choices in an aggregative or a deliberative legislature. In direct democracy, citizens authorize public action by deciding on the substance of public policy. Again, those direct decisions can be made either aggregatively, as some argue is true in referenda, because of their yes/no structure,[18] or deliberatively, as in an idealized town meeting, in which decisions on policy take place after debate on the merits. The essential distinction between direct and representative is not the level of participation but the topic on the agenda: direct democracy requires decisions on substance, whereas representative democracy involves choices on legislators, who decide on substance.[19]

18. See Max Weber, "Parliament and Government in a Reconstructed Germany," in *Economy and Society*, vol. 3, ed. Guenther Roth and Claus Wittich (New York: Bedminster, 1968), p. 1455; Derek Bell, "The Referendum: Democracy's Barrier to Racial Equality," *Washington Law Review* 54, 1 (1978): 1–29; Yannis Papadopolous, "A Framework for Analysis of Functions and Dysfunctions of Direct Democracy: Top-Down and Bottom-Up Perspectives," *Politics and Society* 23, 4 (1995): 421–448.

19. Complexities arise when we think of systems with strong parties with well-defined policy positions and ways of disciplining members who depart from those positions. Such systems have a direct aspect. But we abstract from these subtleties here.

DELIBERATIVE-DIRECT

Forms of democracy that are deliberative-direct seem especially attractive in view of the three reasons for endorsing a democracy as a way to make binding collective decisions. While those reasons support democracy generally, they provide especially strong support for a deliberative-direct democracy.

Consider, for example, the idea that democratic procedures are desirable because they treat citizens with respect, as free and equal. The deliberative conception offers a particularly forceful rendering of this condition. Suppose all participants support their views with considerations that others regard as relevant and appropriate. Nevertheless, because of differences in views about the weight of those considerations, there is disagreement about the right outcome. Still, the minority can scarcely contest the fundamental legitimacy of the decision. After all, not only the procedures but also the arguments themselves treat each as well as one can reasonably demand.[20] Thus the deliberative conception of collective decision extends the idea of treating people with respect from rights and procedures to justifications themselves. A similarly strong case can be made for directly deliberative decision-making on the basis of the arguments about instrumental benefits and learning. But we postpone consideration of these until we have said more about the operations of directly deliberative polyarchy.

Despite these virtues as an expression of democratic values, radical democracy—a system with high degrees of directness and deliberativeness—is subject, we noted earlier, to a series of closely related criticisms: that under modern conditions of political scale, it is not feasible, except as local pockets of direct citizen engagement; that even within those pockets—and certainly as scale increases—cultural heterogeneity thwarts the mutual reason-giving that defines public deliberation; and that the localism characteristic of radical-democratic schemes leaves local minorities at the mercy of their locality.

The starting point of these criticisms is the identification of radical democracy with direct assembly democracy and especially with the Greek *polis* as both the ideal and the practical inspiration for modern critics of centralized, representative democracy. In a direct assembly democracy, legislative power—and the power to review conduct of all officials—is

---

20. It is not reasonable to demand to win: assuming disagreement, any decision will be opposed by some people.

vested in a body that all citizens may attend. In the case of the Athenian *ecclesia*, that often meant meetings of five thousand (with women and slaves excluded from participation). In the polis, the unit of collective decision-making was small, and the members were homogeneous in general outlook and sufficiently disconnected from banausic activities (because sufficiently secure in their social and economic positions) to devote their passions and energies to common affairs. If the combination of directness and deliberativeness can be achieved only under these conditions, then the conventional criticisms of radical democracy are individually damaging and collectively overwhelming.

To vindicate the virtues of deliberativeness and directness, then, we must distinguish these values themselves from familiar ways of institutionalizing them—for example, citizen assemblies, or such modern analogies as workers' councils or economic parliaments—and then describe a modern set of arrangements of collective decision-making suited to these values and to modern conditions of scale and heterogeneity. To guide this elaboration of a workable direct and deliberative alternative to assembly democracy, we need first to establish criteria for "workable" democratic solutions by characterizing the problems democracies now face and the limits of representative, aggregative arrangements in addressing them.

3. Diagnosis of Current Problems

Conventional explanations of current institutional failure range, we said earlier, from too much state (and associated rent-seeking) to too much market (private control of investment under conditions of globalization) to too many civic deficits (decline of trust-building associations). And we indicated, too, that emergent problem-solving institutions suggest the limits of those explanations. But what could an alternative be?

Our own proposal is that existing forms of constitutional democracy— and the associated boundaries between state, market, and civil society that inspire the limited categories of current debate—block democratic and effective strategies of problem-solving in the current environment: where existing political institutions favor uniform solutions throughout a territory, the problems require locally specific ones; moreover, the environment is volatile, so the terms of those local solutions are themselves unstable. In short, because of high diversity and volatility, important problem-solving possibilities are not being exploited by existing institutions. To the extent that this is so—to be sure, it is not the whole story—

the problems of modern democracy arise quite apart from the clash of antagonistic interests or any guileful exploitation by individuals of block-ages created by constitutional arrangements: they are (in the game-theo-retic sense) problems of failed coordination, in which mutual gains are available but different parties are unable to come to terms in a way that captures those gains. If the right arrangements of collective choice were in place, the parties could come to terms on one of the available alterna-tives. In contrast, recognition of the mismatch between solutions and available structures of decision-making leads, by itself, to paralysis, as it reasonably suggests that it is better to do nothing than to do something that will almost certainly fail.

Put another way, we assume that for some substantial range of current problems, citizens agree sufficiently about the urgency of the problems and the broad desiderata on solutions that, had they the means to trans-late this general agreement into a more concrete, practical program, would improve their common situation and would possibly result in the discovery of further arenas of cooperation. This is not to make the fool-ish claim that everyone endorses the same ranking of solutions, only that everyone prefers a wide range of alternatives to the status quo. No sur-prise, then, that the new problem-solving institutions have begun to emerge just in those areas—public safety, public education, economic restructuring—where established institutions have most conspicuously broken down and the problems are agreed to be urgent. For breakdown opens space for new initiatives, and where, as we are assuming, actors are urgently motivated to look for a solution and prefer many alternatives to the status quo, that space is likely to be occupied.

But even in thus qualifying the extent of agreement, we may still be ac-cused of an extravagant confidence in consensus. In its stronger form, this accusation rejects the idea of deliberative problem-solving altogether by criticizing the assumptions about consensus on which it depends. It asserts that the fundamental problem of politics is the pervasiveness of deep disagreement, the consequent fragility of political order, and the immanence of its disintegration into violence. So any assumptions about agreement—and not simply the set just noted—miss the point.[21] The criticism is right in recognizing disastrous possibilities but wrong in the

21. See, for example, Carl Schmitt, *The Concept of the Political* (Chicago: University of Chi-cago Press, 1995); Adam Przeworski, "Minimalist Conception of Democracy: A Defense," in *Democracy's Value*, ed. Ian Shapiro and Casiano Hacker-Cordón (Cambridge: Cambridge University Press, 1999), 23–55.

lessons it draws from them. Assume the setting of a consolidated poly-archy: one in which there is no organized alternative to democracy, in which democracy is "the only game in town."[22] And assume—as is sug-gested by such consolidation—that citizens, who know that they disagree on moral, religious, and political issues, nevertheless accept the impor-tance of conducting political argument on common ground. Those as-sumptions suffice to make deliberative politics possible.

In its more limited form, the objection is straightforwardly empirical: we assert, and the critic denies, that there is currently substantial agree-ment on a list of public problems and on the desiderata to their solution. We point to the diffusion of new problem-solving arrangements; the critic points to congressional gridlock; we think our diagnosis explains the grid-lock; the critic thinks that the new arrangements are too marginal to re-quire explanation. We propose not to adjudicate this disagreement here but to reconfirm that our proposal, like all others, has its empirical com-mitments.

To return to the diagnosis: at the root of this mismatch between prob-lems and problem-solving institutions is, we assume further, a fundamen-tal and familiar characteristic of contemporary political problems: diver-sity. A commonplace of discussion of regulation and administration is that rules and services aimed at achieving any broad end—protection of the environment or training for economic activity—must be tailored to (constantly changing) local circumstances to be effective. Moreover, be-cause the pursuit of such ends often requires the integration of many means—a regime of incentives and fines may have to be combined with monitoring and clean-up programs as well as with research and develop-ment efforts to achieve acceptable levels of environmental protection—local combination of locally specific solutions are required as well.

But fundamental considerations of democracy apparently favor, if they do not mandate, uniform solutions. Thus a basic democratic idea is that citizens are to be treated as equals, which might be thought to imply that state regulations are to be cast in the form of general rules. Why con-strain the free play of interest through aggregation or deliberation only to

22. On the idea of consolidation, see Alfred Stepan and Juan Linz, "Toward Consolidated Democracies," *Journal of Democracy* 7, 2 (1996): 14–33. For doubts about the importance of consolidation, see Adam Przeworski, "What Makes Democracies Endure?," *Journal of Democ-racy* 7, 1 (1996): 39–55. But note that Przeworski and others do not consider the importance of consolidation, as characterized in the text.

allow the powerful to favor themselves by writing laws that accord them benefits directly? It might be thought, too, to imply a requirement of precision or a lack of ambiguity in those regulations. For why prevent directly self-serving regulations, but then permit indirect self-service through exploiting vagueness at the stage of interpretation and application of laws?

Other, related devices of constitutional democracy have the same effects. Thus, a basic institutional expression of the requirement of the rule of law—in particular, of the ban on self-serving interpretation—is the separation of powers, understood as the requirement that rule-making authority be vested in a body that includes representatives of diverse particular interests but that does not itself apply the rules it makes to individual cases. The conventional rationale for this separation of rule-making and rule-applying is that it permits diverse interests to be incorporated into rules, even as it decreases incentives for rule-makers to design rules that favor themselves (either as representatives or as officials). But in obstructing corruption, the separation of powers so understood reinforces the substantive uniformity requirement and thereby tightens the constraint on tailoring solutions to special circumstances.

Hence a familiar and inconclusive tug of war: when problems need to be solved, pressure mounts to violate the constitutional constraints of the rule of law and the separation of powers—to overturn the Tudor polity—precisely because of the restrictions these impose on problem-solving. Then, as the dangers of violations mount, as politics threatens to degenerate into a patchwork of particularistic deals and local privileges, as constitutional democracy approximates pre-Tudor feudalism—pressure mounts to reimpose a system of strict rules. Thus, in the United States, the standard criticism leveled against administrative agencies—created precisely to adopt law to particular circumstances—is that they pave the road back to serfdom. And standard proposals for reform—ranging from Lowi's juridical democracy and Sunstein's post-New Deal constitutionalism to Hayek's neo-liberal constitutionalism—would redeploy rule-making authority to legislatures in order to ensure such substantive uniformity, thus reimposing the very constraints that had prompted earlier constitutional reform.[23]

This to and fro cannot be resolved simply by cutting the Gordian

23. For discussion of these three views, see Cohen and Rogers, *Associations and Democracy*.

knot of constitutional constraint. Absent the most stringent civic sensibilities, a constitutionally unconstrained representative system—in which decisions by a representative body suffice to make the regulation legitimate, irrespective of concerns about substantive uniformity—produces the Hayekian nightmare: a pure bargaining democracy, in which legislative decision-making is under no pressure to be deliberative and hence under no pressure to explore improved solutions or even to meet minimal conditions of coherence and efficiency. Outcomes will simply reflect the balance of political forces, with no obligation to consider how legislative choices will cumulatively solve the problem.[24] (According to public choice views, this is all that democracy is, or could be. But this supposes, improbably, that the real purpose of democracy is to achieve political equilibrium, not to solve problems or establish the legitimacy of solutions.)

Nor can the mismatch of institutions and problems produced by current understandings of the rule of law and the separation of powers be finessed by a strategy of federalist decentralization that would permit local tailoring within a regime of strict rules. Federalism, generically conceived, is a system with multiple centers of decision-making, including central and local decision-makers and separate spheres of responsibility for different units. In such a system, problems requiring local solutions could be delegated to local centers of decision-making, while problems admitting general solutions could be addressed centrally. If log-rolling was Hayek's nightmare of democracy, a radical version of federalism, in which the center did little more than register the generalizable results of local units, was his democratic *arcadia*.

But federalism, thus understood, creates troubles of its own, precisely because it does not require the units of decision-making to communicate and pool their information. To underscore the force of this point, we extend our original characterization of the problem situation of modern democracies beyond the assertion that uniform solutions are not optimal to the further proposition that particular locations, operating in isolation, lack the capacity to explore the full range of possible solutions. For this reason, optimal problem-solving requires a scheme with local problem-solvers who, through institutionalized discussion, learn from the successes and the failures of problem-solving efforts in locales like their own.

24. Moreover, if legislators can secure their own re-election by servicing constituents, then the limits on problem-solving are not a large source of electoral instability.

Through such exchanges, each problem-solving unit would be better situated to capture the benefits of all relevant, locally tailored solutions, thus transcending the limits of localism without paying the price of uniformity such transcendence would otherwise require.

Federalism as currently understood does not foster such mutual learning from local experience; the scheme of a "directly deliberative polyarchy" does. Indeed, abstractly conceived, it simply marries the virtues of deliberation and directness to an ideal of learning by explicitly pooling experiences drawn from separate experiments. Whether this marriage can be made to work is our next subject.

4. Radical Democracy, after the Welfare State

The intuitive idea of directly deliberative polyarchy is to foster democracy in its most attractive—direct and deliberative—form and thereby increase our collective capacity to address unsolved social problems by overcoming current dilemmas of coordination. As background, to remind, we assume that the institutions of polyarchy are in place. More immediately, we assume that citizens—despite conflicts of interest and political outlook—agree very broadly on priorities and goals but cannot translate this preliminary agreement into solutions fitted to the diversity and volatility of their circumstances because of constitutional uniformity constraints. So we look for institutions that are friendly to local experimentation and are able to pool the results of those experiments in ways that permit outsiders to monitor and learn from those efforts.

Consider first the implications for individual decision-making units. Diversity implies that reasoned decision-making in each will need to draw on local knowledge and values; volatility means it will need regularly to update such information. As each unit is distinct, none does best by simply copying solutions adopted by others, though it may do well to treat those solutions as baselines from which to move; as each faces changing conditions, practical reasoning requires a system of collective decision-making that fosters regular readjustment of solutions to those changes. Local problem-solving through directly deliberative participation is well-suited to bringing the relevant local knowledge and values to bear in making decisions. Direct participation helps because participants can be assumed to have relevant information about the local contours of the problem and can relatively easily detect both deception by others and unintended consequences of past decisions. Deliberative participation helps because it encourages the expression of differences in outlook and the provision of information more generally: the respect expressed through the mutual reason-giving that defines deliberation reinforces a commitment to such conversational norms as sincerity and to solving problems rather than to angling for advantage (perhaps by providing misleading information); furthermore, if preferences over outcomes themselves are shaped and even formed by discussion, and mutual reason-giving reduces disagreements among such preferences, then being truthful will also be good strategy.

But the same concern for a form of decision-making that is attentive to unexplored possibilities and unintended consequences requires institutionalization of links among local units—in particular, the institutionalization of links that require separate deliberative units to consider their own proposals against benchmarks provided by other units. Because practical reasoning requires a search for best solutions, decision-makers need to explore alternatives to current practice. A natural place to look for promising alternatives—including alternatives previously unimagined in the local setting—is in the experience of units facing analogous problems. Thus alongside directly deliberative decision-making we need deliberative coordination: deliberation among units of decision-making directed both to learning jointly from their several experiences and to improving the institutional possibilities for such learning. These considerations lead us to our conception of directly deliberative polyarchy—intuitively, a system with both substantial local problem-solving and continuous discussion among local units about current best practice and better ways of ascertaining it.

Before filling out this intuitive idea by exploring its basic operating principles, we underscore that directly deliberative polyarchy describes the form of problem-solving institutions: it is an order in which problem-solving proceeds through connected institutions and organizations that meet a set of abstract conditions of directness and deliberativeness. But the institutions and organizations that meet those conditions might vary widely, from networks of private firms to public institutions working alongside associations. In this respect, the idea of directly deliberative polyarchy operates at a different level of analysis from the idea of associative democracy or workplace democracy. The idea of associative democracy is to solve problems through means other than states or markets: the nature of the "organizational instrument" matters. Similarly, workplace democracy specifies a particular institutional arena—the workplace. With directly deliberative polyarchy, what matters is that the conditions are met, not the organizations that satisfy them.

We emphasize, too, that directly deliberative problem-solving arrangements must operate within a frame of legislative, judicial, and administrative institutions. The role of those institutions changes, from seeking to solve problems to identifying problems and fostering their directly deliberative solution. But in this transformed role, they are essential to the legitimate and successful operation of the new problem-solving arrangements.

CONSTITUTIONAL PRINCIPLES

To describe the basic structure of directly deliberative polyarchy, we need to answer three questions:

1. What are the requirements of democratic process within and among units? More particularly, what does it mean for their decisions to be made deliberatively?
2. What conditions should trigger the operation of these deliberative mechanisms?
3. How should the circle of membership in the deliberative bodies be drawn?

Deliberative Process Within and Among Units. At the heart of the deliberative conception of democracy is the view that collective decision-making is to proceed deliberatively—by citizens advancing proposals and defending them with considerations that others, who are themselves free and equal, can acknowledge as reasons. The shared commitment of citizens in a deliberative democracy is that the exercise of collective power should be confined to cases in which such justification is presented. Citizens contemplating the exercise of collective power owe one another reasons and owe attention to one another's reasons.

But not all reasons are on a par. So the kind of attention owed must be calibrated to the kind of consideration offered. Thus, *constitutional reasons* are considerations that command substantial weight in decision-making. In deciding which considerations are to be assigned such weight, we look for a close connection to the standing of citizens as free and equal members of the political society: considerations affirming that standing have substantial weight, whereas those that deny it are weightless. Thus, citizens must have fundamental political and civil rights because those rights are backed by reasons that affirm the standing of citizens as free and equal, whereas the denial of those rights requires appeal to considerations that throw such standing into question perhaps by denying that members meet all the qualifications for citizenship. But denials of qualification—assertions that some member is not to be regarded as a free and equal citizen—do not count as reasons at all because they are not considerations that command respect from those whose standing is denied. So effective participation rights cannot, except perhaps in very special circumstances (perhaps cases of extreme emergency), permissibly be denied. Similarly, proposals backed by reasons rooted in interests fundamental to the standing of members as free and equal can be rejected only upon offering alternative, more plausible projects for advancing those interests. Thus, a requirement of ensuring a basic educational threshold—a threshold defined relative to participation as a citizen, and more generally, as a cooperating member of society—would be a constitutional reason, and a proposal that would ensure such a threshold would be rejected in a well-ordered deliberative body only in favor of an alternative, better designed scheme.[25]

The first and most fundamental requirement of a directly deliberative polyarchy is, therefore, that it affirm its character as democratically deliberative by giving stringent protection to claims backed by constitutional reasons.

Of course, not all acceptable reasons for public choices are of constitutional magnitude. The class of *policy reasons* comprises those considerations whose endorsement is neither required by nor incompatible with a conception of citizens as free and equal and which are relevant to an issue under consideration. A proposal framed by such considerations may reasonably be rejected by a counter-argument that articulates an alternative balancing of the reasons generally understood as relevant to allocating the resource in question. Consider again the case of education. In deciding how to allocate resources, some relevant and potentially

---

25. Amy Gutmann argues for a democratic threshold principle in her account of the distribution of primary schooling in *Democratic Education* (Princeton: Princeton University Press, 1987), 136ff. But she confines the threshold to "effective participation in the democratic process"—as though there were not an equally good claim to effective participation in labor markets.

competing policy reasons are: helping each student to fully achieve potential; ensuring that students who are performing least well are given special attention; ensuring common educational experience for students of diverse backgrounds. In the case of health care, the reasons include: helping those who are worst off; helping those who would benefit most from medical resources; assisting larger numbers of people; ensuring that people have fair chances at receiving help, regardless of the urgency of their situation and of expected benefits from treatment.[26]

As these examples suggest, the policy reasons relevant to particular domains are complex and varied, and there often will be no clear, principled basis for ranking them: different, equally reasonable participants in deliberative process (and, *a fortiori*, different deliberative bodies) will weigh them differently. Reasonable people and reasonable collective decision-makers reasonably disagree and recognize the results of a deliberative process in which such reasons are aired as legitimate.

This distinction between constitutional and policy reasons brings us to the second broad condition, a requirement of substantive due process on the operation of directly deliberative polyarchy: the process is to give due consideration to reasons of both types, suitably weighted (and allowing for reasonable differences of weight).

Moreover, we require, third, that this consideration be explicit. It is not sufficient to require that outcomes be rationalizable—that the deliberative process issues in decisions for which appropriate reasons could be cited—and to leave it to another institution, say, a court, to determine whether that condition is met. Outcomes in directly deliberative polyarchy are to be arrived at through discussion in which reasons of the appropriate kind are given by participants. Five considerations lead to this conclusion:

1. Though deliberative justifiability itself is important, it must be aimed at being achieved; that is, it will not in general be true that results achieved through a process of exchange or bargaining, or outcomes that reflect a balance of power, will be defensible by reasons of an appropriate kind. So requiring actual deliberation helps establish a presumption that results can be defended through reasons, and thus a presumption that the outcomes of collective decision-making are legitimate.

26. See Norman Daniels and James Sabin, "Limits to Health Care: Fair Procedures, Democratic Deliberation, and the Legitimacy Problem for Insurers," *Philosophy and Public Affairs* 26, 4 (1997): 303–350.

2. Offering reasons to others expresses respect for them as equal members of a deliberative body. So actual deliberation plausibly helps foster mutual respect, which, in turn, encourages citizens to confine the exercise of power, as the deliberative idea requires. No similar result can be expected if we assign the job of assessing the justifiability of outcomes to a separate institution.

3. Actual deliberation provides a better rationale for relying on majority rule, should there be disagreement. With reasons openly stated, everyone can observe that the supporting considerations were relevant reasons, despite disagreements about their proper weight. It is manifest to participants, then, that people are not being asked simply to accede to the larger number but to accept what they can see to be a reasonable alternative, supported by others who are prepared to be reasonable.

4. In actual reason-giving, citizens are required to defend proposals by reference to considerations that others acknowledge as reasons and not simply by reference to their own interests. To the extent that such public reasoning shapes preferences, conflicts over policy will be reduced, as will inclinations to strategically misrepresent circumstances. Moreover, actual deliberation is, by its nature, a form of information pooling: when people take seriously the task of providing one another with reasons and information about circumstances and outlooks, what is relevant to improved policy is then brought to bear by those in possession of it. No similar effects on preferences or on information are likely to issue from non-deliberative processes subject to subsequent review. Indeed, understanding the process of review as the natural forum of principle may well encourage strategic, as distinct from deliberative, conduct.

5. Explicit reason-giving eases the work of other decision-making units and of outside monitors: it provides a record that other decision-makers can consult (and perhaps learn from) in deciding how to solve problems and deciding which monitors (legislators and courts) can refer to in judging whether solutions adopted in particular locations are appropriate and how they might be improved in the light of experience elsewhere.

Requiring explicit reason-giving rather than rationalizable outcomes may, however, have a downside. Critics of deliberative decision-making fault it for being doubly exclusionary.[27] Deliberation, they say, is a partic-

27. See Iris Young, "Communication and the Other: Beyond Deliberative Democracy," in Benhabib, ed., *Democracy and Difference*, 120–135; Sidney Verba, Kay Lehman Schlozman, Henry E. Brady, *Voice and Equality: Civic Voluntarism and American Politics* (Cambridge, MA: Harvard University Press, 1995), 500–508.

ular discursive style, with all the conventional indicia of the rational: formal, deductive, and unemotional. By insisting on abstraction from the personal and particular, deliberation excludes both people and information. People, because it silences citizens whose discursive style is detailed, narrative, and passionate; information, because it invites only contributions cast in general terms. As a result, deliberation is unfair and ineffective. Urging more of it is a reform strategy, but not an especially inviting one.

This objection makes two assumptions, both unwarranted. First, that requiring an explicit statement of reasons implies that nothing other than reasons can be stated—as though a conception of deliberative justification supported a ban on undeliberative humor. Second, that the canonical form of deliberation is the justification of a regulation from first principles: the argument for progressivity in the tax system on grounds of a conception of political fairness. Deliberation may take this form, but nothing in the concept of reason-giving requires that it do so. Nor, more immediately, is the reason-giving that occupies us here naturally expressed in the form of deductions from general political axioms. On the contrary, deliberative problem-solving is by its nature focused on addressing specific problems in local settings. Giving reasons under these conditions is, generally speaking, a matter of offering considerations recognized by others as pertinent to solving the problem at hand. It is simply impossible to limit in advance the kinds of considerations that might be relevant or the form in which those considerations are to be stated. Indeed, deliberation will characteristically involve debating the implications of general principles (standard operating procedures, rules of thumb) in the light of the particulars of local experience and inviting discussion of such experience in whatever terms suit participants—including the ironic "yeah, yeah" that condemns the latest implausible suggestion.

Still, it might be said that requirements of deliberation unfairly bias decision-making in favor of the verbal, that we may end up with a pluralistic logocracy, in which the many forms of verbosity are all on display, but the shy, the quiet, and the reserved are left out. We agree that there is a difficulty here, but why isn't it remediable? In settings of deliberative problem-solving, everyone has something to contribute, so the first task in improving the operation of deliberative arrangements is to ensure that all participants understand that and are encouraged to contribute. The potential for deliberative failure is no argument against efforts at such improvement.

These reasons for preferring decisions by actual deliberation—particularly the last consideration—suggest a fourth requirement of democratic process: that there be like deliberation among units as well. The advantage of actual, deliberate consideration of alternatives by citizens of equal standing but diverse experience and disposition is that the diversity of viewpoints brings out the strengths and the weaknesses of diverse proposals. Moreover, the diversity of proposals reveals strengths and weaknesses in viewpoints that make for more careful assessment in later rounds. Extending deliberation across units allows each group to see its viewpoints and its proposals in the light of alternatives articulated by the others: in effect, it ensures that the exercise of practical reason is both disciplined and imaginative.

To be effective in provoking this kind of informative comparison, information provided for this purpose must be supplied by units in a way that both anticipates and reflects this use: in accounting for their own decisions, decision-making processes, and outcomes, units must take into account information about the relevant practice elsewhere or make a case that apparently better practice is either not genuinely better or not relevant to their circumstances because of differences in population or resources. A standard way of doing this is through benchmarking: evaluation of one's own activities by comparison with others, judged to be similar, by means of metrics inherent in the choice of the comparison. Benchmarking thus requires a survey of possible comparisons, evaluation of possible metrics, and revision, when necessary, of initial choices of both; and the effectiveness of such surveys, evaluations, and revisions depends on the willingness of all participants to disclose information in view of the investigations of the others. This amounts to requiring that, as when acting alone, units actually deliberate among themselves, in the sense of taking account of respective reasons, and not content themselves with deliberative justifiability. This requirement implies that units that show poorly in public comparisons will be under substantial pressure to improve their practice to meet the standard of performance set in other comparable units.

Responsibility for ensuring that deliberation within and among units meets these four conditions falls ultimately to authorizing and monitoring agencies—legislatures and courts. But, in contrast to the conventional "division of deliberative labor," this responsibility is to be discharged by ensuring that the relevant decision-making bodies act deliberatively not—so far as possible—by substituting for their decisions.[28] We return to these points below, in our discussion of institutions.

State/Market? With these core conditions in place, we come to the areas of policy for which directly deliberative polyarchy is particularly well-suited. Generally speaking, the institutions of directly deliberative polyarchy are designed to do well where current political institutions and market exchange do badly.

Consider first the limits on political institutions. These limits are most severe when the following four conditions hold:

1. The sites at which a problem arises and requires address are too numerous and dispersed for easy or low cost centralized monitoring of compliance with regulations. Even if uniform regulations were appropriate, these conditions would suggest a need for decentralizing the capacity to monitor compliance. Discussions of workplace health and safety regulation commonly emphasize this problem: too many workplaces for a central inspectorate to review.

2. The diversity of sites at which similar problems arise suggests that problem-solvers at different sites will want to employ different means to achieve similar aims and specify their aims differently.

3. The volatility of sites suggests a need for continuous reflection on means and ends and the importance of adjusting both in the light of new information about the environment.

4. The complexity of problems and solutions—where problems are substantially the product of multiple causes and connected with other problems, crossing conventional policy domains and processes—implies that the appropriate strategy requires coordination across those domains. Urban poverty, local economic development, and effective social service delivery are among the familiar problems that occupy this class. Solving them plausibly requires cooperation across quite different institutions and groups—for example, lending institutions, health care providers, technology diffusers, education and training establishments, housing au-

---

28. Susan Sturm, "A Normative Theory of Public Law Remedies," *Georgetown Law Journal* 79, 5 (1991): 1357–1446. Also, Rebecca Abers discusses the requirement that citizen-budgeters incorporate considerations of fair distribution in the deliberations in the Porto Alegre system: "Learning from Democratic Practice," in *Cities for Citizens: Planning and the Rise of Civil Society in a Global Age*, ed. Mike Douglass and John Friedmann (Chichester: John Wiley, 1998), 39–65.

thorities, community development corporations, and neighborhood associations.

When all these conditions are in force, we have a strong case for directly deliberative polyarchy, with its linked, local problem-solvers: because of the numerosity and diversity of sites, we want a structure of decision-making that does not require uniform solutions; because of volatility, we want a structure with built-in sensitivities to changing local conditions; because of the complexity of problems, we want a structure that fosters interlocal comparisons of solutions.

To be sure, departures from these four conditions imply a less strong case for directly deliberative polyarchy and a correspondingly stronger case for markets or regulatory solutions. But even in the face of departures from these ideal conditions, two considerations support the case for directly deliberative polyarchy. First, as we have urged, it fits with democratic values, and that fit will tip the balance in unclear cases. Second, our basic premise is that existing strategies of problem-solving are not working well. So we may be aided in diagnosing the shortcomings of those strategies if we try this alternative. Among other things, it will test the thesis that the troubles emerge from a mismatch of problems and institutions of collective choice.

Consider next the circumstances under which problem-solving through directly deliberative polyarchy is preferable to solution through market exchange—here understood as a form of social coordination in which agents need not arrive at a common decision nor defend their separate decisions by giving reasons to others.[29]

Thus suppose we are concerned about the production and allocation of a good that is widely regarded as urgent—that citizens can claim as a matter of basic right or need—and about whose proper production and/or allocation there is disagreement.[30] Because the claims for the good are urgent, arrangements of provision should be open and accountable; moreover, urgency and disagreement together establish a presumption that decisions about the good's provision should be backed by an acceptable rationale. That presumption can be defeated in the case of goods (for example, bread or cars) for which there are a large number of provid-

---

29. Bargaining and command are ways of making collective decisions without mutual reason-giving; confession is the practice of giving reasons to others for individual decisions.

30. The paragraph that follows presents an account of public goods suited to the special setting of a conception of deliberative democracy.

ers and about which it is relatively easy (either for consumers or for a centralized monitor) to acquire accurate information. Assume, then, that the good is best supplied by a restricted range of providers, and that there are high costs to switching among those providers: there can, then, be no presumption of voluntarism in the choice of provider. Add, now, that information about the good is difficult to acquire or summarize because a large number of dimensions are important to its evaluation, people disagree about the relevant dimensions and their relative weights, and the conditions of its production and allocation are volatile. Under these conditions, we want goods to be provided through mechanisms in which decisions are backed by reasons and based on pooled information. In short, we have reason to favor directly deliberative polyarchy over market.

Membership. Finally, as to membership. The basic standard is that directly deliberative arenas are to be open to providers and parties affected by the extent and the manner of provision. (In the case of schools, for example, parents, teachers, and residents of a community served by a school.) Very little can be said in general terms about the requisite representational form: how many members of different groups, affected parties, and so forth. Once more, there is every reason to expect at least as much variation as we currently see in polyarchies. Still, a few considerations are to frame debate about whether deliberative bodies include all who are entitled or are instead objectionably exclusive. In general terms, the considerations pull in two directions, reflecting the ideas of political equality and deliberativeness that define the directly deliberative conception. The value of equality suggests a one-person/one-vote composition of deliberative bodies, whereas the requirement of deliberativeness suggests a constitution that assigns membership in ways that foster the provision of relevant local information and the crisp articulation of alternative views.

More particularly, then, three considerations need to be balanced in decisions about membership. First, citizens can object that the composition and the scope of directly deliberative bodies are objectionably discriminatory—for example, that their geographic range has been gerrymandered on racial or ethnic lines. Second, there is a presumption in favor of equal membership for affected parties—open meetings, with equal rights to participate in discussion and decision-making for all affected parties. Third, rights to participate might also be awarded to organizations with special knowledge that is essential to the problem area in question (for example, neighborhood organizations in the area of public safety) or which are able to articulate a point of view in ways that foster deliberation among alternative solutions.

EFFECTIVENESS

Why expect that such problem-solving will have concrete benefits? How might it be able to overcome the problems of limited information and diversity of sites that vex state action? Five considerations are important.

First, the parties to the discussion are presumed to have relevant local knowledge; moreover, they can put that information to good use because they understand the terrain better and have a more immediate stake in the solution.

Second, assuming a shared concern to address a problem, and an expectation that the results of deliberation will regulate subsequent action, the participants would tend to be more other-regarding in their political practice than they would otherwise tend to be. The structure of discussion—the requirement of finding a solution that others can agree to rather than pressuring the state for a solution—would push the debate in directions that respect and advance more general interests. Other-regardingness would encourage a more complete revelation of private information. And this information would permit sharper definition of problems and solutions.

Third, pursuing discussion in the context of enduring differences among participants would incline parties to be more reflective in their definition of problems and proposed strategies for solution; it would tend to free discussion from the preconceptions that commonly limit the consideration of options within more narrowly defined groups, thus enabling a more complete definition and imaginative exploration of problems and solutions. The same is true for the federalism of problem-solvers that emerges from requirements of discussion across units—here, too, comparisons of solutions at different sites, and benchmarking of local solutions by reference to practice elsewhere, suggest a basis for improving local practice.

Here, notice that directly deliberative polyarchy—understood as a form of problem-solving—is not thwarted by, but instead benefits from, heterogeneity of participants. Of course, the participants must—as our discussion of deliberation indicates—share a view about relevant reasons. But this is, we think, a rather weak constraint that does not demand substantial homogeneity—certainly not homogeneity of comprehensive moral outlook.

Fourth, monitoring in the implementation of agreements would be a natural by-product of ongoing discussion, generating a further pool of shared information.

And, fifth, if things work, the result would be a mutual confidence that fosters future cooperation.

In all these ways, then, deliberation about common problems with diverse participants might thus reasonably be thought to enhance social learning and problem-solving capacity.

INSTITUTIONS

We conclude with a brief discussion of the implications of directly deliberative polyarchy for the design of and expectations on basic political institutions.

First, directly deliberative polyarchy is, as we have indicated, a form of polyarchy. So we assume the continued presence of the legislatures, courts, executives, and administrative agencies, controlled by officials chosen through free and fair elections, in which virtually all adults have rights to suffrage, office-holding, association, and expression, and face alternative, legally protected sources of information.[31] Though the operation of these institutions and arrangements changes, the institutions remain and continue to serve some of the political values with which they are conventionally associated: peaceful transitions of power, restraints on unbridled power, fair chances for effective influence over authoritative collective decisions, opportunities to develop informed preferences, and so forth.

But with the shift in the locus of problem-solving, the operations and expectations of basic institutions change markedly.

Consider first the role of legislatures. Directly deliberative polyarchy is animated by a recognition of the limits on the capacity of legislatures to solve problems—either on their own or by delegating tasks to administrative agencies—despite the importance of solutions. Rejecting the Neo-Liberal Constitutionalist idea that the problems are essentially recalcitrant to collective address, and the modern Civic Republican idea that their address requires only a more vigilant exclusion of private interests from national policy-making (and a correspondingly more acute intervention by technically adept guardians of the common good), the legislature in a directly deliberative polyarchy takes on a new role: to empower

---

31. Dahl, *Democracy and Its Critics*, 221.

and facilitate problem-solving through directly deliberative arenas operating in closer proximity than the legislature to the problem. More particularly, the idea is for legislatures, guided by the conditions of triggering, to declare areas of policy (education, community safety, environmental health) as open to directly deliberative polyarchal action; state general goals for policy in the area; assist potential deliberative arenas in organizing to achieve those goals; make resources available to deliberative problem-solving bodies that meet basic requirements on membership and benchmarking; and review at regular intervals the assignments of resources and responsibility. To be sure, legislatures can play this role only if they are able to identify problems needing solutions and agents with the capacity to solve those problems, even when they cannot themselves produce the solutions. But once we acknowledge the importance of diversity and volatility in shaping acceptable solutions, this assumption is entirely natural.

This changed role for legislatures does not, of course, preclude national solutions through legislative enactment when uniform solutions are preferable (because of limited diversity among sites) or when externalities overwhelm local problem-solving. Instead, the availability of alternative methods of problem-solving imposes on legislatures a greater burden in justifying their own direct efforts: they must explicitly make the case that the benefits of those efforts suffice to overcome the advantages of direct-deliberative solutions.[32]

Administrative agencies, in turn, provide the infrastructure for information exchange between and among units—the exchange required for benchmarking and continuous improvement. Instead of seeking to solve problems, the agencies see their task as reducing the costs of information faced by different problem-solvers: helping them determine which deliberative bodies are similarly situated, what projects those bodies are pursuing, and what modifications of those projects might be needed under local conditions.

And the responsibility of constitutional courts is not simply to inspect procedure for its adequacy as representative, nor to reorganize institutions by reference to substantive constitutional rights, but to require that decision-making proceed in a directly deliberative way: that is, to require

---

32. For related discussions of federalism, see Stephen Gardbaum, "Rethinking Constitutional Federalism," *Texas Law Review* 74 (1996): 795–838; and the account of the "commandeering problem" in Dorf and Sabel, "Constitution of Democratic Experimentalism."

that problem-solvers themselves make policy with express reference to both constitutional and relevant policy reasons. You might describe this as a genuine fusion of constitutional and democratic ideals: a fusion, inasmuch as the conception of democratic process includes a requirement that constitutional reasons be taken into account, as such. The aim is a form of political deliberation in which citizens themselves are to give suitable weight to constitutional considerations and not leave that responsibility to a court.

These remarks sketch, in the sparest terms, how basic political institutions might shift in expectation and responsibility under conditions of directly deliberative polyarchy. Further details will vary greatly, certainly as much as they do in existing polyarchies. Rather than outline the dimensions of such variation, we propose to clarify and deepen this account of transformed conventional institutions by addressing an objection to the very coherence of directly deliberative polyarchy as a form of problem-solving that conforms to basic democratic values. Generally speaking, the objection is that directly deliberative polyarchy is an unstable combination of institutionalization of democratic values: central institutions either will not supervise local arrangements enough to avoid local tyrannies or will over-supervise, thus regenerating the problems of centralized control that directly deliberative polyarchy is supposed to avoid. More particularly, the objection is that directly deliberative polyarchy needs to meet two requirements that are at war with one another: deliberative problem-solvers are supposed to satisfy various conditions (on membership, deliberativeness, and external links to other problem-solvers). But directly deliberative problem-solvers will not meet these conditions as a matter of course, nor is their satisfaction a self-enforcing equilibrium. So the responsibility for ensuring that they are met falls to authorizing and monitoring agencies. If, however, problem-solvers are to achieve the variation in local solutions demanded by conditions of diversity and volatility, then authorizing and monitoring agencies must also ensure them autonomy.

These two conditions are arguably in tension. For directly deliberative problems-solvers can act in ways that conflict with the constitutive values and conditions of democracy itself, either by deciding on the basis of considerations that conflict with those values or by failing to take them fully into account. If a fundamental, generic responsibility of authorizing and monitoring bodies is to ensure that decision-making is democratic, then those authorizing bodies are obligated to review and pass judgment on the decisions of the authorized bodies. But this creates two related troubles for directly deliberative problem-solving: first, reduced autonomy in the name of ensuring democracy may substantially limit interest and enthusiasm for participating in problem-solving bodies. Second, if ensuring democracy means constantly second-guessing the solutions chosen by directly deliberative problem-solvers, then those problem-solvers may decide to avoid troubles by imposing uniform solutions (choosing solutions that have already passed muster), disregarding the suitability of those solutions to their circumstances. This tension, it might be argued, is exacerbated by a tendency of decentralized systems to generate greater inequalities, thus pressuring the center to reappropriate power and impose greater uniformity of circumstance through redistribution.

We have five replies to this problem. The first is to introduce a note of realism. The objection is entirely familiar from current discussions of federalism and of relations between courts and legislatures. Focusing on the latter, it is commonly agreed that courts should, whatever else they do, uphold the democratic process, ensuring that all citizens have rights to participate as equals in that process.[33] Sometimes majorities violate that requirement, and when they do, courts have a responsibility to overturn the results of those violations. The tension noted above is, generally speaking, simply an instance of this problem, which is commonly called the "countermajoritarian dilemma": it is not a problem created by the proposal advanced here, but a reflection, within our proposal, of a problem that any adequate conception of constitutional democracy needs to face.

Second, accepting that the general structure of the problem is familiar, it might nonetheless be argued that a deliberative conception of democracy or an idea of directly deliberative polyarchy inspired by that conception worsens the problem—by imposing more stringent standards of democracy. Though a wide range of views will permit review and rejection of decisions on grounds of incompatibility with democracy, the deliberative view embraces an expansive conception of democracy—and a correspondingly expansive and, therefore, invasive account of—when the judgments of problem-solvers are properly second-guessed. The force of this objection depends on a belief that is widely shared but simply mis-

33. The classic statement of this view is John Hart Ely, *Democracy and Distrust* (Cambridge, MA: Harvard University Press, 1980).

guided: that deliberation, properly conducted, issues in consensus. We have already explained our reasons for rejecting this claim. Deliberation is a matter of balancing relevant considerations and arguing in the light of such balance: competent deliberators will work out the balance differently; and, correspondingly, competent deliberative bodies will typically arrive at different conclusions or will arrive at the same conclusions differently. Indeed, there is no compelling *a priori* argument that the range of acceptable results of deliberative processes is smaller than the range of acceptable results of aggregative processes. So we reject the claim that the deliberative view worsens the familiar problem.

Indeed, third, we think that the deliberative conception may reduce the tension between democracy and autonomy. To see how, recall the idea of a division of deliberative labor. On a conventional view of collective decision-making within a constitutional regime, the division of labor assigns to legislatures the responsibility for devising laws that advance the common good, and to courts the responsibility for ensuring that those laws respect the constitution and the political values implicit in it. As our earlier discussion indicates, the deliberative view rejects this way of dividing deliberative labor. When objections are raised on constitutional grounds to decisions reached by problem-solvers—when it is argued that unacceptable reasons animated the decision, or that fundamental constitutional values were neglected by it—the role of courts (and legislatures) is not to substitute their own judgment about the proper outcome, but to require that the deliberative body revisit the issue, taking the full range of relevant considerations explicitly into account—and exploring the experience of similarly situated problem-solving bodies. Suppose, for example, that a decision to impose an English-only requirement on schools is challenged on grounds that students who are not native English speakers will be disadvantaged by it, and consequently disadvantaged as citizens. The response should be to require that the school committee responsible for imposing the requirement revisit the decision, attending both to the importance of education for equal citizenship and to the experience of other multilingual districts in solving the problem. In short, the deliberative view rejects the conventional division of deliberative labor, proposing instead that all bodies making collective decisions share responsibility for upholding the democratic constitution by treating its principles and values as regulative in their own decisions.

Our fourth reply builds on this last point. Suppose that deliberative decision-makers are required to arrive at decisions with explicit attention to constitutional values and comparable experience. Still, they may make decisions that conflict with the democratic constitution, and courts may be required to review their decisions in this light. But when they are, they will have a record of fact and reasoning to draw on in making their decisions. Because they have imposed requirements of due consideration on problem-solvers themselves, courts will have the information they need to decide whether means are suitably tailored to ends, and whether ends are specified in ways that satisfy constitutional constraints. Judgments about whether or not to defer to problem-solvers will be backed by fact, and not simply by *a priori* estimates of institutional competence.

Finally, without disputing the claim that decentralized systems, as a rule, generate increased inequality, we dispute the extension of the rule to the case of directly deliberative polyarchy and, therefore, do not expect substantial pressures to recentralize in the name of equality.

5. Kicking Radical Democracy Upstairs?

Any plausible conception of democracy requires an interpretation of the idea of the public as the arena in which free and equal citizens reflect on and seek to advance common aims. We conclude our account of directly deliberative democracy, then, by sketching the distinctive conception of the public that has been implicit in our discussion thus far.

First, in directly deliberative democracy (and, by extension, in directly deliberative polyarchy), the public arena is *organizationally dispersed* and *socially heterogeneous*: organizationally dispersed, because public opinion crystallizes not only in reference to the national legislature but also in the work of the local school governance committee and the community policing beat organization, and in their analogies, in areas such as the provision of services to firms or to distressed families; socially heterogeneous, because members are not presumed to share social traits, moral outlooks, or common information. Though the public arena is in both ways pluralistic, its pieces are nevertheless connected by: the requirements of reason-giving, in particular the demand to respect constitutional reasons; the need for explicit comparison with other units, which are themselves conducting similar comparisons; and the need for a wider public debate informed by such comparisons and focused on national projects.

Second, and more fundamentally, the public arena is the place where practicality in the form of problem-solving meets political principle in the form of deliberation through reason-giving among citizens who recognize one another as free and equal. In directly deliberative polyarchy, public deliberation cuts across the distinction between reflection on political purposes and assessment of efforts to achieve those purposes—a central distinction not only in familiar theories of representative democracy but also, and perhaps surprisingly, in current understandings of radical democracy. To underscore this essential feature of directly deliberative polyarchy and point towards the unfinished work of our project, we look briefly at the fate of the modern radical-democratic understanding of the public as it appears in the works of such representative figures as Habermas and Arendt and their innovative followers, and we contrast that fate with the idea developed above.

From this vantage point, the most striking feature of contemporary views of radical democracy is the measure to which they have become defensive, self-consciously chastened, typically directed more to limiting (at times by novel means) the erosion of the institutions of nineteenth-century parliamentary democracy than to transforming and extending them. In part these limited ambitions are a prudent response to the temper of the times, hostile since the fall of the planned economies to any hint of collective control over life choices of individuals, and skeptical, more broadly, about the very idea of public action.[34] More fundamentally, though, this self-limitation reflects a sharp distinction, long established in the social and political theory from which much radical democratic theory stems, between a higher, political world of human self-determination—through an all-encompassing exercise of theoretical and practical reason or innovative public deeds—and a lower realm of workaday conduct governed by calculation, technique, and organization. The idea of the public in directly deliberative democracy questions the underlying assumptions and institutional expression of this distinction.

Consider first the notion of the public as it appears in Habermas's work. According to his theory of communicative action, human interactions differ fundamentally according to whether participants aim to

---

34. Habermas says that he has "no illusions about the problems that our situation poses and the moods it invokes. But moods—and philosophies in a melancholic 'mood'—do not justify the defeatist surrender of the radical content of democratic ideals." *Between Facts and Norms*, xlii–xliii. We agree with the observation about moods and their unfortunate consequences, but—as will emerge—think Habermas has surrendered too much.

achieve worldly success, in part by influencing others, or to coordinate social action through common understandings. When action aims at success, information is manipulated strategically to advance individual or group interests, as in economic exchange or group bargaining. When action aims at understanding, agents acknowledge that they are bound by context-transcendent norms of sincerity (*Wahrhaftigkeit*), truth (*Wahrheit*), and moral probity (*Richtigkeit*), and they are committed to the view that their claims would be vindicated by an unfettered communication of equals.

Within the framework provided by the idea of communicative action, the role of constitutional democracy is threefold: it establishes the system of rights required for autonomous communication among equal citizens (for a discursive formation of public opinion), enables discursively formed understandings of common purpose to achieve legal expression, and ensures that those legally crystallized understandings steer (or, in more anguished formulations, besiege) the state's administrative apparatus, understood as a system of technically constrained instrumentalities for guiding the (still more constrained) activities necessary for society to reproduce and advance.[35] Democratic steering is itself divided into stages, or phases, ordered by their distance from the apparatus of actual decision-making, and hence their freedom from technical constraint and organizational routine: parliamentary debate is limited by its connection to administration, the disputations of political parties by their connection to parliamentary debate. In the "communicatively fluid" public sphere, democracy is most authentic because it is least constrained. Neither hemmed in by specialized vocabularies nor confined to particular social tasks, the public sphere is a dispersed, all-purpose, discursive network within which citizens, connected by the means of mass communication, form currents of opinion in seeking how best to resolve the great questions of the day.[36] Because discussion within that sphere comprises all manner of topic and question, and is guided by each of the three norms mentioned earlier, the dispersed assembly that is the public comes as close as can reasonably be hoped to a free community of equals, autonomously debating the terms of their collective life.

35. "We can interpret the idea of the constitutional state in general as the requirement that the administrative system, which is steered through the power code, be tied to the lawmaking communicative power and kept free of the illegitimate interventions of social power (i.e., of the factual strength of privileged interests to assert themselves)." Habermas, *Between Facts and Norms*, 150, also 176.

36. Ibid., 360.

But the capacity of the public's critical contributions to steer the state must remain, given Habermas's fundamental partition of human action, an open question. The freer the communication within the public—the greater the immunities from state interference with the formation of opinion, the more accessible the newspapers, the less venal the television, the richer the associational life on which public discussion rests—the greater clarification it can attain. Indeed, the call for democratization of the public sphere, which follows naturally from Habermas's emphasis on the role of communicative action in social integration, is exactly the aspect of his general theory that classes it as a type of radical democracy.[37] The basic dualism of understanding and success-oriented action, however, suggests as well that even the most radical extension of the public sphere would be of limited consequence precisely because the technical demands, to which administration, parliament, and party must in turn respond, set limits—but which ones?—to the direction that might issue from a more encompassing, unrestricted discussion among citizens: "Communicative power cannot supply a substitute for the systematic inner logic of public bureaucracies. Rather, it achieves an impact on this logic 'in a siege-like manner.'"[38] At its most paradoxically self-defeating, Habermas's view seems to be that the democratic public cannot be just and effective, because to be just, it must be informal in the sense of constituted freedom of institutions, while to be effective, it must be institutionalized in forms that constrain discussion and hinder the pursuit of justice. In the end, radical democracy serves as a series of reminders—that human communication need not be narrowly technical, that unsolved problems remain outside the purview of conventional institutions—rather than as a program to redirect the ensemble of institutions to ensure a controlling role for communicative power.[39]

As a second illustration of the self-limitation of radical democracy, consider the position of Hannah Arendt. Whereas Habermas sets his account

37. Ibid, 371. Though note the immediately subsequent discussion of the "self-limiting" quality of radical-democratic practice—in particular, the need for a communicatively generated public opinion to work its effects through conventional political institutions.

38. Habermas, "Further Reflections on the Public Sphere," in Craig Calhoun, ed., *Habermas and the Public Sphere* (Cambridge, MA: MIT Press, 1992), 452.

39. See especially Habermas's striking discussion of the "surprisingly active and momentous role" that actors in civil society can play in a "perceived crisis situation." *Between Facts and Norms*, 7, 380–382. This discussion suggests that Habermas is operating with a distinction between crisis situations, in which radical democratic impulses play a central role, and normal politics, in which they do not. For an instructive comparison, see Bruce Ackerman, *We, The People: Foundations* (Cambridge, MA: Harvard University Press, 1991).

of democracy within a general theory of rational discourse and communicative action, Arendt's is framed by a general diagnosis of the human condition and a classification of responses to that condition: thus, human conduct counts as labor if it responds to the rhythmic necessities of biological reproduction; as work if directed to the construction of those durable artifacts, from houses to highways, that provide the scaffolding and outward signs of our "unnatural" social life; and as action if it manifests the fundamental human capacity to begin "something new on our own initiative."[40] Though acting "rests on initiative, it is an initiative from which no human being can refrain and still be human."[41] The public in this view is just the citizens in action, appearing to one another *as human*—as a plurality of initiators—and this citizenry in action embodies democracy in its most radical, constitutional, aspect.[42]

The dilemma for this view is that democracy continues after its initiation; and on Arendt's understanding, concerns arising within the constituted polity would fall from the higher, distinctively human sphere of action and the political to the banausic social spheres of work and labor. For practical purposes, the public would be purposeless and political debate would be a matter of display: as Mary McCarthy said, "If all questions of economics, human welfare, bussing, anything that touches the social sphere, are to be excluded from the political scene, then I am mystified. I am left with war and speeches. But the speeches can't just be speeches. They have to be speeches about something."[43] Thus, if Habermas's view edges radical democracy to the periphery, preserving discursive freedom at the expense of political influence, Arendt's view kicks radical democracy upstairs, preserving its free creativity at the expense of its content.

Recent efforts to modify the idea of the public in both views to respond to these kinds of criticisms by softening the distinctions on which they rest only underscore the constraints of the original schemes. In

40. Hannah Arendt, *The Human Condition* (Chicago: University of Chicago Press, 1950), 177.

41. Ibid., 176.

42. Seyla Benhabib emphasizes that "appearing" is to be taken fully literally: "When Arendt links the public space with the space of appearances she primarily has in mind a model of face-to-face human interactions," within a relatively homogeneous community whose shared ethos makes the meaning of individual action more or less transparent. *The Reluctant Modernism of Hannah Arendt* (New York: Sage, 1996), 201.

43. These remarks, made by Mary McCarthy at a conference on Arendt's work, are reported in ibid., 155; also see 156 for Arendt's reply and a convincing assessment of its plausibility.

both cases the modifications focus on the role of social movements—of women, of racial or ethnic minorities, of citizens concerned about the environment—as forms of the public so dispersed within society to be acting outside of institutions, hence untainted by technical or workaday constraints, yet directly enough engaged with changing particular social arrangements to influence them. In those writings on social movements that refer, critically, to Habermas and others like him, the emphasis is on spontaneous citizen protest against the risks of (increasing) technical manipulation of the social and the natural worlds: the risk of nuclear catastrophe calls forth a social movement against the construction of nuclear power stations, and the industrial use of toxins calls forth a movement for their regulation. But this simply reminds us that a dispersed, discursive public can play a part in limiting only the reach of a "system" whose innermost mechanisms remain beyond political influence.[44]

Writings on social movements that take Arendt as their critical referent, but that reject her public/private, political/social distinctions, are more ethereal still. From this perspective, social movements are seen as the potential precursors to constitutional conventions in the small, or as interstitial, fleeting, fugitive testimony to the human capacity for initiative and, therefore, to the permanent possibility of a higher politics of democratic refounding. In both variants, the newer views accept the defensiveness of their antecedents and reduce radical democracy to an argument about the possibility of protest against the further subjugation of freedom to necessity.

Directly deliberative polyarchy, in contrast, does not seek refuge in social movements; it holds out the promise of transforming the institutions of social steering, not merely of containing their erosion.[45] It claims that the apparent limits on the applicability of democratic principles—

44. For thoughtful discussion of debates on social movements from a viewpoint close to the one adopted here, see Hans Joas, *Die Kreativität des Handelns* (Frankfurt/Main: Suhrkamp, 1992), 348ff.

45. Jeffrey Isaac concludes his thoughtful discussion of Arendt's and Camus' radical democratic, "rebellious politics" by doubting that "such a politics, centred in civil society, can be equally effective in fashioning stable democratic economic and political institutions." He adds that "if rebellious politics is to be something more than a self-actualizing and self-consuming phenomenon, then it must challenge and seek to reshape, however cautiously and imperfectly, existing political institutions." But then Isaac backs off from this need to reshape—however cautiously and imperfectly—by identifying "a more institutional kind of politics" with "a more conventional social democratic politics." Radical democracy thus remains at the margins. See Jeffrey Isaac, *Arendt, Camus, and Modern Rebellion* (New Haven: Yale University Press, 1992), 255, 247, and 258.

and the background dualism of creative or freely reasoning public and banausic life routines—can be overcome by understanding how those principles can contribute to problem-solving, and how problem-solving can contribute to the re-interpretation of those principles. At the core of this mutual re-elaboration, is the idea of deliberation as reason-giving in context—that is, relative to purposes that concern the citizens. Purpose does not vitiate deliberation. Rather, it guides and enables deliberation by suggesting the comparisons and contrasts that give meaning to diverse and mutually informative points of view. And purpose here means purpose of all kinds: the idea of deliberation in directly deliberative polyarchy does not distinguish between constitutional and operational tasks. Indeed, the notion of mutual adjustment of means and ends at the heart of the notion of deliberation in directly deliberative polyarchy—the very feature that recommends it as a method of problem-solving in diverse and volatile environments—undercuts the distinction between these types of activities.

But in stating the contrast between the current, defensive ideas of radical democracy and the possibilities of directly deliberative polyarchy, we are advancing our case by signing promissory notes. We have offered some empirical hints of new institutional developments to warrant our conjectures, subjected those conjectures to the preliminary tests of internal consistency, and noted their appeal as alternatives to the despairing prospects of current debate. If we are right in thinking a new, radically participatory form of democracy is beginning to stare us in the face, the obvious and urgent thing to do is to stare back.

7

DEMOCRACY AND LIBERTY

1. Main Ideas

The fundamental idea of democratic, political legitimacy is that the authorization to exercise state power must arise from the *collective decisions* of the equal members of a society who are governed by that power.[1] That is a very abstract statement of the concept of democracy—as abstract as it should be. Democracy comes in many forms, and more determinate conceptions of it depend on an account of membership in the people and, correspondingly, what it takes for a decision to be *collective*—authorized by *citizens as a body*.

Consider two conceptions of democracy, distinguished by their interpretations of the fundamental idea of collective decision: I will call them *aggregative* and *deliberative*. Both views apply in the first instance to institutions of binding collective decision making,[2] and each interprets the fundamental ideal that such institutions are to treat people bound by

I have presented parts of this essay to the Eastern Division Meetings of the American Philosophical Association, the University of Chicago Workshop on Deliberative Democracy, the Instituto Universitário de Pesquisas do Rio de Janeiro, the North Carolina Philosophy Colloquium, and a seminar with the Graduate Fellows in the Harvard Program in Ethics and the Professions; in my Wesson Lectures entitled "Liberty, Equality, and Democracy" at Stanford University, the University of Nebraska-Lincoln, and Princeton University; and as the Wade Memorial Lecture at St. Louis University. I also discussed these issues in my Fall 1995 political philosophy seminar at MIT. I am grateful for all the comments and suggestions I have received and want especially to thank David Austen-Smith, Zairo Cheibub, Alasdair MacIntyre, Carole Pateman, Adam Przeworski, John Rawls, Elisa Reis, Charles Sabel, T. M. Scanlon, Cass Sunstein, Iris Marion Young, and Judith Jarvis Thomson. Some of the main ideas are presented in "Procedure and Substance in Deliberative Democracy," in Seyla Benhabib, ed., *Democracy and Difference: Changing Boundaries of the Political* (Princeton: Princeton University Press, 1996), 95–119 [reprinted as essay 5 in this collection].

1. "Governed by" rather than "affected by." Democracy is about justifying authority, not about justifying influence. See Michael Walzer, *Spheres of Justice* (New York: Basic Books, 1983); Christopher McMahon, *Authority and Democracy* (Princeton: Princeton University Press, 1995).

2. I am grateful to T. M. Scanlon for emphasizing the importance of this parallel.

collective decisions as equals. According to an *aggregative* conception of democracy, then, decisions are collective just in case they arise from arrangements of binding collective choice that give *equal consideration to*—more generically, are *positively responsive to*—*the interests of each person* bound by the decisions.[3] According to a *deliberative* conception, a decision is collective just in case it emerges from arrangements of binding collective choice that establish conditions of *free public reasoning among equals who are governed by the decisions.* In the deliberative conception, then, citizens treat one another as equals not by giving equal consideration to interests—perhaps some interests ought to be discounted by arrangements of binding collective choice—but by offering them justifications for the exercise of collective power framed in terms of considerations that can, roughly speaking, be acknowledged by all as reasons.

Because the requirements for free public reasoning among equals are not narrowly political—not only a matter of the organization of the state—democracy, on the deliberative view, is not exclusively a form of politics; it is a framework of social and institutional arrangements that:

1. facilitate free reasoning among equal citizens by providing, for example, favorable conditions for expression, association, and participation, while ensuring that citizens are treated as free and equal in that discussion; and
2. tie the authorization to exercise public power—and the exercise itself—to such public reasoning, by establishing a framework ensuring the responsiveness and the accountability of political power to it through regular competitive elections, conditions of publicity, legislative oversight, and so on.

Deliberative democracy, then, is not simply about ensuring a public culture of reasoned discussion on political affairs, nor simply about fostering the bare conjunction of such a culture with conventional demo-

3. See Robert Dahl, *Democracy and Its Critics* (New Haven: Yale University Press, 1989). Dahl holds that the "principle of equal consideration"—which he attributes to Stanley Benn and which states that the good or interests of each must be given equal consideration—is the most compelling interpretation of the deeper "idea of intrinsic equality," according to which individuals are, for the purposes of collective decisions, to be considered equal (85–86). Dahl justifies democracy, as a process for making collective decisions, by reference to the principle of equal consideration, given a "presumption of personal autonomy": the presumption that individuals are the best judges and most vigilant defenders of their own interests. See *Democracy and Its Critics*, chs. 6–8.

cratic institutions of voting, parties, elections. The idea instead is manifestly to tie the exercise of power to conditions of public reasoning: to establish "all those conditions of communication under which there can come into being a discursive formation of will and opinion on the part of a public composed of the citizens of a state"[4] and to generate "communicative power"[5]—an institutionalized impact of that will and opinion on the exercise of political power.

In the large project of which this essay forms one part, I explore the deliberative conception and its implications. Assuming as background a plurality of comprehensive philosophies of life—the fact of reasonable pluralism, which I will explain shortly—I aim to show that democracy, on the deliberative conception, is a substantive, not simply a procedural, ideal and that the substance comprises egalitarian and liberal political values. More specifically, I show the central role within a deliberative conception of democracy of religious, expressive, and moral liberties, political equality, and an egalitarian account of the common good. Egalitarian and liberal political values emerge, then, as elements of democracy rather than as constraints upon it.

In this essay, I focus on the liberties. After sketching the fundamental notions of reasonable pluralism (Section 2) and deliberative democracy (Sections 3 and 4), I discuss religious, expressive, and moral liberty, emphasizing their essential roles in a democracy as conditions of *deliberative inclusion*. The conclusion—on political community and political legitimacy—explains how the deliberative conception presents a compelling interpretation of the democratic ideal.

2. Reasonable Pluralism

I begin with the fact of reasonable pluralism:[6] the fact that there are distinct, incompatible philosophies of life to which reasonable people are drawn under favorable conditions for the exercise of practical reason. By a "philosophy of life"—what Rawls has called a "comprehensive doc-

---

4. Jürgen Habermas, "Further Reflections on the Public Sphere," in Craig Calhoun, ed., *Habermas and the Public Sphere* (Cambridge, MA: MIT Press, 1992), 446.

5. Ibid., 452.

6. For discussion of this fact, see Joshua Cohen, "Moral Pluralism and Political Consensus," in David Copp, Jean Hampton, and John Roemer, eds., *The Idea of Democracy* (Cambridge: Cambridge University Press, 1993), 270–291; John Rawls, *Political Liberalism* (New York: Columbia University Press, 1996); and Joshua Cohen, "A More Democratic Liberalism," *Michigan Law Review* 92, 6 (May 1994): 1502–1546.

trine"—I mean an all-embracing view—religious or secular, liberal or traditionalist—that includes an account of all ethical values and, crucially, provides a general guide to conduct, individual as well as collective. Let us say that people are reasonable, politically speaking, only if they are concerned to live with others on terms that those others, as free and equal, also find acceptable. The idea of reasonable pluralism, then, is that good-faith efforts at the exercise of practical reason, by reasonable people thus understood, do not converge on a particular philosophy of life. Such philosophies are matters on which reasonable people disagree.

The fact of reasonable pluralism is just one of the many forms of human difference, others being differences of preference and ability, life chances and biological endowment, ethnicity and rhetorical style. These differences set a generic task for an account of democracy: to explain how people, different along so many dimensions, are to be recognized and treated as free and equal members of a political society (however we interpret those protean ideas). Though the task is generic, the solution varies according to dimension, and here—as a matter of focus, and not prejudging questions of importance—I concentrate on the dimension captured by the fact of reasonable pluralism.

I said that philosophies of life are matters on which reasonable people disagree, and I mean that as a platitude. But seeing it as such requires that we distinguish the fact of reasonable pluralism itself from various philosophical responses to it. Reflective moral divergence is, for example, commonly taken to provide strong evidence for the conclusion that no moral outlook is true, at least not objectively true,[7] or that moral truth transcends our cognitive powers. But persistent divergence of outlook among reasonable people does not require a nihilist or a relativist explanation. Reasonable people may disagree about a singular truth. Nor does the absence of convergence command skepticism. For the purposes of political argument, all we should say in response to the fact of reflective divergence is that in matters of comprehensive morality, the truth, if there be such, transcends the exercise of practical reason appropriate to expect of others, as free and equal.

Five considerations speak in support of the fact of reasonable pluralism and the force of this response to it. To start with, we observe persistent

---

7. On the importance of moral diversity as a source of pressures toward relativism and nihilism, see Gilbert Harman, "Moral Relativism," in Gilbert Harman and Judith Jarvis Thomson, *Moral Relativism and Moral Objectivity* (Oxford: Basil Blackwell, 1996), 8–14.

disagreements among familiar traditions of ethical thought, each with its own elaborate structure and complex history of internal evolution— disagreements, for example, about the relative importance of values of choice and self-determination, happiness and welfare, and self-actualization, and about the religious and philosophical background of these evaluative views. Second, in addition to the sheer fact of disagreement, the exercise of practical reason generates no apparent *tendency* to convergence on a philosophy of life. Furthermore, third, no compelling *theory* of the operations of practical reason predicts convergence of comprehensive moralities after sufficient evidence or reflection or argument is brought to bear. For moral deliberation, we have nothing comparable to the economists' proof of the existence of a general equilibrium of a competitive market economy with certain minimal optimality properties—much less an argument for convergence on such an equilibrium. Nor, fourth, are there any marginally attractive social or political mechanisms that might generate comprehensive agreement. Finally, we can identify natural explanations for the persistence of disagreement that do not require accusations of "unreason": exercise of practical reason often proceeds within distinct traditions of thought with complex internal structures; personal circumstance and sensibility predispose people to different traditions; and empirical constraints (including the constraints of considered evaluative judgments) are typically too weak to swamp such differences, in part because evaluative concepts themselves are imprecise and their explications are contested.[8]

These considerations may appear to prove too much: to create troubles for the deliberative view, too. For the deliberative view, it will emerge, requires some agreement on political ideas. Why, then, don't the observations that support the fact of reasonable pluralism exclude that agreement, too? By way of response, I need to say something more about the fourth point: the absence of convergence-generating mechanisms in the case of comprehensive philosophies of life. Consider the difference on this point between a comprehensive moral consensus and a narrower po-

---

8. See Rawls's discussion of the burdens of judgment in *Political Liberalism*, 54–58. Leif Wenar argues that these burdens are not widely acknowledged, that, for example, "a religious doctrine characteristically presents itself as universally accessible to clear minds and open hearts," and he cites the Vatican II statement on Divine Revelation in support. See Leif Wenar, "*Political Liberalism*: An Internal Critique," *Ethics* 106 (October 1995): 32–62. But to say that certain religious truths require revelation is to acknowledge that they, unlike truths of natural religion, are not simply available to clear minds and open hearts.

litical agreement.[9] While it is implausible to expect agreement on political values to result from a convergence of practical reasoning conducted
within different, independent moral traditions, it is not so implausible to
expect important elements of political consensus to emerge from the acquisition of ideas and principles embodied in shared institutions. The
acquisition of political ideals and values proceeds in part through participation in common, public institutions of various kinds—families, associations, the state. And the formation of moral-political ideas and sensibilities proceeds less by reasoning or explicit instruction (which may be
important in the case of comprehensive moral views) than by mastering
ideas and principles that are expressed in and serve to interpret these institutions. Thus, people living within institutions and a political culture
shaped by certain ideas and principles are likely to come to understand
those ideas and principles and to develop some attachment to them.

Take the idea of citizens as equal moral persons. This idea is, in several
ways, manifest in the norms and traditions of interpretation associated
with citizenship in a democracy (though practice often fails to conform
to those norms)—for example, equality before the law, and equal civil
and political rights. We can understand how citizens quite generally
might acquire an understanding of one another as moral equals by holding the position of citizen and living in a political culture in which ideas
of equality associated with that position play a central role in political discourse.[10] Different comprehensive views that accept this political understanding of equality will have different ways of fitting it into their broader
conceptions. Some will accept political equality as following from a fundamental religious conviction about human equality or from a general
moral conception of human beings as equally intrinsically valuable; others will accept political equality as an important, nonderivative value.[11]
But what makes agreement possible in this case is that citizens who grow
up within a reasonably stable democracy will find this (self-) conception
familiar and attractive: the political ideas "expressed" in common, public

9. The remarks that follow draw on my "A More Democratic Liberalism."

10. Consider in this connection the virtually unanimous popular endorsement of political
equality and equality of opportunity indicated in Herbert McClosky and John Zaller, *The
American Ethos: Public Attitudes Toward Capitalism and Democracy* (Cambridge: Cambridge
University Press, 1985), 74, 83.

11. Thus, Dahl formulates the "principle of equal consideration of interests," as well as the
"idea of intrinsic equality" on which it rests, to apply solely to processes for making binding
collective decisions, and indicates that both might be adopted by adherents to religious moralities, as well as utilitarian and Kantian moral views. See *Democracy and Its Critics*, 85–87.

institutions and appealed to in the culture to justify those institutions will shape the moral-political education of citizens.

Of course, the acquisition of moral ideas does not proceed exclusively through institutions. So citizens will need to be able to accommodate the political ideas and the self-conceptions they acquire through institutions within their different philosophies of life: to find a way to combine, for example, a conception of human beings as servants of God bound by natural duties with a political conception of citizens as free, equal, and self-governing. And many views—religious, moral, philosophical—have sufficient internal flexibility, or openness, to make such accommodations possible.[12] But while this accommodation may take place when a comprehensive moral or religious view is elaborated in ways that make it compatible with a political conception, we have no reason to expect it to produce agreement extending beyond political values; for no institutional mechanism in a democratic society imposes pressure to reach agreement in ways that would erase fundamental differences between moral, religious, and philosophical traditions. The pressure of the shared institutions in explaining political agreement ends even as considerable disagreement remains.

In short, political values are institutionalized in a democratic society in ways that comprehensive moral (or religious, or philosophical) ideas are not. More precisely, comprehensive ideas are sustained through more particular social associations that are not shared: different churches, for example, advance different comprehensive views. So citizens acquire

12. Consider, for example, the changes in the Catholic doctrine on toleration that emerge in Vatican II. The idea of human dignity, always a central element in Catholic moral and social thought, is developed along new lines as the basis for an account of political legitimacy with principled limits on the state's authority in matters of religious faith and practice. See *The Revised Documents of Vatican II*, "Declaration on Religious Freedom," 1.2, ed. Austin Flannery (Northport: Costello, 1976), 800–801. Dignity imposes an obligation to seek the truth and embrace it. But though the "one true religion subsists in the Catholic and apostolic Church," the pursuit and embrace of truth must comport with our nature as free beings "endowed with reason" and the dignity owing to that nature. And this requires immunity from "external coercion" as well as from "psychological freedom." The introduction to the Declaration ties the force of the sense of dignity and an understanding of its implications to modern experience (the "consciousness of contemporary man"). In an interesting essay on modern Confucian humanism and human rights, Tu Wei-ming suggests a way to reinterpret Confucian doctrine as incorporating a conception of dignity, tied to obligations in social relationships, that could serve in turn as a basis for a conception of human rights. Here, too, the conception of dignity is tied to central Confucian notions, but its formulation is prompted by modern political sensibilities, as articulated through international institutions. See Tu Wei-ming, "A Confucian Perspective on Human Rights," unpublished, 1995.

conflicting comprehensive views through those associations. An account of how consensus might emerge on political values among citizens living in a political society, then, has resources unavailable to an account of a more comprehensive moral consensus.

Despite these considerations, one might still hold out hope for comprehensive moral agreement and for a political community based on such agreement. In response to the observation that there is no tendency to reach agreement, we might, for example, take certain points of moral convergence—on the injustice of slavery or on the value of religious toleration—as at least suggesting a broader tendency toward moral convergence.

Moreover, a political society with comprehensive moral agreement has at least four attractive qualities that might make it a society to be hoped for. In such a society, for example, members respect one another for their determinate, concrete commitments—for the values that animate their lives—and not simply for their abstract though perhaps unrealized human capacities, not merely for their inner, but perhaps unexpressed, dignity. Furthermore, all may believe the truth, whereas moral pluralism implies that some members are bound to endorse false moral ideas; even if we accept that false views have public rights,[13] still, endorsing the truth is an important human good; and endorsing it in common, deepens mutual respect. In addition, agreement gives the members of a society a confidence in the bases of their conduct that is plausibly lacking under conditions of disagreement, thus mitigating pressures to reject the objectivity of ethical thought and embrace skepticism, nihilism, or simple alienation. Finally, as a practical matter, the absence of conflict on comprehensive views may ease communication and coordination.

In response to the proposed extrapolation from cases of convergence—slavery and religious toleration—it must be said that these are not cases in which people agree on comprehensive moral outlooks. Instead, people who belong to different moral and religious traditions come to agree on the injustice of certain especially injurious practices, despite their persistent disagreement on other matters. Thus, the condemnation of slavery is common ground among Catholics, Muslims, Jews, and Protestants; and among Kantians and utilitarians. So the examples are not strong evi-

---

13. For critical discussion of the idea of the "exclusive rights of truth," see John Courtney Murray, "The Problem of Religious Freedom," in J. Leon Hooper, S.J., ed., *Religious Liberty: Catholic Struggles with Pluralism* (Louisville: Westminster John Knox Press, 1993), ch. 2.

dence for the thesis that practical reason generates a more general moral convergence among people working within different moral and religious traditions; rather, they are important cases of agreement on political values among people who have fundamental moral disagreements.

Moreover, let us suppose that comprehensive agreement has important virtues. Still, if the exercise of practical reason does not generate convergence among people who begin with very different outlooks, associated with different traditions of moral, religious, and philosophical thought and practice, then how is comprehensive moral agreement to be achieved? Perhaps through some form of common moral education in a comprehensive view. But how is such education—as distinct from education about requirements of civic responsibility and decency—to proceed in the face of different and competing forms of moral thought, each with its own associational life? Perhaps through the state's coercive means. But it is not so clear that the state can produce genuine moral agreement, as opposed to public spectacles of conformity; and if it could, the price seems unacceptable, despite the values associated with agreement.

I assume the fact of reasonable pluralism, then. And this fact gives shape to the conception of citizens as free and equal that constitutes part of the deliberative conception of democracy I want to explore here. To say that citizens are *free* is to say, inter alia, that no comprehensive moral or religious view provides a defining condition of membership or the foundation of the authorization to exercise political power. Not that religious or moral views are, religiously, morally, or metaphysically speaking, matters of choice. To someone who has a religious view, for example, believing the view is a matter of believing what is true, and acting on it, a matter of fulfilling obligations that are not self-legislated and are perhaps more fundamental than political obligations.[14] But politically speaking, citizens are free in that it is open to them to accept or reject such views without loss of status. To say citizens are *equal* is to say that each is recognized as having the capacities required for participating in discussion aimed at authorizing the exercise of power.

What, more particularly then, can we say about a conception of de-

14. Michael McConnell says, "It would come as some surprise to a devout Jew to find that he has 'selected the day of the week in which to refrain from labor' since the Jewish people have been under the impression from some 3,000 years that this choice was made by God." "Religious Freedom at a Crossroads," *University of Chicago Law Review* 59 (1992): 115. The source of the quotation to which McConnell is responding is Estate of Thornton v. Caldor, Inc., 472 U.S. 703, 711 (1985) (O'Connor, J., concurring).

mocracy suited to conditions of reasonable pluralism? By excluding a comprehensive consensus on values, the fact of reasonable pluralism may suggest that a procedural conception of democracy, limited to such values as openness and impartiality associated with fair process, is the only remaining option. After all, that fact deprives us of a background of shared moral or religious premises—shared reasons—that would give more determinate content to the idea of popular authorization. Without that background, we are left, it may seem, with no basis for agreement on anything more than fair procedures—perhaps not even with that. Faced with disagreement on comprehensive views, what legitimate complaint can a person raise about a framework of collective decision, beyond the complaint that the framework fails to take her interests into account?

I think this conclusion is incorrect and will sketch a view that combines an assumption of reasonable pluralism with a more substantive conception of democracy. I will suggest as well that this combination is a natural result of adopting a *deliberative* understanding of the collective decisions that constitute democratic governance.

3. Public Reasoning

A deliberative conception of democracy puts public reasoning at the center of political justification. I say *public reasoning* rather than *public discussion* because a deliberative view cannot be distinguished simply by its emphasis on discussion rather than bargaining or voting as methods of collective decision making. On any view of democracy—indeed any view of intelligent political decision making—discussion is important, if only because of its essential role in pooling private information, against a background of asymmetries in its distribution.

According to the deliberative interpretation of democracy, then, democracy is a system of social and political arrangements that institutionally ties the exercise of power to free reasoning among equals. This conception of justification through public reasoning can be represented in an idealized procedure of political deliberation, constructed to capture the notions of free, equal, and reason that figure in the deliberative ideal. The point of the idealized procedure is to provide a model characterization of free reasoning among equals, which can, in turn, serve as a model for arrangements of collective decision making—arrangements that establish a framework of free reasoning among equals. Using the model, we can work out the content of the deliberative democratic ideal and its conception of public reasoning by considering features of such reasoning in the idealized case and then aiming to build those features into institutions.

Thus, in an ideal deliberative procedure, participants are, and regard one another, as *free*: recognizing the fact of reasonable pluralism, they acknowledge, as I noted earlier, that no comprehensive moral or religious view provides a defining condition of participation or a test of the acceptability of arguments in support of the exercise of political power. Moreover, participants regard one another as formally and substantively *equal*. They are formally equal in that the rules regulating the ideal procedure do not single out individuals for special advantage or disadvantage. Instead, everyone with the deliberative capacities—which is to say, more or less all human beings—has, and is recognized as having, equal standing at each stage of the deliberative process. Each, that is, can propose issues for the agenda, propose solutions to the issues on the agenda, offer reasons in support of or in criticism of proposed solutions. And each has an equal voice in the decision. The participants are substantively equal in that the existing distribution of power and resources does not shape their chances to contribute to deliberation, nor does that distribution play an authoritative role in their deliberation. In saying that it does not play an authoritative role in their deliberation, I mean that the participants in the deliberative procedure do not regard themselves as collectively morally bound by the existing system of rights, except insofar as that system establishes the framework of free deliberation among equals. Instead, they regard that system as a potential object of their deliberative judgment.

In addition, they are *reasonable* in that they aim to defend and criticize institutions and programs in terms of considerations that others, as free and equal, have *reason to accept*, given the fact of reasonable pluralism and on the assumption that those others are themselves concerned to provide suitable justifications.

Which considerations count as reasons? Generically speaking, a reason is a consideration that counts in favor of something: in particular, a belief or an action. Not an illuminating analysis: I doubt that illuminating analysis is available or that it would be helpful in answering our question.[15] What is needed is an account not of what a reason is, but of which considerations count as reasons. And the answer to this question depends

15. Here I follow discussion in T. M. Scanlon's *What We Owe to Each Other* (Cambridge, MA: Harvard University Press, 1997), ch. 1.

on context. Whether considerations count in favor in the relevant way depends on the setting in which they are advanced. Applying this point to the issue at hand: a suitable account of which considerations count as reasons for the purposes of an account of democratic deliberation will take the form not of a generic account of what a reason is but of a statement of which considerations count in favor of proposals within a deliberative setting suited to the case of free association among equals, understood to include an acknowledgment of reasonable pluralism. This background is reflected in the kinds of reasons that will be acceptable—meaning, as always, acceptable to individuals as free and equal citizens.

I have already specified the relevant deliberative setting as one in which people are understood as free, equal, and reasonable and as having conflicting philosophies of life. Within the idealized deliberative setting that captures these conditions, it will not do simply to advance considerations that one takes to be true or compelling. Such considerations may well be rejected by others who are themselves reasonable—prepared to live with others on terms acceptable to those others, given their different comprehensive views—and endorse conflicting philosophies of life. One needs instead to find reasons that are compelling to others, where those others are regarded as (and regard themselves as) equals and have diverse reasonable commitments. How wide a range of commitments? Because we are addressing the institutional framework for making collective decisions and assume the participants to be free—not bound to their de facto commitments—the range of commitments is similarly wide: not exhausted by de facto commitments. Considerations that do not meet these tests will be rejected in the idealized setting and so do not count as acceptable political reasons. Let us say, then, that a consideration is an acceptable political reason just in case it has the support of the different comprehensive views that might be endorsed by reasonable citizens.

To illustrate these points about the role of the background—the conception of citizens as free, equal, and reasonable—in constraining the set of reasons, let us consider three implications; the first two will be particularly important in my discussion of the liberties.

First, people hold religious commitments on faith, and those commitments impose what they take to be overriding obligations. Such commitments are not, as such, unreasonable: though faith transcends reason, even as "reason" is understood within the tradition to which the commitments belong, citizens are not unreasonable for holding beliefs on faith.

But beliefs held on faith—perhaps beliefs in what are understood to be revealed truths—can reasonably be rejected by others who rely only on the darkness of an unconverted heart and so cannot serve to justify legislation.

Thus, it matters to our response to the case against abortion stated in the encyclical, *Evangelium Vitae*, that Pope John Paul II claims that the gospel of life *"can . . . be known in its essential traits by human reason"* and that the "Law of God" that condemns abortion is "written in every human heart [and] knowable by reason itself"—in short, that the argument is presented as independent of a particular faith position.[16] Though I see no reason to agree with this claim about what lies within the compass of reason, our response to the argument must be different from what that response would be if the argument appealed openly to revealed truths or beliefs held on faith. We must show that the conception of reason it appeals to is itself sectarian and that the argument fails on a conception of reason that is not.

Second, the adequacy of a consideration as a political reason—its weight in political justification—will depend on the nature of the regulated conduct, in particular on the strength of the reasons that support that conduct. Thus, considerations of public order provide acceptable reasons for regulating conduct. Different views have different ways of explaining that value: utilitarians will found it on considerations of aggregate happiness, Kantians on the preconditions of autonomous conduct, others on the intrinsic value of human life and human sociability. Moreover, people are bound to disagree about the requirements of public order: that disagreement may extend to whether a state is necessary to secure the conditions of order. But it will not be acceptable to suppose that, as a general matter, the value of public order transcends all other political values. Except perhaps in the most extreme circumstances, for example, a state may not impose a blanket prohibition on alcohol consumption—including consumption in religious services—in the name of public order. The reasons that support such consumption include considerations of religious duty—more generally, considerations of fundamental duty, which are normally overriding. And those considerations

16. Pope John Paul II, *Evangelium Vitae* (New York: Times Books, 1995), §§29, 62. For critical discussion of these claims and the argument based on them, see Judith Jarvis Thomson, "Abortion," *Boston Review* 20, 3 (Summer 1995): 11–15.

will provide a suitable basis for rejecting a justification cast in terms of the value of public order, except in the most extreme conditions.

These first two points about reasons both generate pressure for liberty. The first point underscores that reasonable pluralism will lead to the rejection of some bases for restricting liberty as politically weightless; the second indicates that other bases of restriction will not be weightless, but they will be insufficient to outweigh reasons that can be acknowledged, consistent with reasonable pluralism, as commending or commanding a course of conduct.

Finally, third, the fact that a policy is most beneficial to me arguably provides me with a reason to support that policy.[17] But this reason carries no weight in public deliberation of the relevant kind, because others, concerned with their advantage and willing to find mutually acceptable reasons, will not accept it as a reason; moreover, it is reasonable for them not to accept it, in part because they can dismiss it while at the same time treating me as an equal and giving my good the same weight in their deliberations that they insist I give to theirs. Thus, I may *prefer* the arrangement that gives me the greatest advantage, and so have a personal reason for promoting it. But in the context of ideal deliberation, I must find considerations in favor of the arrangement that do not neglect the good of others. Similarly, I may wish to reject an arrangement that leaves me less well-off than some others. But I cannot offer as a reason against it that it leaves me less well-off, because every arrangement will leave some people less well-off than some others. So if I need to find reasons acceptable to others, I cannot reject a proposal simply because it does to me what each arrangement must do to someone—and, again, every arrangement leaves some less well-off than others. I can, however, reject it on grounds that an arrangement leaves me less well-off than anyone needs to be.

In presenting the deliberative view in terms of an ideal deliberative procedure in which parties are required to find reasons acceptable to others, I may appear to be tying the deliberative conception to an implausible requirement of political consensus—to the view that "deliberation leads to convergence."[18]

I make no such assumption. Instead, I assume that different views will

17. I say "arguably" because it might be said that reasons are essentially public and capable of being shared. If that is right, then the fact stated in the text would not constitute a reason.

18. See Adam Przeworski, *Democracy and the Market* (Cambridge: Cambridge University Press, 1991), 17.

have different interpretations of the acceptable reasons and of how differ-ent reasons are to be weighted—for example, reasons of equality and of aggregate well-being. As a result, even an ideal deliberative procedure will not, in general, issue in consensus. But even if there is such disagree-ment, and a need to submit the decision to majority rule, still, partici-pants in the ideal case will need to appeal to considerations that are quite generally recognized as having considerable weight and having a suitable basis for collective choice, even among people who disagree about the right result: agreement on political values is not agreement on the proper combination of them. But when people do appeal to considerations that are quite generally recognized as having considerable weight, then the fact that a proposal has majority support will itself commonly count as a reason for endorsing it. Even people who disagree may, then, accept the results of a deliberative procedure as legitimate.

4. Discussion, Deliberation, Motivation

I said earlier that a deliberative conception of democracy cannot be char-acterized by its emphasis on discussion, that any view of democracy will have an important place for discussion because of its essential role in pooling dispersed, private information. Of course, discussion is not al-ways so helpful. As Przeworski puts it, "If people behave strategically in pursuit of their interests, they also emit messages in this way":[19] behavior does not lose its strategic character simply because it involves the use of language. And if people "emit messages"—that is, communicate—strate-gically, they may well have incentives to misrepresent private informa-tion, in which case discussion may play an essential role in creating de-ception and spreading misinformation. The mere fact that conduct is linguistically mediated does not, of course, imply that agents are pre-pared to constrain their conduct by referring to norms of honesty, sincer-ity, and full disclosure rather than simply taking the most effective means to their ends. The use of language may, as a matter of conversational implicature, commit the speaker to such norms—to endorsing them as proper standards of guidance and criticism. But I don't propose to rest anything on this hypothesis.

Though the strategic use of language to advance one's aims always car-ries the potential of deviating from norms of honesty, the strength of in-

19. Ibid.

centives to engage in misrepresentation depends, inter alia, on the underlying diversity of citizen preferences. Intuitively, the more diverse the preferences of individuals—the more they disagree about the best outcome—the greater are the gains from strategically lying, misinforming, or distorting; the greater the gains, the greater are the temptations to undertake such manipulation.[20] The point is familiar in the setting of legislative decision making in legislatures with committee structures. The more extreme the preferences of committee members relative to median legislative preferences (the more they are outliers), the less informative the committees will be (more noise, less signal). For this reason, majoritarian legislatures will not—unless they have a collective preference for self-deception—want to leave important decisions in the hands of a committee composed of preference outliers: members will not expect the committee to provide truthful and complete information.

But—and this is the crucial point—the extent of preference diversity is not fixed, not given in advance of political deliberation. Not that the *aim* of such deliberation is to change citizen preferences by reducing their diversity: the aim is to make collective decisions. Still, one thought behind a deliberative conception is that public *reasoning* itself can help to reduce the diversity of politically relevant preferences, because such preferences are shaped and even formed in the process of public reasoning itself. And if it does help to reduce that diversity, then it mitigates tendencies toward distortion even in strategic communication.

Two points are essential here, one concerning reasons, the other concerning connections between reasons and motives. First, the reasoning that figures in collective decisions need not be exclusively instrumental—only a matter of determining the most effective means for achieving settled aims, given perhaps by desires. Indeed, practical reasoning—understood as reflection on and discussion about what reasons for action agents have—may proceed along deliberative paths with only the most

20. See Keith Krehbiel, *Information and Legislative Organization* (Ann Arbor: University of Michigan Press, 1991), 81–84, 95–96. Apart from this dependence on preference diversity, the effectiveness of speech depends on the ease of verifying information and on whether discussion proceeds sequentially and in public. See David Austen-Smith, "Strategic Models of Talk in Political Decision-Making," *International Political Science Review* 13, 1 (1992): 45–58; on economic institutions that promote verification and sequential, public conversation, see Charles Sabel, "Learning by Monitoring: The Institutions of Economic Development," in Neil Smelser and Richard Swedberg, eds., *The Handbook of Economic Sociology* (Princeton: Princeton University Press, 1995), 137–165.

attenuated connections to the agent's current aims.[21] Citizens are capable of recognizing *as reasons* considerations that conflict with their antecedent preferences and interests, ranking alternatives in accordance with such considerations, and acting on those rankings. I might now recognize that I have good reason to refrain from harming others but not think that I have reason ever to help them, nor have any desire at all to help. Suppose, however, that reflection on *why* I have reason not to harm leads me to see that the explanation for that reason also implies that I have reason to help. Though I have no desire to help, a new reason emerges from a search for reflective equilibrium that, as in this example, proceeds by considering the justification for settled reasons and the implications of the justification for other reasons that agents have. To the extent that I also have preferences that conflict with these reasons, I will continue to have incentives—perhaps strong ones—to strategically misrepresent information. But, coming now to the second point, seeing that certain of my antecedent preferences and interests cannot be expressed in the form of acceptable reasons may help to limit the force of such preferences as political motives.[22]

To illustrate: assume a commitment to deliberative justification—assume, that is, the shared belief that political justification requires finding reasons acceptable to others, understood as free and equal, who endorse that commitment. And assume, alongside that, a desire that others serve my aims, regardless of their own.[23] Though this desire may prompt me to advance a proposal, it does not count as a reason in public argument. To defend the proposal consistent with my commitment to finding justifications of the appropriate kind, then, I need to advance reasons independent of the desire—which I will be prepared to do only if I believe that there are acceptable reasons. And presenting such reasons may lead to the formation of a new desire, say a desire to coordinate with others on mutually beneficial terms. Merely believing that I have such a reason

21. For discussion, see Christine Korsgaard, "Skepticism about Practical Reason," *Journal of Philosophy* 83, 1 (January 1986): 5–25; Scanlon, *What We Owe to Each Other*, ch. 1. For illuminating criticism of instrumental rationality, see Robert Nozick, *The Nature of Rationality* (Princeton: Princeton University Press, 1993), ch. 5. Particularly important for purposes here are the remarks on the symbolic utility of acting on principles.

22. Using Nozick's terminology (see note 21), when I see that a proposal cannot be defended with acceptable reasons, its symbolic utility declines. Assuming that symbolic utility is motivationally important, the motivation for advancing the proposal declines.

23. I am not worrying here about distinctions between "desire" and "prefer," in particular that the latter is a polyadic relation.

may suffice to refashion preferences, but the motivational force of that recognition is likely to be greater if I must state the reasons, thereby lending greater salience to them. That desire, unlike the desire that others serve my aims regardless of their own, is naturally expressed in a reason that is acceptable to others. Moreover, if I develop the desire to cooperate on mutually beneficial terms, my incentive to strategically misrepresent private information will decline. And that means that even if my communications are in part strategically motivated, I will be more likely to provide information that is commonly beneficial.

It should be clear, but it is nevertheless worth emphasizing, that the preference changes with beneficial effects on strategic communication are not simply changes of *induced* preference that result from the acquisition of new information through discussion.[24] Of course, new information may well induce new preferences: I now prefer eating bread to eating cheese because I believe that bread is more nutritious and prefer more nutritious to less nutritious food; if I learn that cheese is more nutritious, and I am rational, I will prefer cheese to bread. And sometimes disagreement among preferences is generated by simple differences of factual belief. Reducing differences owing to lack of common information will often be a good thing. But the kinds of preference changes I am contemplating reflect a sensitivity of motivations—understood as behavioral dispositions—to reasons, understood as standards of criticism and guidance, and not simply a sensitivity of some preferences to information about how most effectively to satisfy other preferences.

Though these are not cases of induced preference change, they are also not cases (like hypnotism or suggestion) of preferences changing without rational explanation. In the kinds of cases I am considering, preferences change because a person comes to understand—through practical reasoning—that his current preferences lack appropriate justification: not because new empirical knowledge is acquired that bears on the achievement of an aim (as in the bread to cheese example), but because the preference cannot be supported by reasons of a suitable kind, the agent recognizes that it cannot, and that recognition has sufficient salience to shape motivations. In the background is the view that the no-

---

24. On the distinction between primitive and induced preferences, and a case for the view that deliberation-induced preference change is a matter of changes in induced preferences as a result of new information, see John Ferejohn, "Must Preferences Be Respected in a Democracy?," in Copp, et al., eds., *The Idea of Democracy*, 236–237.

tion of a reason is essentially normative—a term of justification and of criticism—and that a reason is not a kind of motivation. Practical reasoning, then, is a matter of reflecting on what one is to do, not what one is motivated to do, though the results of such reasoning can motivate.[25]

5. Religious Liberty

I have focused thus far on the structure of the deliberative view. I turn now to its substance, in particular to the thesis that democracy—on the deliberative interpretation of collective choice—must ensure religious, expressive, and moral liberties. This proposal departs from conventional understandings of the relationship between democracy and these liberties. To illustrate that understanding, I want to present a familiar dilemma associated with the idea of democratic legitimacy.

On the one hand, the value of democracy seems too procedural to provide a basis for an account of legitimacy; some democratic collective choices are too repulsive to be legitimate, however attractive the procedures that generate them. On the other hand, the idea of democracy appears to be the authoritative, sovereign requirement of collective decisions. That is because democracy appears to be the form of collective choice mandated by the fundamental political idea that citizens are to be treated as equals. Because the ideal of treating people as equals is so fundamental, and so intimately linked to democratic procedures of binding collective decision making, democracy is naturally identified not simply as one political value to be combined with others but also as the way we must settle the ordering of other political values—the way to ensure equal standing in settling the common environment. To put issues off the democratic agenda appears, by contrast, to establish objectionable spheres of privilege. Thus, Robert Dahl says:

> It seems to me highly reasonable to argue that *no* interests should be inviolable beyond those integral or essential to the democratic process. . . . [O]utside this broad domain [which includes rights of political expression, participation, and association] a democratic people could freely choose the policies its members feel best; they could decide how best to balance free-

25. For suggestive discussion of the role nonstrategic reasons can play in constraining discussion and in improving its effectiveness, see James Johnson, "Is Talk Really Cheap? Prompting Conversation Between Critical Theory and Rational Choice," *American Political Science Review* 87, 1 (1993): 74–86.

dom and control, how best to settle conflicts between the interests of some and the interests of others, how best to organize and control their economy and so on. In short, outside the inviolable interests of democratic people in the preservation of the democratic process [inviolable because of the roots of that process in an ideal of equal intrinsic worth] would lie the proper sphere for political decisions.[26]

Dahl immediately indicates some qualms about this view and explores ways to ensure that conventional democratic process might better protect fundamental interests that are not integral or essential to it.[27] But he has identified a genuine problem, whose most familiar expression arises in connection with what Benjamin Constant called the "liberties of the moderns"—religious liberty, liberty of conscience more generally, liberty of thought and expression, rights of person and personal property. These liberties lack any evident connection to conditions of democratic procedure: to borrow Dahl's words, they are neither integral nor essential to it. So their protection is commonly understood as constraining democratic process—limiting its appropriate scope. In that respect they differ from political liberties, including rights of association, of speech on political questions, and of participation. If a constitution disables a majority from restricting political participation or regulating the content of political speech, that constitution can be interpreted as safeguarding the essentials of democratic process. Assurances of such political liberties help to ensure a connection between popular authorization and political outcome—to preserve the continuing authority of the people, and not simply the majority of them.[28] Those liberties—the liberties of the ancients—are constitutive elements of democratic process.

The liberties of the moderns appear, then, to be based on independent

26. Dahl, *Democracy and Its Critics*, 182.

27. Dahl has long been skeptical about the role of courts with powers of judicial review in providing such protection. See his remarkable essay, "Decision-Making in a Democracy: The Supreme Court as a National Policy-Maker," *Journal of Public Law* 6 (Fall 1957): 279–295; and *Democracy and Its Critics*, chs. 12, 13.

28. See John Hart Ely, *Democracy and Distrust* (Cambridge, MA: Harvard University Press, 1980); Dahl, *Democracy and Its Critics*; and, more generally, on constitutional requirements as enabling democracy, Stephen Holmes, "Precommitment and the Paradox of Democracy," in Jon Elster and Rune Slagstad, eds., *Constitutionalism and Democracy* (Cambridge: Cambridge University Press, 1988), esp. 195–240; and Samuel Freeman, "Original Meaning, Democratic Interpretation, and the Constitution," *Philosophy and Public Affairs* 21 (Winter 1992): 3–42.

values, separate from the ideal of treating people as equals in arenas of collective choice that underlies the appeal of democracy. And that may suggest that, from the perspective of democratic thought, these liberties have roots no deeper than contingent popular consensus. Though abridgments of nonpolitical liberties that emerge from a fair democratic process may be unjust, they face no problems of democratic legitimacy.[29]

On the deliberative conception of democracy, this conclusion is wrong: a deliberative view provides a basis for wider guarantees of basic liberties. The explanation of this feature is that the deliberative conception requires more than that the interests of all be given equal consideration in binding collective decisions; it requires, too, that we find politically acceptable reasons—reasons acceptable to others, given a background of reasonable differences of conscientious conviction. I call this requirement the *principle of deliberative inclusion*.[30]

To illustrate the roots and implications of this principle, I want to start with the case of religious liberty, one of the principal liberties of the moderns and the one that most sharply illustrates the analytical structure.

As I mentioned earlier, religious views set demands of an especially high order—perhaps transcendent obligations—on their adherents. Moreover, if we see these requirements from the believer's standpoint, we cannot see them as *self-imposed*—chosen by the agent. To put the point without benefit of ocular metaphor: if we believe about these requirements (say, as to day and manner of worship) what the adherent believes about them, then we do not believe that the adherent chooses to place herself under these demands. The content and stringency of the demands are fixed instead by the content of the convictions, which the adherent believes true, not by the adherent's endorsement of those convictions. To be sure, if a believer did not endorse the convictions, then she would not believe herself to be bound by them: but given that she does endorse them, she thinks that she would then hold false beliefs and would be more likely to do what is wrong.

29. This is, I believe, Dahl's view. Critics of Roberto Unger's conception of empowered democracy have (mistakenly, I believe) assumed that he endorses it. See his *False Necessity* (Cambridge: Cambridge University Press, 1987), 508–539. And it bears a strong family resemblance to the democracy-based interpretations of the U.S. Constitution advanced by Ely in *Democracy and Distrust*; and Bruce Ackerman in *We, the People* (Cambridge, MA: Harvard University Press, 1991), esp. ch. 1.

30. Of course, not all differences of conviction are reasonable. One implication is that the problem of toleration for the intolerant is a separate issue in an account of religious liberty. Religious liberty generally ought not to be treated as a response to a problem of unreasonableness.

Liberal political conceptions are sometimes said to endorse, if only by way of implicit commitment, a conception of human beings as "bound only by ends and roles we choose" and correspondingly to deny "that we can ever be claimed by ends we have not chosen—ends given by God, for example, or by our identities as members of families, peoples, cultures, or traditions."[31] Liberalism, on this view, rests on moral voluntarism. And such voluntarism implies that religious moralities are false. It is difficult, I think, to find political conceptions that embrace uncompromising moral voluntarism—that conceive of human beings as, in Michael Sandel's compelling phrase, "unencumbered selves." In any case, that philosophy of life cannot possibly serve as common political ground. And once it is rejected as such, we see that reasonable adherents cannot accept, as sufficient reasons in support of a law or a system of policy, considerations that would preclude their compliance with fundamental religious demands or require that they treat those demands as matters of choice.

What, then, of citizens who do not share those views, who reject them as false—or, perhaps, as meaningless? (I will describe the issue from the point of view of a citizen who has fundamental moral convictions but not religious convictions. Broadly parallel remarks could be made from the standpoint of different religious convictions.) They might respond in one of three ways.

First, they might regard all religious views that impose such stringent demands, whatever their content and foundation, as unreasonable. This response might issue from the conviction that all religious views are intolerant, and for that reason politically unreasonable, or that religious convictions cannot withstand reflective scrutiny. But neither of these views is acceptable. The first is simply false. Nothing in religious conviction itself—any more or less than in secular moral conviction—requires endorsement of the view that "error has no rights" or that truth suffices for justification. As to the second, there may be conceptions of "reflective scrutiny" on which religious views cannot withstand such scrutiny. But those conceptions themselves are almost certain to belong to comprehensive views (say, empiricist philosophies) that cannot be permitted to set the bounds on public reasoning, any more than can natural theology's conception of natural reason. Moreover, any account of reflective scru-

31. Michael Sandel, *Democracy's Discontent* (Cambridge, MA: Harvard University Press, 1996), 322.

tiny that condemns religious conviction will almost certainly condemn secular moral ideas as equally unreasonable.

A second possibility is to treat concerns to fulfill religious obligations as intense preferences, to be given equal consideration along with other preferences of equal intensity. This response urges us to put aside the content of the convictions and their special role—as first principles of practical justification—in practical reasoning. The roots of this response lie, I believe, in a misinterpretation of the value of neutrality. Neutrality requires that political justification in a democracy not depend on any particular reasonable view. But it does not require that we neglect the content of views, treat all as matters of mere preference, and let the strength of claims be fixed by the intensity of those preferences.[32] Doing so indicates a failure to take into account the special weight of religious or fundamental moral convictions to the adherent, particularly the weight of requirements that the religious or the moral outlook itself designates as fundamental demands: an unwillingness to see how the adherent's convictions, in virtue of their content, state or imply that the requirements provide especially compelling reasons, and not simply strong preferences.

But if we are not prepared to treat convictions as (without qualification) self-imposed, nor to accept them as true, nor to dismiss them as false, or—putting their truth or falsity to the side—nor to let their weight be fixed by their intensity as preferences, what is left? The alternative is to take seriously that the demands impose what the adherent reasonably regards as fundamental obligations (paradigmatically compelling practical reasons), to accept the requirement—associated with the deliberative view—of finding reasons that might override these obligations, and to acknowledge that such reasons cannot normally be found.[33] The result is religious liberty, understood to include freedom of conscience, which condemns disabilities imposed on grounds of religious belief, and free exercise of religion, which condemns, in particular, limits on public worship.[34] It emerges as the product of three elements. The first is the

32. See Scanlon's suggestion that proponents of subjective criteria for interpersonal comparisons might defend those criteria by arguing that they "would be agreed on by people to the extent that they seek a principle recognizing them as equal, independent agents whose judgment must be accorded equal weight." T. M. Scanlon, "Preference and Urgency," *Journal of Philosophy* 72 (1975): 655–669.

33. On the encumbered self, see Sandel, *Democracy's Discontent*, 14.

34. On the distinction between these two aspects of religious liberty and on the connections between the arguments for them, see Murray, "The Problem of Religious Freedom," 141–144, 148–151.

demanding character of religious requirements, which from the point of view of those who are subject to them, are matters of fundamental obligation. It accepts the idea that free citizens—who accept that no comprehensive moral or religious view provides a defining condition of participation or a test of the acceptability of arguments in support of the exercise of political power—are, in a way, "encumbered": it proposes a rendering of the idea that such citizens have obligations and commitments that are not properly understood, for purposes of political argument, as matters of choice. Second, it draws on the shared concern—fundamental to the deliberative conception—to find reasons that citizens who are subject to what they regard as basic obligations can reasonably be expected to acknowledge. And third, it draws on the fact that citizens who are not religious have fundamental convictions that they take to impose especially compelling obligations.

The first two points are by themselves sufficient, but the third underscores the unreasonableness of failing to acknowledge religious liberty; for those who might be prepared to deny freedom of conscience and liberty of worship to others will typically want to claim freedom of conscience for themselves. And if they are unable to defend that freedom by appealing to the truth of their views, then they will need to defend it by reference to the stringency of the demands imposed by their fundamental and not unreasonable convictions. And then treating others as equals will require that they give similar weight to other demands belonging to that general category.

Suppose, then, that we prevent a person from fulfilling such demands for reasons the person is compelled to regard as insufficient: "compelled," because denying the sufficiency of these reasons follows from a religious or a moral philosophy that not unreasonably commands the person's conviction. This is to deny the person standing as an equal citizen—to deny full and equal membership in the people whose collective actions authorize the exercise of power. And that, according to the deliberative conception, is a failure of democracy. We have denied full membership by failing to provide a justification for the exercise of collective power by reference to considerations that all who are members of the sovereign body that authorizes the exercise of power and who are subject to that power, and are prepared to cooperate on reasonable terms, can accept. There are many ways to exclude individuals and groups from The People, and this surely is one.

To conclude, I want to make two observations about this account of religious liberty. First, my remarks are limited. I have not said anything directly about how to handle claims for religious exemption from general obligations with a strong secular justification (including obligations to educate children); or whether special provision is to be made for specifically religious convictions, as distinct from conscientious ethical convictions with no religious roots;[35] or about tolerating the intolerant. My aim here is not to resolve, or even to address, these issues: any view recognizing rights of free exercise will need to face those hard questions. I am interested only in making the more restricted point that a deliberative conception of democracy is not barred—by its emphasis on an ideal of democracy—from acknowledging a fundamental role for rights of religious liberty: indeed, that it must provide a place for such rights. The basis of such rights, on the deliberative view, lies deeper than contingent popular consensus. Like rights of political expression, they are founded on the idea of democracy itself.

Second, I emphasize that the rationale for the guarantees of religious liberty that fall under the requirement of deliberative inclusion is neither narrowly political nor antipolitical. It is not narrowly political, because those guarantees are not simply about enabling people to participate in normal politics (or to participate without fear), nor simply about improving public discussion by adding more diverse voices to it. It is not antipolitical, because they are not simply about ensuring the strength of organized associations (churches among them) that help to protect individuals from the state's power.[36] The argument does not deny the links between religious liberty and associational liberty. The idea instead is that abridgments of such liberties would constitute denials to citizens of standing as equal members of the sovereign people, by imposing in ways that deny the force of reasons that are, by the lights of their own views, compelling. The reasons for abridgment are unacceptably exclusionary, because they are unsuited to the ideal of guiding the exercise of power by a process of reason-giving suited to a system of free and equal citizens.

The view I am presenting might, then, be contrasted with an approach

35. On this last point: the key to the case for religious liberty is that the content of a view assigns stringent obligations to a person who holds it. But specifically *religious* content is not essential.

36. See the discussion of this rationale in Stephen Carter, *The Culture of Disbelief* (New York: Basic Books, 1993), 17–18, 35–39. As a general matter, Carter's defense of religious liberty seems too exclusively focused on the parallels between religious and associational liberty and, correspondingly, too dismissive of the continuities between freedom of conscience and freedom of public worship. On those continuities, see Murray, "The Problem of Religious Freedom," 148–151.

suggested by Roberto Unger's conception of empowered democracy, as well as with the approach I sketched in an earlier essay, "Deliberation and Democratic Legitimacy."[37] According to Unger, a system of immunities—negative liberties—is one component of a democratic order because "[f]reedom as participation *presupposes* freedom as immunity." The mistake of "critics of traditional democratic theory" is to believe that "participatory opportunities [are] a more than satisfactory *substitute* for immunity guarantees." According to Unger, participation is no substitute; instead, immunity rights are necessary if a citizen is to have the "safety that encourages him to participate actively and independently in collective decision-making." I do not disagree with the claim that immunity rights are necessary, nor with the criticism of other views. But I now think that the deliberative conception of democracy provides the basis for a less instrumental, less strategic rationale for certain liberties, even when those liberties are not needed to ensure appropriate inputs to democratic procedure.

6. Expressive Liberty

The principle of deliberative inclusion extends naturally from religious liberty to a *wide guarantee* of expressive liberty. By a "wide guarantee," I mean a guarantee not confined to political speech, even on very capacious understandings of political speech. Cass Sunstein, for example, defines political speech as speech that is "intended and received as a contribution to public deliberation about some issue."[38] I believe that a deliberative view supports stringent protections of expressive liberty, even when the expression falls outside the political, thus understood.

The deliberative view thus extends a more familiar democracy-based strand of free-speech theory, which defends stringent protections of *specifically political speech* as one prerequisite for a democratic framework of collective choice.[39] Alexander Meiklejohn's version of this theory locates the roots of a strong free-speech guarantee in the U.S. constitutional design of popular self-government. Because popular sovereignty re-

37. Unger, *False Necessity*, 525, emphases added; Joshua Cohen, "Deliberation and Democratic Legitimacy," in Alan Hamlin and Phillip Petit, eds., *The Good Polity* (Oxford: Blackwell, 1989), 17–34 [reprinted as essay 1 in this collection].

38. See Cass Sunstein, *Democracy and the Problem of Free Speech* (New York: Free Press, 1993), 130.

39. See Alexander Meiklejohn, *Political Freedom* (New York: Harper & Brothers, 1960); Sunstein, *Democracy and the Problem of Free Speech*; Robert Bork, "Neutral Principles and Some First Amendment Problems," *Indiana Law Journal* 47, 1 (Fall 1971): 1–35; Ely, *Democracy and Distrust*; Owen Fiss, *Liberalism Divided* (Boulder, CO: Westview Press, 1996).

quires free and open discussion among citizens, the government undercuts the Constitution's defining principle—treats citizens as subjects of government rather than its sovereign masters—when it interferes with such discussion. Others who favor the democracy defense add three considerations that supplement Meiklejohn's constitutional argument: (a) because citizens have diverse views, regulation of speech owing to its content establishes a regime of political inequality by silencing certain views or topics that may be important to some citizens; (b) content regulation effectively restricts the flow of information, perhaps reducing the quality of democratic discussion and decision; (c) content restrictions might limit the range of views in the discussion, and limits on range might confine the capacity of discussion itself to challenge received views and preferences by presenting unconventional outlooks.

Each of these considerations—fairness, quality, and reflectiveness—plays an important role in a full treatment of free expression as essential to deliberative democracy. Here, however, my aim is to indicate how the deliberative view supplements these considerations and thus extends stringent protections beyond political speech—and thus also forestalls the need to stretch the category of "political speech" to cover, for example, *Bleak House, Ulysses,* and Mapplethorpe's photographs (Sunstein's examples) so that they are stringently protected. Restriction to political speech may seem natural, once one has decided to base rights of expression on potential contribution as *input* to a discussion about the proper use of public power. But a deliberative conception must be cautious about accepting such a limit. Though the idea of reasonable discussion aimed at agreement is fundamental to the deliberative view, it does not follow that the protection of expression is to be confined to speech that *contributes to* such discussion. It may also need to extend to speech that cannot permissibly be regulated as an *outcome* of such discussion.

Consider, then, expression that is not part of any process of political discussion—not intended nor received as a contribution to public deliberation about some issue. But assume, too, that it reflects what a citizen reasonably takes to be compelling considerations in support of expression. Such expression advances what I will call an "expressive interest": a direct interest in articulating thoughts and feelings on matters of personal or broader human concern, whether that articulation influences the thought and the conduct of others.[40]

40. For discussion, see Joshua Cohen, "Freedom of Expression," *Philosophy and Public Affairs* 22, 3 (Summer 1993): 207–263 [reprinted as essay 4 in this collection].

As examples, consider artistic expression driven by a concern to create something of beauty; or bearing religious witness with no intention to persuade others; or giving professional advice out of a sense of professional obligation, with no intention to shape broader processes of collective decision making. In the case of bearing witness, an agent endorses a view that places him under an *obligation* to articulate that view and perhaps to urge on others a different course of thought, feeling, or conduct. Restricting expression would prevent the agent from fulfilling what she takes to be an obligation, thus imposing a burden that the agent reasonably takes to be unacceptable. To acknowledge the weight of those reasons, the deliberative view extends stringent protection to such expression. Given the background of reasonable pluralism, the failure to extend such protection represents a failure to give due weight to the reasons that support forms of expression that are not inputs to public discussion. As such, it constitutes a denial of equal standing, and decisions to deny protection are not suitably collective.

Or take expression on matters of political justice. Here, the importance of the issue—indicated by its being a matter of justice—provides a substantial reason for addressing it, regardless of how the message is received. The precise content and weight of the reason are matters of controversy. Aristotelian views identify public engagement as the highest human good; and Brandeis urged that "public discussion is a political duty."[41] But even if political expression is neither the highest good nor a matter of duty, still, it is a requisite for being a good citizen, sometimes a matter of sheer decency. Typically, then, such expression has support from substantial reasons within different moral-political conceptions.

Bearing witness; speaking out on matters of justice; creating things of beauty; giving professional advice: such cases suffice to underscore the importance of the expressive interest. They work outward from fully conscientious expression—the paradigm of expression supported by substantial reasons from the agent's point of view, and therefore expression whose protection is supported by the principle of deliberative inclusion. To be sure, different evaluative conceptions have different implications for what is reasonable to say and to do. But all conceptions assign to those who hold them substantial reasons for expression, quite apart from the

41. Whitney v. California, 274 U.S. 357, 375 (1927) (Brandeis, J., concurring).

value of the expression to the audience, even if there is no audience at all. For this reason, the deliberative view endorses a strong presumption against content regulation, but it does not confine that presumption to political speech.

Other reasons may also support that presumption, understood as part of a wide guarantee of expressive liberty: for example, considerations of reflectiveness (discussed earlier), which suggest that all manner of speech helps to form values and beliefs that also figure in public deliberation. But we need not confine ourselves to considerations of this kind. Content regulation is to be rejected because of the reasons for speech that are captured in the expressive interest, and not simply because such regulations prematurely foreclose public discussion.

To illustrate the point about the deliberative framework, the expressive interest, and a wide guarantee of expressive liberty, let us consider the case of regulations of sexual expression: in particular, regulations of pornography. Part of the trouble with such regulations—for example, the pornography regulations urged by Catharine MacKinnon—lies in this area.[42] An example of such regulation is an Indianapolis ordinance, adopted in 1986, which defines pornography as:

> the graphic sexually explicit subordination of women, whether in pictures or in words, that also includes one or more of the following:
>
> - Women are presented as sexual objects who enjoy pain or humiliation;
> - Women are presented as sexual objects who experience sexual pleasure in being raped;
> - Women are presented as sexual objects tied up or cut up or mutilated or bruised or physically hurt;
> - Women are presented being penetrated by objects or animals;
> - Women are presented in scenarios of degradation, injury, torture, shown as filthy or inferior, bleeding, bruised or hurt in a context that makes these conditions sexual;
> - Women are presented as sexual objects for domination, con-

---

42. The discussion that follows is taken from Joshua Cohen, "Freedom, Equality, Pornography," in Austin Sarat and Thomas Kearns, eds., *Justice and Injustice in Law and Legal Theory* (Ann Arbor: University of Michigan Press, 1996), 99–139.

> quest, violation, exploitation, possession, or use, or through pos-
> tures or positions of servility or submission or display.[43]

In a nutshell, the regulation targets the graphic fusion of sexuality and
subordination.

Turning, then, to the connections of sexual expression and expressive
interest, suppose that concerns about human welfare and the quality of
human life prompt expression; the evident importance of those concerns
provides substantial reasons for the expression. A paradigm is expression
about sex and sexuality—say, artistic expression that displays an antipathy
to existing sexual conventions, the limited sensibilities revealed in those
conventions, and the harm they impose. In a culture that is, as Kathy
Acker says, "horrendously moralistic," it is understandable that such writers as Acker challenge understandings of sexuality "under the aegis of art,
[where] you're allowed to actually deal with matters of sexuality."[44] Again,
in an interview, Kathy Acker says:

> I think you'd agree there are various things in us—not all of
> which are kind, gentle, and tender—readers of de Sade and
> Genet would probably agree on this point! But I think you can
> explore these things without becoming a mass murderer . . .
> without causing *real* damage, without turning to *real* crime.
> One way of exploring these things is through *art*; there are vari-
> ous ways of doing this. We have . . . to find out what it is to be
> human—and yet not wreak total havoc on the society.[45]

The human significance of sexuality lends special urgency to the ex-
plorations Acker describes. Moreover, and here I join the issue about
pornography and the expressive interest, that urgency does not decline
when, as in the case of pornography, sexuality mixes with power and subordination—when, as in materials covered by proposed regulations, it is
not "kind, gentle, and tender." On the contrary, a writer may reasonably
think—as Acker apparently does—that coming to terms with such mix-

43. Indianapolis, Ind., City-Council General Ordinance No. 35 (June 11, 1984). The full text
is cited in Catharine MacKinnon, *Feminism Unmodified* (Cambridge, MA: Harvard University
Press, 1987), 274 note 1. The regulation was overturned in American Booksellers Ass'n. v.
Hudnut, 771 F.2d 323 (7th Cir. 1985), *affirmed without opinion,* 475 U.S. 1001 (1986).

44. See Kathy Acker, "Devoured by Myths: An Interview with Sylvere Lotringer," in
Hannibal Lecter, My Father (New York: Semiotext(e), 1991).

45. Interview with Andrea Juno, in Andrea Juno and V. Vale, eds., *Angry Women* (San Francisco: Re/Search Publications, 1991), 184–185.

ing is especially important, precisely because, in the world as it is, power is so deeply implicated in sexual identity and desire. To stay away from the erotization of dominance and submission—as pornography regulations require—is to avoid sexuality as it, to some indeterminate degree, is.

The connections between pornography (materials covered by the regulation) and the expressive interest may actually be strengthened because, in a world of unequal power, it engages our sexual desires, categories, identities, and fantasies as they are—even if our aim is to transform them. Regulations targeted particularly on the fusion of sexuality and subordination—on the apparent extremes of heterosexual and phallic conventions—will cover too much. For it may be in part by working with that fusion and acknowledging its force, rather than by simply depicting a world of erotic possibilities beyond power, that we establish the basis for transforming existing forms of sexuality.[46]

One difficulty with the regulations, then, is that they make no provision for the importance of the expressive interest—for the weight of the reasons that move at least some people to produce sexually explicit materials that conflict with the regulations. Underscoring that lack of provision, MacKinnon criticizes the exception in current obscenity law for materials with "literary, political, artistic, or scientific value": "The ineffectualness of obscenity law is due in some part to exempting materials of literary, political, artistic, or scientific value. Value can be found in anything, depending, I have come to think, not only on one's adherence to postmodernism, but on how much one is being paid. And never underestimate the power of an erection, these days termed 'entertainment,' to give a thing value." Of course, the expressive interest may be overridden, but the conventional rationales for regulation fail to acknowledge it, and thus fall afoul of the requirement of deliberative inclusion. More particularly, though the connections with the expressive interest do not settle the issue, they do help to increase the burden of argument that must be carried in justifying such regulations: those connections mean that defenders of regulations must make a more compelling showing of the harms of

---

46. See Judith Butler, *Gender Trouble: Feminism and the Subversion of Identity* (New York: Routledge, 1990); Susan Keller, "Viewing and Doing: Complicating Pornography's Meaning," *Georgetown Law Review* 81 (1993): 2195–2228; Duncan Kennedy, *Sexy Dressing: Essays on the Power and Politics of Cultural Identity* (Cambridge, MA: Harvard University Press, 1993), 126–213.

pornography and not simply advance the speculative arguments that are commonly proposed.

7. Moral Liberty

I want now to discuss the implications of the principle of deliberative inclusion in the area of moral liberty, what John Stuart Mill called the "liberty of tastes and pursuits."[47] I propose to concentrate, in particular, on the *enforcement of morality*.

My principal focus here will be on the permissibility of imposing criminal punishment on citizens for violating the ethical code shared by the majority in a society, even when that conduct is neither injurious nor offensive to others: Is it permissible for a political society to use its criminal law to force members to lead lives that are not, by the lights of the majority, immoral or perverse?[48] Criminalization is, of course, a special case, and problems of moral liberty extend well beyond it. Mill's defense of moral liberty was as much a criticism of intrusive collective opinion as of state regulation. And, confining attention to state action, we need to address the codification of morality through regulations that are not backed by criminal sanction: for example, bans on same-sex marriage. But because the issues have important affinities, and can be seen more sharply in the area of criminalization, I will focus on it here.

In two important cases in the 1980s and 1990s—*Bowers v. Hardwick* and *Barnes v. Glen Theatre*—the U.S. Supreme Court affirmed the constitutional permissibility of criminalizing immoral conduct. In the first, "the presumed belief of a majority of the electorate in Georgia that homosexual sodomy is immoral and unacceptable" was offered as a suitable rationale for a law imposing criminal sanctions on consensual homosexual sodomy.[49] To be more precise, the Georgia law itself imposed criminal sanctions on consensual sodomy quite generally, but it was upheld by the Court only as applied to homosexual sodomy. In the second, the Court upheld an Indiana public indecency law requiring dancers to wear pasties and G-strings. As rationale for the law, Justice Rehnquist offers the public's "moral disapproval of people appearing in the nude among strangers in public places." Moreover, he notes traditional common law restrictions on public nudity and the view underlying those re-

---

47. See J. S. Mill, *On Liberty* (Indianapolis: Hackett, 1978), ch. 3.
48. Ronald Dworkin, "Liberal Community," *California Law Review* 77, 3 (1989): 479–504.
49. 476 U.S. 186, 196 (1986).

strictions: that public nudity was an act *malum in se*. Writing in concurrence, Justice Scalia emphasizes that the conduct is prohibited because it is "immoral"—in conflict with "traditional moral belief"—not because it is offensive: "The purpose of Indiana's nudity law would be violated, I think, if 60,000 fully consenting adults crowded into the Hoosier Dome to display their genitals to one another, even if there was not an offended innocent in the crowd." Rejecting Mill's harm principle—which requires a showing of harm to others as a necessary condition for criminal sanction—Scalia says, "Our society prohibits, and all human societies have prohibited, certain activities not because they harm others, but because they are considered, in the traditional phrase, *contra bonos mores*, i.e., immoral"—and he goes on to mention "sadomasochism, cockfighting, bestiality, suicide, drug use, prostitution, and sodomy" as areas in which legal regulation of conduct is constitutionally permitted, though the rationale for the regulations is rooted in "traditional moral belief."

As Scalia's examples indicate, the debate about the enforcement of morals is not confined to issues of sexual morality. Still, that has been a central historical focus—as in *Bowers* and *Barnes*, as well as in disagreements about generic anti-sodomy laws and in disagreements about regulations of prostitution and pornography. I will maintain that focus here.

The debate about enforcing morality implicates in especially profound ways the value of democracy. Indeed, the debate about the permissibility of enforcing conventional ethics is commonly presented as a conflict between democracy, which is said to support the enforcement of morals, and some other value—say, personal liberty or autonomy—which is seen to be compromised by and to condemn that enforcement. Ronald Dworkin, for example, says that the argument from democracy is "politically the most powerful argument against liberal tolerance."[50] And in his classical critique of Lord Devlin's defense of the enforcement of morals, H. L. A. Hart says, "It seems fatally easy to believe that loyalty to democratic principles entails acceptance of what may be termed moral populism: the view that the majority have a moral right to dictate how all should live."[51]

To state the views of the moral populist in more generous terms: on moral issues, the values of the majority ought to be decisive because no

50. Dworkin, "Liberal Community," 483.
51. H. L. A. Hart, *Law, Liberty, and Morality* (Stanford, CA: Stanford University Press, 1963), 79.

other basis for determining our shared "moral environment" is compatible with the equality of citizens—no other basis is fair to citizens as equals. Moral disagreements in the community ought, then, to be resolved by a procedure of decision making that treats citizens as equals—say, majority rule. Lord Devlin himself suggests this case for enforcement in an essay titled "Democracy and Morality": "Those who do not believe in God must ask themselves what they *mean* when they say that they believe in democracy. Not that all men are born with equal brains—we cannot believe that; but that they have at their command—and that in this they are all born in the same degree—the faculty of telling right from wrong. This is the whole meaning of democracy, for if in this endowment men were not equal, it would be pernicious that in the government of any society they should have equal rights."[52]

A first response to the moral populist argues that majority rule on moral questions—like majority rule decisions to establish racially segregated schools—does not treat citizens as equals, because it permits people to act on their view that some citizens are worth less than others. But we ought to resist acceding to this temptation too quickly. It is at least possible to condemn a way of life and the conduct it comprises without condemning those who lead it as being worth less than others: that is, for example, the point of current Catholic doctrine on homosexuality. We may wish to argue, in the end, that this view is hostility barely concealed—that when it comes to matters sexual, moral traditionalism is homophobia and misogyny carried out by other means. Still, the means are different: a complex structure of religious and moral argument. We ought, then, to be cautious about simply *identifying* a willingness to punish conduct judged immoral with either racism or sexism—which are, on their face and without reinterpretation, about people, not ways of life. "Attempting to preclude the entire population from acting in ways that are perceived as immoral is not assimilable to comparatively disadvantaging a given group out of simple hostility to its members."[53] To be sure, regulating ways of life as immoral may in the end be as objectionable as condemning people as being of lesser worth, but we need to distinguish the troubles.

A second response to the argument from democracy is to defend a

---

52. Lord Devlin, "Democracy and Morality," in *The Enforcement of Morals* (Oxford: Oxford University Press, 1965).

53. See Ely, *Democracy and Distrust*, 256. See also John Hart Ely, "Professor Dworkin's External/Personal Preference Distinction," *Duke Law Review* (1983): 985.

Millian harm principle on the basis of the value of autonomy or utilitarian principles. But this strategy may unintentionally lend added force to Devlin-style arguments. Let me explain, concentrating on appeals to the value of autonomy.

The argument from autonomy takes two principal forms. According to the first, the autonomy protected by restrictions on the enforcement of morality is principally the autonomy of the agent whose conduct would otherwise be regulated. According to the second, moral toleration benefits others, whose autonomy is enhanced by a greater range of alternatives.[54] The first version is more familiar, and I will sketch a version of it presented by Ronald Dworkin, who offers it as a reply to one kind of communitarian argument for the enforcement of an ethical code.[55] What matters here are not the details but the central thesis: that we cannot make people's lives go better by requiring them to conform, through threats of criminal punishment, to an ethical code that they reject and would otherwise violate. Dworkin rests this thesis on a theory of the best human life in which the value of autonomy or self-government plays a central role. According to this theory, a person's life is good only if the person chooses the values that guide it—or, if choice conveys the wrong picture, reflectively endorses those values.[56]

Dworkin endorses an especially strong form of the requirement of reflective endorsement, though he needs just such a strong form to defeat the argument for enforcement.[57] Reflective endorsement, he says, has *constitutive*, not merely *additive* value.[58] In particular, no part of a life

54. For an illustration of this strategy of argument, see Joseph Raz, *The Morality of Freedom* (Oxford: Oxford University Press, 1986), ch. 15. According to Raz, the duty of toleration is "an aspect of the duty of respect for autonomy." Autonomy requires a range of choices among different ways of life that include "distinct and incompatible moral virtues." People who endorse those ways of life tend, however, to be intolerant of one another. So ensuring the structure of alternatives required to foster autonomy requires guarantees against intolerance. But as this sketch indicates, the rationale for the guarantees lies not in the benefits conferred on individuals who receive protection but in the preservation of a system of alternative possibilities for others.

55. Dworkin, "Liberal Community."

56. I take the term "reflective endorsement" from ibid., 485–486.

57. The argument closely resembles the "maximalist" strategies for defending freedom of expression that I discuss in my "Freedom of Expression." The difficulties are correspondingly parallel.

58. The roots of this claim about the constitutive value of reflective endorsement lie in what Dworkin calls the "challenge" model of value: the view that a good human life is a life that responds suitably to life's challenges. Dworkin appears to think that an agent's conduct counts as meeting a challenge if and only if the agent engaging in the conduct reflectively endorses it. See his "Foundations of Liberal Equality," in *The Tanner Lectures on Human Values 1990*, vol. 11 (Salt Lake City: University of Utah Press, 1991). I don't find Dworkin's case very plausible but will not pursue the reasons here. I am indebted to John Tully for discussion of Dworkin's view.

contributes to the value of that life unless it is reflectively endorsed. So, for example, the development of intellectual powers makes a life better only if that development takes the form of *self-development*—development guided by the reflectively accepted values of the agent. Altruistic behavior—saving the lives of others, say—makes the saver's life better only if she endorses the value of altruistic behavior.

Dworkin's conclusions about the importance of reflective endorsement closely parallel Locke's defense of religious toleration; indeed, Dworkin's defense of moral toleration might be seen as generalizing Locke's argument. According to Locke, "Although the magistrate's opinion in religion be sound, and the way that he appoints be truly evangelical, yet, if I be not thoroughly persuaded thereof in my own mind, there will be no safety for me in following it. No way whatsoever that I shall walk in against the dictates of my own conscience will ever bring me to the mansions of the blessed. . . . Faith only and inward sincerity are the things that procure acceptance with God."[59] Just as worship is of no value unless accompanied by inner conviction, by faith freely embraced, so, too, decent or socially beneficial conduct—a good impact on the world—adds nothing to the value of a life unless the behavior is accompanied by a freely embraced, inner conviction about the value of the conduct.

Reasoning from this premise about the dependence of salvation on inner faith, Locke argued that the state could not save souls through enforced religious rituals and should not try. Similarly, premising the constitutive value of autonomy, Dworkin concludes that the state cannot make a person's life *better* by forcing that person to live according to an ethical code he rejects. The problem with moral paternalism, then, is not that it fails to be suitably skeptical about the good, or that it provokes civil conflict, but that it rests on an incorrect theory of the good life; it fails to appreciate the constitutive role of reflective endorsement in the value of a life. If this is right, then we cannot defend the enforcement of morals by claiming to show equal concern for the true good of all citizens. Indeed, that argument is, in Dworkin's words, "self-defeating" because, according to the autonomy theory, a life of enforced moral conformity is not better than a life of chosen immorality.[60] On the contrary, the requirement of reflective endorsement supports freedom of personal

59. John Locke, *Letter Concerning Toleration* (Indianapolis: Bobbs-Merrill, 1955), 34.
60. See Dworkin, "Liberal Community," 487.

choice under favorable conditions for considering how best to live (e.g., conditions in which people pursue different "experiments in living," to borrow Mill's phrase).

This argument has considerable force. The premise about autonomy serves as an axiom in a family of reasonable comprehensive moralities; and for the sake of discussion, I assume that the conclusions are well supported by the premises. But as political argument, it has an important shortcoming: it depends on a comprehensive philosophy of life, and the deliberative view requires that, under conditions of reasonable pluralism, we free political argument from such dependence, particularly when such argument bears on the fundamentals of conduct.

Thus, the autonomy theory is a form of comprehensive moral liberalism, rejected by citizens who think, not unreasonably, that human lives are made good at least in part by their compliance with divine law, or their conformity to the order of the universe, or the quality of their impact on the world, or the extent to which they realize human powers. To be sure, citizens who endorse such views may themselves reject the enforcement of morality because they judge it worse or inappropriate to force lives to be as good as they can be. But just as the belief in religious toleration is not and should not be presented as contingent on a religious view about the sufficiency of inner faith to salvation, acceptance of moral toleration is not and should not be presented as contingent on the view that personal autonomy is the supreme moral value and the comprehensive guide to conduct. I mentioned earlier that the autonomy argument for moral toleration generalizes a Lockean argument for religious toleration; whereas the latter rejects enforcement of a religious code because inner faith is required for salvation, the former, more abstractly, treats reflective endorsement as constitutive of the goodness of a life for the person who lives it. I think there is something right in this use of religious toleration as a model, but as I explain in some detail below, the deliberative view presents the parallel in a different way: it emphasizes, in particular, the weight of the reasons that lie behind the regulated conduct and the unacceptability for the purposes of political argument of the considerations that would justify the regulations.

The failure of this argument might suggest that majority rule ought, after all, to extend to moral issues. Precisely by underscoring moral disagreement—indeed, reasonable moral disagreement—the limits of the autonomy argument might suggest that treating citizens as equals requires that the majority be left free to fix the shared moral landscape. Lord Devlin makes just this point. Agreeing that moral differences often cannot be resolved through a good faith exercise of practical reason— that "after centuries of debate, men of undoubted reasoning power and honesty of purpose have shown themselves unable to agree on what the moral law should be"[61]—he concludes that the arbiter of social morality cannot be reason but must instead be the people—"the ordinary man, the man in the jury box, who might also be called the reasonable man or the right-minded man."[62]

But the deliberative account of democracy rejects that conclusion. To see why, notice first that controversies about the *enforcement* of morality characteristically track moral controversies: when enforcement is controversial, so, too, is the moral question itself. The issue, then, is not whether conduct, assumed not to be injurious to others, can permissibly be regulated for moral reasons *on which there is general agreement*. Instead, the issue is whether conduct can permissibly be regulated for moral reasons, despite deep and apparently unresolvable disagreement about the morality of the conduct and the grounds for regulating it.

This point seems easy to miss. In his criticisms of Devlin, for example, Hart asks "why we should not summon all the resources of our reason, sympathetic understanding, as well as critical intelligence, and insist that before *general moral feeling* is turned into criminal law it is submitted to scrutiny of a different kind from Sir Patrick's. Surely the legislator should ask whether the *general morality* is based on ignorance, superstition, or misunderstanding. . . ."[63] Such questions are certainly in order. But in controversial cases of enforcement, the assumption that regulations enforce "general morality" or "general moral feeling" is typically not, unless by "general" we mean "majority," in which case a very large step needs to be filled in—the step that authorizes the majority to speak in the name of the community.

Take the case of homosexuality. It would be preposterous to say that the moral consensus of the community condemns homosexuality, but some people want nevertheless to practice it despite its accepted immorality. Instead, some citizens, for religious or perhaps other reasons, condemn it and perhaps wish to regulate it (though not all who condemn

61. Devlin, "Democracy and Morality," 93.
62. Ibid., 90.
63. H. L. A. Hart, "Immorality and Treason," *The Listener* (30 July 1959): 3, my emphases.

also wish to regulate). Putting aside concededly insufficient appeals to Scripture, two principal arguments have been advanced for condemnation and regulation.[64] First, procreation is the natural end of sexuality (the natural end being the end for which God established sexual desire), natural ends ought to be practically authoritative, and conduct that by its nature is disconnected from or contravenes those ends is base, perverse, and worthless.[65] Second, homosexuality violates a principle of "complementarity," warring against the differentiation—including sexual differentiation—that is essential to God's ordering of the universe: "Human beings are . . . nothing less than the work of God himself; and in the complementarity of the sexes they are called to reflect the inner unity of the Creator."[66]

These lines of argument are parts of philosophies of life that others reasonably reject (indeed, they are very much contested within the traditions of thought to which they belong).[67] Others believe that there is nothing sinful, immoral, or in any other way objectionable about being gay or lesbian. Some reject the view that procreation is *the* natural end of sexuality or, more generally, that human conduct has natural ends or that those ends, such as they are, ought to be authoritative in settling the best way to live. And some reject the particular metaphysics of creation that founds the principle of complementarity.

Parallel points can be made for the other disputes: about sodomy, pornography, or nude dancing. In each case, we ought not to ask whether the state may enforce the *general morality of the community*: on these issues, though the majority may share a morality, the *community* does

64. A third argument, advanced by Roger Scruton, claims that homosexuality exhibits an objectionable form of narcissism and obscene perception, that instead of "mov[ing] out from my body towards the other, whose flesh is unknown to me . . . I remain locked within my body, narcissistically contemplating in the other an excitement that is the mirror of my own." *Sexual Desire* (New York: Free Press, 1986), 310. Though Scruton presents the antinarcissism argument as an alternative to arguments from the natural end of sexuality and complementarity, it is not clear that it stands independently of the latter.

65. For a crisp statement, see C. H. Peschke, *Christian Ethics*, vol. 2 (London: C. Goodliffe Neale, 1978), 379.

66. For discussion of the idea of complementarity, see Scruton, *Sexual Desire*, 309; Andrew Sullivan, *Virtually Normal: An Argument About Homosexuality* (New York: Knopf, 1995); and especially Gareth Moore, *The Body in Context: Sex and Catholicism* (London: SCM Press, 1992), ch. 7. Moore rightly points out that, on natural interpretations, the idea of complementarity depends on the procreation-as-natural-end doctrine. The passage on complementarity comes from the *Letter on the Pastoral Care of Homosexual Persons* of the Catholic Church's Congregation for the Doctrine of the Faith.

67. See, e.g., Sullivan, *Virtually Normal*; and Moore, *The Body in Context*.

not—the democratic community, constituted by free and equal citizens. Disagreements are fundamental and deeply rooted in reasonable differences of outlook, associated with, among other things, different views about our bodies, about the role of our embodiment and the pleasures associated with it in the conduct of our lives, about how to respond to the independence from rational control characteristic of sexual pleasure. Some citizens find the law of sin in our members: they see in the body an obstacle to our highest purposes, or at least the source of temptation to do wrong. Others think, not unreasonably, that embodiment is essential to our nature, that bodily pleasures provide ways to break free of conventional constraint, and that our capacity to transcend such constraints is fundamental to our nature as free agents. These are matters on which—I say this as platitude—people disagree, often profoundly, in thought, sensibility, and conduct: a public basis for justification is absent. The constraints of shared evidence and conceptual precision required for agreement are simply not in view. Law has no place here, not in a democracy committed to treating its members as equals. As Justice Blackmun said in dissent in *Bowers:* "That certain, but by no means all, religious groups condemn the behavior at issue gives the state no license to impose their judgments on the entire citizenry."[68]

Fundamental, reasonable disagreement, then, puts strong pressure against the enforcement of conventional ethics: the principles in the name of which such enforcement might be justified cannot be accepted by all who are subject to them. And that pressure is particularly strong when, as in the case of sexual conduct, the regulations impinge deeply on the lives of those who are regulated. Given the underlying moral division, some members of the community suppose that the regulated conduct is not only permissible but also essential: that sexual intimacy is a fundamental human good and that—particularly in view of the facts of human diversity—its value is contingent in part on its being guided by the judgments, feelings, and sensibilities of the parties to it.[69] Regulations impinge deeply, then, because the reasons that support such intimacy are substantial and can be acknowledged as such by people who reject those

---

68. Bowers v. Hardwick, 476 U.S. 186 (1986).

69. For suggestive remarks about the importance of sexual intimacy—connecting its value to the importance of individuality and imagination, while separating that value from concerns about procreation, see Stuart Hampshire, *Innocence and Experience* (Cambridge, MA: Harvard University Press, 1989), 124–131.

reasons. And because the reasons are so substantial, there is a correspondingly strong case against regulating them in the name of considerations drawn from philosophies of life that some citizens reasonably reject.

At the same time, should regulations not impinge very deeply—should the reasons supporting the conduct be less substantial—then the case against enforcement is less compelling, even if the reasons come from conventional ethics. Thus, regulating boxing because it is immoral—or betting because it is—may be less deeply objectionable than regulating sexuality. Though some may reject the reasons used to support the regulations, they may nevertheless accept majority support as itself sufficient reason. More generally, I think it is very difficult to argue for a blanket condemnation of the enforcement of community morality—in particular, a principled condemnation that does not depend on the complexities of legal categorization and associated slippery slopes—unless we premise the autonomy version of moral liberalism. In any case, no such blanket condemnation is intended here.

I said earlier that the proponents of enforcement often appeal to the value of democracy, urging that the equality of citizens requires that majority values fix the moral environment. This point has considerable force when a collective choice is necessary, as, for example, in the area of security policy: there, we need to arrive at a common decision, so the majority may speak in the name of the community—the majority principle itself may be a matter of general agreement among people who disagree about the right policy.[70] But where regulation is unnecessary, as in the area of sexual morality, this rationale is unavailable.

The case for the majority as tribune of the community is not confined to issues on which collective choice is mandatory. It also has considerable force when regulations do not impinge deeply: when they do not cover conduct rooted in fundamental obligations or supported in other ways by substantial reasons. In such cases, even if a regulation is not required, it is permissible to adopt one with majority support. For example, taxing citizens to support research and development may be unnecessary, but it is unobjectionable: given differences of judgment and interest, it is

---

70. I borrow the example of security policy from the discussion of toleration in Thomas Nagel, *Equality and Partiality* (Oxford: Oxford University Press, 1991), 164–165. The general point—that the case for majority rule weakens when a collective policy is not necessary and that such policy is not required when it comes to moral issues—can be found in both Nagel and Joel Feinberg, *Harmless Wrongdoing* (Oxford: Oxford University Press, 1990), 51.

to be settled by a procedure that treats people as equals. But fundamental interests and substantial reasons are at stake in the area of sexual morality (once more, the key issue of contest about the enforcement of morality). Given the reasonable rejection of the moralities in the name of which the regulations are imposed, the presence of such fundamental interests condemns the regulations.

In short, then, moral liberty—like religious and expressive liberty—is an ingredient in the democratic idea of collective choice by free and equal citizens. The decision to regulate cannot be collective, in a suitable sense: it cannot arise from free reasoning among equals. It is for that reason undemocratic.

8. Community, Legitimacy, Democracy

To conclude, I will sketch some remarks on a fundamental question that I have postponed for the end: What makes the deliberative conception of democracy compelling as an interpretation of the fundamental democratic idea—that the authorization to exercise state power is to arise from the collective decisions of those whose decisions are to be governed by that power?

The principal virtues of the deliberative conception are allied closely with the way that the conception understands binding collective choice. By emphasizing the importance of articulating shared reasons, the deliberative view expresses an especially compelling picture of the possible relations among people within a democratic order; moreover, it states a forceful ideal of political legitimacy for a democracy. I take up these two points in turn.

First, the deliberative conception offers a more forceful rendering than aggregative conceptions do of the fundamental democratic idea—the idea that decisions about the exercise of state power are *collective*. It requires that we offer considerations acceptable to others, understood to be free, equal, and reasonable, and whose conduct will be governed by the decisions. It requires more than that we count their interests, while keeping our fingers crossed that those interests are outweighed.

This point about the attractions of the deliberative interpretation of collective decisions can be stated in terms of ideas of *political autonomy* and *political community*. If a political community is a group of people sharing a comprehensive moral or religious view, then reasonable pluralism ruins political community. But on an alternative conception of political community, deliberative democracy is a form of political community. To see how, notice first that by requiring justification on terms acceptable to others, deliberative democracy provides for political autonomy. Without denying the coercive aspects of common political life, it requires that all who are governed by collective decisions, who are expected to govern their own conduct by those decisions, must find the *bases* of those decisions—the political values that support them—acceptable, even when they disagree with the details of the decision.

Through this assurance of political autonomy, deliberative democracy achieves one important element of the ideal of community—not because collective decisions crystallize a shared ethical outlook that informs all social life generally, nor because the collective good takes precedence over liberties of members. Rather, deliberative democracy is connected to political community because the requirement of shared reasons for the exercise of political power—a requirement absent from the aggregative view—itself expresses the full and equal membership of all in the sovereign body responsible for authorizing the exercise of that power and establishes the common reason and will of that body.

When I say that it expresses "full membership," not simply equal membership, I mean membership in the collective sovereign that authorizes the exercise of power, and not simply membership as a subject of that power. To be sure, an alternative conception of full membership is available: persons might be said to be full members of a political society just in case the values their philosophy of life comprises coincide with the values that guide the exercise of political power. Under conditions of reasonable pluralism, the deliberative view rejects such full coincidence, even as an ideal of practical reason. It acknowledges a separation between, as Michael Sandel puts it, "our identity as citizens [and] our identity as persons more broadly conceived."[71]

But why this separation? Why, Sandel asks, "should political deliberation not reflect our best understanding of the highest human ends?" After all, when it does so reflect, we have an experience of political community unavailable from more truncated political argument, confined to common ground that can be occupied by alternative reasonable views.

The answer is contained in the idea of reasonable pluralism, and I will not repeat the details here. Suffice to say that if we take the fact of reason-

---

71. Sandel, *Democracy's Discontent*, 322.

able pluralism seriously, then we need to watch our third-person plurals as we move from "our identity as citizens" to "our identity as persons": our identity as citizens is shared, our identity as persons is not. Acknowledging this, what are we to make of "*our* best understanding of the highest human ends?" As citizens, we do not have—nor can we expect to secure—a common view about the highest human ends. So the request that *we* make "*our* best understanding" the basis of political deliberation is empty—or, in practice, gets content from the conception endorsed by a particular group of citizens. In contrast, as persons, we each may have such understandings, but they are plural—they are "our best understandings." Because those views are incompatible, we cannot fully incorporate them all into political justification, and to use any one in particular is unacceptable.

This suggestion about deliberative democracy and the value of community may seem strained in light of the role of religious, expressive, and moral liberties in the deliberative view. For such liberties are commonly represented as—for better or for worse—the solvent of community. And that is especially true when we reject the enforcement of community morality.

But the deliberative view offers a reason for skepticism about that claim. Under conditions of reasonable pluralism, the protection of the liberties of the moderns is not a solvent of community. Reasonable pluralism itself may be such a solvent, at least if we define community in terms of a shared philosophy of life. But once we assume reasonable pluralism, the protection of the liberties of the moderns turns out to be a necessary, though insufficient, condition for the only plausible form of political community. For those liberties fall under the "principle of inclusion." As that term indicates, they are conditions required to ensure the equal standing of citizens as members of the collective body whose authorization is required for the legitimate exercise of public power.

Finally, the deliberative conception of democracy presents an account of when decisions made in a democracy are politically legitimate and how to shape institutions and forms of argument so as to make legitimate decisions.

Generally speaking, we have a strong case for political legitimacy when the exercise of political power has sufficient justification. But, as a conceptual matter, a person can believe that the exercise of power is well justified—therefore legitimate—while also acknowledging that others over whom it is exercised reject the justification. As a conceptual matter, legitimacy does not require that the relevant justification be acknowledged as such by those who are subject to the legitimate power: there need be no justification *to* them. But the background of democracy—the idea of citizens as free and equal—and the fact of reasonable pluralism are important in characterizing a more limited conception of justification: because of these conditions, the relevant justification must be addressed to citizens, by which I mean that its terms must be acknowledged as suitable by those subject to political power. Given that citizens have equal standing and are understood as free, and given the fact of reasonable pluralism, we have an especially strong showing of legitimacy when the exercise of state power is supported by considerations acknowledged as reasons by the different views endorsed by reasonable citizens, who are understood as equals. No other account of reasons is suited for this case.

8

MONEY, POLITICS, POLITICAL EQUALITY

1. *Introduction*

In this paper, I discuss and criticize the current system of electoral finance in the United States and the constraints on the reform of that system imposed by the Supreme Court.

1. I begin by stating and discussing a three-part principle of political equality (section 2), which I present as a partial statement of a normative ideal of democracy.

2. I argue that the current system of campaign finance conflicts with the principle of political equality, in particular its requirement of equal opportunity for political influence. Current arrangements establish, in effect, a framework of inequalities of opportunity (sections 3, 4).

3. I discuss the constitutional limits on reform initially set down by the Supreme Court in the 1976 case of *Buckley v. Valeo* and reinforced in a number of cases decided since then. These decisions substantially limit the role that the value of political equality can play in shaping our system of campaign finance. A regulatory scheme that gave weight to that value by aiming to equalize opportunities for political influence would (barring

This essay originally appeared in a volume dedicated to Judith Jarvis Thomson. In it, as in everything I write, I aspire to meet her high standards of clarity. I am sure that I have not succeeded but am deeply indebted to Judy for demonstrating in all her work that it is possible to say important things without sacrificing clarity. The essay started as a talk to a meeting of the Northeast Citizen Action Resource Center. I have presented subsequent and expanded versions to the MIT Club in Washington, D.C., the Tufts University philosophy colloquium, McGill University departments of philosophy and political science, and a Brown University Conference on political equality. I also presented a draft at a meeting of the September Group and earlier versions of the main ideas to political philosophy seminars (in fall 1995 and spring 1998). I am grateful for the comments I received and wish particularly to thank Philippe van Parijs, Erik Olin Wright, and David Estlund for suggestions. I am indebted to Stephen Ansolabehere and James Snyder for discussions of the current system of election finance and to Leonardo Avritzer for discussions of the persisting importance of the Schumpeterian view of democracy in contemporary democratic thought. As always, my debt to John Rawls runs throughout.

special assumptions about diminishing returns to political investment) reduce the overall quantity of electoral speech. But the Court has held that fundamental constitutional principles preclude any restrictions on the amount of speech in the name of equalizing opportunities for political influence (sections 5, 6).

4. I argue that the limits imposed by the Court reflect an unduly narrow conception of democracy and the role of citizens in it, a conception that—like the elite theories of democracy that trace to Joseph Schumpeter—casts citizens exclusively in the role of audience for the messages of elite competitors rather than in the role of political actor, as listeners rather than, so to speak, content-providers.[1] And I suggest that alternatives to the current system, founded on a less narrow conception of democracy and the role of citizens in it—a conception that does not treat the elite-mass distinction as the central fact of political sociology— might achieve a better reconciliation of expressive liberty and political equality (section 7). In short, my central point is that the current system is deeply troubling, not simply because it subordinates democracy to something else—to property, or to an abstract and absolutist view of freedom of expression—but because it can be seen as founded on and as constitutionalizing a narrow conception of democracy and citizenship and thus as precluding experimentation aimed at more fully realizing democratic values.

I will not defend a particular proposal for reforming the system of campaign finance, though for purposes of illustration, I will, from time to time, refer to the voluntary public financing scheme adopted by Maine voters in 1996, a variant of which was adopted in Massachusetts in 1998. In essence, that scheme—whose constitutional standing remains uncertain (though it has been upheld thus far)[2]—finances candidate campaigns through a public fund, on condition that those candidates do not raise or spend private money. So it combines public subsidy with volun-

1. See Joseph Schumpeter, *Capitalism, Socialism, and Democracy* (New York: Harper and Row, 1942), chaps. 21, 22. Not that Schumpeter himself was especially concerned about ensuring more informed electoral judgments. What comes from him is the thesis that we should think of democracy as a particular way of organizing competition for political leadership—that instead of using "birth, lot, wealth, violence, co-optation, learning, appointment, or examination" to resolve the contest for political power, democracies resolve it through voting in regular elections—and think of the role of citizens as analogous to that of consumers in the product market.

2. See Daggett v. Webster, U.S. District Court, District of Maine, slip op. (November 5, 1999 and January 7, 2000).

tary spending limits, incentives to accept the limits as condition for receiving the subsidy (therefore incentives to reduce the overall quantity of speech), some constraints (in the form of reasonably low contribution limits) on private money nonparticipants, and additional support for public money candidates who face large private spending by opponents or large independent expenditures.[3]

One final prefatory note: as I was adding final touches to this paper (in January 2000), the Supreme Court announced its decision in *Nixon v. Shrink*, in which it upheld Missouri's statutory limits on campaign contributions. Were I rewriting the paper now, I would make two changes in light of the opinions in *Nixon*. First, I would change the discussion in section 6 to take notice of the fact that *Nixon v. Shrink* rejects the idea that restrictions on the size of campaign contributions should be subjected to the most demanding level of scrutiny. Second, and more important, I would underscore that the vast majority of the Court now seems willing to uphold campaign finance regulations enacted to ensure a more fair democratic process. This willingness is explicitly stated in Justice Breyer's concurrence and is suggested as well by Justice Souter (writing for the Court), who indicates that corruption of democratic process is not confined to the financial quid pro quo. The implications of this shift remain to be seen. But the apparent departure in constitutional philosophy is cause for hope.

2. A Principle of Political Equality

In a democratic society, the members are conceived of as free and equal persons. A principle of political equality for a democracy presents norms that are suited to persons thus conceived; it articulates values that apply to democratic arrangements for making binding—authoritative and enforceable—collective decisions; and it aims to provide guidance about the appropriate design of such arrangements. In particular, the norms are to guide judgments about the right to vote, the rules of election organization and vote aggregation (ballot access, systems of representation, electoral finance), and the organization of legislative and executive decision making.[4] Thus, a principle of political equality applies to the frame-

3. More precisely, the system allows no private funds beyond the initial seed money required to qualify for public funds. For discussion, see Ellen Miller, David Donnelly, and Janice Fine, "Going Public," in Joshua Cohen and Joel Rogers, eds., *Money and Politics: Financing Elections Democratically*, foreword by Gore Vidal (Boston: Beacon Press, 1999).

4. For illuminating discussion of the terrain, see Charles Beitz, *Political Equality* (Princeton: Princeton University Press, 1989).

work for making authoritative and enforceable collective decisions and specifies, inter alia, the system of rights and opportunities for free and equal members to exercise political influence over decisions that they are expected to comply with and that are made in their name. It does not apply to the dispersed networks of political-cultural discussion, founded on the associational life of civil society—what Habermas calls the "informal public sphere" and Rawls calls the "background culture."[5] It presents, and is framed for the purpose of presenting, an account of, inter alia, demands that free and equal members can legitimately make on the highest-level systems of authoritative collective decision making.

The principle of political equality I rely on here has three components. It states that arrangements for making binding collective decisions are to accommodate the following three norms:

1. *Equal rights of participation,* including rights of voting, association, and office-holding, as well as rights of political expression, with a strong presumption against restrictions on the content or the viewpoint of expression, and against restrictions that are unduly burdensome to some individuals or groups;
2. A strong presumption in favor of *equally weighted votes;* and
3. *Equal opportunities for effective political influence.* This last requirement, what Rawls has called "the fair value of political liberty," condemns inequalities in the opportunities for holding office and influencing political decisions (by influencing the outcomes of elections, the positions of candidates, and the conduct of inter-election legislative and administrative decision making).[6]

To be sure, a principle of political equality is not the only requirement on the authoritative system of collective decision making. Decisions should

5. I return to this limitation and note some reasons for it later, at 277–279. On the informal public sphere, see Jürgen Habermas, *Between Facts and Norms,* trans. William Rehg (Cambridge, MA: MIT Press, 1996); on the background culture, see John Rawls, *Political Liberalism* (New York: Columbia University Press, 1996 [1993]), 14, 382n. 13.

6. See *Political Liberalism,* 327–330. The general idea is familiar. For example, in the 1986 case of *Davis v. Bandemer,* which concerned political gerrymandering, the Supreme Court indicates that equal protection problems emerge when an "electoral system is arranged in a manner that will consistently degrade influence on the political process as a whole," Davis v. Bandemer, 478 U.S. 109, 132 (1986). Notice the importance attached to "influence on the political process as a whole," and not simply electoral influence. Lani Guinier refers to the norm that "each voter should enjoy the same opportunity to influence political outcomes," in *The Tyranny of the Majority: Fundamental Fairness in Representative Democracy* (New York: Free Press, 1994), 152. She emphasizes "the importance of an equal opportunity to influence public policy, and not just to cast a ballot" (134).

also be substantively just, according to some reasonable conception of justice, and effective at advancing the general welfare. But a principle of political equality states norms that will normally override other considerations, apart from the most fundamental requirements of justice. To be sure, conflicts may emerge between and among the norms comprised by the principle. So the force of saying that arrangements for making binding collective decisions are to accommodate all three components is that, when conflicts emerge, we can't say a priori which value is to give way. In particular, if we accept this three-part principle, then we allow that we may need to regulate speech to avoid certain kinds of inequalities in opportunities for political influence.[7]

This third requirement is modeled on the familiar norm of equality of opportunity. Stated intuitively and abstractly, that norm says that one person ought not to have greater chances than another to attain a desirable position because of some quality that is irrelevant to performance in the position. Using some familiar jargon, I will say that this expresses the *concept* of equal opportunity, and that different *conceptions* of equal opportunity are distinguished by the interpretations they give to "irrelevant to performance." For the sake of discussion here, I rely on Rawls's *conception* of equal opportunity, which specifies "irrelevant to performance in the position" as follows: that people who are equally motivated and equally able ought to have equal chances to attain the position.[8]

When this conception of equal opportunity is applied to the political system, the relevant position is *active citizen* in the formal arrangements of binding collective decision making. The requirement, then, is that people who are equally motivated and equally able to play this role, by influencing binding collective decisions, ought to have equal chances to exercise such influence.[9] The Constitution and the surrounding rules governing elections as well as legislative, executive, and administrative decision making establish this position. When suffrage was restricted to property owners, economic position was a formal qualification for hold-

7. To use the standard constitutional jargon, equality of opportunity would provide a compelling interest.

8. John Rawls, A *Theory of Justice*, rev. ed. (Cambridge, MA: Harvard University Press, 1999), 63. Similar requirements of equal political opportunity are found in a variety of accounts of democracy. See, for example, Robert Dahl who attaches considerable importance to equal opportunities to express preferences and citizen control over the political agenda. Robert Dahl, *Democracy and Its Critics* (New Haven: Yale University Press, 1989). I am indebted to Chappell Lawson for underscoring the consistency with Dahl's view.

9. *Theory of Justice*, 197.

ing that position. We now agree that economic position is not a relevant formal qualification. But if economic position is not a relevant formal qualification for voting and other forms of political influence, how could it be acceptable to organize the highest-level system for exercising political influence in a way that makes the opportunity for such influence dependent on economic position? How could it be acceptable to organize the framework so that greater opportunity comes with greater resources?

I do not propose here to defend this principle (though see 292–302 for some relevant considerations) but will confine myself to four comments on the idea of *equal opportunity for political influence*. Three of the comments bear on the content of the principle—why equal *opportunity* for political influence, why *equal* opportunity for political influence, and why equal opportunity for *political* influence—and one bears on its status as "autonomous" or independent.

First, then, political equality demands equal *opportunity* for effective political influence rather than equality of effective influence itself. Inequalities of effective influence are sometimes acceptable, on any reasonable view of political equality. Some citizens may be more influential because, for example, they care more about politics. Differences of influence that trace to such differences in values and choices seem unobjectionable. Similarly, if a person is more influential because her views are widely shared, or her judgment widely trusted, and others are therefore likely to be swayed by her position on the issue at hand: the differences of influence trace to the distribution of political values and commitments in the population, not to the organization of the structure of collective choice. The requirement of equal opportunity for effective influence condemns certain kinds of effective exclusion or dilution, but it does not support charges of objectionable exclusion or dilution merely because I am unwilling to make reasonable efforts to persuade others, or because others regard my views as ridiculous, or because they lack confidence in my judgment.

What about inequalities due to differences in persuasiveness, or in physical attractiveness? In neither case are the greater opportunities for influence due to aspects of the design of arrangements for making collective decisions that we can permissibly control. To be sure, we could make collective efforts to reduce the importance of differential persuasiveness, for example, by investing more in civic education. But the legitimacy and importance of making such investment do not imply that it would ever be permissible to regulate the activities of the persuasive in order to achieve greater equality of opportunity. To regulate those activities would go to the core of the free speech guarantee, by establishing regulations that control viewpoint and are unduly burdensome. Moreover, it would defeat the point of political discussion. After all, differences in persuasiveness are not irrelevant to performance in the position. Similarly, we could try to control the power that flows from being attractive (such as it is) but only by taking measures that would keep people from appearing before one another (only radio spots, no TV). And such regulations would, on their face, be damaging to political judgment.

Underlying this focus on opportunity is the idea that it is unreasonable to demand influence irrespective of one's own actions or of the considered convictions of other citizens. That demand is unreasonable, because a compelling interpretation of the idea of political equality must ensure a place for individual responsibility. Members of a democratic society are represented as free and equal. As free, they are to be treated as responsible for their political judgments and conduct. So if I demand influence irrespective of the judgments of other citizens, then I deny the importance of such responsibility. Once we accept it, then we accept, too, that a regime with equal opportunity for effective influence is almost certain to be associated with inequalities of actual influence.

Second, the norm of equal opportunity for political influence assigns *autonomous* importance to political equality rather than merely *dependent* or *derivative* importance.[10] Thus, suppose we eliminate all inequalities of political influence due to causes that we can identify as unjust apart from their effects on political influence. Assume, in particular, that the distribution of economic resources is fair and that effective participation is not impeded by stereotype or group hostility. Still, unequal opportunities for effective influence might result from inequalities—assumed by stipulation to be fair—in the distribution of resources. In condemning these unequal opportunities, the principle assigns autonomous importance to political equality. It does not require political equality simply as a way to discourage independently cognizable forms of injustice.

Third, the principle requires that we ensure equal opportunity for po-

10. Here, I disagree with Dworkin's account of political equality in "What Is Equality? Part 4: Political Equality," *University of San Francisco Law Review* (Fall 1987). Dworkin there rejects the idea that political equality has autonomous importance.

litical influence, not simply that we ensure a certain threshold level of opportunity—a principle of sufficiency or adequacy of opportunity[11]—or a maximin level of opportunity.[12] Thus, consider a public auction, the winners of which get free television time to present their political views, in particular their electoral views. But the proceeds of the auction go to a fund that subsidizes political activity by low-income citizens: perhaps it subsidizes media access, or internet access with assistance for content provision. So holding the auction expands general opportunities for political influence, but the opportunities are unequal in that greater opportunities for influence are available only to those who have the resources to win the auction.

One response is to deny the premise that underlies the distinction between equalization and the alternatives: that it is possible to improve everyone's opportunity for influence. But that seems mistaken. If we establish a lottery, the winners of which get free television time for presenting their political views, then everyone has greater opportunities for influence (anyone can win the lottery).

Putting this zero-sum response to the side, then, I note two points about the merits of a limit on inequality of opportunity that is more modest than the limit I endorse here. First, from the point of view of the issue that motivates this essay, the distinction between equal opportunity and, say, maximin opportunity is idle. I am concerned here with the issues about liberty, equality, and democracy raised by the (in)famous sentence in *Buckley*: "The concept that government may restrict the speech of some elements of our society in order to enhance the relative voice of others is wholly foreign to the first amendment." Whether the restrictions would serve to equalize opportunity, "adequatize" it, or maximin it, the same issues emerge—unless it could be shown that the need for restrictions emerges only when we are concerned to achieve equal opportunity for political influence.

Second, part of the reason for thinking that a maximin (or sufficiency) view of opportunity is reasonable is that such a view makes sense when it

11. In discussions of equal opportunity in the context of education, the focus is often on adequacy, in part because a number of state constitutions in the United States guarantee an adequate level of education.

12. David Estlund explores these concerns in his excellent paper, "Political Quality," *Social Philosophy and Policy* 17, 1 (Winter 2000): 127–160.

comes to the distribution of economic resources. Although the equality of citizens as moral persons imposes some pressure to reduce socioeconomic inequalities—as a way to express the respect owed to equals—that pressure is limited by the mutual benefits that can flow from inequalities. A parallel case can be constructed, so it may seem, for inequalities of political opportunity. Although the equality of citizens as moral persons imposes some pressure to reduce inequalities of political opportunity—as a way to express the respect owed to equals—that pressure is limited, it might be argued, by the mutual benefits that can flow from inequalities of opportunity. But this parallel is in part illusory. One reason that resource inequalities are not troubling in a world of moral equals is precisely because their equality is already expressed through the equal standing of individuals as citizens in the system of authoritative collective decision making: "The basis for self-respect in a just society is not . . . one's income share but the publicly affirmed distribution of fundamental rights and liberties. And this distribution being equal, everyone has a similar and secure status when they meet to conduct the common affairs of the wider society. No one is inclined to look beyond the constitutional affirmation of equality for further political ways of securing his status."[13] But if inequalities of opportunity extend to the political system itself, as the authoritative system for making collective decisions, then the public basis of mutual respect is less secure. To be sure, an explanation might be given for the inequalities that does not depend on the idea that citizens are unequal (namely, that the inequalities of political opportunity benefit all). But when citizens lack assured equal standing, that explanation may itself provoke suspicion.

Coming back to the principle of political equality, then, my final observation is that the principle requires equal opportunity for political influence. To clarify the force of this condition, I distinguish three interpretations of the idea of political equality, each of which supplements the requirement that votes not be diluted. Thus, equal opportunity for electoral influence condemns inequalities in chances to hold office or to influence the outcome of elections, but it is confined to the electoral

---

13. Rawls, *Theory of Justice*, 477. I trace this idea to Rousseau, in Joshua Cohen, "The Natural Goodness of Humanity," in Christine Korsgaard, Barbara Herman, and Andrews Reath, eds., *Learning from the History of Ethics* (Cambridge: Cambridge University Press, 1996), 102–139.

setting.[14] Equal opportunity for *political* influence (the requirement I endorse here) extends beyond equal opportunity for electoral influence by condemning inequalities in chances to influence decisions made by formal political institutions. Thus, it condemns conditions in which citizens have equal chances to influence the outcome of elections but unequal chances to form or join groups that influence the outcome of legislative decisions. Equal opportunity for *public* influence requires equal opportunities to influence the formation of opinion in the wider, informal public sphere as well as the decisions taken by formal political institutions.

The principle of political equality requires equal opportunity for political influence and is thus more stringent than the norm of equal opportunity for electoral influence. But it does not go as far as the requirement of equal opportunity for public influence. Why not endorse this wider requirement?[15] After all, just as political influence is more important than electoral influence (because of the nonelectoral ways to influence legislative or executive decisions), public influence is arguably more important than political influence. Thus, make the assumption that public opinion is translated into legitimate law. Surely, then, it seems especially desirable to have opportunities for shaping public opinion. So we might

---

14. Bruce Cain and Kathleen Sullivan both accept equal voting influence but reject equal opportunity for electoral influence. See Cain, "Moralism and Realism in Campaign Finance Reform," *University of Chicago Legal Forum* (1995). At p. 136, Cain indicates that equalizing electoral influence through restrictions on political expenditures threatens excessive responsiveness to "ill-formed majoritarian preferences." The basis for that presumption is unclear but appears to derive from the idea that spending limits restrict the flow of information, and thus give too much sway to uniformed preferences. Sullivan's case is far more plausible. See Kathleen M. Sullivan, "Political Money and Freedom of Speech," *University of California Davis Law Review* 30, 31 (Spring 1997): esp. 674–675. She points out, rightly, that the equalizing opportunities for electoral influence will require some regulations of election-related expression, but that no such regulations are required by equally weighted votes, however broadly we interpret the range of unacceptable gerrymanders. So we will need to draw some lines between electoral and political speech that occurs in informal political discussion. The result may be either unacceptable restrictions of political speech in the informal public sphere, if the boundaries around electoral speech are loosely drawn, or only minimal corrections for unequal chances for influence, if those boundaries are drawn more crisply. For if we know one thing from our experience with regulation in this field, it is that every regulation represents an invitation to invest in political strategies that are equally effective but that circumvent the regulation. One might have thought that these "practical difficulties," as Sullivan calls them, would prompt efforts at legal invention. Sullivan puzzlingly treats them as insuperable hurdles.

15. To be sure, the boundaries are vague, as is amply demonstrated by the problem of regulating issue advertising.

suppose that a case for ensuring equal chances for political influence would support equal chances for public influence as well.

I think, however, that we should resist this conclusion and reject the wide interpretation of the principle of political equality.

First, the content of the requirement of equal opportunity for public influence is obscure. The informal process of opinion-formation is not at all well defined, bounded, or understood: it extends throughout life and spreads through all its spheres. So it is not clear what the requirement demands: not clear, that is, when opportunities for influence are suitably equal—when individuals who are equally motivated and equally able have equal chances to influence the formation of public opinion. To be sure, effective chances to persuade others and to discuss cultural and political issues are important, but those chances are ensured both by the protections of expressive and associative liberties that fall under the first part of the principle of political equality and by a fair distribution of resources. Here, I am asking whether there is a further, *independent* requirement of equal opportunities for public influence. To be more precise, I am asking whether such a requirement ought to be included in a principle of political equality, as a fundamental political value to be accommodated along with equal rights of participation and equally weighted votes. If it is not included, it may still be legitimate to reduce inequalities of opportunity for public influence by subsidizing opportunities for people with limited resources: through ensuring more traditional public fora and expanding access to the new fora by, for example, subsidizing internet access (addressing the so-called digital divide) and opportunities for content provision. But the obscurity of the norm speaks against including it in a first principle of political equality, for such inclusion might lead to excessive restrictions on expression.

Second, part of the reason for requiring equal chances for political influence is that the state speaks in the name of citizens, claiming authorization for its binding collective decisions from its equal members; moreover, its decisions are enforceable. So we want to be sure that that claim is founded on arrangements that manifestly treat citizens as equals. But in the wider public sphere, we have no such authoritative statement of results. Although citizens have fundamental interests in chances for public influence, the equality requirement is less compelling.

Third, part of the reason for ensuring equal opportunities for political influence is to establish, in a visible, public way, the respect for citizens as equal members of the collective body that authorizes the exercise of political power. Given the uncertain content of the wider principle of equal opportunity for public influence, it is perhaps unnecessary for ensuring such mutual respect.

3. Facts and Trends

I want now to shift attention in two ways: from political equality in general to the particulars of campaign finance, and from political norms to facts and trends about current campaign finance in the United States. The current system of financing, then, has four fundamental features:

Increasing costs: In the 1996 election cycle, $2.4 billion was raised, and $2.2 billion was spent on candidate campaigns.[16] In addition, another $175 million was spent on independent expenditures and issue advocacy. *Independent expenditures* are funds—roughly $25 million for the 1996 elections—that are used expressly to advocate the election of one candidate or the defeat of another but that are not spent in explicit coordination with a candidate's campaign. In *issue advocacy*, money—roughly $150 million for the 1996 elections—is spent supporting or opposing the stand of an elected official or a challenger on some issue, but without expressly advocating the election or defeat of the candidate. These aggregates nearly doubled the previous record.

Who gives? Though spending is growing steadily, the number of contributors remains small. In 1996, for example, just 0.1 percent of the population gave more than $1000 to candidates and parties. Altogether, the $1000+ contributors accounted for $638 million for the 1996 elections: $477 million to candidates and parties, and another $161 million in soft money and PAC contributions.

Moreover, business spending continues to dominate the scene. "In 1996 . . . the biggest source of campaign money—by far—was the business community. Overall . . . business outspent labor by a factor of 11:1 and ideological groups by 19:1. Looking strictly at contributions to candi-

---

16. I use the 1996 numbers because the essay was originally written in 1999. The $2.4 billion comprises public money for the presidential campaign ($211m), small donors contributing less than $200 ($734m), larger donors contributing more than $200 ($597m), PACs ($234m), "soft money," which is contributed to the parties but not to be spent in connection with federal elections ($262m), and candidates themselves ($262m, led by Steve Forbes's $37m).

dates, business gave nine times as much money as organized labor, and fifteen times as much as ideological donors."[17]

In *Voice and Equality*, Verba, Schlozman, and Brady provide two findings that bear on our understanding of this relatively small pool of citizens who participate in American politics by making financial contributions and who are responsible for a large share of contributions and spending. First, willingness to contribute money is largely explained by income—by the capacity to contribute—and not by political interest. Whereas every other political-participatory act—voting, talking, giving time to a campaign—is substantially explained by the participant's general interest in politics, contributing is explained very little by general political interest and very strongly by income.[18] Second, the pool of contributors is unrepresentative of the citizenry: for example, contributors tend to be more conservative on economic issues.[19]

Unregulated flows. The current system of finance is complex, and contributions to candidate election campaigns are regulated. But here I want to emphasize that certain areas of growing importance are entirely unregulated:

- *Soft money:* Soft money given to political parties for activities allegedly unrelated to federal elections—for example, get-out-the-vote campaigns by a state Democratic or Republican Party—is entirely unrestricted by federal law.[20] Such soft money contributions grew by

17. From an online publication by Center for Responsive Politics, http://www.opensecrets.org/pubs/bigpicture/overview/bpoverview.htm.

18. Level of political interest is measured by responses to survey questions that ask about the respondent's interest in local and national affairs. See Sidney Verba, Kay Lehman Schlozman, and Henry E. Brady, *Voice and Equality* (Cambridge, MA: Harvard University Press, 1995), 553. The finding is striking, but not surprising. Someone with little political interest, thus measured, might be highly motivated to give to a candidate because of a concern about some particular issue, and assuming a declining marginal utility of money, the cost to the contributor is very small. Moreover, people with high capacity but low interest are more likely to give than people with low capacity and comparably low interest, because the former are more likely to be asked for money. My guess is that the finding that financial contributions (unlike other forms of activity) are largely explained by capacity rather than by interest is probably true for a wide range of activities and is almost certainly true of any activity in which professional fundraisers are involved, because they target capacity, not motivation. Perhaps contributions to religious organizations are an exception.

19. *Voice and Equality*, 303, 358, 361–364, 477, 512, 516.

20. Federal candidates are, however, permitted to solicit soft money. For discussion of the complexities of soft money, see Note, "Soft Money: The Current Rules and the Case for Reform," *Harvard Law Review* 111 (1998).

206 percent between 1992 and 1996, to $262 million. Whereas corporations and unions are prohibited from contributing money from their treasury to a candidate, they can contribute soft money, with no restrictions on amounts.

- *Issue ads:* Spending on issue ads is also unregulated by federal law, because such advocacy is not explicit in its endorsement of candidates. So corporations and unions can spend as they wish on issue advocacy, with no disclosure requirements. Absent such requirements, the estimate of $150 million in 1996 is inevitably speculative, but everyone agrees that issue ads are growing in importance.
- *Candidate spending:* Out-of-pocket spending by candidates is unregulated: the cases of Ross Perot, Steve Forbes, and Michael Huffington are the most famously large doses of such spending.
- *Independent expenditures:* Whereas contributions to organizations that engage in independent expenditures are regulated, the extent of such expenditures cannot be regulated. The importance of such spending has grown—fourfold between 1994 and 1996, to $22 million—because the Supreme Court decided that spending by parties on candidate elections cannot be regulated unless that spending is expressly coordinated with the candidate. But contribution limits for donations to parties are much higher than limits on giving to individual campaigns: individuals can give $40,000 to a party in an election cycle (half during the primary season, and half for the general election), but only $2000 to a candidate. So I can give $20,000 to the Democratic Party to spend on vote-for-Kennedy ads promoting Ted Kennedy over other Democratic hopefuls for senator and then another $20,000 to support Kennedy in the general election. So long as the Democrats don't ask Kennedy how to spend the money, there is no problem.

Money matters. In 1996, the candidate who outspent his or her opponent won 92 percent of the House races and 88 percent of the Senate races. These high correlations of spending and winning are typical. But they leave open questions of fact and interpretation about the political difference that money makes, even in the relatively well-defined arena of candidate elections, much less in the wider arena of political influence. For three things are true:

   i. The bigger spender tends to win.

   ii. Incumbents tend to win.

   iii. Incumbents tend to be better fund-raisers.

The trick is to provide a consistent and empirically tenable interpretation of these facts. For example, the correlation between spending and electoral advantage may be spurious, as incumbency may directly confer both. Or perhaps, instead, incumbency confers some fund-raising advantage, and the money in turn directly confers electoral advantage—apart from any direct, nonpecuniary incumbency advantage. The truth appears to be the latter: whereas incumbency makes it easier to raise money and independently easier to win elections, the money itself confers electoral benefit, as we see in open-seat races. Moreover, challengers who spend more than incumbents do have considerably greater chances of winning than challengers who spend less.[21]

Second, if incumbents are good at raising money (which confers electoral benefit), that might be because incumbents are a survivor population of especially talented candidates, and talent attracts money. Or it might be that the powers of officeholding confer an advantage in fund-raising, because contributors (individuals and particularly organized groups) want to curry favor with officeholders as a result of the powers associated with offices, and/or because reelection-seeking officeholders need to please potential contributors and have a capacity to please according to the powers of their office. On this issue, the answer seems not to be that officeholders are a survivor population of high-quality candidates but that officeholding itself creates an advantage in fund-raising. Contributors care about the capacity to deliver results; they therefore pay attention to the offices held by elected officials, and invest in those who, by virtue of their official positions, have that capacity.[22]

21. The literature is vast. See Gary Jacobson, *Money in Congressional Elections* (New Haven: Yale University Press, 1980); Jonathan Krasno and Donald P. Green, "Preempting Quality Challengers in House Elections," *Journal of Politics* 50 (1988): 920–936; Stephen Ansolabehere and James Snyder, "Money, Elections, and Candidate Quality" (unpublished paper, on file with author).

22. If the capacity to raise money (especially from organized groups) reflects the powers of office, we should not conclude that power is therefore a source of money *rather than* money is a source of power, as Ansolabehere and Snyder suggest in "Money and Institutional Power." After all, it is not implausible that greater decision-making capacity (due to greater powers associated with office) is associated with greater fund-raising capacity because funders are interested in influencing the exercise of official powers, and they target their investments accordingly. So powers of office beget money, because money is a source of influence (over the exercise of

Putting the complexities to the side, what seems undeniable is that the success of candidates depends on their fund-raising success, that the capacity to raise money depends on their performance, that the ability to attract support from the groups that give depends on their conduct; contributors, by providing such support, gain some measure of influence over electoral outcomes.

To summarize these four observations, then: formal politics is getting more expensive, just as the flow of money unregulated by sum or by source is increasing. Because of these increasing costs, and because money is important to electoral success, candidates must be especially—arguably increasingly—attentive to the interests and the concerns of the relatively small and unrepresentative group of citizens who spend money on politics and thus provide essential resources for running a modern campaign.

4. Getting the Problem Right

Contemporary discussion of reform tends to focus on one of three issues: that too much money is being spent in the aggregate; that candidates are spending too much time raising money and courting donors; and that donors get political favors in return for their contributions or other forms of spending. I don't think that any of these three concerns gets to the heart of the problem.

The first strikes me as weightless: if campaigns were well run, debated real issues, genuinely reached most citizens, and provided them with essential information, why would we think that $2 billion over a two-year election cycle is too much to spend? Perhaps we are not spending enough.

Are candidates spending too much time fund-raising? Perhaps. Dick Morris reports that President Clinton complained "bitterly" about time spent fund-raising: "I can't think. I can't act. I can't do anything but go to fund-raisers and shake hands."[23] And Vincent Blasi has made a forceful case that time devoted to fund-raising injures the democratic process by limiting the capacity of representatives to do their principal work-infor-

powers). Stephen Ansolabehere and James Snyder, "Money and Institutional Power," *Texas Law Review*, 77, 7 (June 1999): 1673–1704; Stephen Ansolabehere and James Snyder, "Money and Office," in David Brady, John Cogan, and Morris Fiorina, eds., *Continuity and Change in House Elections* (Stanford: Stanford University Press, 2000).

23. Dick Morris, *Behind the Oval Office*, 2d ed. (Washington, D.C.: Renaissance Books, 1998), 150–151.

mation gathering, constituency service, deliberating, legislating.[24] But the case for reducing the sheer time spent raising funds is not so clear. Suppose, once more, that we had a system of campaign finance in which each citizen could spend up to $250 on a candidate election, and that candidates were required to raise all their resources from such contributions. If they spent lots of time fund-raising, perhaps that would be a good thing: they would be required to meet with large numbers of potential contributors and might learn from those discussions, but without the current bias in the pool.

Are contributors getting favors in return for their money? Perhaps; but even if they are not, a large problem of political fairness remains.

The idea of political fairness is captured by the requirement in the principle of political equality mandating that citizens have equal opportunities for political influence. The vote is one form of influence, and the one-person/one-vote requirement is an important implication of the idea of equalizing opportunities for effective political influence. But when money is as important a political resource as it is in our current system, control of it is an important source of political influence. It enables people to run for office, to support electoral efforts financially, and to join together with like-minded others with the aim of persuading fellow citizens on some issue of public concern. A system that does not regulate the flow of money—nor provide (as in a system of public finance) alternatives to relying on private money—provides unequal opportunities for political influence. It provides to wealthier citizens channels of influence that are effectively unavailable to others, who are equally motivated and equally able but lack the resources required for using those channels. Do these channels of influence overwhelm others? Do they establish decisive forms of power? Clearly they are not always decisive. But it seems clear, too, that we will never have conclusive answers to questions about the relative importance of different avenues of influence. What we can say is that the current legal structure establishes a channel of influence that is effectively open to some but not to others. That is itself the problem, however precisely this opportunity translates into power over decisions.

So the principle of political equality—in particular, the norm of equal

24. Vincent Blasi, "Free Speech and the Widening Gyre of Fund-Raising: Why Campaign Spending Limits May Not Violate the First Amendment After All," 94 *Columbia Law Review* 1281 (1994).

opportunity for political influence—raises serious troubles for the current system of finance.

5. Constitutional Landscape

What might be done to remedy this situation? To answer this question, I start with the constitutional landscape.

In the 1976 case of *Buckley v. Valeo*, the Supreme Court heard a challenge to the Federal Election Campaign Act (FECA) of 1971, as amended in 1974.[25] The Court's assessment was mixed: some parts were upheld, some not. But the details of the decision matter less than the framework of analysis and the argument announced in it. That analytic framework comprises two key elements.

First, the *Buckley* Court held that "money is speech": meaning that spending money on politics—both contributions to campaigns and expenditures (by candidates or individual citizens or organizations)—has First Amendment protection. Indeed, as political speech, it lies at the core of the First Amendment. For the First Amendment is centrally (though not exclusively) about protecting political speech from regulation, as a necessary condition for assuring popular sovereignty—rather than governmental sovereignty—that defines the American constitutional system.

The argument that spending is, for constitutional purposes, protected political speech proceeds as follows: "Contribution and spending limitations impose direct *quantity restrictions* [emphasis added] on political communication and association. . . . A restriction on the amount of money a person or group can spend on political communication during a campaign necessarily reduces the quantity of expression by restricting the number of issues discussed, the depth of their exploration, and the size of the audience reached. This is because virtually every means of communicating in today's mass society requires the expenditure of money. . . . The electorate's increasing dependence on television, radio, and other mass media for news and information has made these expensive modes of communication indispensable instruments of effective political speech."[26]

So sending messages requires money, and restrictions on money therefore restrict such sending: they limit the "quantity" of speech. The quan-

25. Buckley v. Valeo, 424 U.S. 1 (1976).
26. Ibid., 19.

tity of speech is an important constitutional value, not simply because speakers have an interest in advancing their views but also because audiences—citizens, as the ultimate political authority—have an interest in the fullest airing of issues, without control by government over what is said or how much is said. Citizens may, of course, tune the messages out, but because of the audience/citizen interest, state restrictions on the quantity of speech face a chilly reception.

More particularly, the Court held that contributions and expenditures both have First Amendment protection, but that regulations of contributions are less offensive to the First Amendment than regulations of expenditures. Contributions are lower in the constitutional scale in part because the principal value of a contribution lies in the fact that it is given, quite apart from its size. Though contributing more reveals greater intensity of support, it does not itself add to the content of the basic message, which is "I support Jones." This claim—here I plead against interest—strikes me as preposterous. Giving lots of money might well express a different belief than giving a smaller amount: namely, the belief that the candidate I contribute to is a *much* better candidate than the competitor, and that it is *very* important that he or she be elected. Apart from this implausible consideration about the independence of the content of the message sent by a contribution from the magnitude of that contribution, the Court also noted that if contributions are regulated, citizens still have other ways to get their messages out—by spending in ways that are not coordinated with a campaign.

Neither in *Buckley* nor elsewhere does the Court contemplate the possibility that electoral speech—though assuredly political—should be, as a general matter, easier to regulate than political speech—more generally easier, say, than nonelectoral, political speech in the public sphere. This possibility might have been defended along the following lines:[27] the Court might have treated speech in the electoral setting generally along the lines that it has treated speech in the setting of ballot access law. Thus the Court has generally taken the view that restrictions on ballot access—say, restrictions on write-in ballots that prevent voters from writing in Daffy Duck or restrictions on fusion candidates that prevent third parties from cross-nominating major party candidates—are permissible because the point of ballots is to select officeholders, not to have open-ended de-

27. C. Edwin Baker, "Campaign Expenditures and Free Speech," *Harvard Civil Rights-Civil Liberties Law Review* 33, 1 (Winter 1998): 1–55.

bate of political ideas: "The purpose of casting, counting, and recording votes is to elect public officials, not to serve as a general forum for political expression."[28] Similarly, the Court might have said that the principal forum for political expression is the informal public sphere, not the electoral setting in particular. The latter is a specific institution, designed for a particular purpose—the selection of officials—and can permissibly be regulated in light of that purpose. So if the purpose of elections is to translate public opinion into an authorization to exercise power—to provide an accurate register of the state of collective opinion rather than to form public opinion itself—then regulations designed to ensure such translation should be permissible, even if they have the effect of reducing the quantity of speech, in just the way that it is permissible to restrict write-in candidacies in light of the institutional purpose of ballots.

One reason for rejecting this approach is that—particularly in a world of virtually permanent campaigning—it would require difficult line-drawing exercises to distinguish electoral speech from other forms of political speech. Those distinctions are much crisper in the ballot setting, where the issue is whether and how a particular person's name will appear on a well-defined ballot. Moreover, some ways of drawing the line and regulating electoral speech might end up providing excessive protection for incumbents. Still, I don't think this criticism is compelling. After all, line-drawing is already necessary, as, for example, in the area of issue advocacy.

More fundamentally, I suspect that the Court would—and should—reject the idea that electoral speech performs a mere "translation function" and the conception of democracy associated with that idea. Elections, they might say, are important not only to translating an antecedently articulated collective opinion into political power but also to crystallizing such opinion in ways that enable the exercise of power to take guidance from it.[29] So we ought not to treat electoral speech as narrowly institutional speech, with a well-defined purpose, nor to make the permissibility of regulation turn on such treatment.

28. Burdick v. Takushi, 504 U.S. 428, 445 (1992); see also Timmons v. Twin Cities Area New Party, 117 S. Ct. 1364, 1377 (1997) (Stevens, J., joined by Ginsburg and Souter, JJ., dissenting), where the dissent attributes this view to the majority.

29. Samuel L. Popkin, *The Reasoning Voter: Communication and Persuasion in Presidential Campaigns* (Chicago: University of Chicago Press, 1991); Arthur Lupia and Matthew McCubbins, *The Democratic Dilemma: Can Citizens Learn What They Need to Know?* (Cambridge: Cambridge University Press, 1998).

Returning to *Buckley:* The second main idea is that the state has a compelling interest in avoiding the appearance and the reality of quid pro quo—dollars for votes—corruption. "Corruption," the Court said in 1985, "is a subversion of the political process," and the "hallmark of corruption is the financial quid pro quo: dollars for political favors."[30] The essential point is that the corruption rationale is narrowly understood—in effect, as a generalization of bribery law.

The Court allows that there may be other compelling rationales for regulating spending but insists that none has yet been identified. In particular, the state is said not to have a compelling interest in "leveling the playing field"—ensuring equal opportunity for political influence. FECA, the Court says, was "aimed in part at equalizing the relative ability of all voters to affect electoral outcomes by placing a ceiling on expenditures for political expression by citizens and groups." But the majority opinion rejects this rationale: "The concept that government may restrict the speech of some elements of our society in order to enhance the relative voice of others is wholly foreign to the First Amendment."[31] In this important remark, the Court does not dispute that restricting the voice of some may enhance the relative voice of others—indeed, that it might be necessary to enhancing their voice. Nor does it deny that such enhancement would be a very good thing, a legitimate and perhaps substantial governmental objective. Instead, the majority asserts that the First Amendment bars the door to achieving equalization through restriction on First Amendment liberties.

With those two elements in place, the rest of the system follows pretty straightforwardly. Because contributions merit lesser First Amendment protection, and because restrictions on "large contributions" are well designed to avoid the appearance and reality of political quid pro quo, restrictions on such contributions are permissible, though only if they are addressed to quid pro quo corruption, and that means only if the regulated contributions are sufficiently large to pose a genuine threat of such corruption. Because expenditures merit especially stringent protection, and because restrictions on expenditures do not advance the one concededly compelling interest in the arena of electoral finance—the interest in avoiding the appearance or reality of quid pro quo corruption—expenditure restrictions are impermissible, unless they are voluntary, as

30. FEC v. NCPAC, 470 U.S. 480, 497 (1985).
31. Buckley v. Valeo, 424 U.S. 1, 48–49 (1976).

under the public financing scheme for presidential elections that was part of FECA.

6. Persisting Constraints

In the period since *Buckley*, the two fundamentals of this framework have been restated and reinforced, but they have not been changed.

Thus, the Court continues to hold that the First Amendment protects both contributions and expenditures and has continued to emphasize the importance of spending in contributing to the *quantity* of speech, and thus to the interest of the audience, even more than it has emphasized the importance of protecting the interests of speakers. Because of this emphasis on quantity of speech, the Court has held that the identity of the speaker is not especially relevant to the permissibility of regulation. Particularly important and revealing in this connection is the 1978 *Bellotti* decision, in which the Court held that states could not regulate corporate spending on ballot initiatives. The fact that the speakers were not individual citizens but corporations did not matter because the protected value was not the corporation's interest in speaking but the audience's interest in a full airing of views.[32] This is "the type of speech indispensable to decision making in a democracy," and its value "in terms of its capacity for informing the public does not depend upon the identity of its source, whether corporation, association, union, or individual."[33] "The Constitution," according to the Court majority, "often protects interests broader than those of the party seeking their vindication. The First Amendment, in particular, serves significant societal interests," in particular the interest in the "free discussion of governmental affairs." So the Court vindicated the expressive liberty of the corporation (in this case, the bank) not because of any special concern for the corporation's interests, or because of a judgment that the regulation was especially burdensome to those interests, but because of a concern for the wider public interest in informed decision making. The essential idea is captured in a paraphrase of Mill's reason for thinking that it is as bad to silence one as to silence all: "Were an opinion a personal possession of no value except to the owner; if to be obstructed in the enjoyment of it were simply a private injury, it would make some difference who the injury was inflicted upon. But the peculiar evil of silencing the expression of an opinion is,

32. First National Bank v. Bellotti, 435 U.S. 765, 767 (1978).
33. Ibid., 777.

that it is robbing the human race"[34]—or if that seems excessively high-minded, let's just say "that it is robbing the voters of relevant information."

As to the second element, the Court shows virtually no disposition to break from *Buckley*'s claim that there is no such thing as a process being corrupt because it is unfair, because it provides citizens with fundamentally unequal chances to influence the political process—more precisely, that even if such inequality is a form of unfairness, it is not of the same constitutional magnitude as quid pro quo corruption and therefore does not justify restrictions on expenditures.[35] Put otherwise, the Court continues to be very solicitous of the interests of citizens as spectators, information gatherers, observers—as consumers of information and argument who can decide for themselves which messages to listen to—but continues to show much less concern for the interests of citizens as activists and participants, seeking fair chances to influence others in the political arena.

In one post-*Buckley* case, the Court majority has acknowledged concerns about fair access—about a corruption extending beyond quid pro quo. In *Austin v. Michigan Chamber of Commerce*, the Court upheld a Michigan law prohibiting corporations from using general treasury funds for independent expenditures in connection with state candidate elections.[36] They upheld it because of concerns about the "corrosive and distorting effects of immense aggregations of wealth that are accumulated with the help of the corporate form and that have little or no correlation with the public's support for the corporation's political ideas." This talk about "corrosive and distorting effects" acknowledges a corruption of democratic process that extends beyond quid pro quo. But the case, which drew a strongly worded dissent from Justice Scalia, has been virtually without impact on subsequent decisions, largely because it has been interpreted as arising specifically from traditional concerns about corporations and wealth accumulated with the help of the corporate form, and not as standing for a more general proposition about the effects of "aggregations of wealth that have little or no correlation with the public's support for the political ideas of the holders of that wealth."

With the two fundamentals of the Court's analysis remaining essen-

---

34. Mill, *On Liberty* (Indianapolis: Hackett, 1978), chap. 2, paragraph 1.

35. As I noted earlier (270), Nixon v. Shrink, 528 U.S. 377 (2000), may signal a change of direction on this essential point.

36. Austin v. Michigan Chamber of Commerce, 494 U.S. 652 (1990).

tially fixed, proposed regulations continue to face very stringent, in practice nearly insuperable, hurdles.

The situation with contribution regulations has not changed fundamentally, though it may be somewhat stricter than it was after *Buckley*, because the Court, as mentioned, has focused principally on the importance of an anticorruption rationale and not on the lesser First Amendment importance of contributions. Because of its focus on corruption, the Court has said that states cannot limit contributions to groups running ballot initiatives: because there is no danger of quid pro quo with a candidate, there is no problem.[37] Similarly, lower courts have been overturning laws with "low limits" on contributions ($100 for state contests). Contribution limits cannot, for example, be justified by "level playing field" arguments, or by the importance of enabling most people to play, or by bringing more citizens into the process. The limit must be set such that there is a plausible concern about quid pro quo: because it seems implausible that you can buy many favors from the mayor of St. Louis for $100, a low limit of that kind provokes suspicion that the aim is to level the playing field not to fight corruption. In addition, there may well be an emerging Court majority for the view that party contributions to candidates are, as it were, born pure: because political parties are coalitions of candidates, those parties cannot be corrupting candidates by directly supporting their campaigns. According to this view, party contributions are to be treated on a par with the candidates' own expenditures, which cannot be regulated because there is no threat of corruption. Justices Rehnquist, Scalia, Thomas, and Kennedy have taken this position, and it may eventually win support from Breyer, O'Connor, or Souter.[38]

The situation with expenditures is similarly crisp, largely stable, with a few signs of increased hostility to anything that suggests limits. Apart from the special case of independent corporate expenditures on candidate campaigns (as in *Austin*), the Court has not upheld mandatory expenditure restrictions, nor are there signs that they will. Thus, in 1985 the Court held that "independent" expenditures cannot be regulated, even if the candidate supported by those expenditures has accepted public money with associated voluntary limits.[39] Moreover, it has adopted a pretty broad interpretation of "independent." The key point is "uncoordi-

37. Citizens Against Rent Control v. City of Berkeley, 454 U.S. 290 (1981).

38. *Colorado Republican Federal Campaign Committee v. FEC*.

39. FEC v. NCPAC, 470 U.S. 480 (1985) (overturning limits on independent expenditures on behalf of Presidential candidates who have accepted public funding).

nated": if spending is not explicitly coordinated with a candidate, then quid pro quo concerns are absent.

So in *Colorado Republican Federal Campaign Committee v. FEC*, the Court opinion held that spending by the Republican Party to defeat Senator Tim Wirth was an independent expenditure because Wirth's Republican opponent candidate had not yet been chosen and no exchange of support for favors could have been in play. In short, party spending in support of a candidate is not, as such, coordinated, and may therefore be protected.

Finally, as the definition of "independent" is capacious, so, too, the solicitude for independent spenders, thus defined, is very great. In a 1994 Eighth Circuit decision, the circuit court rejected a provision of a Minnesota public financing law that would have provided increased support for publicly financed candidates facing opposition from independent spending by PACs.[40] Efforts by the state to match that spending would have amounted, in effect, to chilling the speech of those independent opponents. The theme here is potentially very important: the trouble with this regulation is that it puts the state in the position of trying to reduce the quantity of speech, and that is objectionable.

One case that looks different is a decision in the Eighth Circuit upholding a provision of a Minnesota public financing law that removes expenditure caps from candidates who have accepted such caps as a condition for receiving public money, but who face opponents who do not and who spend more than a specified amount.[41] The challengers said that the state's incentives were too good to be voluntary: that the state was in effect coercing people into the public system and trying to reduce the quantity of speech—likely to be the chief objection to waivers on expenditure limits in public financing schemes. Similarly, the District Court for the Maine District has upheld provisions of the Maine law that provide additional support for clean money candidates facing high-spending challengers.[42]

7. Democracy and Campaign Finance

The current system of campaign finance appears to be at odds with the principle of equal opportunity for political influence. In the name of a

---

40. Day v. Holahan, 34 F.3d 1356 (8th Cir. 1994), cert. denied, 513 U.S. 1127 (1995).

41. Rosensteil v. Rodriguez, 101 F.3d 1544 (8th Cir. 1996), cert. denied, 520 U.S. 1229 (1997). Also, Gable v. Patton, 142 F.3d 940 (6th Cir. 1998).

42. Daggett v. Webster, 74 F. Supp. 2d 53 (D. Me. 1999).

constitutionally basic liberty of speech, however, the Court has resisted reform efforts that appeal to that principle. It is essential to understand exactly what is—and what is not—being said by the Court and the allied critics of reform. To reiterate: the Court has not said that the current system already ensures equal opportunity, or that equal opportunity for influence is a trivial or illegitimate political concern, or that all policies aimed at promoting it are constitutionally infirm, or that proposed reforms would be ineffective at advancing that value. Thus it is not true, as one recent discussion states, that "*Buckley* outright rejected the legitimacy of the asserted interest in equalizing the relative ability of individuals and groups to affect election outcomes."[43] *Buckley* speaks to the magnitude of the asserted interest, not its legitimacy. It is hard to see what, in Buckley, would stand in the way of a redistributive voucher scheme with benefits targeted on low-income citizens, so long as the scheme was not accompanied by expenditure restrictions.[44] Instead, the Court has said that neither governments nor citizens themselves acting directly through initiative can legitimately seek to equalize opportunities for political influence *by means of regulations that reduce the quantity of speech*. Such reduction conflicts with the First Amendment's free speech guarantee. In the name of equality, it puts illegitimate restrictions on freedom of speech.

I want to focus on this claim about illegitimate restrictions. But before getting there, I need to consider an argument to the effect that there is no deep conflict between liberty and equality in this area, and that the *Buckley* framework is not a hurdle to achieving fair equality. Thus it might be said that an ideal scheme of financing would accommodate both expressive liberty and political equality by providing subsidies to all eligible candidates (or to political parties) while attaching no conditions to the receipt of those subsidies—no restrictions on expenditures by candidates who accept them (the current system of financing of presidential elections does attach conditions to the acceptance of public money).

43. Deborah Goldberg, ed., *Writing Reform: A Guide to Drafting State and Local Campaign Finance Laws* (New York: Brennan Center for Justice, 1998), 1–7. The only evidence cited for the proposition quoted in the text is the infamous line in Buckley about the impermissibility of "restricting the speech of some elements of our society in order to enhance the relative voice of others." But the passage is specifically about restricting speech, not about the legitimacy of the interest in ensuring equal opportunity for political influence.

44. Bruce Ackerman's voucher scheme is so accompanied: it excludes real money and permits only voucher-based expenditures. See Bruce Ackerman, "The Patriot Option," in Joshua Cohen and Joel Rogers, eds., *Money and Politics: Financing Elections Democratically* (Boston: Beacon Press, 1999).

By establishing *floors* that enabled candidates to compete without having to appease the interests of contributors, the scheme would go some way to equalizing opportunity for influence. By excluding *ceilings*, it would achieve that equalization without reducing the level of speech, thus eliminating worries about conflict with the first part of the principle of political equality. Worries about public subsidies, because they prompt concerns about incumbency protection, or other forms of official manipulation, could be addressed by using alternative strategies for providing floors: for example, tax credits, deductions, or vouchers that enable individual citizens to finance elections, while eliminating the cost to them of contributing.[45]

Put aside questions about whether such an "all floors/no ceilings" approach, with its focus on candidates, fully addresses the concerns about opportunities for citizen influence. Still, it faces an obvious objection. Private contributions and expenditures may well swamp floors unaccompanied by restrictions, so that no real equalization of opportunities for influence results. In response, the floors-only proponent might say that the benefits of spending more money decline as quantities of money increase; the production function for votes has a negative second derivative. Although this response has some force, it hardly seems sufficient to dismiss the liberty/equality issue. If we take equal opportunity for influence as a basic political value, then we cannot make its satisfaction contingent on a speculative judgment of this kind about the responsiveness of votes to spending.

So a scheme of public financing likely needs to be paired with some limits and some incentives to accept the limits. Consider, for example, a system of voluntary public financing in which public money goes only to candidates who agree to forgo private money; in which nonpublic candidates face reasonably low contribution limits (say, $250 for state-wide offices); and in which additional subsidies go to public money candidates who face independent expenditures or high-spending private money challengers. The Maine system is of this kind, and critics complain that it includes too wide a range of limits. The crux of the worry is that the regulation has the state taking the position that less money, and therefore less speech, is better. And surely they would object still more strenuously to more straightforward limits—for example, a narrower con-

45. See Zach Polett, "Empower Citizens," and Ackerman, "The Patriot Option," in Cohen and Rogers, eds., *Money and Politics*.

ception of issue advocacy that would result in a widening of regulable expenditures, or expenditure ceilings, or a less capacious conception of an independent expenditure. Though the floors-only idea seems very attractive, then, I don't think we can so easily evade the issue.

Returning, then, to the issue of "illegitimate restrictions of speech," I note first that the phrase is not a pleonasm. We have bribery laws, child pornography laws, and contribution limits; restrictions on the time, manner, and place of speech are widely accepted, and sometimes—as with restrictions on campaigning within 100 feet of polling places—those restrictions apply exclusively to political speech: in short, some restrictions of speech are acceptable. Moreover, the kinds of restrictions of speech that are most profoundly objectionable—that offend most directly against the value of freedom of expression—are restrictions very different from those contemplated by campaign finance regulations.[46] First, they are directed against speech with certain contents or viewpoints. Such regulations threaten to freeze the existing state of opinion and, perhaps, to insulate the government from popular criticism. But campaign finance regulations are neutral with respect to content and viewpoint.

Second, restrictions are objectionable when they are directed against certain persons or groups. They say in effect that some person or group is not worthy of being heard or have the objective effect of imposing an undue burden on the expression of some group. Again, the regulations under contemplation appear not to be of this kind.

Suppose, then, that regulations are content- and viewpoint-neutral and do not impose undue burdens on some citizens or groups. Why might they still represent unacceptable burdens on freedom of speech? It might be—third—that they restrict more speech than is necessary for achieving their goal of ensuring equal opportunity for political influence: perhaps, that is, we can find alternative regulations that are less restrictive but more or less as effective. But absent optimistic and highly speculative assumptions about declining marginal benefits of money, I see no reason to suppose that the proposed regulations are, in this way, unreasonable.

Consider, then, a content- and viewpoint-neutral regulation that is not unduly burdensome to any group and that is no more restrictive of speech than is necessary—given available alternatives—for ensuring equal opportunity for political influence. Why should the sheer fact that it re-

---

46. This paragraph and the next two draw on Rawls's discussion of the three conditions that an acceptable regulation must meet. See *Political Liberalism*, 357–358.

duces the quantity of speech make it so objectionable? Why does that suffice to trump the importance of equal opportunity for influence?

Two answers come to mind. The first is instrumental and concerns threats to the quality of decisions that might result from restrictions. Recall the Court's statement in *Buckley* that "a restriction on the amount of money a person or group can spend on political communication during a campaign necessarily reduces the quantity of expression by restricting the number of issues discussed, the depth of their exploration, and the size of the audience reached." Here, the restrictions on money, which lead to limits on the quantity of speech, are tied to a threat of making worse collective decisions, because the restrictions limit the flow of information and prevent a sufficiently close examination of the issues. In short, the restrictions make the outcomes worse.

This first, instrumental argument against reducing the quantity of expression seems very weak. It is not true that restrictions on money "necessarily" restrict issue range, depth of exploration, or audience size. Though they do limit quantity, the effects of quantity limits—whether they transform into limits on quality—are contingent on the extent and character of the restrictions and on what the money would have been used for: if the money goes to more attack ads, then quantity declines, but not range, depth, or audience size. Indeed, if Steve Ansolabehere and Shanto Iyengar are right, spending on negative ads turns voters off. So an increase in expenditures may produce a decline in audience size.[47]

A second argument is intrinsic and plays a large role in hostility to regulation: it claims that restrictions on the quantity of speech are objectionable, not because they worsen political outcomes, but because they worsen the democratic process itself by distorting the proper role of citizens within it. In short, such restrictions conflict with the ideal of democracy itself. The intrinsic argument is founded on an idea about individual responsibility and its role in democracy. It says that democratic process, properly understood, assigns to individual citizens the right and the responsibility to decide how much information is sufficient and to distinguish between reliable and unreliable sources—just as democracy assigns to individual citizens the responsibility to decide how much they wish to participate, as indicated by the embrace of an equality of opportunity rather than an equality of influence principle. But this assignment

47. Stephen Ansolabehere and Shanto Iyengar, *Going Negative* (New York: Free Press, 1995).

of responsibility is undermined when collective judgments about appropriate levels and kinds of information replace individual judgments, whether those collective judgments come from legislatures or from citizen majorities acting directly through referenda. It is incompatible with this idea of democracy to seek to correct, through collective means, for biases or imbalances in available information, except perhaps by increasing the level of speech. We cannot restrict the quantity of speech on the ground that citizens may be misled by what they hear or that they may be put off because they hear too much or because what they hear is so relentlessly negative. Thus the Court's essential claim in *Buckley*: "The First Amendment denies government the power to determine that spending is wasteful, or excessive, or unwise. In the free society ordained by our constitution it is not the government, but the people—individually as citizens and candidates and collectively as associations and political committees—who must retain control over the quantity and range of debate on public issues in a political campaign."[48]

"The people," as the passage between the dashes underscores, must here be understood distributively, as the set of individual citizens and associations of citizens, not as a single collective authority. The Court here denies that collective responsibility extends to the issue of how much should be said in an election, or to the range of issues that ought to be covered. Though the intrinsic argument emphasizes the role of individual responsibility, it does not deny the importance of a division of labor within democracy between collective and individual responsibility. Instead it holds that we discharge our collective responsibility to uphold democracy by ensuring an open process of communication—with no restrictions on the flow of information or the content of communications—that enables citizens to act with political responsibility by making their own judgments about political affairs, including judgments about what to pay attention to.

This intrinsic argument has considerable force. It does not commit the critic of regulation to saying, for example, that property rights or private liberties take precedence over democracy. Kathleen Sullivan correctly observes that "arguments for greater limits on political contributions and expenditure typically suggest that any claims for individual liberty to spend political money ought to yield to an overriding interest in a well-

---

48. Buckley v. Valeo, 424 U.S. 1, 57 (1976).

functioning democracy."[49] The critic I have described here turns that argument around. This critic accepts the overriding interest in a well-functioning democracy but argues that a "well-functioning democracy," properly conceived, does not permit regulation of speech in the name of equal opportunity for political influence. The critic who endorses the intrinsic argument does not say: "Yes, the current regime of campaign finance injures democracy, but this injury is justified by the need to ensure that citizens can freely use their private property" (though, of course, some critics may say that). Instead, the argument is that the value of democracy itself condemns regulation, because of the conception of responsibility ingredient in the best conception of democracy. The dissent in *Nixon v. Shrink* suggests just this point: "The right to free speech is a right held by each American, not by Americans en masse. The Court in *Buckley* provided no basis for suppressing the speech of an individual candidate simply because other candidates (or candidates in the aggregate) may succeed in reaching the voting public. Any such reasoning would fly in the face of the premise of our political system—liberty vested in individual hands safeguards the functioning of our democracy."[50]

Observing the earlier discussion of equal *opportunity* for influence, the critic argues that a plausible principle of political equality, suited to a political society of free and equal persons, needs to include some account of individual political responsibility. So the argument might be put this way: the principle of political equality includes a right of free political speech and an associated idea of political responsibility, implicit in its hostility to content and viewpoint regulation and the distinction between equalizing opportunity for influence and equalizing influence itself. That's part of what is involved in treating democratic citizens as free. But once we embrace this notion of political responsibility, we must accept, too, that collective regulation of the quantity of speech is incompatible with democracy.

Though forceful, this argument is doubly deficient. First, it misconceives the case for regulation by representing it as dependent on a judgment about who is entitled to decide whether the quantity and the kind of information are sufficient. The argument for regulation based on the principle of equal opportunity for influence is not of this kind. Though it

49. Kathleen M. Sullivan, "Political Money and Freedom of Speech," 671.
50. Slip op., 17.

leads to restrictions on the quantity of speech, those restrictions are the by-product of a principle of political fairness not of the claim that the legislature or the majority of citizens are better judges of the value of political messages than are citizens and their associations acting separately. The problem that the regulations are designed to address is not that citizens may be misled or put off by what they hear, but that they have a powerful objection to a process whose organization does not even make an effort to ensure equality of opportunity for influence among citizens who are said to be equal. No insult to the freedom of citizens, or to their capacity for responsible judgment, is implied or suggested.

Second, though the intrinsic argument against restrictions stakes its case on the value of democratic process, it neglects an essential point about that process. The point might be put in terms of the different interests of citizens in a democracy or in terms of roles associated with those interests.[51] The *Buckley* framework—like much democratic theory in the "elite" tradition associated with Schumpeter—casts citizens principally in the role of audience. As participants in democratic process, they have a fundamental interest in listening to debates, acquiring information through both formal political communications and more informal processes of discussion,[52] arriving at judgments about policies and candidates, and acting as political agents when they express those judgments at the polls, making informed judgments among competing candidates. But in a democracy, citizens are also agents, participants, speakers, who may aim to reshape both the terms of political debate and its results, by running for office or by seeking to influence the views of candidates, the outcomes of elections, and the interelection conduct of politics.[53] A requirement of equal opportunity for political influence aims to ensure that they are in a position to play that role, should they wish to take it on. Of course, they may also wish to influence politics through conduct in the informal public sphere. But, once again, the principle of political equal-

---

51. For a parallel discussion, see Ronald Dworkin, "The Curse of American Politics," *New York Review of Books* 17 (October 1996): 19–24. Dworkin emphasizes the dual role of citizens, as judges of electoral contests and as participants in those contests.

52. See Samuel Popkin's *The Reasoning Voter*, on the acquisition of information through informal discussion.

53. See my discussion of the deliberative and expressive interests, in "Freedom of Expression," *Philosophy and Public Affairs* 22, 3 (summer 1993), 224–229 [reprinted as essay 4 in this collection].

ity is confined to the organization of the arrangements of authoritative collective decision making.

The claim that "democracy" casts citizens in this role and respects their expressive-participatory interests might appear to depend on some special philosophical view, whether Aristotelian or Rousseauean, about the value of political participation in a well-lived human life. But it need not be presented as so dependent. The idea that citizens have a fundamental interest in bringing their conceptions of justice to bear on the conduct of political life is common to a range of philosophies of life.[54] A characteristic feature of different philosophies—different comprehensive doctrines, in Rawls's phrase—is that they assign to us strong reasons for exercising responsible judgment about the proper directions of collective life and for aiming to correct those directions particularly when they are unjust; and those reasons are all the more compelling when authoritative collective decisions are made in the name of those over whom they are enforced. Aristotelians found those reasons on the central role of civic engagement in a flourishing human life; Rousseaueans on the fundamental value of individual autonomy and the connection of such autonomy with political participation in a democratic polity; and some religiously based philosophies on the commanding personal obligation to ensure social justice and to respect human dignity. These alternative philosophies of life each acknowledges that citizens have substantial, sometimes compelling, reasons for addressing political affairs and a correspondingly fundamental "expressive" interest in favorable conditions for forming judgments about the proper directions of policy and for acting on those judgments—by presenting them to others and by seeking to correct for injustices by acting in the political arena. Failure to acknowledge both the weight of those reasons for the agent and the claims to opportunities for effective influence that emerge from them reflects a failure to respect the democratic idea of citizens as equals.

The weight of these reasons is reflected in part by the first component of the principle of political equality, which requires equal rights of political speech, association, and participation. But these reasons do not simply support a right to participate. They also yield a right to opportunities for effective influence on the political environment. Moreover, because claims for effective influence reflect the standing of citizens as equals,

54. Ibid., 224–226.

those claims are for an equal chance to influence: a failure to provide such is a failure to acknowledge that equal standing.

More particularly, the aim must be to mitigate the impact on effectiveness in the role of citizen of irrelevant facts about economic position—particularly when that impact is a result of the design of arrangements of binding collective decision making. And that means a different understanding of the division of individual and collective labor. Individuals remain responsible for finding the signals in the political noise that surrounds them and for judging how far they wish to go in taking on the role of participant, agent, speaker. Thus we keep free political speech, without content or viewpoint restrictions, and maintain the influence/opportunity-to-influence distinction. When it comes to acquiring the information needed to play this role, collective responsibility is to ensure open communication and perhaps to encourage, in the familiar Brandeisian phrase, "more speech." But collective responsibility extends to ensuring that when citizens do decide to operate as political agents, they have a fair chance for influence. We cannot reasonably expect people to respect the results of a political process whose basic organization effectively assigns greater opportunities for political influence to those who are economically advantaged.

What makes the current constitutional framework so disturbing is that it says that the people cannot permissibly adopt this conception of democracy and citizenship nor experiment with ways to secure equal opportunities for political influence while also protecting political speech. It says that the Constitution enacts Joseph Schumpeter's *Capitalism, Socialism, and Democracy*. To underscore the point, I conclude by contrasting the framework of constitutional reasoning described here with the framework presented by the European Court of Human Rights in the case of *Bowman v. The United Kingdom* (1998).[55] The case involved a challenge to a 1983 British law (the Representation of the People Act) that prohibited individuals from spending more than five pounds either favoring or opposing the election of a particular parliamentary candidate in the period immediately preceding an election. The case was decided under Article 10 of the European Convention on Human Rights, which states that the exercise of freedom of expression "may be subject to such formalities, conditions, restrictions or penalties as are prescribed by law

55. Bowman v. United Kingdom, *European Court of Human Rights*, 19 February 1998, slip op.

and are necessary in a democratic society." More particularly, the court needed to decide whether the regulation was more stringent than necessary to foster a democratic society, where such fostering was understood to comprise three legitimate aims: establishing fair conditions for competing candidates, ensuring the independence of candidates from interest groups, and preventing political debate around election time from focusing on single issues rather than on matters of broad concern. The court found the five-pound limit excessive. The crucial point here, however, is not the conclusion but the court's recognition that the three aforementioned values are aspects of democracy, and that promoting them provides an entirely legitimate reason for restricting the quantity of speech in the period just prior to an election. Whatever the wisdom of the court's judgment in the *Bowman* case, the framework—with its recognition that political fairness and freedom of expression are both ingredients of democracy—is more suited to a democracy than the *Buckley* framework is.[56]

8. Conclusion

A fundamental proposition of democratic thought is that our collective decisions should reflect our judgments (the judgments of individual citizens), formed through open processes of communication, unconstrained by collective judgments about what and how much we should hear. But this important principle must not lead to the undemocratic proposition that citizens are equals only when we sit in the audience, listening to what others say, and unequals when we take to the political stage. The principle of political equality requires that we accommodate the interests of citizens as audience and actor. We need to preserve a system of open political communication that enables citizens to exercise their deliberative responsibilities by forming their views against a background of adequate information and rich debate and also that ensures equal access to the public arena: we should not organize the political arena as a system of unequal opportunities. Designing a regulatory scheme that promises both will be hard: we need some experimentation. But we do not solve the conundrum by throwing out half the democratic ideal.

56. I should add that it is very much consonant with the view suggested in the concurrence by Justice Breyer in *Nixon v. Shrink*, which states that contribution limits are based on the "need for democratization" and not simply on the concerns about quid pro quo corruption. Slip op., 10.

9

PRIVACY, PLURALISM, AND DEMOCRACY

> So the spheres of the political and the public, of the nonpublic and the private, fall out from the content and application of the conception of justice and its principles. If the so-called private sphere is alleged to be a space exempt from justice, then there is no such thing.
>
> Sometimes those who appear to reject the idea of public reason actually mean to assert the need for full and open discussion in the background culture. With this political liberalism full agrees.
>
> —JOHN RAWLS[1]

Privacy is a controversial idea of law and political morality. The controversy it provokes can be divided into two areas. The first is about the *right to privacy*, which requires protections of certain kinds of information and conduct from public disclosure and regulation. Debate about the privacy right considers how we should characterize its content; whether that content (if there is such a right) transcends concrete rights that protect reputation, property, and bodily integrity; what connection, if any, there is between the protection of interests in personal independence characteristic of constitutional privacy and the protections of inter-

I presented earlier versions of this essay at a meeting of the Eastern Division of the American Philosophical Association, at the Universidad Torcuato di Tella, at the University of Georgia, at the Graduate Center, City University, at the Inland Northwest Philosophy Conference, and as a Donald Kalish Memorial Lecture at UCLA. I am indebted to Martha Nussbaum, Judith Thomson, Frances Kamm, David Estlund, Eduardo Rivera-López, Andrew Sabl, Seana Shiffrin, and Erik Olin Wright for their helpful comments on earlier versions. I would like to think that my friend Don Kalish would have endorsed the combination of privacy rights and cultural democracy that I endorse here.

1. John Rawls, "The Idea of Public Reason Revisited," *University of Chicago Law Review* 64 (1997): 791, 769.

ests in nonintrusion and nondisclosure of personal information associated with tort privacy; and what special challenges to such protections may arise from new communications technologies. Stylizing greatly, we might distinguish two parties to the dispute: *privacy skeptics* think we should reject, as uncontrollably capacious, a right to privacy that transcends protections of reputation, property, and bodily integrity; *antiskeptics* think that an expansive privacy right protects a distinct set of interests in personal independence and need not be objectionably open-ended, even if the relevant set of interests is not crisply circumscribed.

A second concern, more cultural than constitutional, is about conventions of privacy—about the informal social norms that distinguish *public* topics, which are fit for discussion, revelation, or disclosure, from topics that are unsuitable for public consideration. Once more, we have two stylized positions. The skeptic worries that solicitude for privacy masks protection for privilege. Fueled by reflection on the history of appeals to the family and to the firm as spheres of private ordering, skeptics fear that a crisp public-private distinction in cultural debate will put the roots of too much injustice and unreason beyond the reach of public criticism. The antiskeptic argues that inattention to the boundaries between private and public damages both private and public life: it damages private life, because it threatens to "normalize" private diversity and complexity by subjecting them to public scrutiny; it damages public life by swamping deliberation about common concerns with therapeutic *self*-disclosure and the intrusive revelation of personal information. Thus Hannah Arendt expressed concern about our "eagerness to see recorded, displayed and discussed in public what were once strictly private affairs and nobody's business."[2] And Thomas Nagel has urged that "something has gone wrong, in the United States, with the conventions of privacy"—that more or less any topic is now seen as fair game for public discussion.[3]

In this essay, I explore both topics—privacy rights and privacy conventions—within the framework of a deliberative conception of democracy. I will proceed in three steps. First, I sketch the rudiments of the deliberative conception and indicate how its three essential elements—reasonable pluralism, reasoning, and equality—provide a basis for rights to per-

2. Cited in Seyla Benhabib, "The Personal is not the Political," *Boston Review* 24 (1999): 45.
3. Thomas Nagel, "Concealment and Exposure," in *Concealment and Exposure and Other Essays* (Oxford: Oxford University Press, 2002), 3.

sonal liberties, and thus assign an essential place in democracy to the liberties of the moderns.

Second, I extend this framework to the specific case of privacy rights and focus on the issues of life, death, and sex that have been the subject of constitutional privacy debates in the United States since the mid-1960s. Rejecting skepticism, I argue that privacy rights—which I understand as protecting *independence of judgment*—have an essential place in a democracy understood as a society of equals. Once we acknowledge the pluralism of philosophies of life characteristic of such a society, I argue, we should understand privacy rights as expressing democracy's central values not as constraining such expression.

Finally, third, I discuss conventions of privacy. Here I am more skeptical. Drawing on the distinction between an informal sphere of public discussion and cultural argument and the formal political sphere of authoritative collective decision making, I argue that the case for strong norms of reticence is more compelling in the latter than in the former. I accept what Rawls has called the *duty of civility* in the political public sphere of a democracy and agree that duty imposes restrictions on appropriate forms of public justification. But I do not think there is a comparable case for the application of that duty to the informal public sphere: to what I will call the system of *cultural democracy*. The idea of democracy as a society of equals has different implications in the political sphere than in the informal public sphere. In particular, the fundamental pluralism that makes privacy rights essential to a deliberative-democratic system of authoritative collective decision making should achieve more open expression in the informal, democratic public sphere.

Deliberative Democracy

1. The deliberative-democratic idea is that authoritative collective decisions should issue from public reasoning among equals.[4] Three ideas play a central role in this conception:

  1. The fact of reasonable pluralism, according to which citizens endorse a plurality of politically reasonable philosophies of life;
  2. The requirement of deliberation, which states that the justification

---

4. The discussion that follows draws on Joshua Cohen, "Democracy and Liberty," in Jon Elster, ed., *Deliberative Democracy* (Cambridge: Cambridge University Press, 1998) [reprinted as essay 7 in this collection].

of authoritative collective decisions should be founded on public reasoning;

3. A conception of the members of a democratic society as free and equal.

These three conditions, I suggest, impose restrictions on the principles and values that provide the proper terms of public-political justification in a democracy: that is, they circumscribe the content of democracy's public reason. After sketching these three ideas, then, I will indicate how they support a conception of the content of public reason that includes a constitutive role of personal, nonpolitical liberties.

First, then, the fact of reasonable pluralism is the fact that there are distinct and incompatible philosophies of life to which people, who are reasonable politically speaking, are drawn under favorable conditions for the exercise of practical reason. By a *philosophy of life*—what Rawls calls a "comprehensive doctrine"—I mean an all-embracing view, religious or secular in foundation, liberal or traditionalist in substance, that includes an account of all ethical values and, crucially, provides a general guide to conduct, individual as well as collective. People are *reasonable, politically speaking*—in short, politically reasonable—only if they are concerned to live with others on terms that those others, understood as free and equal, can also reasonably be expected to accept.

I say "politically reasonable" because the relevant notion of reasonableness is suited to the context of political questions. Generically speaking, a reasonable person is someone who gives due attention to the considerations that bear on an issue and whose judgments and conduct reflect that attention. So a person is politically reasonable if he or she gives due attention to *the facts about the political relation of citizens in a democracy*—in particular, the fact that political power is the collective power of equals: that it belongs to us all, and that government of the people is to be by and for the people. The fact of reasonable pluralism, then, is the fact that when politically reasonable people engage in conscientious, good-faith efforts at the exercise of practical reason—aimed at deciding how to live—those efforts do not converge on a particular philosophy of life, but lead to different views, many of which are compatible with democracy itself.

The fact of reasonable pluralism does not express a skeptical or nihilist or relativist view about conceptions of the right way to live and the place of human beings in the world: it does not say that the truth in these matters is unknowable, or that there is no truth, or that the truth varies across persons, or cultures, or places; nor does it deny any of these views. Certainly, people who hold different outlooks think of their views as true: they believe them, and believing is believing true. The fact of reasonable pluralism does not conflict with what they believe but says that the truth in such matters, if there be such, *transcends the exercise of practical reason that we can appropriately expect of others, as equals in the political society.* So it affirms a kind of toleration of reasonable differences in ultimate outlook. As the italicized formulation indicates, when we assert the fact of reasonable pluralism, we are already operating within the domain of political argument. We are not relying on a philosophical theory about the scope and competence of reason that provides common ground for different outlooks: the nature and competence of reason, both theoretical and practical, is one matter on which such outlooks disagree. Instead, we are making a point about what we can appropriately expect of others, as free and equal.

A crucial point for the issue of privacy is that liberalism itself is both a political outlook and a philosophy of life.[5] As a philosophy of life, liberalism emphasizes the importance of autonomous choice—of reflective self-direction—as a guide to conduct. As a political outlook, liberalism is committed, inter alia, to securing basic personal and political liberties through a system of rights, whose precise content is a matter of controversy. One such controversy is about the scope and content of privacy rights, and about whether such rights depend on a liberal philosophy of life. I believe that they do not, for reasons I will discuss later.

Second, the deliberative conception of democracy puts public reasoning at the center of political justification, which I understand as the justification of coercively enforced regulations. To clarify, let's distinguish two conceptions of democracy, *aggregative* and *deliberative*. The basic distinction lies in their interpretations of the fundamental idea of a democratic society as a society of equals, and thus of a collective decision made or authorized by citizens as equals. Both views apply in the first in-

---

5. A central point of Rawls's political liberalism is to show that liberalism as a political conception does not depend on liberalism as a broader philosophy of life, with a distinctive moral, metaphysical, and epistemological outlook. See John Rawls, *Justice as Fairness: A Restatement,* ed. Erin Kelly (Cambridge, MA: Harvard University Press, 2001). For the alternative view, see Roberto Unger, *Knowledge and Politics* (New York: Free Press, 1974); and Michael Sandel, *Liberalism and the Limits of Justice* (Cambridge: Cambridge University Press, 1982).

stance to *institutions* of binding collective decision making, and each interprets the basic democratic ideal that such institutions are to treat people bound by collective decisions—subject to them and expected to comply with them—as equals. According to *aggregative* conceptions of democracy, decisions are collective just in case they arise from procedures of binding collective choice that assign equal weight to—or, more generically, are positively responsive to—the interests of each person bound by the decisions.[6] According to a deliberative conception, a decision is collective just in case it emerges from arrangements of binding collective choice that foster *free public reasoning among equals who are governed by the decisions.*

The two views—aggregative and deliberative—share a conception of political power as the collective power of equals. And they share the idea that that power is exercised over members who typically do not have effective exit options from the political society.[7] The deliberative view then adds that the exercise of this power is rendered suitably collective—appropriately by and for the people—only if the considerations that figure in public argument used to justify its exercise (at least on fundamentals) belong to the common reason of members.

According to the deliberative interpretation, then, democracy is a system of social and political arrangements that ties the exercise of collective power to free reasoning among equals. Which considerations count as reasons? The answer will not take the form of a generic account of what a reason is, but a statement of which considerations count in favor of proposals within a deliberative setting suited to the case of free political association among equals, understood to include an acknowledgment of reasonable pluralism. This background is reflected in the kinds of rea-

6. See, for example, the discussion of intrinsic equality and equal consideration in Thomas Christiano, *The Rule of the Many* (Boulder: Westview, 1996); and Robert Dahl, *Democracy and Its Critics* (New Haven: Yale University Press, 1989), 85, 87. Also, conditions imposed on social choice functions—in particular, anonymity and independence—are sometimes motivated in ways that suggest an identification of the requirement that people be treated as equals with the requirement that interests be given equal consideration. See William Riker, *Liberalism Against Populism: A Confrontation Between the Theory of Democracy and the Theory of Social Choice* (San Francisco: W.H. Freeman, 1982).

7. Rawls suggests that we model the political relation by thinking of it as a relation in a "structure we enter only by birth and exit only by death." See Rawls, "The Idea of Public Reason Revisited," 769. To be sure, this modeling assumption is not literally true, but it captures the idea that political decisions are binding on citizens, and that they cannot be made compatible with the freedom of citizens simply by establishing a right to emigrate.

sons that will be acceptable: meaning, as always, acceptable to individuals as free and equal.

Third, then, in democratic deliberation, participants are and regard one another as *free:* recognizing the fact of reasonable pluralism, they acknowledge that no comprehensive moral or religious view provides a defining condition of participation or a test of the acceptability of arguments in support of the exercise of political power. Moreover, a democracy is a society of equals. Everyone with the deliberative capacities—which is to say, more or less all human beings—has and is recognized as having equal standing at each of the stages of the deliberative process. Each, that is, can propose issues for the agenda, propose solutions to the issues on the agenda, and offer reasons in support of or in criticism of proposed solutions. And each has an equal voice in the decision.

2. I have sketched the deliberative conception of democracy, with its three main ideas—reasonable pluralism, reasoning, and equality. Subject to these assumptions, political justification cannot proceed simply by advancing considerations one takes to be true or compelling. For those considerations—whether about the importance of personal autonomy in the conduct of life or the value or rightness of willing submission to divine command—may well be rejected by politically reasonable equals, with conflicting philosophies of life, founded on opposing religious and moral outlooks. One needs instead to find considerations that can reasonably be expected to be acceptable to others, as equals: with political power as the power of all as equals—imposed on all and in the name of all—political justification is to proceed on common ground. Interpreted by reference to pluralism, equality, and deliberation, democracy emerges as an arena not only of public rights but also of autonomous public argument—a space of public reasoning and justification open to all on equal terms.

These considerations have implications for the content of democracy's public reason: they constrain suitable political reasons in a democracy. What is of immediate interest is that they provide a way to show the essential place of nonpolitical liberties in a democracy and underscore that that place does not require an appeal to a moral-liberal philosophy of life. In particular, pressure for liberty comes from at least two sources within the political ideal of democracy.

First, because of the pluralism of philosophies of life among politically reasonable citizens, some bases for regulating conduct are politically weightless. To take the clearest case, people hold some commitments on faith, and take those commitments to impose overriding obligations. Such nonnegotiable commitments are not as such unreasonable, nor is there anything unreasonable about embracing them as true. But because they are expressly held as truths known through faith, they are matters on which reasonable people disagree, and adherents cannot reasonably expect others to accept those considerations as having any weight and, therefore, cannot use them in justifying regulations. And the fact that they cannot, will impose pressure for personal liberties—say, religious and moral liberty—which are often restricted for such unacceptable reasons.

Second, acceptable considerations—which are not weightless—will have different weights in political justification. Even if they are not weightless, they may be insufficient to override the reasons that can be acknowledged, consistent with reasonable pluralism, as commending or commanding the conduct whose regulation is under contemplation. And the weight will depend on the nature of the regulated conduct and, in particular, on the weight of the reasons that support the conduct.

Take, for example, the value of public order. It provides an acceptable rationale for regulating conduct. Different outlooks have different ways of explaining the value of public order—as a precondition of the full exercise of personal autonomy, as an expression of submission to God's law—and people are bound to disagree about what public order requires. But it will not be acceptable to suppose that, as a general matter, the value of public order transcends all other political values. Except perhaps in the most extreme circumstances, for example, a state may not impose a blanket prohibition on alcohol consumption—including consumption in religious services—in the name of public order. After all, the considerations that support such consumption include considerations of obligation, which will provide a suitable basis for rejecting a justification cast in terms of the value of public order, except in the most extreme conditions. To be sure, not all citizens acknowledge the obligations in question. But even those who do not can see the weightiness of those reasons, within the outlooks of other politically reasonable citizens.

I will come back later, in the discussion of privacy, to this idea about the weightiness of reasons that support a course of conduct. Suffice to say here that if we take these two considerations together, we have the basis for a strong case for rights to religious, moral, and expressive liberties as elements of democracy's public reason. Thus, conduct in these areas is supported by strong (perhaps compelling) reasons, as when religious exercise is a matter of obligation according to a person's reasonable religious outlook. At the same time, standard reasons for restriction—religious and sectarian moral reasons—will often be weightless. More generally, we can see, at least in general terms, how a case for personal liberties emerges without resting on ideas—of personal autonomy, individuality, or self-ownership—drawn from liberalism, understood as a general philosophy of life. The ideas of pluralism and deliberative justification addressed to equals together establish a stricture against religious and moralistic justification (along with the stricture against secular-liberal moral justification); moreover, they require attention to the burdensomeness of regulations, as defined by the nature of the reasons that support the regulated conduct.

Given this rationale for personal liberties, we can see why they are elements of democracy. For imposing regulations in the name of reasons that are either weightless or of insufficient force to override reasonable demands violates the fundamental democratic idea: the idea that a democracy is a society of equals and that authorization to exercise state power must arise from the *collective decisions* of the equal members of a society who are governed by that power, that such authorization must be supported by reasons that can be shared by the addressees of the regulations.

Privacy Rights

1. Thus far I have sketched a general framework of ideas about democracy and indicated how at least some personal liberties might be understood to have a constitutive place in democracy's public reason. Under conditions of moral pluralism, the collective authorization that lies at the heart of democracy has limited scope.

What, then, about the right of privacy—in particular, a right to personal independence in areas of life, death, and sex? Can it be defended without appealing to a liberal philosophy of life? Skepticism in American constitutional argument about a capacious right to privacy derives in part from the concern that such a right *does* depend on a liberal philosophy of life. In particular, constitutional theorists who interpret the constitution as fundamentally a design of democracy, whether aggregative or deliberative, have typically been skeptical about a constitutional privacy right, in part for this reason.[8] Because the constitution is a shared, fundamental, public-political framework, they are troubled—as they should be—by the constitutionalization of a liberal philosophy of life.

Although their concerns are reasonable, their conclusions are incorrect. A fundamental right of privacy does not depend on a liberal philosophy of life. Or so I hope to show.

2. To focus the discussion, I will begin with a widely cited remark in the 1977 Supreme Court case of *Roe v. Whalen*. The details of the case do not matter here. Suffice to say that Justice Stevens there distinguishes two kinds of interests that privacy rights are commonly thought to protect: "The individual interest in avoiding disclosure of personal matters . . . and the interest in independence in making certain kinds of important decisions."[9] The former is the constitutional analogue of one of the interests protected by the privacy tort, and I will not discuss it here—apart from noting that it overlaps the latter, inasmuch as disclosure may itself undermine independence in decision making.[10]

So my focus will be on Stevens's remark about the interest in "independence in making certain kinds of important decisions"—what might be described as *independence of judgment*. The phrase "certain kinds of important decisions" invites the question: Which kinds of decisions? One familiar kind of answer strikes me as not very helpful. In particular, I cannot see how we could possibly identify the private arena with the family, or with the economy, or with any arena of social life, identified—either spatially or institutionally—prior to normative political argument. My doubts are founded on a familiar line of thought. Once we acknowledge that the organization of any sphere is in part a result of collective decisions, and may have decisive bearing on the lives of equal citizens, then we cannot adopt a hands-off policy to a sphere identified in advance. In the United States, the New Deal taught this lesson about the economy; and feminism, both as a movement and a theory, taught this lesson about the family.[11] Thus the thesis that a decision is private, and ought not therefore to be regulated except for especially compelling reasons, is not

8. See John Ely, *Democracy and Distrust* (Cambridge, MA: Harvard University Press, 1980); and Cass Sunstein, *One Case at a Time* (Cambridge, MA: Harvard University Press, 1999), esp. 250–252.

9. Roe v. Whalen, 429 U.S. 589, 599–600 (1977).

10. If having an abortion, for example, meant that your name appeared in the newspaper, then the decision about whether to have one would to that extent be less independent.

11. See the quote from Rawls about the public-private distinction at the start of the essay.

best understood as a premise in political argument—*because the decision is private, we should not regulate it*—but as a conclusion of such argument.

3. How, then, are we to characterize the kinds of decisions that ought to be protected as private? I propose that we do so by reference to the weight of the reasons that support them, in the judgments of those who makes the decisions. I do not have a precise characterization of this idea (I am not sure that a precise characterization is appropriate), and I do not wish to suggest that there will be general agreement about the relative weight of different sorts of reasons. Still, the idea strikes me as essential.

Consider some examples that may help explain it. When I say that a course of conduct is a matter of obligation, I claim that it has support from an especially weighty reason. If, in contrast, I say that I prefer one course of conduct to another, even that I prefer it intensely, I am down-grading the kind of reason that supports the conduct. If I say that something is essential to a decent human life, then the reason has considerable weight. If I say that it is a good thing to do, then the weight is greater than if it is a matter of preference (even intense preference) but is not as substantial as when it is a matter of obligation or an essential of a decent life.

Of course different philosophies of life will interpret these categories differently and assign different content to them: such philosophies will differ, for example, on the nature and content of our obligations to preserve human life or on the scope and weight of duties of charity. The essential point is that, once we accept the three essential elements of the deliberative conception of democracy—reasonable pluralism, equality, and deliberative justification—then we need to let political ideas of burdensomeness track the weight of reasons within the reasonable views of those we are regulating. Thus it will not be acceptable to say that we will make special efforts not to burden people by preventing them from fulfilling their fundamental obligations, but then deny that their own politically reasonable views about what those obligations are have any weight—to say that we respect people's obligation to keep the Sabbath, but then to insist that, after all, the only Sabbath they have any obligation to keep falls on Sunday.

4. Consider now how these observations apply to some of the issues about life, death, and sex—issues that are arguably to be covered by a

constitutional privacy right and that have been at the center of the debate about that right in the United States. I will be very brief on these extraordinarily complex issues, because I mean to be illustrating the framework rather than saying anything very distinctive about the issues themselves.

Thus, in the case of abortion, three considerations suggest the conclusion that restrictive regulations are especially burdensome. First, there is the burden on women's equality if women are required to carry unwanted pregnancies to term. This point is acknowledged in the Supreme Court's 1992 *Casey* decision, with reference to the consequences of a twenty-year adjustment to the *Roe* regime—"The ability of women to participate equally in the economic and social life of the nation has been facilitated by their ability to control their reproductive lives"[12]—but the same point could have been made without the reference to issues of adjustment to *Roe v. Wade*.

Second, restrictive regulations burden women's liberty, by restricting choices of a deeply personal kind, thus impinging on a woman's exercise of personal responsibility about the course of her life. They represent a substantial denial of judgment about the conduct of elementary aspects of life. There is of course an equality aspect to the issue here, inasmuch as no comparable denial is contemplated for men. But the relevant burden would not be alleviated by generalizing it.

A third burden—the burden on judgment—results from the kinds of reasons that commonly support decisions about continuing life and is especially pertinent here. In its *Casey* decision, the U.S. Supreme Court says that "at the heart of liberty is the right to define one's own concept of existence, of meaning, of the universe, and of the mystery of human life,"[13] and it supposes that women take guidance from such judgments

12. Planned Parenthood of Southeastern PA v. Casey, 505 U.S. 833 (1992).

13. Ibid.; Justice Scalia disparages this remark as the "famed sweet-mystery-of-life passage" in Lawrence et al. v. Texas, 539 U.S. 558 (2003). He finds two problems with it: laws, he says, never restrict the right to define concepts (he has "never heard of a law" that restricts the "right to define" concepts); and laws standardly restrict conduct based on a self-defined "concept of existence." Thus the famed passage is either vacuous or massively destructive ("the passage that ate the rule of law"). But some laws do restrict beliefs—for example, they attach sanctions to holding them—and laws restricting beliefs do not contain escape clauses that permit defendants to plead that their belief is a matter of definition ("it is impermissible to deny the Trinity, except when the essential unity of God is asserted to be a matter of definition"). As for "eating the rule of law": the famed passage asserts that conduct that is closely associated with certain kinds of important beliefs (say, in the way that wine consumption is closely associated with belief in the doctrine of transubstantiation) should only be regulated for especially compelling reasons. To be sure, it is important to say which beliefs and in what way the conduct is closely

in making decisions about childbirth. And in *Life's Dominion*, Ronald Dworkin has characterized the relevant judgments as "spiritual" disagreements about the relative importance of natural and human contributions to the value of a human life.[14]

The burdens on equality and liberty are not especially controversial: someone may think that they are overridden, but surely they are substantial. Moreover, as to the burden on judgment, we can argue over how precisely to characterize the relevant judgments, but however they are characterized, the point is that they have considerable weight. Moreover, we can debate how to explain the disagreements about these judgments and offer views about why they have the weight that they do. But for the purposes of political argument, this debate is unnecessary. Suffice to say that the judgments are about when we have compelling reason to ensure the continuation of life: that content indicates their weight and shows why they are covered by a privacy right and can be overridden only by reasons of considerable weight.

To be sure, that right could be overridden by an argument that abortion is, as the papal encyclical *Evangelium Vitae* asserts, the taking of innocent human life: such an argument would provide grounds for regulation, despite the three burdens.[15] But that argument cannot be made, except by appealing to a particular outlook about the nature and value of life that is rejected by many who are reasonable, politically speaking. This criticism is driven not by the idea that judgments about the continuation of life are in some way intrinsically private: instead, the claim that they are private matters expresses the thesis that there is a strong case for leaving women to their own judgment on these matters, in part because of the weight of the reasons that support their conduct. Requirements of reason giving under conditions of a pluralism of philosophies of life drives the argument.

But there may appear to be a sleight of hand at work here. After all, the pro-life and pro-choice positions seem completely symmetrical. That is, either abortions are restrictively regulated or they are not. If they are re-

---

associated. But it is not clear why the effort to draw such distinctions is bound to undermine the rule of law, except of course if the rule of law means a law of rigid rules. See Antonin Scalia, "The Rule of Law as a Law of Rules," *University of Chicago Law Review* 56 (1989): 1175–1188.

14. Ronald Dworkin, *Life's Dominion* (New York: Knopf, 1993), 91.

15. See Pope John Paul II, *The Gospel of Life [Evangelium Vitae]* (New York: Random House, 1995).

strictively regulated, the side that favors restrictive regulation wins. If they are not, then the side that has a liberal view wins. So yes, some people do reject the justification for regulation: and let's say that they are politically reasonable. But why should their objections carry the day? After all, some people reject the current settlement, which permits abortion. Why do their objections to a permissive regulatory regime not carry as much weight as the objections to a restrictive regime?

This alleged symmetry is illusory. The restrictive regime imposes undeniably substantial burdens on women's liberty, equality, and independence of judgment; in a society of equals, those burdens need to be justified, and the terms of that justification must carry some weight with those whose liberty and equality are impaired. Otherwise, we fail to respect them as equals. The restrictive regime cannot stand, then, because no such acceptable justification is available.

The case for a right to die, understood as comprising a right to assisted suicide, is importantly different. To be sure, there is a compelling case for the conclusion that regulations of assisted suicide are burdensome: like restrictive abortion regulations, they regulate conduct governed by judgments about when we have compelling reason to ensure the continuation of life. The considerations that support regulations in this area are, however, of a different kind. In particular, the defense of such regulation should appeal not to a conception of when life ends or what makes a whole life (or parts of it) worth living but to concerns about when we have a conclusive showing of a person's willing decision to end her own life, and worries about pressures to make that decision as a way to reduce burdens on family and friends. A compelling case for the conclusion that these decisions about death should be treated as private matters would need to address these concerns. Absent such address, it is not unreasonable for a democratic process to regulate, and thus to hold that the interest in independent judgment, although present and substantial, is overridden (though it would also be reasonable to have a more permissive regime).

In the case of sexual intimacy, there is a strong case for concluding that democracy's public reason must treat it as a private matter—an arena to be regulated by the independent and diverse judgments of individuals. On the one hand the reasons for regulation—a religiously founded moral outlook—are arguably weightless because they are objectionably sectarian.[16] Moreover, the regulations are burdensome, for a reason that Justice Harry Blackmun rightly identified in his powerful dissent in *Bowers v. Hardwick*, and which the Supreme Court more recently embraced in *Lawrence v. Texas*: that intimate relations are an important setting in which we do something of fundamental importance in a decently lived life, namely, work out a sense of our identity. But this importance of sexual intimacy—often one aspect of a personal relationship—is contingent in part on its being guided by the judgments, feelings, and sensibilities of the parties to it.[17] Because of the importance of such intimacy, the reasons that support it are substantial.[18] So democracy's public reason provides a compelling case for treating this as a private matter. But, once more, the claim that it is private does not serve as a premise in the case against regulation. Instead it is a conclusion drawn from reflection on the kinds of reasons that support the regulated conduct and the considerations that might be used to defend a case for its regulation.[19]

Conventions

1. I turn now to the second privacy issue: the social conventions that mark the boundaries between the public and the private. This is a sprawling territory, and to narrow it I will focus here on a discussion of these issues by Thomas Nagel. According to Nagel, we ought to embrace strong

16. The majority opinion in *Lawrence v. Texas* notes that the moral reasons that support regulation have, among other things, a religious background (they are "shaped by religious beliefs, conceptions of right and acceptable behavior, and respect for the traditional family"), and asserts their weightlessness, though the weightlessness does not turn on their provenance in religious morality.

17. Bowers v. Hardwick, 478 U.S. 186 (1986).

18. The majority in *Lawrence v. Texas* cites *Casey's* "sweet-mystery-of-life" passage in explaining the importance of the conduct regulated by restrictions on sexual intimacy. Autonomy in intimate conduct is important because such conduct is tied to independent self-definition.

19. The issue of gay and lesbian marriage raises questions that extend beyond my concerns here, though the considerations I have presented bear on the issue in three ways, which I will simply mention. First, the regulated conduct is supported by important reasons. Second, some of the considerations appealed to in arguments against legal status are weightless: for example, the argument in the Vatican's "Considerations Regarding Proposals to Give Legal Recognition to Unions Between Homosexual Persons" that "marriage is holy, while homosexual acts go against the natural moral law." Third, although arguments about the "best interests of the child" (also in the Vatican statement) are certainly not weightless, they need to be made in a sufficiently compelling way, given the importance of the regulated conduct. The statement is available at http://www.vatican.va/roman_curia/congregations/cfaith/documents/rc_con_cfaith_doc_20030731_homosexual-unions_en.html.

norms of reticence to preserve "smooth functioning" in the public domain when we don't need collective decisions and cannot expect agreement. Nagel's discussion of these issues was animated by what he perceived as overreaching in the American public debate surrounding Bill Clinton's impeachment—overreaching by the public, the media, and the political officials who presumed that Clinton's sexual appetites and habits were fit subjects of public discussion. Prompted by the Clinton controversy, Nagel's argument proceeds well beyond Clinton and sex to a defense of "cultural liberalism." Though fugitive in its precise content, cultural liberalism is (roughly) the view that we ought to respond to fundamental disagreements in our informal public culture with a restraint—a reticence about criticism—parallel to that which we arguably ought to respect in our formal system of law and politics. Let me explain.

In the formal political system—what Habermas calls the "political public sphere"—where the stakes are authoritative, coercively enforced legal regulations, we should not enforce a particular moral or philosophical outlook; but we ought to justify laws and policies by reference to values that can reasonably be embraced by reasonable people who endorse different outlooks: that is the idea of democracy's public reason. Similarly, in the public culture more broadly—what Habermas calls the "informal public sphere," and Rawls "the background culture"—where the stakes include discursive presuppositions, as well as social conventions and norms backed by decentralized sanctions, cultural liberalism requires that, as a general matter, we steer clear of controversial topics about which we cannot expect to reach agreement and that do not demand a collective decision. In the particular case of sex, Nagel says: "We should stop trying to achieve a common understanding in this area and leave people to their mutual incomprehension, under the cover of conventions of reticence."[20] Nagel extends these points to religion, and concludes, quite generally, that it would be "a good idea to leave the public space of a society comfortably habitable, without too much conflict, by the main incompatible elements that are not about to disappear."[21] To be sure, in a culturally liberal world, old-fashioned, "healthy mutual contempt"[22]—for example between and among the communicants of differ-

20. Nagel, "Concealment and Exposure," 23.
21. Ibid., 24.
22. Ibid.

ent religions—would flourish, but it would be obscured by tight-lipped, ironic smiles.

So cultural liberalism means two things. First, it rejects communitarian aspirations to control the public culture and to establish cultural uniformity, and it requires instead what might be called a "cultural democracy," in which all members are entitled to participate as equals in shaping the public cultural environment. Second, cultural liberalism takes a particular view about what such participation and cultural democracy involve: it commands reticence about the public expression of fundamental disagreements. These two elements are independent; reticence does not follow from opposition to communitarianism. To be sure, the attractions of permanent Kulturkampf are themselves a matter of persistent conflict. But those who are drawn to it—a group that arguably extends from Machiavelli and Mill to the postmodernist friends of an agonistic public realm—are all anticommunitarian. So we need additional argument in favor of cultural liberalism with its norms of reticence as an alternative to cultural democracy with more open public contestation yet with no expectation of agreement. And the case for it does not seem very compelling. The connection observed earlier between democracy and liberalism (including rights of privacy) in the political sphere does not extend to a comparable connection between democracy and reticent liberalism in the cultural sphere.

To explain why not, I will make three points: about the costs of reticence, about why the case for political reticence (a duty of civility) does not extend to a more general case for public reticence, and about the benefits of more open public argument even when no agreement is in view.

2. As to the costs of reticence: let's say that a strong convention of reticence or restraint with respect to some area of disagreement requires that we not get into that area at all (anyway, not outside the sphere of close friends and intimates). Thus there might be a strong convention against any open, public discussion of sex or religion or attitudes toward groups different from one's own. The case for such strong conventions of restraint is that they are mutually beneficial. Still—and as ever—legitimate questions can be raised about the distribution of those benefits.

For example, we are all better off with a norm condemning all discussion of who is sleeping with whom, than with a completely permissive view of sexual gossip. But although such a blanket condemnation is facially neutral, men—especially in positions of power—may be especially large beneficiaries of this particular convention: they get multiple sexual partnerships with reduced danger of discovery (because of the convention). For this reason, strong reticence may be perceived—in Nagel's words—"as a form of male mutual self-protection."[23]

To appreciate the force of this observation about the distribution of the benefits, note that a range of different conventions might be adopted toward regulating discussion in this area—all weaker in the restraints they impose on discussion but better for all than an unregulated free-for-all. Consider the norm: "Don't talk about who is sleeping with whom, unless the target is a powerful man who should know better." That norm—whatever its ultimate merits—would be better for all than the regime of open gossip, would be less likely to be rejected as a form of male mutual self-protection, and would be arguably helpful in undermining cultural sensibilities that support the abuse of power.

The general problem is familiar from discussion of problems of social coordination with mixed motives: we have a plurality of conventions; each such convention is mutually beneficial compared with the absence of normative regulation; different conventions are associated with different distributions of benefits; and there is nothing obviously right about the status quo distribution. Under these circumstances, to opt for strong norms of reticence—to insist on strong cultural norms of privacy that would effectively put existing conventions beyond challenge—seems simply to be a matter of endorsing the current distribution and seems to deny the importance of cultural democracy. Thus, it is right to worry that the "elevation of reticence" is "too protective of the status quo and that it gives a kind of cultural veto to conservative forces who will resent any disruption," at least if we interpret reticence as requiring a *generalized restraint* on any contentious, open public discussion about a topic.[24]

Nagel acknowledges this concern: "Those who favor confrontation and invasion of privacy will think it necessary to overthrow pernicious conventions like the double standard of sexual conduct and the unmentionability of homosexuality. To attack harmful prejudices, it is necessary to give offense by overturning the conventions of reticence that help to support them."[25] But he appears to believe that these costs must

23. Ibid., 23.
24. Ibid., 25.
25. Ibid.

be paid—perhaps worrying, with Lord Devlin, that a rejection of regnant cultural norms may put us on the slippery slope that ends in the rejection of civilization itself, on the road to hell in a handbasket. I conclude instead that there is something to classic worries about conventions of privacy: that under the color of neutral norms of decorum, civility, decency, and sheer discretion, they effectively mute criticism of social practices.

3. Strong conventions of reticence, then, impose costs. But perhaps we ought to bear the costs to avoid even greater damage: after all, less reticence may impose greater pressures to conformity not more disruptions of a stifling status quo. This is a large issue, and I can only address a piece of it here. In particular, I want to consider whether the case for restraint in political argument, aimed at the collective exercise of power, carries over to the informal politics of a democratic public culture—to public conversation and interaction quite generally.

Let's start with the idea—associated with democracy's public reason—that there is a duty of civility that requires that we cast our justifications for fundamental laws and policies on the common ground of political values.[26] Although it is permissible to offer justifications that draw on our own philosophy of life, arguments that lie on the common ground of democracy's public reason must—here I follow Rawls—be available and offered "in due course."[27] Thus moral liberals must, for example, present a case for a right to die that does not rely on the thesis that autonomy is the supreme value or that individuals own themselves. They can also present arguments that do depend on such premises. But the duty of civility requires that they, roughly speaking, also present ("in due course") *some* argument that lies on common ground. And it requires, too, that when they present an argument on a fundamental political question, and do appeal to their own comprehensive outlook, they are not to expose the underlying philosophical, religious, or moral outlooks of their opponents, and subject those outlooks to challenge: they are beyond reproach. So the duty of civility requires a kind of restraint or reticence in the political arena with respect to matters of fundamental disagreement.

I accept the duty of civility, understood as applying to public political argument. But its plausibility, thus applied, reflects two special features of the political domain. First, political debate issues in collective deci-

26. On the duty of civility, see John Rawls, *Political Liberalism* (New York: Columbia University Press, 1996), 216; and John Rawls, "The Idea of Public Reason Revisited," 768–769.
27. Rawls, "The Idea of Public Reason Revisited," 793.

sions that are made in the name of all: the majority is the tribune of the people. But the fact that laws are made in the name of all, in the name of citizens as equals, naturally suggests that they ought to be justifiable—and be shown to be justifiable—by reference to values that all can reasonably accept, and that they should provide for everyone a secure place in the debate: this, as I indicated earlier, is the deliberative interpretation of the idea that democratic decisions should be suitably collective. When the supreme political authority speaks in a democracy, it ought to be manifest that it speaks in the name of equal citizens. In the informal public culture, we find no such corresponding authoritative statement of a conclusion: "cultural democracy" names a social practice of argument among equals, not a form of authority. With no agent authorized to speak for all, there is no corresponding case for restraint in the terms of debate.

Second, collective decisions apply to all and are backed by the collective power of the state. If we wish to reconcile this coercive imposition of regulation with the recognition of citizens as politically autonomous self-legislators, then the best we can hope for is that the justification of basic laws and policies rests on political values that can be shared. But, once more, there is no comparable coercive imposition in the case of the public culture, and so no comparable requirement of restraint.

I have said that cultural democracy is not a form of authority, and that it does not involve a coercive imposition of constraints comparable to the formal political system. I do not, however, wish to deny that cultural democracy is a form of power or to deny that cultural norms constrain conduct. To the contrary. Equal standing in the system of cultural democracy is important in part because of the importance of the common environment of cultural norms and standards of taste and value: we do not want to leave these matters in the hands of others, even if we can count on an exercise of collective political authority that is governed by democracy's public reason. For we may still find the public culture and the constraints it fosters deeply uncongenial. Thus Scanlon says: "I have no desire to dictate what others, individually, in couples or in groups, do in their bedrooms, but I would prefer to live in a society in which sexuality and sexual attractiveness, of whatever kind, was given less importance than it is in our society today." Or again, "What I fear is not merely the legal enforcement of religion but its social predominance."[28] In both cases,

---

28. Thomas Scanlon, "The Difficulty of Tolerance" in David Heyd, ed., *Toleration: An Elusive Virtue* (Princeton: Princeton University Press, 1996), 30.

it is difficult to see how we can challenge the regnant cultural norms, while remaining within the bounds fixed by a duty of civility extended to the informal public sphere. Nevertheless, the two differences—about authority and constraints—remain, and because of these differences, the case for a duty of civility—for reticence about fundamental criticism— seems less forceful in the informal public sphere. A democratic society is a society of equals; but the implications of this idea for the public political sphere differ from its implications for the informal public sphere.[29]

4. So strong reticence carries costs, and there is no case for it comparable to the case for the duty of civility in the political arena. Still, suppose we accept the fact of reasonable pluralism and reject the communitarian aspiration of achieving agreement on fundamentals through open-ended public discussion. Once we accept that we cannot, in any case, expect agreement on these matters, why bother getting into them? What is the point of a more open, democratic public culture, freed from strong conventions of reticence on matters on which agreement is not in view? Why put up with the conflicts ingredient in the informal public sphere; that's a cost, too. Why not reticence?

Consider three kinds of public speech, each of which might break with strong norms of reticence, none of which is presented with any expectation of achieving deeper agreement, but all of which can contribute something important to informal public argument: bearing witness, expressive presentation of information, and fundamental criticism.

In bearing witness, I present my stand on an issue, act from a sense of personal responsibility in presenting my view, and may feel it necessary to condemn opponents' views at their roots. I do not aim to change minds or to present someone else with information that they lack but only to state my convictions.

In the expressive presentation of information, people present their hostility to some aspect of the public culture that they find stifling, oppressive, humiliating, or demeaning, in view of who they are—in view of some particular aspect of their identity. The form of this discourse is, "As an X, I feel. . . ." I describe this as an expressive presentation of information because I want to emphasize that others may learn something from

29. On this point, see my discussion of the distinction between equal opportunity for electoral, political, and public influence in "Money, Politics, Political Equality," in *Fact and Value*, ed. Alex Byrne, Robert Stalnaker, and Ralph Wedgwood (Cambridge, MA: MIT Press, 2001), 153–157.

the complaint, even if presented not with the aim of enlightenment but simply as a way of expressing a hostile attitude toward a social practice, perhaps with the suggestion that the speaker's finding the practice to be objectionable suffices to condemn it. The speaker need not expect a collective response nor act in the hope of prompting agreement, but instead may be seen as providing information about how a feature of the culture is not universally appreciated.

By fundamental criticism, I mean an explicit attack on the moral, religious, or philosophical foundations of someone's political outlook—precisely the kind of thing that violates the duty of civility when it happens in political discourse. But there are three reasons for pursuing fundamental criticism rather than adopting a general policy of reticence as a response to fundamental disagreements.

The first reason is, once more, simply informational: I may want to let my opponents know that others who share the public culture with them find their public displays of religiosity creepy, or find their views false or childish.

Second, I may entertain the more ambitious thought that an awareness of deeper and persisting disagreements will result in some modification of opposing views, particularly if fundamental criticism is coupled with the political respect reflected in the duty of civility. This point has particular force when there are political disagreements that we think are probably rooted in deeper religious or moral disagreements: certainly true in issues about sexuality, life, and death that provided the focus of my discussion of privacy rights. If a duty of civility restrains us from pursuing these disagreements in the political arena, it will be important that there be a setting in which they can be openly aired. Here I offer a speculation about the cultural basis of political democracy: namely, that we are more inclined to keep political deliberation within the confines of democracy's public reason and to respect the duty of civility if we think that opponents have been subjected to more open-ended pressure elsewhere. A vibrant cultural democracy may be both supportive of a liberal political democracy and philosophically consistent with it.

Third and finally, I may think that the public culture itself is now one-sided: that it is far easier to express conventional religious sentiment or to deploy conventional religious symbols than to express skeptical or hostile views about religion, or to embrace unconventional religious views. Think again of Scanlon's examples. Believing that the public culture is important—that cultural norms do constrain conduct—and rejecting the idea of regulating the culture politically, I think it important that it be open to expressions of fundamental disagreement that do not have a proper place in politics. The point of such expressions is neither to produce agreement nor to create a comfortably communitarian public culture. Instead, the point is to create a public culture more fully expressive of the pluralism that democracy promises.

To be sure, there are dangers here. As Nagel says, "Revolution breeds counterrevolution." Nagel is surely right about the United States: the cultural revolution of the 1960s eventually bred a cultural counterrevolution, filled with nonsense about how the civilization was in much better shape in the 1950s when it was dominated by white Protestant men. More fundamentally, though, my argument here suggests an answer to worries about counterrevolution in response to cultural democracy: with strong protections of privacy rights acting as limits on the exercise of political authority by a society of equals, the informal public sphere of that same society of equals can more easily afford to reject cautious reticence—really, deference to the status quo—as a response to persistent disagreement.

10

REFLECTIONS ON DELIBERATIVE DEMOCRACY

1. Introduction

For more than two decades, egalitarian-democrats have sought to describe a "post-socialist" political project. The socialist project, including its social democratic variant, comprised a set of political values and an institutional and political strategy for advancing those values. The values were egalitarian and participatory. The institutional models and the political strategy focused on the state.

Contemporary debate among egalitarian-democrats begins in the conviction that this approach is misguided and moves along two paths.

The first, growing out of appreciation of the state's limits as an economic manager is sometimes called "asset-egalitarianism." The idea is to shift the distribution of income by changing the distribution of income-generating assets. It is an important idea, particularly with pressures from globalization on income security, but not my topic here.[1]

A second—and this will provide my focus here—is more political. Building on what I will describe as "radical-democratic" ideas, it seeks to construct models of political decision in which "local" players can be involved more directly in regulation and in collective problem solving, with a center that coordinates local efforts, rather than dictating the terms of those efforts. Thus, local—or, more exactly, lower-level actors (nation-states or national peak organizations of various kinds; regions, provinces,

I presented earlier versions of this essay at the University of Southern California Law School and as a keynote address at a Princeton University conference on deliberative democracy. I am grateful to the audiences on both occasions for their comments and criticisms.

1. For representative ideas, see John Roemer, *Equal Shares: Making Market Socialism Work* (New York: Verso, 1996); Samuel Bowles and Herbert Gintis, *Recasting Egalitarianism: New Rules for Communities, States and Markets* (New York: Verso, 1999); Stuart White, *The Civic Minimum* (Oxford: Oxford University Press, 2003); Bruce Ackerman and Anne Alstott, *The Stakeholder Society* (New Haven: Yale University Press, 2000); Richard Freeman, *The New Inequality* (Boston: Beacon Press, 1998).

or sub-national associations within these, and so on down to whatever neighborhood is relevant to the problem at hand)—are given autonomy to experiment with their own solutions to broadly defined problems of public policy. In return they furnish higher-level units with rich information about the goals as well as the progress they are making towards achieving them. The periodic pooling of results reveals the defects of parochial solutions and allows the elaboration of standards for comparing local achievements, exposing poor performers to criticism, and making good ones (temporary) models for emulation.

This "radical-democratic" project builds on two distinct strands of thought.[2]

With Rousseau, radical democrats are committed to broader *participation* in public decision-making—though not, as Rousseau supposed, through regular meetings of a legislative assembly open to all citizens.[3] According to this first strand, citizens should have greater direct roles in public choices or, in a less demanding formulation, should participate in politics on the basis of substantive political judgments and should be assured that officials will be responsive and accountable to their concerns and judgments. Though more participatory democrats disagree on the precise locus of expanded participation, they all are troubled when democratic participation is largely confined to a choice between parties competing for control of government, and particularly when that choice is not founded on clearly articulated substantive programmatic-political differences between and among parties and pursued with the expectation that the parties will be held accountable to their announced programs. The underlying participatory idea is that citizens in a democracy are to

2. I have written elsewhere on this radical-democratic project: with Joel Rogers (on associative democracy), Chuck Sabel (on deliberative polyarchy), and Archon Fung (on participation and deliberation). In writing this essay, I have drawn freely on this joint work, and I am very grateful to my co-authors for the collaborations that produced it. See Joshua Cohen and Joel Rogers, *Associations and Democracy* (London: Verso, 1995); Joshua Cohen and Charles Sabel, "Directly-Deliberative Polyarchy," *European Law Journal*, vol. 3, no. 4 (December 1997): 313–342 [reprinted as essay 6 in this collection]; Joshua Cohen and Joel Rogers, "Power and Reason," in Archon Fung and Erik Olin Wright, eds., *Deepening Democracy: Institutional Innovations in Empowered Participatory Governance* (New York: Verso, 2003); Joshua Cohen and Charles Sabel, "Global Democracy?," *New York University Journal of International Law and Policy* 37, 4 (2006): 763–797; Joshua Cohen and Archon Fung, "Radical Democracy," *Swiss Journal of Political Science* 10, 4 (2004).

3. Rousseau himself explored other forms of democratic participation, particularly in his *Constitution of Poland*, where considerations of size precluded direct citizen participation in lawmaking.

engage with the substance of law and policy and not simply delegate responsibility for such substantive engagement to representatives.

Along with participation, radical democrats emphasize *deliberation*. Instead of a politics of power and interest, radical democrats favor a deliberative democracy in which citizens address public problems by reasoning together about how best to solve them—in which, at the limit, no force is at work, as Jürgen Habermas said, "except that of the better argument."[4] According to the deliberative interpretation, democracy is a political arrangement that ties the exercise of collective power to reason-giving among those subject to collective decisions. Once more, we see substantial differences among different formulations of the deliberative-democratic ideal. Some see deliberative democracy as a matter of forming a public opinion through dispersed and open public discussion and translating such opinion into legitimate law; others as a way to ensure that elections—or legislative debates, or perhaps discussions within courts or agencies—are themselves infused with information and reasoning; others as a way to bring reasoning by citizens directly to bear on addressing regulatory issues. But in all cases, the large aim of a deliberative democracy is to shift from bargaining, interest aggregation, and power to the common reason of equal citizens—democracy's public reason—as a guiding force in democratic life.[5]

In this essay, I will explore these two distinct strands of the radical-democratic project—participatory and deliberative—though I will focus on the deliberative because that is the topic here. My central point is that participation and deliberation are both important, but different, and they are important for different reasons. Moreover, it is hard to achieve both, but the project of advancing both is coherent, attractive, and worth our attention. I begin by presenting an idea of deliberative democracy. Sec-

4. Jürgen Habermas, *Legitimation Crisis*, trans. Thomas McCarthy (Boston: Beacon Press, 1973), 108. In this passage, Habermas is not describing an idealized democracy but a hypothetical situation suited to the justification of norms.

5. We now have many statements of the deliberative conception. For my own, which I draw on here, see Joshua Cohen, "Deliberation and Democratic Legitimacy," Alan Hamlin and Phillip Petit, eds., *The Good Polity* (Oxford: Blackwell, 1989); "Procedure and Substance in Deliberative Democracy," in *Democracy and Difference: Changing Boundaries of the Political*, ed. Seyla Benhabib (Princeton: Princeton University Press, 1996); "Democracy and Liberty," in Jon Elster, ed., *Deliberative Democracy* (Cambridge: Cambridge University Press, 1998); and "Privacy, Pluralism, and Democracy," *Law and Social Justice*, eds. Joseph Keim Campbell, Michael O'Rourke, and David Shier. (Cambridge, MA: MIT Press, 2005). [All these essays are reprinted here.]

ond, I will sketch three attractions of deliberative democracy. Third, I discuss four lines of skeptical argument. Fourth, I sketch three tensions between deliberation and participation. Fifth, I consider two political and institutional strategies for blunting those tensions. I conclude by mentioning two large challenges.

2. *Deliberation*

Carl Schmitt said that deliberation belongs to the world of the parliament, where legislators reason together about how to address public problems. It does not belong to the world of mass democracy, where ethno-culturally homogeneous peoples find leaders who pick the people's friends and enemies. According to Schmitt, "The development of modern mass democracy has made argumentative public discussion an empty formality."[6] Rejecting Schmitt's view, as well as its more benign contemporary progeny, deliberative democrats explore possibilities of combining deliberation with mass democracy. And not just explore: we are hopeful about the possibilities of fostering a more deliberative democracy.

Deliberation, generically understood, is about weighing the reasons relevant to a decision with a view to making a decision on the basis of that weighing. So an individual can make decisions deliberatively, a jury has a responsibility to deliberate, and a committee of oligarchs can deliberate: deliberation, in short, is not intrinsically democratic. The "democracy" in "deliberative democracy" is not pleonastic.

Democracy is a way of making collective decisions that connects decisions to the interests and the judgments of those whose conduct is to be regulated by the decisions. The essential idea is that those governed by the decisions are treated as equals by the processes of making the decisions. Democracy, as Tocqueville emphasized, is also a kind of society—a society of equals—but I will be confining myself as a general matter to the more specifically political understanding of democracy. Of course, even if we think of democracy politically, as a way to make binding collective decisions, constructing a more deliberative democracy is not a narrowly political project: deliberative democracy requires attention to encouraging deliberative capacities, which is, inter alia, a matter of edu-

---

6. Carl Schmitt, *The Crisis of Parliamentary Democracy*, trans. Ellen Kennedy (Cambridge, MA: MIT Press, 1985), 6.

cation, information, and organization.[7] I will return briefly to this point near the end.

Deliberative democracy, then, combines these two elements, neither reducible to the other. It is about making collective decisions and exercising power in ways that trace in some way to the reasoning of the equals who are subject to the decisions: not only to their preferences, interests, and choices but also to their reasoning. Essentially, the point of deliberative democracy is to subject the exercise of power to reason's discipline, to what Habermas famously described as "the force of the better argument," not the advantage of the better situated. Deliberative democracy does not aim to do away with power, an idea that makes no sense, nor does it aim simply to subject power to the discipline—such as it is—of talking, because talking is not the same as reasoning (consider verbal assaults, insults, racial slurs, lies, blowing smoke, exchanging pleasantries, exploring common experiences); nor is it simply to reason together, because reasoning together may be without effect on the exercise of power.

Moreover, the notion of reason's discipline is not nearly definite enough. Plato's philosopher-guardians subject power to reason's discipline—that, at any rate, is what they say they are doing. But deliberative democracy is a kind of democracy, so the reasoning must be in some recognizable way the reasoning of the equal persons who are subject to the decisions. And not just the process of reasoning but also the content of the reasons themselves must have a connection to the democratic conception of people as equals. Deliberative democracy is about reasoning together among equals, and that means not simply advancing considerations that one judges to be reasons but also finding considerations that others can reasonably be expected to acknowledge as reasons. That's why deliberation focuses, as a constitutive matter, on considerations of the common good, and also why—or so I have argued elsewhere—basic personal liberties are essential elements of a deliberative democracy. Deliberative democracy is not majoritarian, and these substantive conditions—the common good and the personal liberties—are essential to

7. In *Is Democracy Possible Here?* (Cambridge, MA: Harvard University Press, 2006), Ronald Dworkin emphasizes the importance of education in a well-functioning, deliberative democracy, and he asserts that "the most daunting but also most urgent requirement is to make a Contemporary Politics course part of every high school curriculum" (148). The idea of such a course is sensible enough, but it hardly seems the most urgent issue about the reform of our educational system, for the purposes of fostering the partnership in argument that is so central to democracy.

democratic deliberation, under conditions of reasonable pluralism. In short, the ideal of deliberative democracy is to discipline collective power through the common reason of a democratic public: through democracy's public reason.[8]

To be sure, discussion, even when it is founded on reasons, may not—and often does not—issue in consensus. No account of deliberative democracy has ever suggested otherwise. All complex practical problems—from trade and security to organizing schools and transportation, providing clean water and public safety, allocating health care and ensuring fair compensation—implicate a range of distinct values, and reasonable people disagree about the precise content of and weights to be assigned to those values. In any allocative decision, for example, there are likely to be people who think that the worst-off person should have priority, others who think there should be equal chances, others who think the person who benefits most should get the good. In allocating medical resources, some will think that priority goes to the worst off; others, to those who would benefit most; others will think we should assist the largest number of people; others may hold that we should ensure that all people have fair chances at receiving help, regardless of the urgency of their situations and of expected benefits from treatment. So no matter how deliberative the democracy gets, collective decisions will always be made through voting, under some form of majority rule. Indeed, deliberation may work best when participants do not (as in a jury setting) feel the pressure to adjust their views for the sake of consensus—as if attention to reasons ensured convergence, and disagreement revealed bias or incapacity or some other failure.[9]

There may be some temptation to think that the prospect of majority rule defeats deliberation: because collective decision-making concludes with a vote, participants—anticipating that final stage of resolution—will not have any incentive to deliberate in earlier stages so will focus instead on counting heads rather than on weighing reasons: aggregation at the end of the day, then aggregation all day. But that temptation should be resisted. Even if everyone knows that, at the end of the day, heads may be

8. As Rawls observes, an idea of public reason is one of the "essential elements of deliberative democracy." See "The Idea of Public Reason Revisited," in *Law of Peoples* (Cambridge, MA: Harvard University Press, 1999), 139.

9. On problems with deliberation under a unanimity rule, see David Austen-Smith and Timothy Feddersen, "Deliberation, Preference Uncertainty, and Voting Rules," *American Political Science Review* 100 (2006): 209–218.

counted, they may still accept the idea of arriving at a collective judgment based on considerations that others acknowledge as reasons. They may, for example, believe that reason-giving is an important expression of respect or that it is the right way to acknowledge the collective nature of the decision. If they do, they will be willing to deliberate in the stages leading up to the vote, even when they know a vote is coming.

Deliberative democracy, thus understood, is a distinctive interpretation of democracy: democracy, no matter how fair, no matter how informed, no matter how participatory, is not deliberative unless reasoning is central to the process of collective decision-making. Nor is democracy deliberative simply because the process and its results are reasonable: capable of being given a rational defense, even a rational defense that would be recognized as such on reflection by those subject to the decisions. The concern for reasonableness must play a role in the process. Thus the contrast between deliberative and aggregative democracy. In an aggregative democracy, citizens aim to advance their individual and group interests. If the process is fair, the results may well be reasonable. But unless the reasonableness is aimed at by participants in the process, we do not have deliberation.

Of course, it might be argued that reasonable results must be aimed at to be achieved and that democracy must therefore be deliberative to be reasonable. So, for example, if we have a hypothetical test for the rightness of decisions, where the hypothetical process involves reasoning under idealized conditions about what is best to do, then it might be said that the actual process must look something like the hypothetical to provide a basis for confidence in the rightness of results.[10] Still, it is best to see this connection between reasonableness and deliberation as a broadly empirical claim and to keep deliberation as a way of deciding—a way that comprises both the nature of the process and the content of the reasons—distinct from reasonableness as a property of decisions.

Aggregative and deliberative democracy do not exhaust the space of interpretations of democracy. Consider a community of politically principled citizens, each of whom endorses a conception of justice. The conceptions they endorse differ, but each person accepts some conception as setting bounds on acceptable policy and decent institutions. Assume further that they do not see much point in arguing about what justice re-

10. See, for example, Jürgen Habermas, *Between Facts and Norms*, trans. William Rehg (Cambridge, MA: MIT Press, 1996), 296, 304.

quires, though they discuss issues with an eye to generating information, and each conscientiously uses his or her own conception in reaching political decisions. No one in this political community thinks that politics is simply about advancing interests, much less a Schmittian struggle between friends and enemies. But reasoning together plays a very restricted role in public political life: the members accept that they owe one another an exercise of conscientious judgment but not that they owe a justification by references to reasons that others might reasonably be expected to accept. I will not develop this distinction further here. I mention it to underscore that the case for deliberative democracy needs to be made not simply in contrast with accounts of democracy that focus on interests and power but also in contrast with views that assume a conscientious exercise of moral-political judgment by individual citizens, although not deliberation.

This emphasis on subjecting power to reason's discipline is a thread that runs through much of the literature on deliberative democracy.[11] Thus, Amy Gutmann and Dennis Thompson say that "deliberative democracy's basic requirement is 'reason-giving.'"[12] Jon Elster also emphasizes that deliberation is about argument—in fact, arguments addressed to people committed to rationality and impartiality.[13] John Dryzek says that a "defining feature of deliberative democracy is that individuals participating in democratic processes are amenable to changing their minds and their preferences as a result of the reflection induced by deliberation."[14] Elsewhere he emphasizes "communication that encourages reflection upon preferences without coercion."[15] But Dryek's characterizations of deliberative democracy are not literally *defining*: they follow from the more fundamental characteristics of deliberative democracy. The *point* of deliberative democracy is not for people to reflect on their pref-

11. The emphasis on deliberation as reason-giving is not captured in models of deliberation as cheap talk signaling, where the point is to convey some piece of private information and success depends on beliefs about the trustworthiness of the speaker (see Austen-Smith and Feddersen, "Deliberation, Preference Uncertainty, and Voting Rules"). For an interesting effort to model deliberation as reasoning—arguing from premises to conclusions, where individuals can check the quality of the reasoning themselves—see Catherine Hafer and Dimitri Landa, "Deliberation as Self-Discovery and Institutions for Political Speech," *Journal of Theoretical Politics* 19, 3 (2007).

12. Amy Gutmann and Dennis Thompson, *Why Deliberative Democracy?* (Princeton: Princeton University Press, 2004), 3.

13. "Introduction," *Deliberative Democracy* (Cambridge: Cambridge University Press, 1998), 8.

14. *Deliberative Democracy and Beyond* (Oxford: Oxford University Press, 2004), 31.

15. Ibid., 8.

erences but to decide, in light of reasons, what to do. Deciding what to do
in light of reasons requires, of course, a willingness to change your mind,
since you might begin the deliberative task with a view about what to do
that is not supported by good reasons. But the crucial point is that Dryzek
emphasizes that deliberation is basically about reasoning—about rational
argument—and that other kinds of communication need to be "held to
rational standards."[16]

3. Reasons for Deliberative Democracy

Why is deliberative democracy a good thing? It is of course hard to deny
that the exercise of collective power should be supported by appropriate
reasons. But deliberative democracy is not simply the undisputed idea
that the exercise of power should be rationally defensible, thus non-
arbitrary. The question is why it is important to discipline the exercise of
power by actually reasoning together. I will mention three considerations.

The first is about promoting justice. Thus suppose we think that requirements of justice are fixed by idealized reasoning under conditions of
full information and equal standing. One argument for deliberative democracy is that actual deliberation is needed if collective decisions are to
meet the standards of political right that would be accepted under idealized conditions of information and equality. So if justice is fixed by impartial reasoning in hypothetical conditions in which agents aim to justify principles to others, then, arguably, we will only achieve justice if we
make collective decisions using reasoning of a similar kind. We cannot
trust the achievement of justice to the pursuit of individual and group interests, even under fair conditions.

A second line of argument is that reason-giving is a distinctive form of
communication and it may have desirable consequences, apart from promoting justice. Thus, the requirement that I defend my proposals with
reasons that are capable of being acknowledged as such by others, will—
whatever my own preferences—impose some desirable constraint on the
proposals I can advance and defend. Of course if every proposal can be
rationalized in an acceptable way, then the requirement of defending
proposals with acceptable reasons will not have much effect: but I am
skeptical about this claim. Moreover, the need to give reasons that are ac-

16. Ibid., 167; and, in general, chap. 3.

ceptable to others might produce desirable consequences if reason-giving itself changes preferences, or at least saliences. So while I start preferring most what is best for me or my group, the practice of defending proposals with reasons may change my preferences, dampening the tension between my beliefs about what is right or politically legitimate and my preferences: not because that is the point of deliberation but because that is its effect. In addition, deliberation may improve results by eliciting information: though there are certainly truth-telling equilibria for strategic actors, I assume that the informational effects of deliberation depend in part on a commitment to truthfulness or sincerity in communication, which may itself be reinforced through deliberation, although it is hard to construct from nothing. But that is true about the entire account of deliberation: though deliberation may reinforce a prior commitment to argue on terms that others can acknowledge as reasons, some such prior commitment must be in place if the enterprise of mutual reason-giving is to get off the ground and be sustained.

A third case for deliberative democracy, not about consequences, is that the deliberative view expresses the idea that relations among people within a pluralistic, democratic order are relations of equals. It requires that we offer considerations that others, despite fundamental differences of outlook, can reasonably be expected to accept, not simply that we count their interests, while keeping our fingers crossed that those interests are outweighed. The idea of collective authorization is reflected not only in the processes of decision-making, but also—as I said earlier—in the form and the content of democracy's public reason.

This point about the attractions of the deliberative interpretation of collective decisions can be stated in terms of an idea of self-government. In a deliberative democracy, laws and policies result from processes in which citizens defend solutions to common problems on the basis of what are generally acknowledged as relevant reasons. To be sure, citizens will, as I mentioned earlier, interpret the content of those considerations differently and assign them different weights. The reasons relevant to particular domains are complex and often competing, and there often will be no clear, principled basis for ranking them: reasonable people may reasonably disagree on how they should be weighted, even after all the reasons have been aired. Nevertheless, they may accept the results of the deliberative process in part by virtue of the process having given due consideration to reasons that all reasonably accept.

When citizens take these political values seriously, political decisions are not simply a product of power and interest; even citizens whose views do not win out can see that the decisions are supported by good reasons. As a result, members can—despite disagreement—all regard their conduct as guided, in general terms, by their own reason. Establishing such political deliberation would realize an ideal of self-government or political autonomy under conditions of reasonable pluralism. It may be as close as we can get to the Rousseauean ideal of giving the law to ourselves.

4. Skepticism about Deliberation

I want now to consider four objections that have been raised against the deliberative conception of democracy. The interest of exploring the tensions between deliberation and participation will be greater if some of these concerns can be dispelled.

1. The first is about inequality. It begins with the observation that reasoning is an acquired capacity, one that is not equally distributed among all. So collective decision-making through reason-giving may not *neutralize* power, but it may, instead, create a "logocracy," in which political power is effectively shifted to the rhetorically gifted (or at least to the verbally uninhibited), which may well compound existing social inequalities and deliver political power to the educated, or economically advantaged, or men, or those possessed of cultural capital and argumentative confidence.[17]

While the concern is important and understandable, the evidence, such as it is, suggests that this objection exaggerates the feared effect, in part by "depoliticizing" it—more precisely, by underestimating the capacity to recognize and alleviate it, should it arise. Democracy, to borrow a phrase from Jane Mansbridge, is always a work in process, and much can be done to address this concern. Thus Archon Fung finds that citizen participation in Chicago policing efforts is greater in poorer neighborhoods (not a very large surprise, given crime rates in different neighborhoods), and that the city, cognizant of obvious concerns about cultural and class bias, invested resources in training participants in policing and schooling efforts.[18] Studying the case of participatory budget-

17. I believe that Lynn Sanders was the first to raise this objection, in "Against Deliberation," *Political Theory* (1997): 347–376.
18. Archon Fung, *Empowered Participation: Reinventing Urban Democracy* (Princeton: Princeton University Press, 2004), chap. 4.

ing in Porto Alegre, Abers and Baiocchi find high rates of involvement by poorer, less-educated citizens and discover substantial rates of participation by women and Afro-Brazilians.[19] The thread running through these and related cases is that participation is not exogenously given. Deliberative bodies can undertake affirmative measures to address participatory biases. In particular, they can help to train participants in the issues decided by the body and in how to frame arguments about the relevant policies.

Now it might be argued that in the favorable cases just noted, the deliberative bodies aim to solve relatively concrete problems—to improve policy in relatively well-defined areas (say, pertaining to the provision of local public goods)—not to have an open-ended public debate. Inequalities of argumentative skills on broader matters may resist remedy.[20] But evidence from deliberative polling suggests otherwise: deliberative capacities seem reasonably widely shared, even when issues are more abstract and less locally focused. Critics of deliberation, it seems, were too quick to conclude that deliberative decision-making empowers the verbally agile.

2. A second objection is about effectiveness. Thus it might be said that a deliberative process does not mitigate the effects of power on outcomes of collective decisions. In addressing this issue, we face a large methodological problem. As a general matter, and putting aside the issue of deliberative democracy, it is hard to make an empirically compelling case that process changes produce outcome changes, because changes in process and in result may well both be produced by some third factor: as, for example, when a party with a redistributive project empowers the less advantaged and promotes a shift in economic resources as well, thus suggesting (incorrectly) that the change in process produced the change in result.

A few studies, though not of deliberative democracy, have forcefully addressed these problems of spuriousness. Ansolabehere, Gerber, and Snyder have shown that court-ordered reapportionment in the 1960s

19. See Rebecca Abers, "Reflections on What Makes Empowered Participatory Governance Happen," in Fung and Wright, *Deepening Democracy*, 206, and more generally her *Inventing Local Democracy* (Boulder, CO: Lynne Riener, 2000); Gianpaolo Baiocchi, *Militants and Citizens: The Politics of Participatory Democracy in Porto Alegre* (Stanford: Stanford University Press, 2005).

20. In his critique of deliberative democracy, Richard Posner is less hostile to locally focused discussion about the provision of public goods, perhaps for reasons of the kind noted in the text. See *Law, Pragmatism, and Democracy* (Cambridge, MA: Harvard University Press, 2003).

shifted public goods spending in the states in the direction of previously underrepresented districts: a special case because reapportionment was a court-ordered exogenous shock.[21] Similarly, Chattopadhyay and Duflo have made the case that reserved seats for women on Indian village councils have led to shifts in public goods spending, with greater spending on goods that are preferred by women when the head of the village council is a woman.[22] Here the problem of spuriousness is solved by randomness in the process that determines which village councils will be headed by women. We have no comparably compelling case that increased deliberativeness leads to changes in the content of the decisions.

Still, we have some suggestive evidence. Thus, participatory budgeting in Porto Alegre and the village councils in Kerala appear to have produced substantial shifts in the allocation of public resources to the poor: in Porto Alegre, for example, there is now full coverage of water and sewers and there is a three-fold increase in school attendance.[23] Similarly, Lucio Baccaro has argued that internal democratic reform in Italian unions produced large shifts in union policy in directions more favorable to the interests of outsiders (pensions, employment, and regional development issues). To be sure, the results in these cases may come not from deliberation but from broader participation or the dominance of a left party. But deliberation seems to be part of the story, both because deliberation shifts preferences and because it shifts collective decisions by making some proposals harder to defend: namely, proposals that cannot be defended in public on the basis of acceptable reasons. (Baccaro makes a good case that deliberation made the difference).[24]

3. A third concern is about deliberative pathologies. A social-psychological variant of this concern says that group discussion imposes normative pressure on group members: a variance-reducing pressure not to be less extreme than the group median, and a mean-shifting pressure not to be less extreme than the group mean. A cognitive story claims that group discussion in a relative homogenous group is dominated by argu-

21. Stephen Ansolabehere, Alan Gerber, James M. Snyder, "Equal Votes, Equal Money: Court-Ordered Redistricting and the Distribution of Public Expenditure in the American States," *American Political Science Review* (August 2002).

22. Raghabendra Chattopadhyay and Esther Duflo, "Women As Policy Makers: Evidence from a Randomized Policy Experiment in India," *Econometrica* 72, 5 (2004): 1409–1443.

23. Gianpaolo Baiocchi, The Citizens of Porto Alegre, *Boston Review* 31, 2 (March-April 2006).

24. Lucio Baccaro, "The Construction of Democratic Corporatism in Italy," *Politics and Society* 30, 2 (June 2002): 327–357.

ments embraced by the majority, so that when people update on a relatively homogenous argument pool, they consolidate. In either case, it is bad for outsiders.[25]

These are very serious concerns, but at least in principle, the remedies seem straightforward, whatever the likelihood of their adoption. If deliberation under conditions of homogeneity drives polarization, then it is important to ensure that deliberative settings in some way reflect the wider diversity: in some deliberative settings, the competitive quality of the decision—when the issue at stake is the allocation of scarce resources—engenders such expression. In other settings, ensuring diversity of opinion may be a matter of institutional principle or the responsibility of a moderator. In settings of group discussion, this might mean ensuring that some time is devoted to expressing beliefs or judgments that are assumed not to be shared by others in the group: ensuring that this happens seems to be well within the reach of moderators or participants themselves.

Put more generally, the point is that studies of deliberative pathologies need to be treated with some care. Those pathologies may emerge from group decision-making conducted without efforts to avoid the pathological results. So such studies may often be interpretable as sources of cautionary notes and recommendations for improvement rather than being interpretable as undermining the case for deliberation. That said, it is also true that the more fragile deliberation is, the more structure that needs to be in place to move from discussion to good deliberation, the less confidence we can reside in the project of building a more deliberative democracy. A naïve version of the deliberative ideal supposes that people are waiting to deliberate and need only to get competitive political structures out of the way. Deliberation may be a more fragile accomplishment.

4. The final objection is about naïveté concerning power.[26] Because constraints on what counts as a reason are not well defined, the advantaged will find some way to defend self-serving proposals with consider-

25. Cass Sunstein, "Group Judgments: Statistical Means, Deliberation, and Information Markets," *NYU Law Review* 80 (June 2005): 962–1049; and Tali Mendelberg's very instructive discussion of deliberation and small-group decision-making, in "The Deliberative Citizen: Theory and Evidence," in *Political Decision-Making, Deliberation, and Participation: Research in Micropolitics*, vol. 6, ed. Michael X. Delli Carpini, Leonie Huddy, and Robert Shapiro (Greenwich, CT: JAI Press, 2002), pp. 151–193.
26. See Cohen and Rogers, "Power and Reason."

ations that are arguably reasons. For example, they may make appeals to ideas of the common advantage but press a conception of the common advantage that assigns great weight to a deeply unequal status quo. Or if they fail in this, the advantaged will simply refuse to accept the discipline of deliberation.

If this objection is right, then proposals for deliberative democracy that are inattentive to background relations of power will waste the time of those who can least afford its loss: those now subordinate in power. The time and energy they spend in argument, laboring under the illusion that sweet reason will constrain the power that suppresses them, could have been spent in self-organization, instrumental efforts to increase their own power, or like efforts to impose costs on opponents.

The complaint that deliberative democracy is touchingly naïve about power betrays vertiginously boundless confusion.

First, the importance of background differences in power is not a criticism of the deliberative ideal per se, but a concern about its application. Deliberative democracy is a normative model of collective decision-making, not a universal political strategy. And commitment to the normative ideal does not require commitment to the belief that collective decision-making through mutual reason-giving is always possible. So it may indeed be the case that some rough background balance of power is required before parties will listen to reason. But observing that does not importantly lessen the attraction of the deliberative ideal; it simply states a condition of its reasonable pursuit.

Thus, in Habermas's account of the ideal speech situation, or in my own account of an ideal deliberative procedure, inequalities in power are stipulated away for the sake of presenting an idealized model of deliberation.[27] These idealizations are intended to characterize the nature of reasoned collective decision-making and, in turn, to provide models for actual arrangements of collective decision-making. But actual arrangements must provide some basis for confidence that joint reasoning will actually prevail in shaping the exercise of collective power, and gross inequalities of power surely undermine any such confidence. So discussion that expresses the deliberative ideal must, for example, operate against a background of free expression and association, thus providing minimal conditions for the availability of relevant information. Equally, if parties

27. See Cohen, "Deliberation and Democratic Legitimacy," and Habermas, *Between Facts and Norms*, chap. 7.

are not somehow constrained to accept the consequences of deliberation, if "exit options" are not foreclosed, it seems implausible that they will accept the discipline of joint reasoning and, in particular, reasoning informed by the democratic idea of persons as equals. Firms retaining a more or less costless ability to move investment elsewhere are not, for example, likely to accept the discipline of reasoned deliberation about labor standards, with workers as their deliberative equals.

Saying, "If you don't listen to reason, you will pay a high price" is not a joke: it is sometimes necessary to resort to destabilization, threats, and open conflict as answers to people who won't reason in good faith. A sucker may be born every minute, but deliberative democracy is not a recommendation that we all join the club. But if the willingness to reason does depend on the background distribution of power, doesn't that defeat the point of deliberative democracy by reducing deliberation to bargaining under a balance of power? Not at all. Once people do listen to reason, the results may reflect not only the balance of power that defeated their previous imperviousness but also their attentiveness to reasons that can be shared. If I need to drink some espresso to concentrate hard enough to prove a theorem, it does not reduce theorem-proving to a caffeine high. So similarly, paying attention to power and threats to exercise it doesn't reduce deliberation to bargaining. To suppose otherwise is like thinking that if you need to trust your math teacher in order to learn how to do a proof then there is nothing more to proof than trust. It confuses conditions that make an activity possible with that activity itself.

5. Some Tensions between Participation and Deliberation

I started by noting two strands in the radical democratic tradition: participatory and deliberative. But I have not said much at all about political participation: deliberative democracy is about political reasoning, not the breadth and the depth of participation. To be very brief: participation is particularly important in connection with achieving fair political equality, because shifting the basis of political contestation from organized money to organized people is a promising alternative to the influence conferred by wealth. Similarly, expanding and deepening citizen participation may be the most promising strategy for challenging political inequalities associated with traditional social and political hierarchies. Moreover, it may be important in encouraging a sense of political responsibility.

But participation is one thing, and deliberation is another, and they may pull in different directions. Consider three sources of tension.[28]

1. Improving the quality of deliberation may come at a cost to public participation. Suppose, for example, that legislators, regulators, and judges were to embrace a deliberative form of decision-making. Instead of seeking to advance the interests of their constituents or single-mindedly maximizing their prospects of re-election, for example, legislators would engage in reasonable discussion and argument about policies. Judges would, in turn, reinforce the legislators by requiring explicit attention to reasons in legislative and administrative decision-making. But doing so might require insulation from public pressures.

2. Expanding participation—either the numbers of people or the range of issues under direct popular control—may diminish the quality of deliberation. Initiatives and referenda, for example, allow voters to exercise more direct and precisely targeted influence over legislation, policy questions, and even elected officials. But far from improving deliberation, such measures—in part because they ultimately focus on a yes/no decision on a well-defined proposition—may discourage reasoned discussion in creating legislation. And even bringing people together to discuss specific laws and policies may—with a homogenous collection of people or a lack of commitment to addressing a common problem—diminish deliberation, as discussion dissolves into posturing, recrimination, and manipulation.[29]

3. More fundamentally, social complexity and scale limit the extent to which modern polities can be both deliberative and participatory. Deliberation depends on participants with sufficient knowledge and interest about the substantive issues under consideration. But on any issue, the number of individuals with such knowledge and interest is bound to be

28. Diana Mutz explores a different tension between deliberation and participation in her important book, *Hearing the Other Side: Deliberative Versus Participatory Democracy* (Cambridge: Cambridge University Press, 2006). Mutz argues that deliberation among the diverse encourages greater toleration but dampens participation because of a desire to avoid conflict with the people to whom one talks. Participation, in turn, is animated by a sense of passion that is dampened by deliberation. I am not sure that Mutz's results extend outside participation in highly competitive political settings. But the challenge she raises is deep and needs to be addressed.

29. See, for example, Derek Bell, "The Referendum: Democracy's Barrier to Racial Equality," *Washington Law Review* 54, 1 (1978): 1–29; Yannis Papadopolous, "A Framework for Analysis of Functions and Dysfunctions of Direct Democracy: Top-Down and Bottom-Up Perspectives," *Politics and Society* 23 (1995): 421–448.

relatively small, and so the quality of deliberation will decline with the scope of participation. Of course, knowledge and interest are not fixed, and deliberation may improve both. Still, time and resource constraints make it undesirable for any particular area of public governance to be both fully deliberative and inclusively participatory.

6. And So?

These three tensions notwithstanding, public decision-making in liberal democracies could become both more participatory and deliberative. The challenge is to devise practical projects that can incorporate both. Radical democrats have two broad strategies for achieving that aim, which I will sketch in very broad strokes.

The first aims to join deliberation with mass democracy by promoting citizen deliberation on political matters, in what Habermas calls the "informal public sphere," constituted by networks of associations in civil society.[30] Because such informal discussion does not aim at a practical decision but—insofar as it has an aim—at an informed public opinion, it can pursue an unencumbered discussion about political values and public goals. Moreover, these dispersed discussions—one element of a political society's process of collective decision-making—are potentially very broadly participatory, for they take place through structures of numerous, open secondary associations and social movements. For this mix of mass democracy and deliberation, the essential ingredients, apart from ensuring basic liberties, are diverse and independent media; vibrant, independent civil associations; and political parties that operate independently from concentrated wealth and help to focus public debate. All of this arguably helps to foster deliberative capacities—a point I mentioned earlier and promised to return to. The marriage of open communication in the informal public sphere with a translation—through elections and legislative debate—of opinion formed there into law provides, on this view, the best hope for achieving a greater mix of participation and deliberation under conditions of mass democracy and a rule of law.

Much of the attractiveness of this view, then, hinges first upon the deliberativeness of discourse in the public sphere and then upon the strength of the links between such deliberation and the decisions of legislative bodies and administrative agencies. But because dispersed, infor-

30. Habermas, *Between Facts and Norms*, chap. 8; John Rawls, *Political Liberalism* (New York: Columbia University Press, 1996), 14, 382–383.

mal public deliberation and public policy are only loosely linked, a more participatory and deliberative informal public sphere may have little impact on decisions by formal institutions. Citizen participation in the informal public sphere, then, may be of limited political relevance, and the marriage of reason with mass democracy may proceed in splendid isolation from the exercise of power. To be clear: I am not here objecting to this first approach, only pointing to a concern and a possible limitation.

A second radical-democratic approach builds on the distinctive practical competence that citizens possess as users of public services, as subjects of public policy and regulation, or as residents with contextual knowledge of their circumstances. The idea is to draw on these competencies by bringing ordinary citizens into relatively focused deliberations over public issues. Typically, such strategies create opportunities for limited numbers of citizens to deliberate with one another or with officials to improve the quality of some public decision, perhaps by injecting local knowledge, new perspectives, and excluded interests or by enhancing public accountability.

One approach randomly selects small groups of citizens to deliberate on general political issues, such as laws and public policies. Citizen juries in the United States and planning cells in Germany, for example, empanel small groups (12–40) of randomly selected citizens to discuss issues such as agriculture, health policy, and local development concerns.[31] Fishkin and his colleagues have sponsored larger gatherings of 300–500 citizens—with randomization—to deliberate upon such issues as the adoption of the Euro in Denmark, the regulation of public utilities in Texas, and the extent of foreign assistance.[32] On an ambitious *analytical* interpretation, post-deliberation polls provide insight into what *the people* think about a policy issue. Political impact is another matter. As with citizen juries and planning cells, their political impact—to the ex-

---

31. Julia Abelson, Pierre-Gerlier Forest, John Eyles, Patricia Smith, Elisabeth Martin, and Francois-Pierre Gauvin, "Deliberations about Deliberative Methods: Issues in the Design and Evaluation of Public Participation Processes" in *Social Science and Medicine* No. 57 (2003): 239–251; Ned Crosby, "Citizens' Juries: One Solution for Difficult Environmental Questions," in O. Renn, T. Webler, and P. Wiedelmann, eds. *Fairness and Competence in Citizen Participation: Evaluating Models for Environmental Discourse* (Boston: Kluwer Academic Press, 1995): 157–174; G. Smith and C. Wales, "The Theory and Practice of Citizens' Juries," in *Policy and Politics* 27, 3 (1999): 295–308; John Gastil, *By Popular Demand* (Los Angeles: University of California Press, 2000).

32. For a sketch of polls and implications, see Bruce Ackerman and James Fishkin, *Deliberation Day* (New Haven: Yale University Press, 2005), esp. chap. 3.

tent that they have impact—comes from their capacity to serve in advisory roles and to alter public opinion or to change the minds of public officials.

Another strategy convenes groups of citizens to deliberate and develop solutions to particular problems of public concern. Such participatory-deliberative arrangements—characteristic in different ways of associative democracy and directly deliberative polyarchy—differ from political juries in two main ways. Whereas political juries usually consider *general* issues, such as economic, health care, or crime policy, these deliberations aim to address more specific problems, such as the management of an ecosystem, the operation of a public school or a school district, the prevention of crime in a neighborhood, or the allocation of a city's resources across projects and neighborhoods. Whereas political juries recruit impartial and disinterested citizens by randomly selecting them, participatory-deliberative arrangements recruit participants with strong interests in the problems under deliberation.

Because of the specificity of these arrangements, citizens may well enjoy advantages in knowledge and experience over officials. In Chicago, for example, residents deliberate regularly with police officers in each neighborhood to set priorities on addressing issues of public safety, using their background knowledge as a basis for deliberation. And in Porto Alegre, citizens meet regularly at the neighborhood level to agree on priorities for public investment (for example, street paving, sanitation, and housing); the capital portion of the city's budget is produced by aggregating the priorities that emerge from those deliberations.

Participatory-deliberative arrangements—in areas such as education, social services, ecosystems, community development, and health services—show promising contributions to political equality by increasing popular engagement in political decision-making. As I mentioned earlier, in Chicago's community policing program, for example, participation rates in low-income neighborhoods are much higher than those in wealthy neighborhoods. Similarly, poor people are substantially over-represented in both the budgeting institutions of Porto Alegre and the local development and planning initiatives in Kerala, India. Directly democratic arrangements that address problems of particular urgency to disadvantaged citizens can invert the usual participation bias in favor of wealth, education, and high status. They can also, however, create large potential political inequalities. If systematic and enduring differences—

in deliberative capabilities, disposable resources, or demographic factors—separate those who participate from those who do not, decisions generated by participatory-deliberative arrangements will likely serve the interests of participants at the expense of others.

The proliferation of directly deliberative institutions fosters democratic self-government by subjecting the policies and actions of agencies such as these to a rule of common reason. But these contributions to self-government are, however, limited by the scope of these institutions. Most participatory-deliberative governance efforts aim to address local concerns and do not extend to broader issues of policy and public priorities. Moreover, there is the danger of administrative "capture": that by entering the circuit of regulatory problem-solving with its pragmatic concern about the effectiveness of policy, participating citizens and groups lose their capacity for independent action and their sense of the importance of open-ended reflection and morally motivated criticism and innovation.[33] They may become dependent on the state and its official recognition for power and resources, and their political horizon may come to be undesirably confined by attention to policy constraints. If this is right, then the alleged limitation of informal, society-wide deliberation—the fact that its impact is so indirect—is really its virtue. The precondition of the unconstrained discussion on which public deliberation depends requires distance between a civil society's associative life and the state's decision-making routines.

7. Final Reflections

So achieving both participation and deliberation is complicated. But because of their more direct bearing on the exercise of power, participatory-deliberative arrangements have a particular promise as a strategy for achieving the ends of radical democracy. Two large challenges, however, lie on that path.

The first concerns the relationship between conventional institutions of political representation and participatory-deliberative arrangements.[34] Participatory-deliberative arrangements make it possible to address practi-

33. See Lucio Baccaro and Konstantinos Papadakis, "The Downside of Deliberative Public Administration" (unpublished).

34. For discussion of the issues sketched here, see Cohen and Sabel, "Directly-Deliberative Polyarchy"; Cohen and Sabel, "Global Democracy?"; and Joshua Cohen and Charles Sabel, "Sovereignty and Solidarity in the EU," in Jonathan Zeitlin and David Trubek, eds., *Governing Work and Welfare in a New Economy: European and American Experiments* (Oxford: Oxford University Press, 2003), 345–375.

cal problems that seem recalcitrant to treatment by conventional political institutions. But those arrangements are not a wholesale replacement of conventional political institutions: they have limited scope and limited numbers of direct participants. To the extent that they are successful, however, participatory-deliberative arrangements and conventional political representation can be transformed and linked so that each strengthens the other. If such arrangements became a common form of local and administrative problem-solving, the role of legislatures and public agencies would shift from directly solving a range of social problems to supporting the efforts of many participatory deliberations, maintaining their democratic integrity, and ensuring their coordination. Conversely, those who participated directly in these new deliberative arrangements would form a highly informed, mobilized, and active base that would enhance the mandate and legitimacy of elected representatives and other officials.

The second challenge is to extend the scope of radical democracy. Can participatory deliberation help democratize large-scale decisions about public priorities—war and peace, health insurance, public pensions, and wealth distribution? One way to address these larger questions is to connect the disciplined, practical, participatory deliberations about solving particular problems—say, efforts to reduce asthma rates in a low-income community, or efforts to provide decent medical care in New Orleans or Los Angeles—to the wider public sphere of debate and opinion formation about the costs of and the access to health care and the importance of health relative to other basic goods. Participants in direct deliberations are informed by the dispersed discussions in the informal public sphere, and those more focused deliberations in turn invest public discussion with a practicality it might otherwise lack. The ambitious hope is that citizens who participate in constructing solutions to concrete problems in local public life may in turn engage more deeply in informal deliberation in the wider public sphere and in formal political institutions as well.

In the end, then, radical democracy—understood as an effort to combine the values of both participation and deliberation—has promise to be a distinctive form of democracy, in which the informal public sphere and conventional democratic institutions are reshaped by their connections with participatory-deliberative arrangements for solving problems. Whether it will deliver on that promise remains, of course, a very open question.

11

TRUTH AND PUBLIC REASON

In 1958 I wrote the following:

> There are no hard distinctions between what is real and what is
> unreal, nor between what is true and what is false. A thing is
> not necessarily either true or false; it can be both true and false.

I believe that these assertions still make sense and do still apply
to the exploration of reality through art. So as a writer I stand
by them but as a citizen I cannot. As a citizen I must ask: What
is true? What is false?

HAROLD PINTER, Nobel Prize Lecture (2005)

Political constructivism does not use (or deny) the concept of
truth; nor does it question that concept, nor could it say that
the concept of truth and its idea of the reasonable are the
same. Rather, within itself, the political conception *does without the concept of truth.*

JOHN RAWLS, *Political Liberalism*

Democratic politics comprises, among other things, public discussion about laws and policies on the basis of reasons of justice. How
large a part is not my concern here. I assume that such reasoning, mixed

I presented earlier versions at the Catholic University of Leuven; LUISS Guido Carli; the
Harvard Graduate Conference in Political Theory; the philosophy departments at Columbia
University, Union College, Northwestern University, and Cornell University; the September
Group; the Stanford Law School Legal Theory Colloquium; and as the 2008 Mala Kamm Lec-
ture at NYU. I am grateful to audiences on all these occasions, to the Editors of *Philosophy &
Public Affairs*, and to Bradley Armour-Garb, Alex Byrne, David Estlund, Erik Freeman, Samuel Freeman, Barbara Fried, David Hills, Erin Kelly, Cristina Lafont, Jon Mandle, Sebastiano
Maffetone, Richard Miller, Ingrid Salvatore, Thomas Scanlon, Seana Shiffrin, and especially
to Paul Horwich for comments and suggestions. I also benefited greatly from generous and illuminating comments by Richard Rorty at the Stanford colloquium. I sketch his concerns below in note 55.

with bargaining and hectoring, confession and accusation, self-pity and compulsive self-display, provides some part of democratic politics. Focusing on this deliberative part, I want to consider the role that the concept of *truth* might properly play in it.

I will defend two conclusions about that role.

First, the concept of *truth*, and judgments and assertions deploying that concept—including judgments and assertions that apply the concept to basic principles of justice—have a legitimate role to play in public, political argument. Here I endorse Pinter's Nobel lecture view about the place of truth in the reflection of citizens (not his comments on the artistic license to violate the law of noncontradiction) and disagree with Rawls's claim in *Political Liberalism* that a political conception of justice "does without the concept of truth."[1]

Second, the conception of truth that plays a role in public justification should be *political*. A "conception" or "understanding" of truth is a set of claims about truth, though not offered as an analysis of the concept.[2] By a political conception of truth, then, I mean (very roughly) a set of claims about truth—for example, that truth is distinct from warrant, and that it is important—that is suited for the purposes of political reflection and argument in a pluralistic democracy, characterized by doctrinal disagreements. I will explain later (section 3) the special aim and distinctive content of a political conception of truth. Suffice it to say here that the aim is to present a view of truth that suffices for public reasoning and that could reasonably be endorsed by the adherents of conflicting doctrines, which may themselves employ richer conceptions of truth, for example, the view that truth consists in a correspondence of truth bearer and fact, or in some sort of idealized justification.

A political conception of truth is thus a genuine conception of truth,[3]

---

1. To be sure, Pinter was thinking about the truth and the falsity of assertions about matters of nonnormative fact: for example, about the absence of weapons of mass destruction from Iraq in 2002. Nevertheless, because he states his point in more sweeping terms, just as he had earlier stated a perfectly general claim about truth, I think it is appropriate to interpret him as making a more general claim about the place of truth in the discourse of citizens.

2. I say "conception" or "understanding" rather than "theory," because I am not supposing that a conception needs to have the internal structure that we associate with a theory. See below, 372–373 (final two paragraphs of sec. 3).

3. In the way that the political conception of objectivity, associated with political liberalism, is a genuine conception of objectivity, though different from, and in a way less committal than, rational intuitionist and Kantian conceptions of objectivity. See John Rawls, *Political Liberalism* (New York: Columbia University Press, 1996), 110–116.

although less committal than the conceptions that have traditionally occupied philosophical attention and that have deep roots in our practices of making and defending assertions (including logically complex
assertions), in our reasoning, and in ordinary understandings about the
content and the correctness of thoughts. Because a political conception is less committal, it bears some similarity to antimetaphysical, "deflationary" theories of truth. Those theories are inspired by the redundancy theories of Frege and Ramsey, according to which the content of
the claim that a proposition is true is the same as the content of the proposition.[4] Their main thrust is that truth is not a philosophically deep idea;
the concept is fully captured by the infinitely many instances of the truth
schema (T):

(T) *The proposition that p* is true if and only if p.[5]

Deflationary theories thus deny that truth is correspondence, or warranted assertibility, or consensus in inquiry's ideal limit, or a cheerfully
solidaristic backslap. In denying these claims, such theories are *conceptually* deflationary and thus to be distinguished from the *evaluatively*
deflationary view that truth is not something to which we should attach great importance. A political conception cannot endorse an antimetaphysical, conceptually deflationary theory. That endorsement is not
needed for public reasoning and would put the political conception
needlessly at odds with religious or philosophical views that comprise
more ambitious conceptions of truth. Endorsing an antimetaphysical
deflationism would make the political conception of truth unacceptably
sectarian. Instead, a political conception aims to be nonmetaphysical
rather than antimetaphysical.

Two points of clarification before proceeding. First, while disagree-
ing with Rawls's claims about truth, I endorse the ideal of *public reason*.[6]
According to that ideal, political justification, at least on certain funda-

4. See Gottlob Frege, "The Thought: A Logical Inquiry," *Mind* 65, 259 (July 1956): 293.

5. There are many versions of the deflationary approach and not all treat propositions (as op-
posed to sentences) as truth bearers: I have made that assumption here, but nothing in my dis-
cussion turns on it. For discussion of some of the variety, see Scott Soames, *Understanding
Truth* (Oxford: Oxford University Press, 1999), chap. 8; Bradley Armour-Garb, "Deflationism:
A Brief Introduction" (unpublished). On propositions as truth bearers, see Soames, chap. 1;
Paul Horwich, *Truth*, 2d ed. (Oxford: Oxford University Press, 1998), 16–17.

6. On public reason, see *Political Liberalism*, lecture 6; John Rawls, "The Idea of Public
Reason Revisited," in *Collected Papers*, ed. Samuel Freeman (Cambridge, MA: Harvard University Press, 1999): 573–615.

mental questions, should proceed on a terrain of argument that can be shared. In the case of democracy's public reason, the shared terrain comprises values that can reasonably be shared by people who regard themselves as free and equal, despite irreconcilable doctrinal disagreements and disagreements about justice. Although I find the idea of public reason compelling, I disagree with Rawls's claim that the concept of truth finds no place in it. That claim makes the idea of public reason unnecessarily contentious, as if it were committed to the view that the truth about justice does not matter. And it makes the idea of pubic reason hard to understand, because it proposes to leave the concept of truth behind while preserving notions of belief, assertion, judgment, reason, and objectivity, all of which are essential to an idea of public reason. In making his case for putting truth aside, Rawls suggests that we face a dilemma: that we can have truth or public reason, but not both. My aim in presenting a political conception of truth is to show that this is a false dilemma and that we can have both. The political conception of truth, then, is presented as part of a defense of the idea of public reason.

Second, I emphasize that the political conception is not, to borrow a phrase from Rawls, "political in the wrong way." A political conception of truth does not say that a proposition is true just in case it solves our problems or is part of a broad consensus. Still less does it say that a proposition is true just in case authorities say that it is true or it confers advantage on the powerful. Such Thrasymachean theses about truth and politics are best understood as critical claims about how the term "true" and its cognates are used. They derive their critical edge from the fact that they do not express conceptions of truth. Instead, they present the charge—understandable to anyone who has the concept of truth, troubling to anyone who cares about it—that "true" is systematically applied to propositions in virtue of their satisfying a condition that does nothing to make them worthy of belief.[7] The political conception is not political in virtue of tracing cognitive appraisals to an exercise of authority or to the effects of power. It belongs to a very different conception of the political, and it is classified as political because it can reasonably be endorsed as common ground for the purposes of consequential collective decisions.

To defend my two claims, I start (section 1) by sketching the back-

---

7. For discussion of the charge, and the ways that it puzzlingly deploys a passion for truthfulness against the concept of truth, see Bernard Williams, *Truth and Truthfulness* (Princeton: Princeton University Press, 2002).

ground of Rawls's idea that public reason "does without the concept of truth." Second, then, I discuss (section 2) why it is hard to understand the idea that public reason leaves truth aside. To clarify the puzzlement, I distinguish four views that diminish the place of truth in political argument: the No Concept view (Rawls's position), No Truth Bearers, No Substantive Judgments, and No Big Deal. Third, I sketch a political conception of truth and offer an account of what having such a conception available in public political argument comes to (section 3). Fourth, I criticize three arguments that might be offered in support of the No Concept view that truth does not belong to public reason (section 4). Finally, I distinguish the idea that public reason does without truth from an evaluatively deflationary view, which I will call the "cultural proposal." Drawing on this cultural-political distinction, I suggest (section 5) that a political world that does without the concept of truth is missing something important.

1. Truth and Public Reason

The intellectual context for the discussion is provided by Rawls's idea of a specifically *political* liberalism. The phrase "political liberalism" may have the air of a pleonasm. Liberalism has always been, inter alia, a political outlook, defined by an emphasis on personal freedom, religious tolerance, open inquiry, the rule of law, social mobility, and, in its modern formulations, democratic politics.

The point of the phrase, then, is that the liberal political outlook has also often been presented as the political department of a broader philosophical position, mixing an ethic of self-direction, religious latitudinarianism, suspicion about the normative force of tradition and authority, metaphysical and epistemological modesty. But as, for example, the twentieth-century Catholic accommodation to modernism illustrates, a liberal political perspective can derive support from other philosophical starting points, including religious views that downplay autonomous choice in favor of substantively correct decisions, regard tradition as a deposit of evolving insight, are metaphysically and epistemologically ambitious, and see religious commitments as providing less latitude and greater density of demands.[8] Presentations of liberal political commit-

8. See "Declaration on Religious Freedom," *The Teachings of the Second Vatican Council: Complete Texts of the Constitutions, Decrees, and Declarations* (Westminster, MD: Newman Press, 1966), 366–367; John Courtney Murray, "The Problem of Religious Freedom," in *Religious Liberty: Catholic Struggles with Pluralism* (Louisville, KY: Westminster, 1993).

ments that tie them to a general philosophical liberalism may, therefore, impose unnecessary barriers to a broad embrace of liberalism. To the extent that such presentations take hold in the political culture, they may work to intolerantly exclude people from the political public sphere. Political liberalism aims to free the formulation of liberalism as a political outlook, so far as possible, from that wider set of philosophical and religious commitments, and thus to "put no unnecessary obstacles in the way of . . . affirming the political conception."[9] Moreover, it would honor the value of tolerance and the ideal of the political arena as a space of public reasoning open to equal citizens.

Rawls's concerns about truth emerge from this background. To explain how, I need to say a little more about why political liberalism might seem a forceful response to doctrinal conflict, particularly in a democratic society.

The trouble with truth begins, then, with *doctrinal* pluralism, the pluralism of incompatible "comprehensive doctrines"—views about the world, the place of human beings in it, the appropriate ways to acquire an understanding of the world, and the way that human beings should accordingly live their lives. Doctrinal pluralism is not the *only* political problem: conflicts of interest—or of ethnicity, race, or nation—are not, at root, doctrinal. Moreover, doctrinal conflict is not only a *problem*. As Mill and others have observed, it can work as a basis of social learning, as we pool information drawn from the varieties of human experience and reflect in light of thoughts and patterns of conduct that we would never otherwise have entertained. Too, doctrinal conflict may be seen as having some intrinsic attraction, as an expression of the scope of human possibilities.

Doctrinal pluralism is *also* a problem, however, and presents a distinctive challenge in a democracy. Democracy is not simply a matter of living together but also, ideally at least, a society of equals, whose members decide together how to live together. People who disagree fundamentally, however, have trouble occupying a common ground on which they can justify to one another those joint decisions.

One response to this trouble is to try to characterize such a common ground of political justification. I will call this "democracy's public reason." Democracy's public reason is a terrain of political reflection and judgment that equal persons, drawn to conflicting doctrines, can reasonably be expected to occupy and endorse as a basis for addressing public

9. John Rawls, *Justice as Fairness: A Restatement*, ed. Erin Kelly (Cambridge, MA: Harvard University Press, 2001), 37.

issues. The essential point here is that common ground, if it is available at all, requires that the content of public reason is restricted relative to the doctrines endorsed by members.

For example, concepts of self-realization, associated with the view that there is an essential human nature that consists in the possession of certain self-governing powers, and of salvation, associated with the idea of a transcendent God, are not available to public reason. Moreover, Rawls thinks that the concept of truth is unavailable.

This claim about truth is not founded on any general philosophical doubts about truth, nor on general doubts about the place of normative notions in public reason. Ideas of rightness, justice, reasonableness, correct judgment, and objectivity all have a proper place in public reason. His concern is specifically about public reason and truth, and he locates this concern at the heart of his account of political liberalism and public reason.[10] When Rawls first proposed the idea of a conception of justice that would be "political, not metaphysical," he defined a political conception as one that avoids claims about truth: "The aim of justice as fairness as a political conception is practical, and not metaphysical or epistemological. *That is* [emphasis added], it presents itself not as a conception of justice that is true, but one that can serve as a basis of informed and willing political agreement between citizens viewed as free and equal persons."[11] Later formulations of political liberalism remained emphatic about steering clear of the concept of truth.[12] "Political liberal-

10. In emphasizing Rawls's concern specifically with truth, I disagree with Joseph Raz's claim that Rawls is equally concerned with a variety of terms of normative appraisal, including "reasonable." See his "Facing Diversity: The Case of Epistemic Abstinence," *Philosophy & Public Affairs* 19, 1 (Winter 1990): 15 (and esp. note 34). Raz's article was written before Rawls had developed a number of the main ideas of political liberalism, so the (mis)interpretation is understandable. More broadly, I agree with Raz in thinking that Rawls was mistaken in putting the concept of truth aside. But there are several important points of difference between his view and mine: (1) Raz does not have the idea of a political conception of truth, and thus does not see that doctrinal disagreement imposes any conditions on the understanding of truth that falls within public reason (or perhaps see any need for an account of public reason at all); (2) I think that Rawls, in emphasizing the importance of the political and the practical, was never concerned simply with what Raz calls "consensus-based social stability." Because Raz misconstrues Rawls's concern with the political and the practical, he misinterprets the reasons for abstaining from judgments about truth; (3) Raz appears to endorse what I will later call the Sufficiency and the Full Display arguments, an endorsement that may be associated with skepticism about the idea of public reason.

11. John Rawls, "Justice as Fairness: Political Not Metaphysical," in Joshua Cohen, *Collected Papers*, ed. Samuel Freeman (Cambridge, MA: Harvard University Press, 1999), 394.

12. The passages that follow are from *Political Liberalism*, xxii, 116, and 94. In "The Idea of Public Reason Revisited," Rawls does not address the issue of truth at all, though he does not suggest (except perhaps by the sheer omission) any change of mind.

ism," Rawls says, "rather than referring to its political conception of justice as true, refers to it as reasonable instead." Moreover, political liberalism, he says, "has an account of objectivity" that is connected to an account of "reasonable judgment" and suffices for the purposes of public justification and "may *leave the concept of a true moral judgment* to comprehensive doctrines" (emphasis added). And, perhaps most fundamentally, political liberalism "does not use (or deny) the concept of truth; nor does it question that concept, nor could it say that the concept of truth and its idea of the reasonable are the same. Rather, within itself, the political conception *does without the concept of truth*" (emphasis added). Reasonableness, not truth, is the "standard of correctness,"[13] and the objectivity of judgments about justice is characterized without reference to the notion of truth. In response to Jürgen Habermas's claim that political liberalism cannot avoid issues of truth, Rawls forcefully replies that people will "[c]ertainly . . . continue to raise questions of truth and to tax political liberalism with not discussing them. In the absence of particulars, these complaints fall short of being objections."[14]

Rawls's point, I emphasize, is that the *concept* of truth is unavailable (later I will contrast this *No Concept* view with a few other views that are skeptical about a role for truth in political argument). Thus we cannot, while operating within democracy's public reason, make claims about the nature of truth (and whether it has a nature), about its importance, or about its relationship to justification, objectivity, and reasonableness. Nor can we make assertions about the truth of any elements of our views, including our comprehensive doctrine, or our views about justice, or our understanding of how the society works.

Consider, for example, justice as fairness, with its two principles of justice. Assume that justice as fairness is one of several reasonable conceptions of justice that would win support among citizens in a democratic society. The idea, then, is that it would be appropriate in political argument to think or assert that justice as fairness is reasonable—indeed the "most reasonable" conception of justice[15]—and thus to use its principles

---

13. *Political Liberalism*, 127.

14. "Reply to Habermas," in *Political Liberalism*, 394–395.

15. Political officials and candidates for office have a "duty of civility" to explain their positions on fundamental issues by reference to the political conception that they take to be most reasonable. See "The Idea of Public Reason Revisited," in *Collected Papers*, 576. The point is not that it is advisable or obligatory to *assert* that one's view is the most reasonable. Instead, there is a duty to argue by reference to the view that one judges to be most reasonable. Judgments about the reasonableness of one's views thus belong to the terrain of political reflection and argument.

in judging political arrangements.[16] But it would be an inappropriate departure from the norms of public reason to assert its truth, and it would be inappropriate, in one's capacity as a citizen assessing laws and policies, to think that justice as fairness is true and to act on the basis of that thought. More particularly, it would be inappropriate to affirm the truth even of the proposition—uncontested among the competing reasonable conceptions of justice—that individuals have a right to liberty of conscience. And this would be inappropriate even though it is entirely in order to assert that people have a right to such liberty as a matter of justice, that it is reasonable to believe that they have a right to liberty of conscience as a matter of justice, and that that thesis about the right to liberty of conscience is objectively correct in virtue of being reasonable.[17]

Advancing claims about truth is, then, needlessly divisive: it undermines public reason and conflicts with the equal standing in public, po-

16. Rawls states that he takes justice as fairness, with its two principles, to be the most reasonable conception. See *Political Liberalism*, xlvi.

17. Samuel Freeman proposed in correspondence that Rawls wishes to avoid claims only about the truth of principles of justice not about the truth of consequences drawn from those principles. We cannot, then, affirm, within public reason, that the principle of equal basic liberties is true, nor can we affirm that it is true that justice requires equal basic liberties. If that principle is, however, part of the most reasonable conception of justice, then there is no objection to saying about a law infringing freedom of worship that it is true that it is unjust. The acceptable claim of truth is made from "within" the conception of justice, whereas the unacceptable claim is made about the conception itself. The same distinction, however, does not apply to the notion of being reasonable (or most reasonable). I do not see a case for interpreting Rawls this way, and do not, in any case, see the basis for the proposed restriction on the concept of truth. First, if we cannot say that the principles are true, can we nevertheless affirm the principles, or are we limited to asserting that the principles describe the most reasonable conception? If we affirm the principles, assert them, and believe them, what is the force of withholding the judgment that they are true? Second, suppose it is permissible to judge, from "within" a conception of justice, that it is true that certain policies are unjust. Let's say that is because we confine claims about truth to what we can argue for from common ground (not that I wish to accept that thesis). But then why is it not permissible to judge, from "within public reason"—which provides a terrain of argument that different conceptions of justice share—that certain principles of justice are true because they can be argued for from common ground? Third, the case for confining truth to judgments made "within" a conception of justice seems to turn on a sharp distinction, reminiscent of Carnap, between internal questions, which arise within a linguistic framework, and external questions, about whether to adopt a framework. But Carnap's distinction did not permit judgments about which framework or which language (say, a thing-language or a sense-datum language) is "most reasonable." Our attitude to a framework, on Carnap's account, is a matter of acceptance, not of belief or of assertion: it is, he says, "not of a cognitive nature." So it is nonsense to describe a framework as true, but that is because the framework is not a matter of belief at all. See "Empiricism, Semantics, and Ontology," reprinted in Rudolf Carnap, *Meaning and Necessity*, 2d ed. (Chicago: University of Chicago Press, 1956), 205–221. The idea that cognitive appraisal is entirely internal is foreign to public reason.

litical argument that democracy promises. "Once we accept the fact that reasonable pluralism is a permanent condition of public culture under free institutions, the idea of the reasonable is more suitable as part of the basis of public justification for a constitutional regime than the idea of moral truth. Holding a political conception as true, and for that reason alone the one suitable basis for public reason, is exclusive, even sectarian, and so likely to foster political division."[18]

Rawls does sometimes hint, if only indirectly, an alternative view. "Rational intuitionism," he says, "conceives of truth *in a traditional way* [emphasis added] by viewing moral judgments as true when they are both about and accurate to the independent order of moral values."[19] Rational intuitionism, which Rawls associates with Cudworth, Clarke, Grotius, Pufendorf, and Locke, is a species of nonreductive moral realism, treats our moral thought as an exercise of theoretical reason, and is arguably an ingredient in much natural law theory.[20] His remark about a "traditional way" of understanding truth and an independent order of values suggests that it endorses a correspondence theory of truth, and the phrase "a traditional way" suggests that other conceptions of truth are available. If there is such an alternative, then it might have a role in public deliberation.[21]

Moreover, such a conception might fit with the spirit of political liberalism. Political liberalism distinguishes comprehensive doctrines, which include moral ideas that guide people in all aspects of their lives, from political conceptions, which comprise moral ideas and values expressed in political judgments. I will not try to characterize the distinction here. Suffice it to say that ideas with a role in comprehensive doctrines can also play a role in political conceptions, if those ideas are given a "political" interpretation, as with political conceptions of justice, the person, objectivity, reasonableness, autonomy, and liberalism itself. The political

18. *Political Liberalism*, 129. I will come back later to this passage, which ties together two arguably very different ideas, one about holding a political conception as true, the other about holding it as the one suitable basis for public reason in virtue of its being true.

19. Ibid., 92. See also 111 ("in the familiar way") and 114 ("this idea of truth").

20. On rational intuitionism and the idea of an independent order of moral values, see *Political Liberalism*, 91–92; John Rawls, *Lectures on the History of Moral Philosophy*, ed. Barbara Herman (Cambridge, MA: Harvard University Press, 2000), 69–83, esp. 70–72.

21. When Rawls states that political liberalism "does without the concept of truth," he identifies this as one of four elements in the contrast between rational intuitionism and political constructivism. See *Political Liberalism*, 91–94. But, logically speaking, the alternative to endorsing a "traditional conception" of truth is to not endorse a traditional conception. There are two ways to do that: do without the concept of truth altogether, or endorse a nontraditional (that is, noncorrespondence) interpretation of truth.

conceptions are intended, roughly, to play a role when citizens reason together about political affairs. Thus, a political conception of persons as
free says, for example, that no particular ends are mandatory or obligatory
from a public point of view, that obligations a person has in virtue of his
or her moral or religious outlook do not have public standing *as obligations*, and that civil standing does not shift with shifts in fundamental aims, no matter how much or how deeply a person's self-conception is
bound up with those aims.[22] This political conception of persons as free
is meant to be available to adherents of views that endorse distinct and
incompatible philosophical conceptions of the free person, as an autonomous self-legislator with a will sensitive to reflective judgments, or as created in God's image, subject to His laws, and free when in willing compliance with those laws. Similarly, a political conception of liberalism as
assigning equal liberties to all is meant to be available to both proponents
and critics of the moral-liberal view that individual, reflective self-direction is essential to a good life.

Why not, then, a *political conception of truth*, understood as a conception of truth suited to play a role in democracy's public reason? Rawls
did not pursue this path. Perhaps he thought that the concept of truth is
unavoidably metaphysical, originally owned by Platonists, and passed
along to their rational intuitionist descendants. As applied to moral
thought, he might have supposed that truth comes packaged with the rational intuitionist's notion of an independent order of values. Or perhaps he thought that the alternatives are a correspondence theory, a
coherence theory, an antimetaphysical deflationism, or some other unacceptably philosophically demanding theory. In any case, he proposed to
"leave the concept of a true moral judgment to comprehensive moral
doctrines."

I think that Rawls is mistaken and that affirmations of the truth of propositions about justice are a perfectly legitimate part of democracy's public
reason. But to address the animating concerns about the tensions between truth and public reason, we need a political conception of truth.
To understand why, it will help to say more about Rawls's proposed response to these tensions and about why that response is deeply puzzling.

---

22. On the political conception of the person, see *Political Liberalism*, 18–20, 29–35, 48–54,
and 86–88.

2. Doing without Truth?

How could we "do without the concept of truth"? Truth is of course a controversial idea. But however it is best understood, the concept of truth—like concepts of cause, object, fact, reason, and evidence—is deeply rooted in our thought and reasoning. Truth is intimately linked to the notions of belief and meaning, both fundamental in an account of thought. Thus, beliefs are said to "aim at" the truth, in that truth is their standard of correctness; correspondingly, coming to believe that p is not true is typically "fatal" to the belief that p. Moreover, because truth is the standard of correctness for beliefs, while we may come to believe that p without deliberating about whether p (is true), when we deliberate about whether to believe that p, we try to determine whether p (is true).[23] As for meaning, Donald Davidson has observed that we often figure out what someone's utterances mean by assuming that they are saying something true, at least when they are saying something about publicly observable surroundings.[24]

The notion of truth is also fundamental in our understanding of reasoning. Thus, truth is tied to judging, in that judging whether p is closely connected to judging whether p is true (judgment is the "acknowledgement of the truth of a thought");[25] to assertion, inasmuch as asserting is commonly understood to involve presenting the asserted content to others as true ("What distinguishes [truth] from all other predicates is that it is always asserted when anything at all is asserted");[26] to assuming that p for the sake of argument, in that when we assume that p we assume that it is true; to reasons for believing, which are reasons for believing true; and to ideas of a logical consequence, as a proposition whose truth is assured by the truth of other propositions, and of deductive argument, whose spe-

---

23. On the relevant kind of fatality, see Williams, *Truth and Truthfulness*, 67–68. On truth as standard of correctness, see Nishi Shah, "How Truth Governs Belief," *Philosophical Review* 112, 4 (October 2003): 447–482; and Nishi Shah and David Velleman, "Doxastic Deliberation," *The Philosophical Review* 114, 4 (2005): 497–534.

24. See Donald Davidson, *Truth and Predication* (Cambridge, MA: Harvard University Press, 2005), chap. 3.

25. Gottlob Frege, *Basic Laws of Arithmetic*, sec. 5, in *Translations from the Philosophical Writings of Gottlob Frege*, ed. Peter Geach and Max Black (Oxford: Blackwell, 1970), 156.

26. Frege, *Posthumous Writings*, ed. H. Hermes, F. Kambartel, and F. Kaulbach, trans. P. Long and R. White (Chicago: University of Chicago Press, 1979), 129. Neither this remark of Frege's about assertion, nor the previous remark about judgment, depends on his redundancy theory of truth, much less on his view that true sentences denote the same object.

cial virtue is to be truth preserving. Truth is connected as well to norms of thought and interaction that call for accuracy in representation, sincerity in expression, consistency, "getting it right," and being attentive to how things are and not simply how we wish them to be.[27]

These observations are all familiar. I register them to distinguish the concept of truth from a variety of other concepts that public reason might arguably do without. Suppose someone proposes that public reason should avoid concepts of salvation, or of self-realization, soul, personal autonomy, purity, courage, or honor. Whatever the merits of such abstention, we have some idea of what is being proposed. We can imagine what it would mean to conduct political justification without recourse to such concepts. But the idea of locating a common ground of political reflection and argument that does without the *concept* of truth—like doing without the concept of an object, or a cause, or a thought, or a reason, or an inference, or evidence—is hard to grasp. Truth is so closely connected with intuitive notions of thinking, asserting, believing, judging, and reasoning that it is difficult to understand what leaving it behind amounts to.

Keep in mind that what is at stake here is the concept of truth, not a theory of truth. It is easy to see reasons for avoiding philosophical controversy about truth: whether the truth of a proposition consists in its correspondence with a world of facts that exist determinately and independently or, instead, it consists in the beliefs on which ideally conducted inquiry would ultimately converge; or whether, as the minimalist theory claims, grasping the concept of truth consists in being disposed to assert instances of the truth schema, or the Heideggerian, that truth is the disclosure of being.[28] Such disagreements may be seen as needlessly divisive, because they invite controversies that are politically idle. What matters is what we think is right or just, not what we think the truth of normative propositions consists in.

There are good reasons for steering democracy's public reason clear of such philosophical controversies and for leaving it to competing traditions of thought to add their own philosophical interpretation of truth to public discourse (if they have such an interpretation). Similarly, they may add different interpretations of the nature of justice to a public understanding of justice or may add different accounts of the competence

27. On the good of accuracy and sincerity, see Williams, *Truth and Truthfulness*, chap. 3.
28. For an illuminating discussion of Heidegger on truth, see Cristina Lafont, *Heidegger, Language, and World-Disclosure* (Cambridge: Cambridge University Press, 2000), chap. 3.

of reason to a conception of the politically reasonable. But the fact that there is more to be said about justice does not exclude considerations of justice from public reason; disagreements between empiricists and rationalists about the nature and powers of reason do not exclude a conception of the politically reasonable; and disagreements between Kantians and rational intuitionists about objectivity do not keep the idea of objectivity out of public reason. So, too, the fact that there is more to be said about truth does not provide a rationale for excluding truth.

What could it be for the shared public terrain of argument to do without the *concept* of truth? I have expressed some puzzlement about this, but skeptical attitudes about the place of truth in political argument are familiar. Is it really so puzzling? To explain why it is, I want to distinguish the idea under consideration—I will call it the *No Concept* view—from three other skeptical views: that truth has no role because no truth-apt claims are in play *(No Truth Bearers)*; that truth-apt claims are in play and the concept is available, but we should refrain from applying it to substantive political claims *(No Substantive Judgments)*; and that truth-apt claims are in play, the concept is available, and there is no problem applying it to substantive normative judgments, but it is of no real interest *(No Big Deal)*. The distinctions will help to clarify the view and the puzzlement.

1. *No Truth Bearers.* The idea that democracy's public reason does without the concept of truth must be distinguished, first, from a noncognitivist view of political discourse, akin to the views taken by classical, metaethical noncognitivists about evaluative discourse generally (though rejected by many contemporary noncognitivists). According to the classically noncognitivist emotivist, for example, the concept of truth has no application to normative discourse, because no truth-apt claims are being made.[29] Statements with the surface form of assertions that are made in

---

29. Allan Gibbard initially defended an expressivist account of normative discourse and argued that such discourse is not fact-stating or truth-apt. See *Wise Choice, Apt Feelings* (Cambridge, MA: Harvard University Press, 1990), 8, 10. For criticisms, see Paul Horwich, "Gibbard's Theory of Norms," *Philosophy & Public Affairs* 22, 1 (1993): 67–78. More recently, Gibbard proposes an expressivist explanation of normative discourse but recognizes that the expressivist strategy—which starts by asking what states of mind normative claims express—can help itself to notions of *truth* and *fact*. See *Thinking How to Live* (Cambridge, MA: Harvard University Press, 2003), esp. chap. 9.

normative discourse are devices for emotional appeal, rhetorical manipulation, and badgering.

If we say, with a variant of classical noncognitivism, that political argument is a matter of decisions (say, deciding on friends and enemies and expressing the decisions) or expressions of attitude (cheering for your side, shouting at the other) or words used to provoke behaviors, then the concept of truth would arguably have no hold. Despite the surface forms of political discourse—apparently asserting logically simple propositions and embedding them in logically complex ones ("If slavery is not unjust, then nothing is unjust," or "If the fetus is a person, then abortion is morally wrong"), seeming to reason to and from those apparent assertions—it would not involve claims that could be either true or false. Saying that a political conception does without the concept of truth, then, would be like saying that cheerleading does without the concept of truth. You do without the concept because you are not trafficking in anything to which the concept applies. Of course, cheers often have the form of assertions. But when cheerleaders say, "We are number one" in the final minutes, with the team down 46–0, no one thinks that they are really expressing the belief that theirs is the best team.[30]

Whatever the merits of this view, it is not public reason. Rawls proposes to leave truth out, but not because he is endorsing an interpretation of political argument in which no claims are being made that are apt to be either true or false. While public reason is to do without the concept of truth, it is an exercise of practical reason, of reflection, and of judgment: "So if the idea of reasoning and judgment applies to our moral and political statements, as opposed simply to our voicing our psychological state, we must be able to make judgments and draw inferences on the basis of mutually recognized criteria and evidence; and in that way, and not in some other way, say by mere rhetoric or persuasion, reach agreement by the free exercise of our powers of judgment."[31]

My point about the truth-aptness of claims made in the domain of pub-

30. Anticipating what will come later: If public reason includes the concept of truth, does this impose a barrier for noncognitivists, who traditionally have thought that truth is not in play in normative discourse? The answer lies in the content of the political conception of truth. Noncognitivists have no reason to object to that use, given the relatively minimal commitments that come with it. See Gibbard, *Thinking How to Live*, chap. 9; Simon Blackburn, *Truth* (Oxford: Oxford University Press, 2005).

31. Rawls, *Political Liberalism*, 110–111. For a forceful statement of the point, see John Rawls, *Lectures on the History of Political Philosophy*, ed. Samuel Freeman (Cambridge, MA: Harvard University Press, 2007), 7.

lic reason can be put more strongly. The reason that the concept of truth has no place *cannot be* that the claims made by a political conception are not truth-apt; those claims *must* be truth-apt, even if the political conception itself somehow abjures the concept of truth. They must be, if there is to be a common ground of argument under conditions of doctrinal disagreement. To deny the truth-aptness of the claims made on the terrain of public reason would offend against the essential idea of public reason. That is because the *very propositions* advanced in public political argument—even if not taken as or presented in that context as true—might be judged true by the religious or moral doctrine affirmed by a citizen.

Consider an example. Suppose I endorse a Catholic natural law view. I will say with *Dignitatis Humanae* that it is true that citizens have a right to religious freedom. But also, with *Veritatis Splendor*, I will say that "the splendour of truth" is the foundation of morality and political justice, that there is a "moral obligation, and a grave one at that, to seek the truth and to adhere to it once it is known," and that there is an "inseparable connection between truth and freedom—which expresses the essential bond between God's wisdom and will."[32] Moreover, with the conviction that Christ is "the way, the truth, and the life," and, resisting the temptation of "detaching human freedom from its essential and constitutive relationship to truth,"[33] I will hold that the truth of the (political) proposition—that individuals have a basic right to religious freedom—follows from the truth of an account of human dignity founded on the doctrine that human beings, created in God's image, are bound by His laws. If that is all correct, then the political claim expressed on the terrain of public reason—that there is a right to religious freedom—must be truth-apt. It must be capable of being true or false, because *that very proposition* can be judged to be true from the standpoint of Catholic doctrine, and it is said to be derivable from the underlying truths about human dignity.

It would conflict with the essentials of public reason to deny any of this: to deny that the proposition that individuals have a right to liberty of conscience is true or to deny that its truth follows from the basic truths about the right way to live as fixed by natural law. Lacking the concept of truth, a political conception used for public reasoning can issue no such

32. *Veritatis Splendor*, paragraphs 34, 99. This is an encyclical by Pope John Paul II on moral theology. See http://www.vatican.va/holy_father/john_paul_ii/encyclicals/documents/hf_jp-ii_enc_06081993_veritatis-splendor_en.html.
33. Ibid., paragraph 4.

denial. At the same time, the Rawlsian proposal is that *the very proposition about religious liberty that the natural law adherent affirms as true* and as a consequence of more fundamental truths *is* available for assertion in political reflection and argument, available to be used as a premise in reasoning. The natural law adherent is simply not permitted to say everything he or she believes about that proposition—in particular, that it is true and a consequence of more fundamental truths.

In short, Rawls's proposal is to endorse a cognitivist understanding of political conceptions of justice and political argument on which notions of judgment, reasoning, and argument are fully in play, while denying the availability of the concept of truth within such conceptions. The concern is specifically with the concept of truth, and the reason for leaving it out cannot be that political discourse traffics in something other than truth bearers. Someone might offer that rationale for the view that truth has no place in political argument, but not if they think of political argument as an exercise of public reason.

2. *No Substantive Judgments.* A second view is that the contents of political conceptions are truth-apt, the concept of truth is available, and certain kinds of judgments using it are permissible, but in public reason we are to abstain from making substantive moral or political judgments using that concept. David Estlund appears to attribute this combination of views to Rawls. The attribution is, I think, mistaken, but characterizing the view will help in clarifying the No Concept view.

Estlund summarizes Rawls's view this way: "Truth," Estlund says, "is held to be neither necessary nor sufficient for a doctrine's admissibility [in public political argument]."[34] But the claim that the truth of a propo-

---

34. David Estlund, "The Insularity of the Reasonable: Why Political Liberalism Must Admit the Truth," *Ethics* 108 (January 1998): 253. Habermas also misinterprets the claim that the concept is unavailable. He attributes to Rawls the view that "a theory of justice cannot be true or false" and mentions a "weak interpretation" of this thesis on which it asserts that "normative statements do not describe an independent order of moral facts." See "Reconciliation Through the Public Use of Reason," *Journal of Philosophy* 92, 3 (March 1995): 123. A political conception of justice cannot make either of these claims, on Rawls's account. Lacking the concept of truth, it cannot make any claims about the truth or the falsity of conceptions of justice, including the claim that they cannot be true or false. Moreover, endorsing the moral constructivist thesis that normative statements do not describe an independent order of moral facts (the so-called weak interpretation) would put it directly in conflict with rational intuitionism. See *Political Liberalism*, 113. What political constructivism does say is that "once, if ever, reflective equilibrium is attained, the principles of political justice (content) *may be represented* as the outcome of a certain procedure of construction (structure)" (Rawls, *Political Liberalism*, 89–

sition is neither necessary nor sufficient in licensing appeal to it in public argument—if understood an assertion within public reason—belongs to a very different view from the one that Rawls endorses and that we are exploring. Asserting that truth is neither necessary nor sufficient requires having the concept of truth available. It is thus quite different from neither holding truth to be necessary nor holding truth to be sufficient for a doctrine's admissibility, which does not require the concept.

Consider a parallel. It is one thing to say that a view holds that conduciveness to salvation is neither necessary nor sufficient for the rectitude of conduct. It is quite another to say that it neither holds that salvation is necessary nor holds that it is sufficient. You can only endorse the first if you have the concept of salvation. But you can, consistent with holding neither, lack the concept. So a public understanding of justice for use in public reason does not hold salvation to be necessary nor hold it to be sufficient for rectitude. But it would be a serious misunderstanding to say that it holds that salvation is neither necessary nor sufficient. Lacking the concept of salvation, the public understanding makes no judgments about it at all.

If public reason works without the *concept of truth*, then, it cannot hold that truth is neither necessary nor sufficient for admissibility as a premise in political argument, much less make any claims about the truth or the falsity of substantive propositions of political justice. Estlund in effect, then, urges a modified political liberalism, which has the concept of truth available, affirms that truth is neither necessary nor sufficient for admissibility in public justification, also affirms as true the proposition *that reasonable acceptance is necessary for admissibility*, but does not apply the concept to substantive moral and political claims. Adding this proposition about reasonable acceptance would be a natural extension of a view that has the concept of truth available and that holds truth to be neither necessary nor sufficient for a doctrine's admissibility. But this is a very different view from the No Concept conception.[35]

Rawls's *No Concept* thesis is that public reason lacks the concept. *No*

---

90). The italicized phrase is essential. It would defeat the purpose of political constructivism to say that the principles of justice *are* the product of a procedure of construction and, therefore, "do not describe an independent order of moral facts." The rational intuitionist may well agree with the political constructivist claim about how the principles "may be represented," while rejecting the moral constructivist claim about what those principles are.

35. In saying that it is very different, I am not criticizing the view. My aim in this section is simply to clarify the No Concept account.

Substantive Judgments says that public reason has the concept but abjures substantive applications of it. I will not discuss this view further. Suffice it to say that the motivations for it are not very clear. After all, it is perfectly consistent to say that reasonableness is necessary and sufficient for the admissibility of a consideration into public reason—for its use in public justification—and to say that it is permissible to present substantive moral and political claims views as true. Once truth is available, it is not clear why it should be cabined in the way suggested.

3. *No Big Deal.* A third view—normative-political positivism—accepts a role for assertions of truth and falsity in political argument. It says, as distinct from *No Truth Bearers*, that the contents presented in political argument are (at least sometimes) truth-apt. It says, as distinct from *No Substantive Judgments*, that the application of the concept of truth to substantive moral and political judgments is legitimate. But because of the normative positivism, truth does not play a substantial role in political reflection and argument.

To appreciate the point, consider Hobbes's claim that "the authority of writers, without the authority of the commonwealth, maketh not their opinions law, be they never so true": auctoritas non veritas facit legem.[36] Hobbes's thesis is about legal validity, not about justice. The idea is that legal validity is fixed entirely by an act of authority and not at all by moral rectitude. I think it is a useful, deflationism-inspired anachronism to think that Hobbes expresses a point about the independence of legal validity from moral rectitude in convenient shorthand when he says that truth does not make the laws. He might have said: If lying is right, that is irrelevant to legal validity; if lying is wrong, that is irrelevant; if stealing is right, that is irrelevant; if stealing is wrong, that is irrelevant; if kindness is nice, that is irrelevant; if kindness if not nice, that is irrelevant; and so on, ad infinitum. Instead, taking semantic flight, he generalizes over all propositions of any content and says that truth does not make the laws.

That position is legal-positivism, which is consistent with the view that there are natural standards of rectitude to be used in evaluating laws.[37] But Hobbes was arguably (only arguably) led to his legal positivism from positivism about justice itself: *auctoritas non veritas facit justitiam.* As

36. Thomas Hobbes, *Leviathan* (Indianapolis: Hackett, 1994), 180.

37. See John Austin, *The Province of Jurisprudence Determined* (Amherst, NY: Prometheus Books, 2000). According to Austin, the moral rectitude of laws depends on conformity with natural law, understood as God's law for humankind.

Hobbes says, there are no unjust laws, because, antecedent to the sovereign's law-making activity, there is no just or unjust distinction for laws to be answerable to. So when Hobbes says that truth does not make law, he means that legal validity does not depend on truths about rightness. But that is in part because there are no normative truths available prior to authority that might enter into determinations of legal validity. If that is indeed the rationale for legal positivism, then it follows as well that the truth—that is, truths about what is just and unjust, right and wrong—cannot figure in *assessing* valid laws as just or unjust, because the justice-making facts, too, are exercises of sovereign legislative authority.

Once more, in semantic ascent, we might report this view by saying that truth does not *make* justice. Nevertheless, the concept of truth can be used in assertions about propositions concerning the justice of valid laws. There is no trouble affirming that the proposition that theft is unjust is true, no more trouble than in affirming simply that theft is unjust or that theft violates the law. What makes theft unjust is that authorities make laws defining and enforcing property rights. Nothing beyond that illegality is needed to make theft unjust and therefore to make the proposition that theft is unjust true. As a result, claims about the truth of propositions concerning justice are available in political argument, even though truth does not make the justice of the laws.

Truth is available for the normative-positivist, then, but its relevance is limited. The limits come not from the conception of truth as a device for expressing generalizations but from the positivist view that justice is fixed by the social facts of sovereign enactment. That view limits the force of worries about whether our views about justice are true, about whether we have it right about justice. The concern is intelligible. I might think that I have been misinformed about the laws in a jurisdiction and so wonder whether my beliefs are true. But once I know what the social facts are—in particular, what the authority has decided—I have no basis for further concern about whether justice is what I suppose it to be.

Drawing these points together, we have four views in play, each interpreting the general idea that, roughly stated, truth is not important in political argument:

1. *No Concept*: Though public, political justification is an exercise of reason, and the contents presented are truth-apt, the concept of truth is not available.
2. *No Truth Bearers*: The concept of truth has no application, be-

cause the contents presented in normative political discourse are not truth-apt.

3. *No Substantive Judgments*: the contents are truth-apt, and the concept is available, but the concept is to be left on idle when it comes to substantive issues of justice.

4. *No Big Deal*: The concept is available and exercisable but does no significant work, because it is simply available to report the results of exercises of authority that are not constrained by norms of justice (or any other norms).

Rawls, I said, in effect suggests that we face a dilemma: that we can have truth or public reason, but not both. He embraces the idea of public reason as common ground under conditions of doctrinal disagreement, and concludes that we should leave truth aside. But for the reasons I have been suggesting, it is hard to see how we can. It is difficult to understand what leaving truth aside comes to. Moreover, if political argument involves (as the idea of public reason indicates) beliefs, assertions, judgments, and reasoning, then truth also seems to be in play. And if justice is not—as the normative-positivist holds—fixed by authoritative decision, then there is plausibly something important about getting justice right. Is there some way to reconcile these competing pulls?

To see how we might free ourselves from the dilemma, we need first to have an account of what is involved in the idea that the concept of truth is available to political reflection and argument.

3. *Including Truth*

I said at the beginning that political argument in democracies is in part a matter of reasoning and judging on the basis of considerations of justice. Such reasoning and judging might appeal, for example, to the principle that all citizens are entitled to the same basic liberties, to the abstract idea that a just society must treat its members as being of equal importance, and to the arguments showing that a just society must secure equal basic liberties in part because securing those liberties is essential to treating members as being of equal importance. All of this—the principles as well as the reasoning—lies, I will assume, on the terrain of democracy's public reason.

What, then, would it mean to say that a conception of justice—say, a conception that includes the proposition that justice requires equal basic liberties—includes the concept of truth? The issue is not about a word, but about what it is for the concept of truth to be part of the conception. Rawls says that a political conception of justice does without the concept of truth, and leaves the concept to comprehensive moral doctrines. We want to know what this "doing without" consists in, or, more precisely, what it would be to "do with" the concept.

Think of a political conception, used to formulate arguments in public reason, as a set of propositions. Let's say it includes, among others, the proposition that persons are entitled to a fully adequate scheme of equal basic liberties, that fairness is a fundamental political value, and that the original position models the ideal of fair cooperation among persons understood as free and equal. Consider a formulation of the conception in English, including the word "true" and the biconditional. Speakers—by virtue of their mastery of English—can say what propositions are expressed by various sentences; they can also say that the sentences expressing those propositions are true; and they can formulate biconditionals connecting the propositions and their truth conditions. So, for example, the sentence "Justice requires assurances of equal fundamental liberties" expresses the proposition that justice requires assurances of equal fundamental liberties, and *the proposition that justice requires assurances of equal fundamental liberties* is true if and only if justice requires assurances of equal fundamental liberties. So the formulation of the conception enables them to state and endorse instances of the truth schema: *the proposition that p* is true if and only if p. For example, they can say that the proposition that justice requires equal basic liberties is true if and only if justice requires equal basic liberties.

But more than this is needed to have truth available in public reason. To see why, consider a deflationary theory of truth, which tells us that truth is not a substantial property—not, for example, a relation of correspondence between a truth bearer and an independent order of facts—and that the truth schema tells us all there is to be said about the concept of truth. I assume that that schema is not itself in dispute between deflationary theories and their opponents. The point of contention is whether the schema exhausts the concept, or if there is anything more to the concept or nature of truth than is captured by the schema (or by a truth-definition that entails instances of the schema).

Consider, in particular, a version of the deflationary theory that says, among other things, that the truth schema, itself unexplained by any deeper theory, fully explains everything about the property of being true; that a grasp of the concept of truth consists in a disposition to affirm all the instances of the truth schema; and that truth is not a substantial property and lacks a nature. Moreover, it says that the sole point of having a truth predicate is to be able to express generalizations: for example, to say that everything that Einstein said is true, or that all propositions of a certain form are true, or that the truth of normative propositions is not relevant to legal validity.[38] If you hold such a minimalist theory, then you will think that having the phrase "is true," and all the sentences that can be used to express instances of the truth schema are—assuming competent speakers, who are disposed to affirm all instances of the schema—what having the concept of truth in the political conception consists in.

But neither minimalism of this kind, nor any other form of deflationism, can provide the account of what it is to have the concept of truth in the political conception. Although the instances of the schema and the inferences deploying the schema can be part of democracy's public reason, the minimalist theory of truth cannot be, and for two reasons (parallel considerations apply to other forms of deflationism).

First, minimalism does not say, on its face, anything about the fact that truth is important or about why it might be important: that our beliefs and assertions ought to be true; that it is good that they be true. Understanding the equivalence schema and being disposed to assert its instances while not knowing anything about the point of classifying propositions as true and as false is like knowing the rules of a game without knowing that the point of the game is to win. Grasping the significance of truth is arguably (I come back below to the force of this qualification) not something you understand simply by virtue of understanding that the use of the concept of truth is captured by the instances of the schema or that mastery of the concept consists in a disposition to affirm those instances.[39] A conception of justice, even when its formulation is understood to include the term "is true" and all the instances of the schema,

38. See Paul Horwich, *Truth*.

39. See Michael Dummett, "Truth," in *Truth and Other Enigmas* (Cambridge, MA: Harvard University Press, 1978), 2–3; on the importance of giving an account of the point of the concept of truth, see as well, Davidson, *Truth and Predication*; Williams, *Truth and Truthfulness*; and Crispin Wright, *Truth and Objectivity* (Cambridge, MA: Harvard University Press, 1992). Dummett focuses on Frege's redundancy theory. "It is part of the concept of truth," Dummett says, "that we aim at making true statements," but Frege's account of truth "leaves this quite out of account." For criticisms, see Tyler Burge, "Frege on Truth," in *Truth, Thought, Reason* (Oxford: Oxford University Press, 2005), 130, and more generally, 88–93 (esp. note 3).

may nevertheless arguably be said not yet to include the concept of truth. Including the concept as part of public reason also requires incorporating some account of the point of judging claims to be true and of the classifications that employ the concept of truth. I will return to this point in a moment.

More fundamentally, second, minimalism is a contested theory about truth. In contrast to correspondence, coherence, and pragmatic theories, it says that truth has no nature and is not a substantial property. It thus puts public reason needlessly at odds with philosophical doctrines—say, the rational intuitionism associated with some formulations of natural law theory—that embrace metaphysically more demanding theories of truth. It says more than is necessary for the purposes of including the concept of truth within democracy's public reason. Minimalism is an antimetaphysical theory of truth. In contrast, a political conception of truth cannot—as I said earlier—be antimetaphysical. It should be, however, nonmetaphysical, which will give it significant overlap with an antimetaphysical theory: it will not make claims about the real nature of truth or affirm that it is substantial property, nor will it make claims about what substantial property it is. But it needs to say less than minimalism does so that it does not impose unnecessary barriers to entry onto the terrain of public reason (it will not deny claims about the nature of truth either).

In short, minimalism says too much (denies too much) and perhaps says too little to serve as a conception of truth in public reason. For the concept of truth to have a place in public reason, we need both more and less. The political conception of truth needs, first, to avoid asserting any theory about the nature of truth or its lack of a nature. Such assertions impose unnecessary hurdles and seem to serve no purpose within public reasoning.

Then, second, the political conception needs to include at least four commonplaces about truth:[40]

- *Attitudes:* Believing (asserting, judging) is believing (asserting, judging) true, where this slogan is understood to mean that truth is the norm governing beliefs, assertions, and judgments;

40. See Crispin Wright, "Truth: A Traditional Debate Reviewed," in *Truth*, ed. Simon Blackburn and Keith Simmons (Oxford: Oxford University Press, 1999), 203–238; and Wright, *Truth and Objectivity*, chap. 2.

- *Correspondence:* True beliefs present things as they are (they "say of what is that it is and of what is not that it is not"), and in that uncontroversial sense correspond to how things are, although it will not add (or deny) that such beliefs present things as they really are in themselves, determinately and mind-independently;
- *Contrast:* There is a distinction between truth and warrant or justification, so that an account of justice, for example, may be warranted—we may have grounds for endorsing it—but may not be true:[41] although, to reiterate, it will not say that truth is a substantive property different from warrant, nor will it offer an account of what property truth is that distinguishes it from warrant; but it will avoid claiming that nothing informative can be said on this issue;
- *Value:* Truth is important; and, given that truth is different from warrant, that truth is important in a way that is different from the way that warrant is important.

I mentioned before that minimalism may say too little to serve as an acceptable political conception of truth, and I need here to clarify the point. Minimalists do not dispute these four claims but argue that the truth predicate is a device of generalization, that our grasp of the concept consists in our disposition to affirm instances of the truth schema, and that these additional claims—for example, about the value of truth—are derivative. They are explained in terms of the truth schema: according to minimalism, everything about truth can be so explained.[42] The political conception of truth, in contrast, takes no position on whether the truth schema is "explanatorily basic" in this way: it neither affirms nor denies the minimalist's explanation. It is agreed that an adequate account of truth must in some way include the commonplaces about truth. The political conception of truth can simply treat these commonplace claims as elements in the shared understanding of truth without claiming that they

41. A distinction of some kind between truth and warrant seems important to understanding the practice of deductive argument. Deductive argument is both compelling and useful. It is compelling because it is truth-preserving. But it is useful because often we are not antecedently warranted in endorsing the conclusion of a deductive argument or warranted in endorsing the conclusion independently of its issuing from that argument. See Michael Dummett, *The Logical Basis of Metaphysics* (Cambridge, MA: Harvard University Press, 1991), chap. 7.

42. Horwich, *Truth*; idem, "Norms of Truth and Meaning," in *Reflections on Meaning* (Oxford: Oxford University Press, 2005), 104–133; and "The Value of Truth," *Noûs* 40 (2006): 347–360, esp. sec. 10, on how to explain the desirability of truth without supposing that the concept is "constitutionally normative."

are part of the concept or without aiming at an explanation (or denying the plausibility of some proposed explanation). In contrast, minimalism either lacks an account of the value of truth, in which case it says too little, or offers a theory about the value of truth, in which case it says too much.

If our aim is to provide a philosophical theory of truth, then abstaining from investigating the structure of this whole cluster of claims is bound to seem unsatisfying, a dereliction of intellectual duty, or simple laziness. But that is not the point of an account of public reason. Here, the aim is simply to show that the concept, understood in a certain way, is available as part of a shared ground of argument. We should not exclude the concept, but we need not incorporate a philosophical theory of truth, any more than we need to incorporate a philosophical theory of reason when we include an account of reasonableness. We have an understanding that serves the purposes of public political argument, but it does not go beyond those purposes.

4. Three Reasons for Keeping Truth Out of Public Reason

Having sketched a political conception of truth, I want now to consider in more detail some considerations that might be advanced for excluding truth from public reason, for what I have called the No Concept view. I presented an intuitive case earlier (section 1), but I want now to discuss three lines of argument, each of which exemplifies some general reason for thinking that concerns about truth do not belong to politics, at least not to the kind of deliberative politics on common ground under conditions of doctrinal disagreement associated with the idea of public reason. The first is that the "singularity of truth" makes it practically divisive, perhaps intolerant, thus at odds with the animating concerns of public reason; the second is that the inclusion of truth encourages the idea that truth is sufficient, which in turn encourages sectarianism; and the third, that truth introduces a concern with depth that is inappropriate to public reason. Rawls and others suggest each of these three, and each has some force. But with the political conception of truth available, we can accommodate the force while also preserving public reason.

Singularity. Assertions about the truth of a view may be seen as needlessly divisive, perhaps intolerant, because of a fundamental logical property of truth, namely, that truth is singular, whereas reasonableness is plural. Thus, inconsistent propositions cannot both be true, and their adherents cannot therefore all believe the truth, whereas inconsistent propositions can both be reasonable to believe, and their adherents can all hold reasonable beliefs. It is not a philosophical theory, but a commonplace about the concept of reasonableness that reasonable people disagree about certain matters. The *singularity argument* turns this logical distinction between truth and reasonableness into a rationale for dropping truth while keeping reasonableness.

Rawls suggests the singularity argument when he says, "Holding a political conception as true, and for that reason alone the one suitable basis of public reason, is exclusive, even sectarian, and so likely to foster political division."[43] I will return later to the phrase "and for that reason alone." Putting it aside for now, the essential point is that if I assert that my account of justice is true, and if yours conflicts with mine, then I am committed to denying that yours is true. But I may assert that my view is reasonable, while accepting that yours is, too. Why bring truth in, with this potentially troubling exclusiveness? Hannah Arendt gives forceful expression to this concern, suggesting that truth claims are divisive in ways that are hostile to political life: "Factual truth, like all other truth, peremptorily claims to be acknowledged and precludes debate, and debate constitutes the very essence of political life. The modes of thought and communication that deal with truth, if seen from a political perspective, are necessarily domineering; they don't take into account other people's opinions, and taking these into account is the hallmark of all strictly political thinking."[44]

A first trouble with the singularity argument is that truth has close competitors in the divisive singularity market. Even if truth is not in play, other standards of appraisal seem not only divisively singular but also unavoidable, at least on the broadly cognitivist understanding of political discourse associated with public reason. So, for example, while there are a variety of different political conceptions of justice, and though reasonableness is plural, only one can be the *most reasonable* conception; "most reasonable" is as singular as "true."[45] Indeed, even "more reasonable"

43. *Political Liberalism*, 129.

44. Hannah Arendt, "Truth and Politics," in *Between Past and Future* (New York: Penguin, 1977), 241. For an instructive discussion of the complexities of Arendt's views, see Linda Zerilli, "Truth and Politics," *Theory & Event* 9, 4 (2006).

45. Rawls says that citizens fulfill their duty of civility when they explain their positions to other citizens by reference to "the political conception of justice they regard as the most rea-

might be seen as divisive, since conflicting views can both be reasonable, but each cannot be more reasonable than the other. When, in political reflection and argument, I rely on a particular conception of justice, I must distinguish mine from others on some relevant dimension of appraisal. Saying it is the most reasonable conception (or at least more reasonable than others)—that it is more strongly supported by the range of relevant reasons—is one such distinction.

Of course, it might be argued that the fluidly continuous more/less reasonable distinction is less needlessly divisive than the rigid true/false binary. But closer inspection reveals that this observation has little force. After all, I can say that someone has it more or less right, or is close to the truth, or that what he thinks is approximately true, or more or less true, but not quite. Indeed, in the spirit of nondivisiveness, I can say that it is very reasonable, even if it is not true.

A second problem with the singularity argument lies in its supposition that "is true" causes the trouble. We should resist shooting the semantic messenger. I think that justice requires equal basic liberties; you think it requires maximin basic liberties; I think that privacy is among the basic liberties required by justice, while you do not. We agree that these views come to the same thing in most circumstances, and I accept that what you think is reasonable. Still, we disagree, and we seem to disagree not simply about which view is "most reasonable" but also about what justice requires. I think that unequal liberties are unjust, even when the inequality is associated with greater liberty for those with lesser liberty. We cannot both be right, though our views may both be reasonable. I want, then, to reject the claim that the concept of truth (or the deployment of that concept) provokes disagreement. Its use, insofar as it is used in public reason, expresses the disagreement that we have.

The first two responses to the singularity argument both emphasize that we can have divisiveness and perhaps intolerance without truth. A third observation is that we can have truth without divisiveness. Consider again the passage in which Rawls suggests what I am calling the singularity argument: "Holding a political conception as true, *and for that reason alone the one suitable basis of public reason*, is exclusive, even sectarian,

---

sonable" ("Idea of Public Reason Revisited," 576). To be sure, as Philip Kitcher reminded me, several views may be tied for the most reasonable. The relevance of this is uncertain, because you are still left with the judgment that some are less reasonable. Public reason is animated by concerns about tolerance, not by an unwillingness to make judgments.

and so likely to foster political division" (emphasis added). The point is that divisiveness does not come from the concept of truth, with its singularity, but from the thought that there is one suitable basis for public reason. If that is objectionable, then it is wrong to think that because a conception is true, it alone has a role to play in public argument. But that inference can be resisted, while preserving a place for the concept of truth. It makes perfectly good sense to say, "My view is true, but other views, while not true, are reasonable to believe, and what matters for democracy's public reason is reasonableness not truth." We need not drop the concept of truth in order to drop the thesis—suggested in this passage—that the truth of a proposition is a necessary condition for its playing a permissible role in public reason, or the thesis—to be investigated next—that its truth suffices to license appeal to it in political reflection and argument.

Sufficiency Argument. The sufficiency argument, with its concern about fostering sectarianism, begins from the suspicion that the concept of truth would serve in public reason as a general license for introducing considerations that might otherwise be of suspect appropriateness. I call this the "sufficiency argument," because the claim is that a proposition's truth suffices to make an appeal to it appropriate in political justification.

If truth did work as a license, there would be troubles for including truth within democracy's public reason. But this provides a rationale for leaving truth behind only if we think that the concept of truth, once available, will end up serving as a rationale for treating any true proposition as a relevant consideration in political argument. Thus Rawls worries about a "zeal for the *whole* truth" and about people who think of politics as a "relentless struggle to win the world for the *whole* truth," and he emphasizes "that politics in a democratic society can never be guided by what we see as the *whole* truth."[46] But should concerns about the *whole* truth provide a rationale for excluding truth? Only if its inclusion leads to an endorsement of its sufficiency.

Suppose someone asserts that abortion after eighteen weeks should be stopped because, as Aquinas argued, God ensouls the fetus at quickening thus transforming it into a living human being. Or consider the view that

46. *Political Liberalism,* 42; "Idea of Public Reason Revisited," 766; *Political Liberalism,* 243. Emphases added. A number of other passages in *Political Liberalism* also focus their concern on appeals to the "whole truth." See 216, 218–219, 225, 242–243.

gay marriage should not be permitted because it violates the duality essential to God's creation, or that social insurance ought to be eliminated because the best human life is a life of personal independence at odds with social insurance that protects against life's risks. In each of these three cases, an argument can be made for excluding the consideration from democracy's public reason, because proponents cannot reasonably expect others to endorse the consideration. (I am not defending this idea here: it is part of the background to the discussion.) But when presented with that case, the proponent might say, for example, "But it is *true* that God ensouls the fetus at quickening, and therefore *true* that abortion after 18 weeks is murder. How could these truths—universal and objective—not matter in deciding what to do?"

This appeal to truth carries no weight, and the availability of the concept changes nothing. If the proposition that God ensouls the fetus at quickening is not relevant, then the truth of that proposition is not relevant. After all, the case for its being irrelevant in public justification could not depend on the claim that it is false, since that claim would defeat the point of public reason. Correspondingly, the assertion that it is true does not add anything to the case for its relevance.

This point—that if *the proposition that p* is not relevant, then *it is true that p* is also not relevant—may seem to depend on endorsing a redundancy theory of truth, according to which the attributing truth to a proposition adds nothing to an assertion of the proposition itself. That is, the argument against truth as a license may be seen as semantic: If a person who asserts the truth of some proposition says nothing more than a person who asserts the proposition, then how could the former be relevant if the latter is not? Consider a person who rejects the redundancy theory and says that when he claims that the proposition about the fetus is true he is adding something. He is asserting, he might say, that the proposition corresponds to the facts about the fetus—to how things really are—and that it is true that abortion is murder because God decided the issue and our belief fits the facts as they are, independently of our decisions and judgments. How, he might say, could that not be of decisive relevance?

These claims indicate that the proponent rejects the redundancy theory but add no politically relevant argument. They tell us what makes it wrong to have an abortion, from which it follows that it is true. If someone, then, argues for the relevance of truth along the lines just suggested, the answer is that if the wrong-making facts did not suffice to establish the relevance of the consideration, then the truth-making facts cannot, that the understanding of truth as correspondence does not yield any additional facts of moral importance. If God's making abortion murder was not relevant, given the constraints of public reason, then how could the additional fact of correspondence with the divine-instituted wrongness make the wrongness relevant? Truth, in short, has no power to lift an otherwise irrelevant consideration into relevance.

A similar point is familiar from other settings and does not have to do with the theory of truth or with any judgment about the importance of the truth. Suppose I am on a jury, deliberating on a charge of theft. If I mention in the deliberations that the defendant stole my wallet, I will be ruled out of order, and it will not make any difference to insist, "But I am telling you the truth." The objection by the other jurors was to the pertinence of my claim in this setting, not to its veracity. And denying the relevance of my claim to be speaking the truth does not depend on a particular theory of truth.

But these reasons for rejecting the claim that truth operates as a general license are not reasons for steering clear of the concept of truth, unless the concept itself—or the practice of using it in political argument—invites us to slide to an assumption of its sufficiency. There appears to be some temptation to make this slide. For example, in explaining why Rawls refrains from presenting his conception of justice as true, Raz says: "Asserting the truth of the doctrine of justice, or rather claiming that *its truth is the reason for accepting it*, would negate the very spirit of Rawls's enterprise."[47] By "accepting it," Raz must mean "accepting it as an appropriate basis for public justification." Thus interpreted, Raz is certainly right that the claim that the truth of a proposition is "the reason for accepting it"—and contrapositively, that doubts about acceptability require denial of truth—is at odds with the fundamentals of political liberalism and of public reason. But if we were not tempted to slide from truth to sufficiency, why would we think that this observation provided a good reason to "refrain from claiming" that a view is true—and correspondingly, that if we have good reason to think that assertions about truth are permissible, then we ought to accept that truth is sufficient for acceptability?

The way to resist the slide from affirming the truth of concededly rele-

47. Raz, "Facing Diversity," 9.

vant normative claims to the view that all truths are relevant, the slide from nothing but the truth to the whole truth, is by pointing to the error in that inference, not by denying a role for truth. The inference may be tempting because of the thought that there would be no good reason to affirm the truth of a proposition in the practical setting of a political discussion if the sufficiency thesis were not true, that it would be practically idle to affirm the truth of a claim unless an affirmation of truth sufficed to establish the relevance of a claim and the use of it as a conversation-stopping rebuttal to all objections. But familiar reasons about the use of truth as a device of generalization show that this is wrong.[48] Consider again the jury setting. Imagine that the jury hears from a particularly convincing witness, and one of the jurors says: "I think that everything she said was true." (Assume that nothing the juror said was ruled out of order.) Alternatively, one of the jurors might say that the essential thing the jury needs to settle on is whether "Jones is speaking the truth." The other jurors agree, and that common conviction is a working premise in their subsequent deliberations. But the fact that that working premise is expressed using the concept of truth does nothing to establish the relevance of my claim to be speaking the truth when I say that the defendant robbed me.

In short, truth may be relevant without being sufficient. Our (intellectual) response to those who aim to win the world for the whole truth is not to yield the concept of truth. Instead, the response is to underscore the phenomena of reasonable doctrinal disagreement, explain the value of a shared ground of argument among equals, point out that the case for a shared ground is not founded on a skeptical or a relativist outlook, and clarify the appropriate but limited role of judgments about truth on that shared ground—thus denying the sufficiency of truth.

Limited Display. The "limited display" argument suggests that we should leave the concept of truth out of public reason because its inclusion leads to a concern with philosophical depth that is unsuited to public reason. Suppose that everyone in a group accepts a principle of equal basic liberties and accepts it in part because this principle would be agreed to by

48. For a sketch of the familiar point, see Horwich, *Truth*, 2–5. Horwich begins his discussion by saying that "the truth predicate exists solely for the sake of a certain logical need." The political conception does not include any such story about the sole reason, but it can incorporate the rest of what is said.

the members as a way to live together as equals with conflicting fundamental religious and moral convictions. They all see the principle as supported by a set of reasons—about living together as equals, about permitting conduct guided by basic convictions, about finding terms that others can reasonably be expected to accept—that, we are assuming, are accepted by all.

At the same time, the common acceptance of this argument is founded on different and conflicting doctrines about the bases of those shared reasons. Now someone might say: "I see that the principle of equal basic liberties is reasonable, and I see how the case for its being reasonable can be presented by reference to a procedure of construction that brings together the relevant reasons. But is the principle of equal basic liberties *true?*" This question can be interpreted in two ways. It might be understood as asking whether justice requires some other principle, even if equal basic liberties are an acceptable accommodation. Or it might be understood as asking for a "full display" of the case for equal basic liberties: not simply for a case that operates on common ground but for an argument issuing from more fundamental values, principles, and reasons. The argument might, for example, be founded on the idea of human dignity associated with creation in God's image or on an idea of human autonomy associated with the powers of reflective thought. The line of thought underlying full display might go like this (suggested by general norms governing assertion): in asserting a principle of justice to be true, the speaker communicates to the listener that he believes that he has some grounds for making that assertion. Moreover, the speaker commits him or herself to presenting a justification that gives the case for the truth of the principle. But such a justification must derive the principle (or the conception of which it is a part) from true moral principles: that is, a full display of the case for it. But such a derivation—a full display—cannot be part of public reasoning.[49] Since the assertion about truth commits the speaker to the full display, and only a limited display is permissible, claims about truth should be excluded.

The second interpretation is the relevant one, and it invites four responses. First, even if we agree that asserting that p, or asserting that it is true that p, commits the speaker to offering a justification for the claim that it is true that p, it does not follow that assertions of truth invite or commit the speaker to a full display of the speaker's entire ethical view

---

49. Habermas suggests that Rawls endorses the full display argument. See "Reconciliation Through the Public Use of Reason," 124–125.

(assuming that he or she has one)—that the rule, in the space of reasons, is in for a penny, in for a pound. Recall that democracy's public reason is a terrain of argument, and it may suffice, when challenged, to present a case for liberty of conscience, for example, that lies on common ground, with shared premises. If the premises are assumed to be true, then nothing more is needed to make a case for the assertion that that proposition is true. An assertion about truth need not be understood as committing the speaker to presenting a full display, any more than the assertion that justice requires liberty of conscience needs to be understood that way. Even if assertions commit a speaker to presenting a justification, they need not express commitments to depth. Truth is not depth. Sometimes, as Rawls observed, the point of philosophy is "to extend the range of some existing consensus."[50]

Second, whatever commitments about presenting reasons may follow from asserting that a proposition is true presumably also follow from asserting the proposition itself. If we are required to get into excessively deep waters when we assert that it is true that justice requires liberty of conscience, we also get into those waters when we assert that justice requires liberty of conscience. If there is a culprit, it is assertion (and the norms governing it), not truth.

Third, assertions about truth may not call for any display of argument at all. Suppose Smith says that he agrees with Mill's harm principle but not with Mill's views about equality and democracy. If Jones says in response that she thinks that more or less everything Mill said was true, I cannot see that she has advanced any claim at all about the kind of argument that can or needs to be given for Mill's conclusions—in particular, and following on the second point, that she now has a justificatory burden greater than the one she would have had if she had simply said that she agreed with various claims Mill made about equality and democracy and had not said anything about truth.

Fourth, even if claims about truth do invite a full display, there may be nothing objectionable about presenting a full display of a doctrine that leads one onto common ground. I might say that I have a case, founded on a broader doctrine that underwrites my view that a principle of equal basic liberties is true. At the same time, I am fully aware that others disagree with the doctrine and have their own reasons for endorsing the liberty principle. What we share is an understanding of what justice re-

50. John Rawls, A *Theory of Justice*, revised edition (Cambridge, MA: Harvard University Press, 1999), 509.

quires and a conviction about the truth of that requirement. I understand that others endorse that requirement and assert it to be true for reasons different from mine. A full display need not be divisive, then, but it may involve my presenting my reasons for accepting the common ground we are all assumed to occupy.[51] Of course, the full display will not provide a public justification, but it may nevertheless play a constructive role.

5. Getting It Right

The political conception of truth, I have argued, spares us from the horns of a dilemma. It enables us to respect the limits of public reason and to preserve a place for truth. The political conception thus addresses what might be seen as a fundamental objection to the idea of public reason. I want to conclude now with some comments that will set the discussion in a wider context and will clarify what is at stake.

Consider the following remarks:

1. "[Fania Pascal's] statement ['I feel just like a dog that has been run over'] is grounded neither in a belief that it is true nor, as a lie must be, in a belief that it is not true. It is just this lack of connection to a concern with truth—this indifference to how things really are—that I regard as the essence of bullshit."[52]

2. "The truth of an opinion is part of its utility. If we would know whether or not it is desirable that a proposition should be believed, is it possible to exclude the consideration of whether or not it is true? In the opinion, not of bad men, but of the best men, no belief which is contrary to truth can really be useful: and can you prevent such men from urging that plea, when they are charged with denying some doctrine which they are told is useful, but which they believe to be false."[53]

3. "[We] need to take seriously the idea that to the extent that we lose a sense of the value of truth, we shall certainly lose something and may well lose everything."[54]

51. Here I follow Rawls's discussion of "declaration," in "Idea of Public Reason Revisited," 594.
52. Harry Frankfurt, *On Bullshit* (Princeton: Princeton University Press, 2005), 33–34.
53. John Stuart Mill, *On Liberty* (Indianapolis: Hackett, 1978), chap. 2, paragraph 10.
54. Williams, *Truth and Truthfulness*, 7.

Set against the background of these remarks by Frankfurt, Mill, and Williams, Rawls's claim that the concept of truth has no place in public reason may seem startling. Is political liberalism an invitation to the bullshitter's indifference to truth and falsity; to tying the hands of the "best men" from pleading the truth of unconventional beliefs; or, by losing the distinction between belief with its characteristic discipline and undisciplined wishful thinking, losing everything? Certainly not. Rawls's point about truth and its place in public reason is less starkly at odds with the claims of Frankfurt, Mill, and Williams than these passages might suggest and is so in at least two ways that by now should be clear.

First, in his defense of truth and truthfulness, Williams was especially concerned about a kind of infantilization of discourse consequent on losing the distinction between belief and wishful thinking. But there may be barriers other than truth to the encroachment of wishful thinking—perhaps the Rawlsian standard of reasonableness suffices.

Second, and more fundamentally, the idea that democracy's public reason should do without the concept of truth is not the idea that "we" can do without the concept of truth and, therefore, need not, in any straightforward way, provoke Williams's concern, or Frankfurt's about a culture of bullshitting, or Mill's about indifference to truth. To explain, I will call the proposal that *we* do without the concept of truth "the cultural proposal." The thought is that the culture, broadly speaking, should do without the concept of truth. More particularly, suppose we accept (as the political conception says) that truth is a norm for belief distinct from the norm of justification and that a concern for believing the truth is a concern for getting things right, for how things really are, and not simply for having warranted beliefs, even ideally warranted. The proposal, then, is that the culture would be better off—and we would be better off—if we lacked the notion of truth and the associated distinct norm in public discourse. We would be better off if concerns about the correctness of belief were correspondingly understood to be exhausted by concerns about having beliefs that are supported by the best available reasons and that help us to navigate our way in the world.

Richard Rorty's view of truth is, I think, best understood along the lines of the cultural proposal.[55] Although Rorty sometimes presented a

55. See in particular Richard Rorty, "Is Truth a Goal of Inquiry? Donald Davidson versus Crispin Wright," in *Truth and Progress: Philosophical Papers*, vol. 3 (Cambridge: Cambridge University Press, 1998), esp. pp. 41–42. In his comments on my paper at a Stanford Law School

reductive theory, on which truth is understood as acceptance in a community, or as warranted assertibility, or as warranted assertibility at the idealized end of inquiry (or as a jocular slap on the back for ideas we agree with), he agreed that none of these reductive proposals gives an adequate account of truth.[56] The problem with the concept of truth, on the cultural proposal, is precisely that it *is* irreducibly distinct from justification, that it makes perfectly good sense to ask, relative to any account of what justification is, whether a proposition that meets that standard of justification, and that we are, therefore, warranted in believing and asserting, is *true*.[57]

Because of this irreducible difference from justification, the adherent of the cultural proposal urges that we drop the concept of truth from our repertoire and aspire to a cultural world in which people regard the concern for truth—for getting it right, latching onto things as they really are—as a thankfully transcended preoccupation, like the concern about whether ghosts are in the cellar or an incubus is upstairs. "[A]ttaining truth as distinct from making justified statements *is* a goal for metaphysically active inquirers. We metaphysical quietists deplore the fact that most people in our culture can be incited to this sort of activity. . . . [W]e pragmatists hope our culture will eventually replace itself with the culture that James and Dewey foresaw." Pragmatists, Rorty says, "should see themselves involved in a long-term attempt to change the rhetoric, the common sense, and the self-image of the community"[58]—all deposits for the detritus left by decaying metaphysical doctrine. Pragmatism, thus understood, is not a thesis that truth is what works in the long-run, or any other run, but a recommendation that we figure out what works, get down to the business of doing it, and stop worrying about truth.

Of course, that counsel is hard to follow. Foucault says that "the question for the West" is: "How did it come about that all of Western culture began to revolve around this obligation of truth which has so far taken a lot of different forms? Things being as they are, *nothing so far has shown that*

---

colloquium in October 2006, Rorty disagreed that truth is a norm distinct from warrant, for reasons that struck me as assuming some form of pragmatism, and resisted my attribution to him of the cultural proposal. But once we accept that truth and warrant are distinct norms, and distinguish the word "true" from the concept of truth, then we must conclude that Rorty is endorsing something along the lines of the cultural proposal. Or so it still seems to me.

56. Rorty notes the wavering in ibid., 21–22.

57. See Hilary Putnam, "Does the Disquotational Theory Solve All Problems," in *Words and Life* (Cambridge, MA: Harvard University Press, 1994), 264–278.

58. Rorty, "Is Truth a Goal," 29, 41.

it is possible to define a strategy outside of this concern [emphasis added]. It is within the field of the obligation to truth that it is possible to move one way or another, sometimes against the effects of domination which may be linked to structures of truth or institutions entrusted with truth."[59] These hardships notwithstanding, the pragmatist urges that we soldier on.

According to the cultural proposal, concerns with truth foster anxiety about whether we have things really right, or skepticism because we might not, or despair because we do not or cannot. Those concerns reflect a failure to take a proper sense of responsibility for our convictions as our own. We would live better, freer, happier, less fraught lives if we gave up worrying about getting things really right, stopped fretting that the world might be other than what we justifiably take it to be, focused on solving problems, and—with cheerful irony—embraced our convictions and our culture wholeheartedly and without embarrassment as . . . ours. And we should unburden ourselves not because we finally have found the philosopher's stone—a way to answer the skeptic, or a grip on the idea of correspondence with reality, or an understanding of precisely what substantial property distinct from warrant truth really is—and are entitled to some rest after an intellectual job well done. The critique of truth is a cultural intervention, not a philosophical argument—a recommendation for living, not a theory. We should drop the concept of truth because it does not help us get on with life's business.

Williams and Frankfurt are, I think, worried about the cultural proposal. But the cultural proposal is different in three important ways from the idea that democracy's public reason lacks the concept of truth. First, public reason is about political justification, not about the culture generally. Second, in presenting a political conception as available on common ground, the idea is precisely not to take a view on the correct theory of truth or the proper attitude to it in the culture but to assume a range of views and to avoid unnecessary controversy: the political proposal begins from the assumption, suggested by the idea of doctrinal conflict, that "the public culture" is unalterably divided in its understanding of, inter alia, the nature of truth. Third, the point of finding a conception that can serve as common ground is to provide a basis for cooperation among equals on a basis of mutual respect; the cultural proposal, in contrast, appears to express a specifically romantic ideal of self-creation and rejects the concept of truth because it burdens such creation.

59. Michel Foucault, "The Ethics of Concern for Self as a Practice of Freedom," in *Ethics: Subjectivity and Truth*, ed. Paul Rabinow (New York: New Press, 1997), 295.

Suppose, then, we put aside the cultural proposal about dropping truth from the culture, not because the cultural proposal is wrong, but because it is not our topic. The disagreement at issue here is not between Rorty and Williams (or Frankfurt or Mill), but between Rawls and Pinter. Assume, then, a culture in which the concept of truth is available: some people think we have already lost this culture; others regret that they are wrong. And suppose that we are tempted to reject the Rawlsian view about keeping truth out of public reason: we agree that it is hard to understand what it means to drop the concept (unless we are also prepared to drop, among others, the concepts of belief, assertion, judgment), that a nonmetaphysical (not antimetaphysical) understanding of truth is available, and that the reasons for dropping it are not compelling. So we are prepared to keep the concept of truth (interpreted along the political lines I described earlier) in political justification and to acknowledge that truth is different from (even ideal) warrant. In rejecting the Rawlsian proposal, aren't we still recommending the public anxiety that the cultural proposal condemns? The objection to keeping the concept of truth raised by the cultural proposal may still have force even when our focus is narrowed to the arena of public political discourse.

It may. But should the alleged anxiety be laid at the doorstep of truth? Why not say instead that it comes with the territory of justice, thus with the territory of public reason?

We are concerned to do what justice requires: anyway, that is what we say; that is what we want other people to think we are committed to; it is what we want to take ourselves to be committed to. Not simply what we think justice requires, or what we warrantedly believe it to require, but what justice requires. But caring about justice, as the political conception indicates, requires caring about the truth about justice. If a concern about justice has—as I said at the outset—a place in democracy's public reason, then so, too, does a concern about getting it right, that is, about the truth about justice. We of course should, while keeping a concern for the truth, steer clear of needless controversy about the nature of truth: the political conception of truth suffices to meet that aim; nothing either so extreme or so fugitive as leaving the concept of truth out is needed.

As for the anxiety that comes with the concern to get justice right: that comes with the territory of taking justice seriously. We can live with it, should not live without it, and should not enlist philosophy to provide therapy for that anxiety.

INDEX

Abers, Rebecca, 207n28, 337

abortion, and privacy rights, 18–19, 313–316, 314–315n13, 317n16

Acker, Kathy, 116, 118, 252–253

Ackerman, Bruce, 293n44

aggregative conception of democracy: deliberative democracy and, 157–160, 163–164, 168; directly deliberative polyarchy and, 191–192; liberty and, 223–224, 224n3, 264–266; privacy rights and, 307–308, 308n6

Amar, Akhil Reed, 148n131

Anarchy, State, and Utopia (Nozick), 5

Ansolabehere, Stephen, 282n22, 296, 337–338

Aquinas, Thomas, 376

Arendt, Hannah, 204, 220, 220n42, 221, 221n45, 374, 374n44

"Associations in Democratic Governance" (Cohen and Rogers), 13, 36n40, 61

associative democracy: alternative governance and, 69–70; comparative experience lessons and, 70–74, 72n16; directly deliberative polyarchy and, 200–201; education of citizens and, 69; egalitarianism and, 63–66, 64nn5–7, 67; equalizing representation and, 68–69; groups, and potential contributions to, 67–68; ideal, 16, 21–22, 37; impossibility argument and, 75–76; participation/deliberation tensions and resolution using, 175–180, 177nn46–47, 179nn49–50; response to problems with, 74–75; summary of, 5, 10, 12–13, 61–63, 62nn3–4, 96–97; undesirability argument and, 76–83, 77n21, 82n25; unions and, 80–81; vague delegations of power, and risks of abused discretion in, 80, 82–83, 82n25

Austin, John, 366n37

Austin v. Michigan Chamber of Commerce, 290, 291

autonomy: deliberative democracy and, 17, 25, 27–28; directly deliberative polyarchy and, 215; freedom of expression and, 120; liberty and, 257, 257n54, 259

Baccaro, Lucio, 338

"background culture," 271, 303, 318

Baiocchi, Gianpaolo, 337

Baker, C. Edwin, 127n81

Barnes v. Glen Theatre, 254, 255

Beitz, Charles, 138n110, 171nn32–33, 270n4

Bellotti decision, 289

Benhabib, Seyla, 220n42

Black, Hugo L., 127n80, 129

Blackmun, Harry, 262, 317

Blasi, Vincent, 283

Bollinger, Lee C., 114n31, 122n70, 124n76

Bowers v. Hardwick, 254, 255, 262, 317

Bowman v. The United Kingdom, 301–302

Brady, Henry E., 280

Brandeis, Louis D., 102, 118n60, 123, 134, 136, 139, 140, 250, 301

Brandenburg v. Ohio, 126

Brazil, and participatory democracy, 207n28, 337, 338, 345

Breyer, Stephen G., 270, 291, 302n56

British law, and electoral finance, 301–302

Bruce, Lenny, 116

Buckley v. Valeo: democracy and, 11–12, 302; electoral finance issues and, 173–174, 174n38, 268–269, 285–286, 288, 290–291, 293,